Football in Africa

Football in Africa

Conflict, Conciliation and Community

Gary Armstrong
Department of Sport Sciences
Brunel University, UK

and

Richard Giulianotti
Department of Sociology
Aberdeen University, UK

palgrave
macmillan

First published 2004 by
PALGRAVE MACMILLAN
Houndmills, Basingstoke, Hampshire RG21 6XS and
175 Fifth Avenue, New York, N.Y. 10010
Companies and representatives throughout the world

PALGRAVE MACMILLAN is the global academic imprint of the
Palgrave Macmillan division of St Martin's Press LLC and of
Palgrave Macmillan Ltd.
Macmillan® is a registered trademark in the United States,
United Kingdom and other countries. Palgrave is a registered
trademark in the European Union and other countries.

ISBN 0 333 91979 3 hardback

This book is printed on paper suitable for recycling and
made from fully managed and sustained forest sources.

A catalogue record for this book is available
from the British Library.

Library of Congress Cataloging-in-Publication Data
Football in Africa : conflict, conciliation, and community / [edited
  by] Gary Armstrong & Richard Giulianotti.
      p. cm.
   Includes bibliographical references and index.
   ISBN 0–333–91979–3
   1. Soccer—Social aspects—Africa. I. Armstrong, Gary, lecturer.
II. Giulianotti, Richard, 1966–

   GV943.9.S64F68 2004
   796.334'0968—dc22

                                                            2003069123

10   9   8   7   6
13   12   11   10   09   08   07   06

Printed and bound in Great Britain by
Antony Rowe Ltd, Chippenham and Eastbourne

Contents

List of Figures and Tables

Acknowledgements

The authors are indebted to the following people, listed in alphabetical order, for their contributions to the production of this text: Andrew Blaikie, Steve Bruce, Irmani Darlington, Mark Gleeson, Matti Goksyor, Geoff Hare, Rosemary Harris, Rolf Husmann, Pierre Lanfranchi, Murray Last, Emanuel Maradas, Phyllis Martin, Alison Moir, Anne-Gaël Plais, Rolf Schwery, Sally Scott, Peter Sloane, Eric Worby, Malcom Young.

We appreciate the separate contributions of Geoff Hare and Anne-Gaël Plais in helping our translation of Chapter 2. Thanks also to Sally Scott for typing up a draft.

Our thanks are also due to Karen Brazier for commissioning this text, and Jennifer Nelson and Briar Towers for tolerating us during the production process. Sincere gratitude is also due to Ray Addicott of Chase Publishing Services and to Tracey Day for her editorial work.

As always we owe a great deal to Hani Armstrong and Donna McGilvray who lived with the evolution and denouement of this work.

Every effort has been made to trace copyright holders of any third-party material included in this book.

Contributors

Peter Alegi is Assistant Professor of History and Director of the African American Studies Program at Eastern Kentucky, USA. He has lectured in African history at Harvard University and Boston University, and in sport history at Tufts University. His research on the social and political history of sport in southern Africa has been published in international journals and collections. His book *Laduma: Football, Politics and Society in Modern South Africa* is forthcoming.

Gary Armstrong is a lecturer in the Department of Sport Sciences, Brunel University, London. He is the author of *Football Hooligans: Knowing the Score* and *BladeRunners: Lives in Football*. He has also co-edited (alongside Richard Giulianotti) *Entering The Field: New Perspectives in World Football, Football Cultures and Identities* and *Fear and Loathing in World Football*. He is currently researching the role of football in the reconstruction of Liberia and the role that football has played in the politics of Malta.

John Bale teaches and researches at Aarhus University, Denmark and Keele University, UK. He has published many books and articles on various aspects of sports. Among his most recent works are (with Joe Sang) *Keynan Running: Geography, Movement Culture and Global Change* and *Imagined Olympians: Body Culture and Colonial Representation in Rwanda*. He has lectured in many universities in Europe and North America and has been a visiting professor at the University of Jyvaskyla, Finland, the University of Western Ontario, Canada, and the University of Queensland, Australia.

Wiebe Boer is a doctoral student in African History at Yale University. A Fulbright Fellow, he is presently in Nigeria attached to the University of Jos researching and writing his doctoral dissertation on the transmission of British culture, particularly football, in colonial Nigeria. He was born and raised in Jos, Nigeria to Dutch/American/Canadian missionary parents, and completed his secondary schooling in Nigeria before undertaking his first degree at Calvin College, Grand Rapids, Michigan.

Tim Edensor is author of *Tourists at the Taj* and teaches Cultural Studies at Staffordshire University. He has recently completed a book, *National Identity, Popular Culture and Everyday Life*, and is engaged in an ongoing project on the aesthetics of British industrial ruins. Other work has focused on cultures of walking, cars, tourism, the film *Braveheart*, and rural and urban cultures.

Laura Fair is an Associate Professor of African history at the University of Oregon. Her research focuses on leisure and popular culture in colonial East Africa, and her publications include *Pastimes and Politics: Culture, Community and Identity in Post-Abolition Urban Zanzibar, 1890–1945*. She is currently working on a history of commercial cinema in Tanzania, Kenya and Uganda.

Youssef Fates is Docteur d'Etat en Science Politique at the University of Paris x-Nanterre. He is the author of *Sport et Tiers Monde*, and of numerous articles on the relations between sport and development, Islam, gender, international systems, and violence, as well as papers on Algeria's colonial history and its young people.

Richard Giulianotti is a Senior Lecturer in Sociology at the University of Aberdeen. He is the author of *Football: A Sociology of the Global Game*, and the author of numerous articles on football. He is the co-editor of several collections on football, most recently (with Gary Armstrong) *Fear and Loathing in World Football*.

Hans Hognestad is a social anthropologist and works as a researcher at the Norwegian University of Sport and Physical Education. He has published a variety of articles on football since 1995, mostly based on fieldwork within fan cultures in Norway and Scotland. His most recent project is focused on Norwegian fans of British football clubs, looking specifically at the construction of transnational identities and processes of hybridization. Other areas of research interest include sport and development and sport and space. He has also worked as an adviser on culture and development issues for the Norwegian Commission for UNESCO.

Ibrahim Koodoruth has taught sociology at the University of Mauritius for the past seven years. His areas of interest are methodology of social research, social theory and criminality and deviance. He has been working as national consultant for the UN Joint Programme on youth on the island of Rodrigues, and collaborated as national consultant with UNICEF in a study on the commercial sexual exploitation of children in Mauritius.

Alex Last is a freelance journalist who lived in Eritrea between 1998 and 2002. A Manchester University graduate in history, he later studied Arabic history at the American University in Cairo. Having lived for a time in Nigeria he is currently living in London.

Gareth Stanton is a lecturer in the Department of Media and Communications at Goldsmiths College, University of London. He has a PhD in anthropology and has conducted fieldwork in North Africa and southern Europe. Among his recent publications is a critical edition of *Une enquête au pays*, a novel by the Moroccan writer Driss Chraïbi. He is currently working on questions of world cinema.

Arvid Tollisen is teaching Sport and Physical Education at Fredtun College in Stavern, Norway. He is also working on completing his Masters Degree at the Norwegian University of Sport and Physical Education, Oslo. His fieldwork analyses development through sport in the Mathare Youth Sports Association, Nairobi, Kenya.

Bea Vidacs teaches anthropology at Baruch College, City University of New York. She has published extensively from research which examined the social and political significance of football in Cameroon. Her research interests include nationalism and ethnicity, the social imagination and postcolonial societies.

Peter Woodward held positions working for the VSO in Kosti, Sudan between 1966 and 1967 before becoming a lecturer at the University of Khartoum between 1968 and 1971. He is currently Professor of Politics and International Relations at the University of Reading. He has authored books on Egypt, Sudan and the Horn of Africa and is the former editor of *African Affairs*, the journal of the Royal African Society.

Drama, Fields and Metaphors: An Introduction to Football in Africa

Richard Giulianotti and Gary Armstrong

When Nigeria defeated Argentina to win the football (or soccer) tournament at the 1996 Olympic Games, that victory was no single victory for one nation over another. For most Africans with an interest in football, Nigeria's triumph was a continental rather than a national success. It marked the competitive arrival of African football on the world stage.

Reflecting on the contemporary context, we can say that international interest in African football has never been higher. The world's leading teams and league competitions typically feature African players, and not just those from the biggest football nations. The African Nations Cup has been covered live on the European television broadcaster Eurosport since the mid-1990s, and in the UK it gained similar coverage from BBC television in 2002. Surprisingly, set against the boom in cosmopolitan football-related literature since the early 1990s, informed and full-length literature on the African game is relatively scarce.[1]

This book seeks to highlight and to help fill that lacuna with the first detailed collection of analyses of football in each region of Africa. We seek to provide an open and wide-ranging critical exploration of football in Africa. All our authors have first-hand knowledge of African football, the vast majority having personally conducted fieldwork on the continent. In line with the book's intellectual spirit, the authors examine the African game from a diversity of disciplinary perspectives, including anthropology, history, sociology, political science and geography.

As any football follower is aware, there is obviously more to the game than a collection of naked facts regarding teams, results and championships. Football cultures in any location tell us much about the societies that play and understand the game in the distinctive ways that they do. Equally, put in reverse, it is important to grasp the general aspects of a society before we can make adequate sense of the particularities surrounding that location's sport. This constant interpretative movement between the general and the particular has been termed the 'hermeneutic circle' and, we would suggest, provides a common if latent intellectual impulse that connects our authors' approaches to their respective nations and questions.

In the context of this introductory chapter, we seek to provide a short analysis of African football's history and contemporary condition. For matters of explication, we begin with the general, with the history of modern Africa through its colonial and postcolonial phases, before seeking to explore the particularities of African football since the late nineteenth century.

Marking out the field: the making of modern Africa

Africa's contemporary structural and cultural condition is largely due to the consequences of long-term European colonization. Britain, France, Germany, Portugal, the Netherlands and Belgium were the most prominent emissaries of European 'civilization', invading the continent to subjugate its peoples and expropriate its natural resources. It is hard to estimate the number of Africans enslaved between the fifteenth and nineteenth centuries, many of them dying in bondage in the filthiest conditions en route to the New World. Perhaps around 15 million were exported during this period, while others suggest as much as 70 million were lost in total at all stages in the slave trade (Coquery-Vidrovitch 1988: 19–22). Subsequent urbanization and industrialization marked the formation and routine oppression of a new mass proletariat, notably in southern Africa. European traders and businessmen plundered Africa's natural wealth in gold, diamonds, iron ore, copper, nickel, tin and ivory. European farmers and corporations seized the most fertile land to cultivate crops – such as maize, coffee, tea, tobacco, groundnuts, fruits and vegetables – for commercial purposes, particularly to reach export markets.

Colonization proceeded at different speeds, and mapped out a geopolitical mosaic of diverse European influence and control across the continent. Many trading stations on the east and west coasts had been established by Europeans since the sixteenth century; the Portuguese had held a fortified post in Ghana since the late fifteenth century. British and Dutch colonization of the south began in the seventeenth century, and was subsequently dominated by the British who advanced north into the former Rhodesia. Conflicts between the rival European nations intensified through the late nineteenth century, as their military-industrial complexes became more sophisticated, and as Africa's interior was entered and charted for the purposes of annexation.

In the north, colonization was somewhat slower: the French took control of what is now Algeria in the 1830s, settling on the best land, and subsequently annexed neighbouring Morocco and Tunisia, as well as the vast territory of 'French West Africa' that spanned much of the north-western interior. Further east, the British established important strategic control over the Suez Canal, and retained major ruling influence over Egypt and the Sudan in the late nineteenth century. In more central African locations, notably current-day Cameroon and Tanzania, Germany held control, while in neighbouring Congo the Belgians had gained a particularly brutal dominance.

The subsequent foundation of African cultural identities bore the heavy imprint of colonial domination. The subdivision of African territories that form the borders of today's postcolonial nation-states depended not upon local cultural traditions but upon the negotiation of land by rival European war machines. Local populations were forcibly assimilated or divided with little regard for continuities or differences in language, belief-systems or customs. Smith (1999: 167) has argued that in these 'nations of design', the dominant elites have sought to implant 'a spurious unity and fraternity in their heterogeneous and divided populations' within dubious circumstances bequeathed to Africans by colonialism.

European penetration of African culture extended to the construction of particular African traditions and identities. Colonial states established control over African populations by forging links with the precolonial 'big men' who had previously dominated local peoples (Berman 1998). African 'tribal' categories were themselves largely constructed by the colonial powers, as a way of knowing, segmenting and controlling indigenous populations.[2] Europeans came to write African social history, and to map Africa's cultural geography, for the Africans – tasks made all the easier by uprooting and directing African labour power to service European farmsteads and industries.

After the Second World War, the colonial era's time was up. The old European powers, notably Britain, could no longer afford to sustain imperial hegemony across Africa. Locally, the African struggle for political independence and emancipation was often bloody but ultimately irresistible. Between 1956 and 1968, and beginning with Morocco, 35 African nations freed themselves from formal European control. In parts of Africa where large European minorities had become established, the white elites were most resistant to African nationalism and liberation. Kenya and particularly Rhodesia (today's Zimbabwe) only transferred to majority rule after substantial armed struggle. The French departure from Algeria in 1962 occurred after a sustained liberation battle and the loss of up to 1.1 million lives. Portugal retained its 'overseas territories' until

1974, whereupon the white evacuation destroyed much of the modern infrastructure in these newly independent states. In South Africa, where sizeable white settlement had occurred since the seventeenth century, the most industrialized, modern nation on the continent was the most systematically oppressive towards the black majority. The apartheid system was not replaced by majority rule until 1990, after strong international pressure led by independent African nation-states and movements such as the Organization of African Unity.

Following independence, many African nations were caught in the Cold War's global political chessboard. Civil wars fought between rulers and rebel groups have occurred across the continent with conflicts in Ethiopia, Angola, Nigeria and Sudan among the most prominent. The most settled nations aligned to the West were encouraged to maintain a policy of 'development' or 'modernization' with the official aim of catching up with industrialized societies, but with the real consequence of accumulating crippling international debts that simply reintroduced Western 'neocolonial' hegemony across much of the continent.[3] Africans had enjoyed few opportunities to participate in colonial politics and civil leadership, and that lack of training and experience complicated the transition to effective postcolonial rule. The Europeans' creation of export-dependent mono-economies in Africa – such as copper-led Zambia – meant that the independent states' viability was impossibly reliant on good price-setting by powerful Western states, transnational corporations (TNCs) and the volatile international commodity markets. In some nations, notably Libya and Nigeria, the wealth of oil deposits has promised a strong economic future. In Nigeria's case, the oil economy has been sharply vitiated by environmental pollution and disasters, the oppression of local peoples (notably the Ogoni and the Ijaws), corruption, and the shadowy political influences of major TNCs (Frynas 2001; Simonsen 1995).

Development has entailed major social and cultural changes for the indigenous populations. Africa's 'mega-cities' – such as Lagos, Nairobi and Kinshasa – continue to grow rapidly and chaotically. There has been little scope for the managed distribution and support of migrants, while extensive kinship systems have fragmented and have not been adequately replaced by new social networks. Crime, unemployment and the 'informal economy' have all spiralled since the 1960s.

Most of Africa continues to struggle with the basic, existential dangers of war, disease and famine. Since 1960, around half of the African states have experienced some levels of militarized strife, not counting wars of independence. The causes of these conflicts are typically poverty, low education and political oppression (*African Development Report 2001*: 189–91). Fundamentalist Islamic movements have engaged in paramilitary violence, primarily in north and east Africa. In Algeria, thousands of civilians have died in the ongoing struggle between Muslim fundamentalist movements and the military-backed regime. In Egypt and east Africa, American institutions and Western tourists have been targeted by paramilitary movements. In central Africa, the continuation of internal wars within nominal nation-states has varying cultural dimensions, such as 'tribal' divisions (such as Rwanda and Burundi) and religious antagonisms (Sudan). Yet there are more significant, political economic roots to Africa's numerous conflicts: in Sierra Leone, Liberia and the Democratic Republic of the Congo (DRC), various external states and bands of unrecognized 'warlords' struggle to acquire territorial access to rich mineral deposits, notably diamond mines.

Health disasters in Africa have their main roots in poverty and political marginalization. Malaria kills up to 2 million Africans annually, and markedly impairs national economic growth and development (Gallup and Sachs 2000). The leading industrial nations contribute barely a tenth of the sum needed to control the disease. The most prominent African health disaster concerns the HIV/AIDS pandemic. In southern Africa adult infection rates are the highest in the world, as large as 39 per cent in Botswana and 22 per cent in South Africa. Life expectancy has fallen to as little as 39 years in these nations, producing an estimated 21 million orphans across the continent, and thus an unbearable burden of care on grandparents (*Economist*, 29 November 2002). High levels of HIV transmission have strong sociological roots in the contemporary sub-Saharan African experience: high unemployment and poverty levels, chaotic migration patterns allied to rapid urbanization, food shortages, and weak health education policies. The long delay in acquiring cheap anti-retroviral drugs has led to millions of infected Africans quickly developing AIDS.

Famine continues to be a dominant signification of the modern African condition within the international media. Although the continent has the natural resources to feed itself, and more, internal wars and dependency on cash crops produce regular famines. All regions of sub-Saharan Africa have suffered chronic food shortages in the postcolonial era, notably Biafra during the Nigerian civil war (1967), Ethiopia in the mid-1980s, and central and southern Africa in the new millennium. Overseas food aid, hewn from genetically modified crops, carries the possible introduction of new dependencies within the African primary sector for the products and technology of Western agribusinesses.

Since the late 1980s, the structural and social condition of most African nations has declined further through the imposition of Washington Consensus economic policies. Bretton Woods institutions, the IMF and the World Bank, with the political backing of the United States and its rich allies, have dictated that indebted African nations must introduce neoliberal economic policies to secure future crisis loans. These structural adjustment programmes prioritize debt repayment, curtailing the state's public role dramatically, while compelling local industries to compete in a 'free market' that is rigged to protect Western TNCs and nation-states.[4] The typical effects are disastrous for most Africans: state budgets in education, health, transport and social welfare are slashed; nationalized industries are sold off cheaply; unemployment, homelessness, and absolute poverty (living on about $1 a day) have risen to unprecedented levels. In the mid-1960s, around 55 per cent of Africans lived in absolute poverty; that figure had risen to 65 per cent by 2002. Ghana, for example, was the star African pupil of the Washington Consensus in the early 1990s, but a decade later had become one of the world's most indebted poor nations. High HIV levels compound the problems and poverty levels in the era of structural adjustment (Poku 2002).

As the state withers, international non-governmental organizations (NGOs) have stepped in, allowing foreigners to take control of whole sections of health, education and welfare provision. Some have argued that NGOs are new forces of neocolonialism. NGO workers are not democratically accountable to local people, their main leadership and strategies are formulated in the West, and they serve to promote new forms of African dependency upon Western institutions (Ranger and Vaughan 1993: 258–9).

It is within this context that the rise in corruption within African society can be properly understood. To outside eyes, African politics is riddled with an indigenously nurtured system of chronic corruption and clientelism. The analyses of Bayart (1993) and others, through the notion of the 'politics of the belly', understand corruption as a traditional form of patronage, in apparent contradistinction to Western values of governance, such as honesty, integrity and transparency that must be imposed from outside if they are to take root. This argument underplays the European role in helping to sustain the precolonial patron–client relationships among Africans as a way of securing broader influence and control through the colonial and postcolonial eras. The argument has also been criticized for its cynicism and misunderstanding of African politics, and for ignoring the 'ideals, struggles for justice, notions of equality' throughout the continent (Szeftel 1998: 223, 235). The obsession of Western academics and donor institutions with corruption in Africa thus tends to misread it as a cause of political and economic underdevelopment rather than as a symptom. Deeper political and economic forces are at play in setting the conditions for secondary practices of governance, including corrupt ones.

Colonialism, neocolonialism and neoliberalism thus provide the circumstances within which African peoples make and remake their cultural identities and practices. Cultural nationalism has been promoted by the (often state-controlled) institutions of the mass media and the education system. Yet all nations contain linguistic diversity, whether in official European terms – such as Cameroon, with its French-, English- and German-speakers – or in the many local languages that often differentiate populations internally. African cultural nationalism is more likely to arise through international exchanges and interrelations with other cultures. Cultural globalization brings with it pressures of 'relativization' that force specific societies to respond to each other. Hence African engagement with international culture also provides strong studies in pragmatic cultural 'creolization' or 'glocalization', to use the respective phrases of Hannerz (1992) and Robertson (1992), each of which describes the capacity of local people to engage creatively with global cultural forms. In music, for example, Western instruments and traditions have been refashioned to produce new, 'creole' techniques and aesthetics within specific local cultures, notably in southern Africa.

Sport and other physical cultures within Africa have been destroyed, introduced and refashioned through this interplay of historical, political economic and cultural influences. Africa's precolonial movement cultures were generally annihilated during the systematic reorganization and subjugation of Africans by Europeans.[5] Some indigenous traditions did survive, notably the pan-African games known in southern Africa as *mancala* and *moraba-raba*. More commonly, the fledgling European sports traditions were taught to young African males by Western missionaries, teachers, soldiers, administrators and businessmen. Britain again led the way. In the Sudan, the political service was staffed particularly by Oxbridge graduates with excellent athletic backgrounds. In tropical Africa, elite missionaries endeavoured 'to create Tom Brown in Africa' through linking moral training to muscularity (Mangan 1985: 87, 120–1). In turn, aspiring Africans typically differed from the colonial elites by placing far greater emphasis on acquiring education and professional accreditation than in shaping themselves into athletic, muscular Christians through sport (Mangan 1987: 164–5). Where white elites were most sizeable, the right to use the most sophisticated sport facilities, or to represent the colonized nation, was denied to black competitors. European nations such as Portugal, which viewed their colonies as overseas territories, were able to field the occasional, great African athlete as Portuguese, and enter that person into the national team. The football stars Eusebio and Mario Coluna are the most prominent example. Yet with the rise of postwar African nationalism, sport took on major symbolic significance. Sport participation placed the new African nations in highly favourable, and unusually fair, international competition while promoting national identification at home. At the Mexico Olympics in 1968, Africa won a ground-breaking 13 athletics medals (Baker 1987: 277). Sport enabled African athletes and their clubs to generate forms of social and symbolic capital, and to assert particular strains of identity and difference, in the new villages and towns emerging from colonial rule. All of this was 'glocalized' further through the Africans' generation of particular aesthetic codes and tactical systems that differed from those in other nations and continents.

Football in Africa: from colonial import to cultural reinvention

Football's introduction and inculcation within Africa is a story both of cultural colonization by Europeans and of cultural adaptation or 'creolization' by the African people. Certainly, British influence was most prevalent at the outset. Football was introduced first into South Africa in the 1860s, and then into territories controlled in the south, east and west, as well as Egypt in the north. The French played the next most important role, bringing the game to the Maghreb and beyond, stretching from Algeria south through modern-day Mali, Niger, and Mauritania, and then into Benin, the Ivory Coast, and the Central African Republic, and as far down as Congo in the west, plus the island of Madagascar in the east. Portuguese influence was prominent along the Atlantic seaboard, from the Cape Verde islands, through Guinea-Bissau and Angola, as well as Mozambique on the east. Germany promoted football in the central regions, in what are now Cameroon, Rwanda and Tanzania. The Spanish played an important pioneer role in two small Atlantic loci that are today Western Sahara and Equatorial Guinea. Belgian colonizers played football in what is now the Democratic Republic of Congo (DRC) while Italians developed the game in Libya and Eritrea.

The colonial groups associated with football's spread varied little: teachers and missionaries, soldiers, and colonial settlers were the most prominent practitioners. Most favoured playing among themselves, but African involvement was often a *sine qua non* when European numbers ran low. For white educators, football was a cheaper, more accessible game to have local people play than alternatives such as cricket that required both expensive equipment and a more intense commitment to patrician British mores. In each new colonial conurbation, Africans watched Europeans play football, and sought to emulate their skills in township games using bundles of rags as makeshift balls. In turn, local African football teams were founded and competed in township tournaments, developing their own rivalries and styles of play.

Politically, the more autonomous north has always been the leading player in African football. Egypt was the first African association to be accepted into FIFA (Fédération Internationale de Football Association), in 1923, and eleven years later became the continent's opening representative at the World Cup finals, in Italy. Only four African football associations (Egypt, Sudan, South Africa and Ethiopia) were recognized by FIFA by the time that the African football federation CAF (Confédération Africaine de Football) was founded in 1957 (Murray 1996: 130–1). Egyptian officials have since retained a strong hegemony as CAF has grown into a 52-member association, the largest continental governing body in the world.

In the postwar era of rising pan-African independence, the political capabilities of the indigenous peoples were highlighted in football through the creation of international and club competitions across the continent, which produced a wide geographical spread of winners.[6] The African Nations Cup began in 1957, before its European equivalent, and has been played biennially since then. Cameroon have been most successful, winning four times; other winners come from the north (Egypt, Morocco, Algeria), the west (Ghana, Nigeria, Ivory Coast), the Sahara region and central Africa (Sudan, Ethiopia, the former Zaire), and the south (South Africa). A similar plurality of sides has taken the annual African Champions Cup, contested since 1964, though it has become increasingly dominated by the biggest teams, such as Raja CA Casablanca in the north, or ASEC Mimosas from the west. Other tournaments such as the Cup Winners Cup (played since 1975) and the CAF Cup (since 1992) have followed the European club tournament format, culminating in the foundation of a Super Cup in 1992.

Independent African states did succeed in pressurizing FIFA into ejecting the racist states of South Africa and Rhodesia from world football. Yet the African voice remained relatively muted until João Havelange gained backing from developing nations in his successful bid to become FIFA

President in 1974 (Darby 2002). African nations gained directly from Havelange's stated aim to expand the game competitively. Without a guaranteed place at the World Cup finals since 1934, African nations were represented in turn by Morocco, Zaire and Tunisia at successive tournaments during the 1970s.

In 1982, two African nations were allocated finals places and demonstrated the continent's potential. Algeria defeated the eventual cup finalists West Germany in a preliminary fixture. Only a shameful, contrived victory over Austria allowed the Germans to qualify for the later stages at the Algerians' expense. Cameroon, meanwhile, held the eventual winners, Italy, to a goalless draw, and were edged out of qualification on goal difference. Four years later, in Mexico, Morocco became the first African side to reach the second phase, winning their qualifying group in the process. In 1990, Cameroon (and in particular, veteran star striker Roger Milla) set the Italian World Cup finals alight by defeating world champions Argentina in the opening fixture. The West Africans went on to lose unluckily to England in the quarter-finals. As the World Cup finals continued to expand, Africa was awarded five places at the 32-team finals in France in 1998. At the 2002 tournament, Senegal provided the strongest African threat, defeating world champions France and reaching the quarter-finals. These early successes of African teams have fuelled international expectation that is both excessive and unfulfilled. Nigeria's victory in the men's football tournament at the 1996 Olympic Games in Atlanta represents the greatest achievement by an African international team to date. Liberia's George Weah has been the most internationally lauded African player, winning the World Player of the Year competition in 1995 during his time at top Italian club AC Milan. African international victories have occurred four times in the Under-17 World Championships, won twice apiece by Nigeria and Ghana, but the victors have failed to turn these teams into adult world-beaters.

Africa's arrival on international football's world stage has been hampered by the failure to attract the World Cup finals to the continent. The regular bids by northern nations such as Morocco are rarely considered as serious. Most damagingly, South Africa were pipped by Germany in the 2006 finals bid, despite FIFA President Sepp Blatter's earlier insistence that it was 'Africa's turn' to host the world's biggest single-sport event.

Football's development in postcolonial Africa has been strongly shaped by neocolonial and neoliberal forces. From the 1970s onwards, European coaches and agents have sought to identify and develop African football talent for export purposes. Young players are recruited to European-controlled clubs under highly exploitative contractual relations with the hope of moving to the top leagues run by the former colonial powers in England, France, Germany, Holland, Belgium, Spain, Italy and Portugal. Some European coaches that control professional club or national sides are inclined towards forms of racism in dealing with their players. The Dutch coach Clemens Westerhof, who has coached in several African nations, was recognized as 'a racist and a militarist' by Nigerians when he controlled their national team, but was credited as an effective coach (Hoberman 2000: 120–1). However, opposition to the recruitment of foreign coaches is often strong, particularly regarding the national level; defeats are often blamed on these coaches, and on the sense of postcolonial dependency that their earlier recruitment had continued to foster among Africans (Vidacs 1998).

The western states of Nigeria, Cameroon and Ghana have produced some of the most prominent African players at European level. Many players fail to make the grade after transfer, and so are left to struggle with minimal resources on European city streets. Inevitably, for the vast majority of African boys, football offers no real prospect of positive social or geographical mobility. Mass migration of players inevitably devalues the quality of domestic club competitions. Most African nations struggle to bring back all of their overseas players to compete in international fixtures. Those players who do break through internationally seek proper financial rewards from national associations in an attempt to avoid the pitiable fate that has befallen most of their predecessors upon retirement. On several occasions African players have gone on strike to ensure decent payment from the leaders of their football associations. In the worst scenarios, monies earmarked for players can disappear into the private coffers of football officials.

However, football's international system is not entirely negative for young African players. For the handful that succeed, social status and economic security go alongside the pleasure of playing the game regularly. For many who miss the European 'big time', it is better to stay in the West and to work or to retrain than to return to a nation in major decline. For the millions that fail to attract scouting interest, football represents a personally pleasing leisure experience and a healthy social pastime, an albeit temporary escape from the personal hazards of African city-life.[7]

The broad structural decline of African economies, and the implementation of Washington Consensus policies, has adversely affected the African football infrastructure. State-owned enterprises had helped to run football clubs that were important community resources. Following their takeover by TNCs, the newly privatized institutions have tended to reduce expenditure in all social programmes, including sports-related associations. In Zambia, for example, the Nkana Red Devils, sponsored by a local copper mine, reached the African Club championship quarter-finals during Kaunda's reign, but subsequently fell into decline after mining privatization.

Highly indebted national governments lack the resources or political freedom to introduce new capital projects within sport, such as the erection of new stadiums and sports centres. In Zaire, for example, a stadium-building project that would have enabled the nation to host the African Nations Cup was subsequently abandoned, in part through lack of funds. Stadium maintenance is a further major problem: taxation and gate-receipts decline during tough economic times, leading to the decline and dereliction of existing sporting venues.

High unemployment, rising poverty levels and long hours spent scratching a living in the informal economy do not establish the stable environment needed for healthy young football players to learn and hone new skills. Attracting investment and sponsorship from the private sector is more difficult than in Europe or Asia as comparatively few TNCs identify great potential markets across an impoverished Africa. Through a deal struck with FIFA, Coca-Cola has donated thousands of footballs to African nations. Alternatively, somewhat more negatively, the most prominent sponsors of African club football are often beer and cigarette corporations.

FIFA has sought to enhance football development in African states through its GOAL! projects that provide direct aid, such as coaching clinics and the delivery of equipment. However, there remain concerns that the money that does come into African football, whether from local or international sources, is often restricted or redirected by corrupt practices. Zimbabwe's football chief, Leo Mugabe (the nephew of national president Robert Mugabe) was voted out of office in December 2002 by the national association after over $60,000 of FIFA monies disappeared. In July 2001, Ghana's former sports minister was jailed for four years after being convicted of stealing around $46,000 in bonus money intended for the national football team. Other forms of corrupt practice involve bribing referees or opposition teams and players. Malawi were accused of bribing match officials prior to a fixture with Kenya, while a reported $25,000 changed hands before the Nigeria–Ghana match that the host team won 3–0, thereby edging Liberia out of a place at the 2002 World Cup finals.

There are strong correlations between poverty and human risk, and in turn African football has had to contend with greater disasters than we find in other continents in recent years. In terms of health, the HIV/AIDS pandemic, which strikes particularly at young adults, has ravaged much of the football infrastructure in southern Africa. At elite level, African nations have been robbed of many brilliant talents, such as Size Motaung (South Africa), Rogers Lupiya, Pearson Mwanza and Gibby Mbasela (all Zambia), and Frank Sinalo, Clifton Msiya and Holman Malunga (all Malawi). At the everyday level, HIV infection has greatly shortened the lives of young people, and irreversibly damaged their quality of life, such as in active sports engagement.

Football can only be one of many mediums for the communication of health messages by state health authorities and international NGOs. The United Nations' children's charity, UNICEF, has entered collaboration with FIFA in order to communicate disease-prevention messages through organized football matches. Some specific projects have targeted tournaments with predictably large audiences. At the east and central African football tournament held in Kenya in November 1999, health messages and the distribution of condoms were aimed at the 120,000 supporters who held a minute's silence before games to reflect on the social impact of AIDS.

Other forms of high daily risk have undermined football engagement. Chemical pollution makes for unsafe landscapes in which to practise football informally. High levels of transport-related deaths or serious injury are also related to poverty and have significantly affected football. The most notable disaster saw the entire Zambian national team killed by a plane crash after a fixture in Gabon in 1993. To save the national football association some money, the team had been flying in aircraft belonging to the armed services, rather than using a more reliable, commercial airline. Rather damningly, the report into the cause of the crash was suppressed without explanation by the Zambian government (Liwewe 1999). Violence and lawlessness have also pushed players towards destitution, such as Ndaye Mulamba, the great Zaire forward of the 1970s, maimed by looting soldiers after his retirement and left to count out his days in southern Africa.

While crowd safety in other parts of the world has been strengthened, recent disasters at African football stadiums have become more prominent internationally. These tragedies have been caused mainly by poor facilities and crowd-control techniques by undertrained and badly managed security services. 126 supporters were killed at a club fixture in Ghana in May 2001 when police overreacted to minor crowd disturbances and generated a major stampede. A month earlier, 43 spectators were killed at a derby match in Johannesburg due to ineffectual policing at the turnstiles and intense crushing inside stands.

The strength of African football is to be found at grassroots level, where the game is unquestionably the dominant athletic pastime among children and young men. Proper football matches played in African suburbs and villages are either organized into a league system under the auspices of the local football associations, or are part of a wide, independent, informal network of 'social football' programmes. Football clubs are liable to be formed from highly informal roots. In Kano, Nigeria, for example, clubs are formed by boys who then look to adults to make the team more official and help with finance (Haruna and Abdullahi 1991: 117–18). More prominent, powerful clubs often emerge in townships under the influence of local 'big men' whose patronage is gained in exchange for the club becoming a more personalized symbol of the success of charismatic leadership (Jeffrey 1992). The oldest teams have generated support among local Africans that is expressed in familial terms, as a bond between the current generation and their ancestors who founded these cultural institutions. Making football clubs 'family' serves to further the cultural Africanization of the game (Martin 1995: 120).

As they are founded upon competition and the generation of rivalries, African football fixtures may dramatize underlying forms of political conflict and cultural tension. Urbanization, social differentiation along linguistic and ethnic lines, and postcolonial nationalism provide the more salient ingredients that feed into the cultural identities within Africa's complex football system. As in any other continent, African club football is peppered with major rivalries and derby fixtures. The most intense intracity derbies include Zamalek v. Al-Ahli in Cairo and Orlando Pirates and Kaizer Chiefs around Johannesburg; others include Canon v. Tonnerre in Yaoundé, St George v. Mechal in Addis Ababa, Mighty Barolle versus Invincible Eleven in Monrovia, and WA v. Raja in Casablanca. Major rivalries suffused with ethnic and regional dimensions include Hearts of Oak (Accra) v. Ashanti United (Asante) in Ghana; the Shooting Stars (Lagos), Enugu Rangers and Nationale (Oweri) power struggle in Nigeria; and the Highlanders (Bulawayo) and Dynamos (Harare) battle in Zimbabwe. African football crowds highlight the strong creolization of the European game by local peoples. Generally, African crowds have long departed from the restrained behavioural codes that their colonial masters favoured within sport. African football fans are strongly partisan, highly vocal, and advocate unambiguous views regarding events on the field of play. The supporters, as well as the significant number of football journalists, establish and sustain popular traditions surrounding specific clubs, as conveyed through their nicknames, songs, reminiscences about great former players, and the fluctuations in their team's fortunes and relations with rival clubs. Other aspects of football's Africanization include the pre-match entertainment that can feature performances by local artists. Before kick-off and during half-time, football crowds can enjoy the delicacies of local African cuisine, such as skewered mice (sugar cane rats) in Malawi, peanut-flavoured kebabs in Ghana, and heated nuts in most northern nations. The different aesthetic codes within African football have complex cultural histories. Compared to Europeans, African players must adapt their play to different environmental and economic circumstances. Most pitches are in poor condition, lack grass and possess bumpy surfaces. African players typically learn to play without boots, in crowded and dusty townships while kicking around a self-made 'ball'. African football societies that learned skills and tactics from videos and foreign coaches (notably Yugoslav, French and Brazilian) were more inclined to favour technical styles of play. For example, the great Ashanti side of Ghana during the late 1960s were strongly influenced by their Brazilian coach; Cameroon has an essentially French style dating back to at least the 1960s; while the Yugoslav-coached national sides of Zaire and Zambia during the mid-1970s were highly technical. In the old British colonial footholds across east, southern, and parts of west and central Africa, the more physical British style has remained particularly influential.

Perhaps the most fascinating aspect of African football culture concerns the role of traditional belief-systems, notably those surrounding witchcraft or 'juju' as performed by 'muti-men'. Large numbers of African football clubs consult or employ religious specialists to perform rituals and prescribe medicines that will protect players and upset the opposition (Leseth 1997; Martin 1995: 121–2). Favoured juju practices include smearing players' bodies in magical powders or bathing in treated liquids, and daubing the goalposts or the stadium entrances with the blood of animals that have been ceremonially slaughtered. Leading African football officials seek to counter juju to promote the continent's game according to Westernized, orthodox ideals of scientific rationality, professionalism and managerial efficiency. Prior to the 2002 African Nations Cup finals, CAF officially banned the involvement of 'muti-men'. Nevertheless, several teams found ways of importing these 'assistants' under alternative professional titles. The struggle came to a chaotic conclusion in the hours before the semi-final fixture between Mali and Cameroon when several police officers arrested several Cameroonian officials on suspicion that a muti ceremony was occurring on the pitch. Cameroon won the match 3–0.

In general, juju represents the African cultural solution to a universal football problem: quelling pre-match anxiety in a sport marked by uncertainty of outcome. Training and coaching advice can prepare players tactically and technically for their test on the field, but confidence, the will-to-win and motivation can require other sources of professional guidance. Juju's strongest critics argue that it can promote fatalism among players, thereby undermining their training, fitness, and thus their performance (see *The East African*, 1 April 2002). More commonly, juju provides players with the extra psychological edge that can enhance their competitiveness. In the West, sport psychologists are recruited to instil self-belief among players. In Africa, it is the divination of the spirits rather than the discovery of the athlete's 'inner child', that places players in a state of mental equilibrium. Let us not forget too that African juju provides more sophisticated versions of the 'lucky' pre-match rituals that are still employed by many of the world's top players.

National football teams, such as that of Cameroon, are an important public source of symbolic identification for peoples that are differentiated linguistically and ethnically (Clignet and Stark 1974). Some international fixtures have acquired a strong sense of rivalry and serve to enhance that national solidarity. The Cameroon–Nigeria match is one of Africa's major encounters, while southern African nations are always keen to secure a strong performance against South Africa, the region's economic superpower. When Zaire won the 1974 African Nations Cup, President Mobutu's power was cemented through the stronger sense of national unity that resulted.

However, beneath the unity of the national side, the cultural politics of identity difference are often contested. In which city should the national team play? What club background should the national team coach have? Which club players should be selected? These kinds of questions and their ensuing public debates capture the processes by which religious, ethnic and regional groups typically struggle for symbolic hegemony over the nation's representation through football. In Ghana, Christian and Muslim groups dispute player selections. In Egypt, some Christians complain that players of their faith need to be exceptionally good to displace inferior Muslim players. In Nigeria, ethnicity is the focus of analysis as biases by national team coaches and captains are seen as undermining the representative chances of players from other ethnic groups. The successful Zaire side of the 1970s was comprised entirely of players of Baluba ethnicity from the Lumbashi district.

In some circumstances, cultural difference will be sufficiently strong for some minorities to place their allegiances outside of the national team. During the 2002 African Nations Cup in Mali, the Tuareg and Arab minorities in the host nation were notable supporters of North African teams, to mark their cultural difference from the wider Malian population. At some football fixtures in Libya during September 2000, Nigerians and other immigrant Africans were caught up in serious crowd disturbances with local people that escalated into violent rioting, resulting in several reported deaths.

The underlying problems in nation-building through football may be focused primarily on the incumbent political regime. Many African states either prohibit or persecute those who formally criticize the state, such as through literature or public rallies. Football can provide an important, alternative public sphere for the expression of popular discontent towards ruling elites. For example, in Cameroon, Zambia and Ghana, vociferous football crowds expressed their opposition to the unpopular regimes of Paul Biya, Kenneth Kaunda, and Jerry Rawlings respectively. In Libya in July 1996, at least 20 fans were killed when security forces opened fire at a football crowd attending the El-Hilal versus Al-Hal Benghazi fixture, after supporters had been chanting anti-Gaddafi slogans.

In the most problematic circumstances, football has a modest though notable role to play in regions where ethnic divisions and political struggles have fuelled long-running military conflicts that traumatize soldiers and civilians alike. Football has been employed to assist processes of positive resocialization and reconciliation, to mediate across cultural conflicts, and to try to develop forms of positive symbolic dialogue between rival populations. In war-torn states such as Rwanda and Burundi, international NGOs seek to organize young players from different ethnic backgrounds into games. More commonly, football and other sports are introduced by aid agencies as therapeutic measures for resocializing former child soldiers and other young victims of military conflicts. In Sierra Leone, for example, one priority is to train referees to enhance the building of rule-following play (Richards 1997).

Nevertheless, it would be naive to suggest that football is some kind of cross-cultural panacea that can incapacitate complex, embedded social conflicts. In sport, as in the rest of life, the dice are loaded against the disadvantaged. But African football also provides recurring studies of how these groups declare their presence, and enhance their standing, within the public sphere through physical culture. During colonial times, this was obviously evident in football's adoption and adaptation by the indigenous populations. In the postcolonial era, football provides one venue of symbolic mobility for those communities that are denied entry to apparently more conventional forms of social advancement (notably education and employment). In the past decade, African women's football has grown strongly and places women within a very visible and culturally valued male domain.

Book contents: competition, conflict and conciliation

The book is divided into four parts. In Part One, 'Contested Selections', we consider the modern social history of football within four African nations – Eritrea, Algeria, Nigeria and Zimbabwe.

Located on the horn of Africa, Eritrea, the youngest nation of the continent, is one African setting to have suffered particularly from the ravages of war. In this opening chapter, Alex Last details the history of conflict in the region and the role that football and its clubs have played during these difficult times. Football began with the Italian colonists, but the indigenous peoples were excluded and forced to create their own leagues in emulation. When the British took over after 1941, football provided a social space for cross-cultural communication, while allowing remaining Italians to express their antipathy towards the new rulers. The subsequent Eritrean struggle for independence was enacted in football, as Eritreans established their own separate federation, despite Ethiopian resistance. As Last shows, football has continued to be a significant domain of political and cultural struggle. The post-conflict situation of the late 1970s saw a radical change to Eritrean football which reflected the Soviet backing the country had received during the war and whose legacy remains to this day primarily in the nomenclature of football clubs. In the late 1980s and early 1990s in times of armed struggle, football and football clubs played an important role in the creation of the Eritrean diasporas and the sustaining of morale amongst armed combatants and prisoners of war.

The history and politics of Algerian football are assessed by Youssef Fates. French colonists and visiting British people played a major role in sparking local fascination with football. Politically, football became an important venue in various struggles. During colonial times, popular support for the cause of Algerian nationalism was voiced by local football supporters. Spectator violence was commonplace and a source of major concern for the colonial authorities. In the postcolonial era, the struggle has shifted to that between the ruling nationalist elites and the fundamentalist movements. In football, this means the observation of religious instructions by crowds and some players, and further incidents of social breakdown within the stadium.

The history and politics of Nigerian football is then explored by Wiebe Boer. Although Nigeria is one of Africa's most successful football nations, there has been little attempt to chronicle its history. The game was introduced by British colonists and spread from the coast across the country. Boer notes that football served to cement notions of Nigerian identity, notably in the postcolonial period, while being patronized by ruling elites, notably the Abacha regime. The successes of Nigeria internationally have made the national football team a key symbol of African pride.

In the following chapter, Richard Giulianotti examines the social history and contemporary sociology of football in Zimbabwe. Giulianotti breaks the history into three parts, covering colonialism, the period of state-formation following independence, and the ongoing period of neoliberal globalization. Football, as an important element of black popular culture, has sustained a significant distance from its domination by the most powerful elites. Under colonialism and the post-independence period, clubs were foci for the complex symbolic interplay between ethnolinguistic groups. Zimbabwe's serious decline since the mid-1990s, however, has significantly undermined the football infrastructure.

Part Two, 'Footballing Colours' examines the role that football has played in the debate over playing style, ethnicity and nation building in four African countries. In the first of these, Laura Fair examines football's early development and creative adaptation by local African people on the island of Zanzibar, a semi-autonomous region of Tanzania located off Africa's east coast. British colonial administrators had hoped sport would instil disciplined behaviour among young male Africans, but football rapidly grew into the 'national' game with a strong local cultural underpinning. Zanzibar football was infused with the aesthetic meanings and pleasures associated with *ngoma* (indigenous drum and dance competitions). Distinctive playing styles, spectator cultures, and fusions of music and football were soon central to the Zanzibar game, reflecting African cultural vitality despite structural and historical inequalities.

The oldest football nation on the continent – South Africa – is discussed in the chapter by Peter Alegi. The author's focus is a specific one, concerning the South African Soccer League (SASL) that ran from 1960 to 1966 under the control of non-whites at the height of apartheid. Alegi argues that SASL revolutionized South African football and sport in general, producing spectacular fixtures and highly popular new clubs, and confirming the potential of 'blacks' and 'coloureds' to run major institutions with marked success. The racist state recognized the danger and effectively 'strangled' the SASL, serving to retard further the development of South African football within the international context.

Tim Edensor and Ibrahim Koodoruth explore the relationship of football to forms of ethnicity within Mauritius, a polyethnic island off the east coast of Africa in the middle of the Indian Ocean. They argue that football, like music, helps convey the intense fluidity of ethnic identity and expression on the island. Violence around club fixtures culminated in lengthy rioting, arson and several deaths in 1999. The government suspended and reorganized the football system, seeking to negate the ethnic allegiances of leading sides. However, football remains strongly marked by ethnicity, not least through its domination by Creole players who seek alternative forms of social mobility.

Arguing that football can be a form of liberty to the oppressed and feared by those in power for the emotions it releases, Gareth Stanton's study of the role of the game in the making of Morocco details the popularity that the game holds in the collective imagination and the way the game has been linked to the institution of the monarchy. The relative paucity of documentary record should in no way detract from the achievements of migrating Moroccans who have graced the leagues of Western Europe since the 1930s and the World Cup finals on four occasions since 1970. The popularity of the game was realized by King Hassan II seeking a unifying factor in nation building and football clubs have had the patronage of royalty and have at times acted as surrogate form of nationalist activity against the colonialists of the French Protectorate who excluded them from their competitions. In the postcolonial situation of the mid-1950s the game's players and administrators have had a huge burden of expectation placed on them, particularly those involved with the national team, thus illustrating the precarious nature of investing too much nationalistic baggage in a 90-minute athletic competition.

Part Three, 'Off the Ball Movements', takes analysis beyond the game itself to the epi-phenomenon created around it. This analysis examines the legacies of colonialism in Cameroon as well as projects that seek to provide for a 'civil society' in countries devastated both economically and by armed conflict.

The most successful national football team of the African continent – the Indomitable Lions of Cameroon – are analysed by Bea Vidacs in relation to their former French colonizers. The chequered colonial history of Cameroon saw no fewer than three European powers attempt to impose their political will here; however, the outstanding legacy remains that of the French who, despite granting independence to Cameroon in 1960 following a bloody struggle for independence, sustain close links with the people who wanted them gone. This relationship is manifest in football where accusations about French duplicity and involvement in results that go against the national team are never far from the surface of football discussions. Analysis focuses on the 1998 World Cup tournament hosted by France which saw Cameroon managed by a French coach eliminated in the first round whilst the host nation went on to win the final. The Cameroonians supported all the teams that provided opponents to the French in what the author presents as a multifaceted opposition based in various postcolonial and racial resentments. That France would beat Brazil in the final was to many Cameroonian observers a foregone conclusion, because the match, manifesting as it did the First World against the Third, would see the former bribe the latter. Such an assumption raises the question as to whether the same people would expect their own players to be so susceptible to similar financial inducement. In the absence of an agreed answer the Cameroonians are left to debate whether footballing success is more a product of the 'politics of the belly' or arises out of more scientific and cultural factors.

A metaphor that likens a biscuit to a game of football should provoke the curiosity of many a seasoned football observer. In this chapter Gary Armstrong examines the role that the game has played in the history of Liberia, one of the continent's most fascinating places. Whilst the first independent nation of Africa, Liberia was subject to a de facto colonization in the early nineteenth century by the arrival of former slaves from the southern states of the US. The returning people were to subject the indigenous ones to a form of living not too far from that they had been freed from. The resentment of this subjugation combined with economic factors eventually produced, in the late twentieth century, some 20 years of civil conflict which continues to this day. The author examines the hypothesis that football can integrate people at odds over and above other peace initiatives and chronicles the attempts made by various Liberian politicians to achieve national consciousness via football. The rhetoric and reality behind the claims made about both the funding and the power of football as a vehicle for reconciliation are critically presented and make for pessimistic reading. Optimism survives, however, with the discovery of a grassroots scheme that exists beyond formal politics and celebrity endorsement.

The highly acclaimed football-led project of the Mathare Youth Sports Association (MYSA) in Nairobi, Kenya, is chronicled and placed in the context of the role of sport and social development in the chapter by Hans Hognestad and Arvid Tollisen. Begun on the initiative of a Canadian humanitarian worker, the MYSA scheme was an attempt to unite diverse and sometimes antagonistic people via collective action in a milieu burdened with the problems of poverty and its usual accompaniments – violence and ecological chaos. In its 15 years of existence the project has become Africa's largest youth organization. From humble origins and with minimal equipment and funding, but inspired by a self-help philosophy, MYSA now has a respected professional football club and 1000 feeder teams held together by elected representatives, and is funded by both internal and external sources. The project has duties beyond the field of play and plays a huge part in making the neighbourhood habitable and healthy via its multifarious environmental schemes which have gained accolades from the United Nations. Other issues the project addresses via its footballers are: AIDS awareness, the vulnerability of street children, and the necessity of education enshrined within its emphasis on fair play and mutual responsibility both on and off the field of play. The 'pulling together' philosophy of postcolonial Kenya is exemplified in sport which successive governments have promoted as a way of nation-building. Not all rhetoric is realized, however, and violence around football is prevalent. With this reality the MYSA project seems to offer an alternative to entrenched and often tribally-led political and ethnic loyalties and offers a beacon of hope for those who love the game, standing as it does as an institution with integrity in a game which faces endemic accusations of domestic corruption.

In two of the chapters that contribute to the fourth and final section entitled 'Moving with the Ball', various explanations on a grand scale are offered as to African footballer migration, before a specific case study of the great Esuebio of Mozambique and Benfica of Portugal.

The migration patterns and the reception offered to African footballers seeking fame and fortune in Western Europe is explored. Mapping the geographical variations in such movement, John Bale excavates the processes of recruitment before examining how Europe 'writes' the African footballer. Citing the extent of migration and locating it in the growing commercialism of the football industry, the author presents the varieties of migrations available to the varieties of 'African footballer'. Accepting that some movement is self-initiated, the author notes the often concomitant practice of 'passports of convenience' enabling the player to construct a mythical ancestry which permits him to ply his trade within the European laws governing the game. Once in Europe the migrant may well face poor playing conditions, racist abuse and, if the gamble does not pay off, destitution. Pondering on the postcolonial situation, Bale examines the 'imaginative geographies' that the African player inspires. While imagery provided by footage provokes comments from the European audience on footballing abilities which liken the

African players to European predecessors, the perception of some fatal flaw as a product of their assumed surfeit of 'instinct' and untutored purity over the 'modern' and 'technical' European-born footballer nevertheless insinuates a widespread personal state of chaos and irrationality.

The migration of one individual – the great Eusebio of Mozambique – is the subject of the chapter by Gary Armstrong. Aged 60 at the time of the interview in 2002, the Lisbon-residing Footballing Ambassador for both his native country and his adopted country of Portugal is a universally recognised figure even though his playing days ended close to 30 years ago. The man known as the 'Black Panther' recalls his journey from the poverty of colonial Mozambique in 1961 to the highest pinnacles world football could offer over the next 15 years. His story comes complete with interclub intrigue and enlightens the reader as to the extent of the intrusion of politicians in shaping his career. It also details the role of core–periphery relations in the migration of talent under Portuguese colonialism. His opinions on the role of European clubs in Africa and the nature of some of the African players provide interesting contrasts to those evident in the previous chapter.

By way of conclusion, the final chapter by Peter Woodward sees this long respected scholar on African affairs play the metaphorical role of *libero* as he offers his reflections on this volume whilst adding his own stories about the role that the game played in his time on the continent.

Acknowledgements

Our thanks are due to to Mark Gleeson, Emmanuel Maradas (editor of *African Soccer* magazine) and Peter Woodward for their generous assistance with empirical information in this chapter.

Notes

1. Alegi is working on an authoritative book on South African football; Darby (2002) has chronicled aspects of African football politics in relation to FIFA; Broere and van der Drift (1997) provide a highly informative study of African football in a book initially published in Dutch. See also Apraku and Hesselman's (1998) contribution to this area, written in German.
2. See, for example, Worby (1998) on 'tribal' identities in Zimbabwe.
3. The chief protagonist of modernization theory was Rostow (1960).
4. Historical lessons, of course, dictate that free market policies in emerging economies do not work. Indeed, the major Western nations such as the US, the UK and Japan built up their own industrial and corporate power by pursuing highly protectionist policies, with varying levels of state investment, to bolster local businesses against any international competitors. Denied such

protection, Latin American or African economies remain underdeveloped, producing cash crops (such as foodstuffs) to fill niche markets in the West, rather than advancing to become the industrial and intellectual powerhouses of the twenty-first century.

5. On the sociocultural changes in Kenya, from precolonial to postcolonial times, see Bale and Sang (1995).

6. Alegi (2000b) examines in detail what has been termed the 'first sub-Saharan African football championship', contested in 1949–50 by teams from the Belgian Congo and South Africa.

7. On these issues, see the documentary *Sold Out: From Street to Stadium*, produced by Fish Film, Vienna, April 2002.

Part One
Contested Selections

1
Containment and Counter-Attack: A History of Eritrean Football

Alex Last

The small stadium in Eritrea's capital city of Asmara was packed to its 10,000 capacity as local fans, clapping and cheering and sounding klaxons, supported the national team in a crucial African Nations Cup qualifier against Mozambique in 1999. Along the running track around the pitch, special red motorized tricycles were parked, in which were sat some of Eritrea's disabled veterans of their long War of Independence from Ethiopia which had officially ended in 1991. Eritrea needed to score. On the break, the Mozambique goalkeeper fumbled a long shot, the Eritrean forward scooped the ball over the keeper and it dropped just under the bar. The crowd erupted and Italian residents of Eritrea, the legacy of Italian colonialism, jumped for joy alongside indigenous Eritreans. The running track below witnessed the bizarre sight of disabled war veterans in their motorized tricycles doing furious laps of honour, waving flags and swerving around the hapless policeman standing in the way in a vain attempt to halt the 'traffic' so the game could continue.

The victory celebrations continued long after the game, but the joy masked the everyday reality of a difficult time for the country at large. After just seven years of peace Eritrea was once again at war with its giant southern neighbour Ethiopia. The day of the match itself coincided with the eve of the country's Martyrs Day, similar to Remembrance Sunday in Britain, except in Eritrea the memories of sacrifice were much closer at hand. As hundreds of thousands of Eritreans walked down the main avenue that evening, holding candles to commemorate the occasion, one old women I interviewed stated, 'It's a very sad day for us, to remember our lost relatives ...', adding after a long pause, 'but at least we beat Mozambique at football.'

Football, however, has not been one of the priorities in Eritrea in recent years, war and survival of the nation were considered more important. The success of the game against Mozambique was more about having

27

something to celebrate amidst the trauma of a society coping with conflict. At the same time, the success of the Eritrean national football side in football is a reminder of the glory days before the trouble really started, when, in 1963, nine of the eleven players who made up Ethiopia's victorious African Nation's Cup team were Eritrean.

Eritrea is a small nation about the size of England, with its half Christian, half Muslim population currently estimated at 3.5 million. Eritrea is bordered to the east by the Red Sea, with stunning mountains rising to over 2000 metres running like a backbone through the middle of the country, and with flat lowlands to the west meeting the border of Sudan. To the south on the coast lies the small French-dominated country of Djibouti and Eritrea's giant landlocked neighbour Ethiopia. As colonial powers carved up Africa in the late nineteenth century, Italy belatedly wanted some of the action. After being humiliated in battle by the Ethiopian emperor, Menelik II in 1896, Italy settled for what is now Eritrea.

Football and foreign rule[1]

Football in Eritrea developed through Italian colonialism from the turn of the century. With the Italian colonial administration came the Comitato Nazionale Olympico Italiano (CONI), the Italian Olympic Committee founded in 1914, which oversaw sports both in Italy and its new colonies. Football, cycling, motor racing, show jumping, swimming and sailing were among the sports officially organized in Eritrea. They were also the strict preserve of Italians; no indigenous Eritreans could participate. Eight stadiums were built in the highland capital of Asmara alone. Italian football teams were created which competed in their own league. By the 1930s there were two Italian sports newspapers for Eritrea, *Luce Sport* and *Vita Sportiva*.

In 1916, the Italian designers of the city were already thinking in terms of racial segregation. But it was not until the mid to late 1930s that racial segregation took on its dramatic forms, mostly in response to the influx of troops for Mussolini's invasion of Ethiopia in 1935, and then the arrival of 60,000 Italian civilian workers from 1936 onwards. Mussolini, who had come to power in 1922, was trying to impress on the colonial administration the need for racial segregation. Buses and cinemas were segregated, even the main avenue was split, with indigenous Eritreans not allowed to walk on one side of the boulevard. Despite this, in December 1936 the first six indigenous Eritrean teams were organized to compete in their own league. This was the year after Italy's successful conquest of Ethiopia in which tens of thousands of Eritrean troops had been used by the Italian army. An area of open ground where the University of Asmara now stands, was termed the Campo Nativo, and was given over for Eritreans to play amongst themselves. The indigenous teams had Italian names, like Ardita, Savoia and Vittoria.

Addressing the colonialists' tactics: 1935–50

The separate league system developed from 1936. The Eritreans held their own cup competition, the Directors Cup, on the path of separate development. In schools, for example, Eritreans were only allowed to be educated up until the standard of 4th grade (today's equivalent would be the education given to a ten-year-old). The Second World War ended all football competition, both Italian and Eritrean. After the defeat of the Italian army in Eritrea by British forces in 1941, the British took over the administration of Eritrea. However, they left most of the Italian infrastructure intact and paid Italian civil servants to continue running the country. The Italian Olympic Committee, CONI, was left in charge of sport.

The British did, however, abolish the colour bar. The new administration also began to train Eritreans for the civil service, and allowed the development of newspapers and the formation of political parties. In this new political atmosphere, football gradually made a return. It marked the start of Eritrean attempts to be accepted into the exclusively Italian league in Eritrea, Serie A.

Such attempts began in 1944 by accident. An Eritrean footballer had broken his leg but could not afford medical treatment. The indigenous football clubs held a meeting to discuss the lack of money and how best to help the player. At the meeting, the issue of joining the CONI-run Italian league was raised. The Eritreans came up with a solution. They would put forward one team, drawn from the best players of the indigenous clubs, to join the Italian league. Naturally, there were disputes over what to call the new superteam. Names were written on slips of paper, placed in a hat. The one drawn out was Hamasien, the name of the central highlands region.

The new team appealed to the British to be allowed to join the Italian league. The British deferred to CONI, which refused, citing an article in its constitution which did not permit non-Italians to participate. The Eritreans then sought the advice of an Italian man working for the Melotti brewery in Eritrea. He advised the Eritreans to buy a cup and invite an Italian team in the league to play for it. The invitation was made, and an Italian team, ironically named Eritrea, agreed to play. The game was played at the stadium of Chicero in Asmara, and the covered seating was reserved for whites only. To the delight of the native locals, Hamasien beat Eritrea 3–2.

The Eritrean press wrote positively about the game and support seemed to be growing to allow Hamasien to join the Italian league. More friendly games were organized with other Italian teams. However, Hamasien was often deducted some of its gate receipts because of the mass of Hamasien fans who turned up to watch the games that were accused of damaging the fences around the ground. In 1945, Hamasien was finally allowed to join the Italian league, nine years after the first indigenous teams were formed. That season, Hamasien finished second out of the seven Serie A clubs. In 1946/47, a second indigenous team, Mar Rosso (Red Sea), was also accepted into the league. The arrival of the new team had more of an effect on the other purely Eritrean team, splitting the fan base of the club. That season, Hamasien finished third, Mar Rosso last and the latter eventually pulled out of the league.

Eritrean football identities

Eritrean football manifested the divisions evident within the society. In the 1940s, there was religious tension in the capital between Orthodox Christians and Muslims.[2] Religious differences also affected the two clubs; Muslim supporters tended to root for Mar Rosso, while Hamasien became associated with Christians. It also appears to have led to players moving between the two teams. However, how long this situation continued is not clear. Firstly, Mar Rosso dropped out of the league within one year, which could well have increased support across the board for the Hamasien team. Secondly, there was a famous and well publicised meeting between an Eritrean Muslim leader, Ibrahim Sultan and a Christian Eritrean nationalist leader, Woldeab Woldemariam, in which they sat and ate together and called for Eritreans to unite. The effectiveness of this appeal is subject to debate; some historians think that religious violence did not die down until 1949.

The success of teams like Hamasien had not gone unnoticed. In 1949, CONI decided that Italian teams could now select up to three native-born players. It was perhaps an indication of a new social realism in postwar Eritrea, or at least a recognition that footballing victories were more important than debate about race. By that time, the economy in Eritrea was collapsing due to a postwar depression and both Eritreans and Italians were facing economic hardship.

Others, however, suspect a deliberate attempt on the part of the CONI to weaken the upstart Hamasien club. The new regulation decimated the purely Eritrean team as the Italian clubs poached virtually all their players. Hamasien withdrew from the league in protest – an ironic twist in that it was the Eritrean club which was damaged by the new mixing of Eritreans in the Italian teams. Hamasien, or what was left of it, went off to play with Sudanese teams, but soon re-formed and requested to be readmitted into the Eritrean Serie A. However, CONI appeared reluctant, so Hamasien continued playing Sudanese teams.

The close ties between Eritrea, Italy and Italian football proved to be another source of conflict between the Eritreans and the Italians. In 1949, the entire team of the famous Italian football club Torino were killed in a plane crash on their way back from a European game in Portugal. In Eritrea, a cup competition, the Coppa Torino, was organized by Italian expatriates in their honour. The Hamasien football club sent letters of condolence to Torino, and was in return invited to play in the Italian organization's cup competition, alongside Italian teams and two British teams formed from the army regiments still stationed in Eritrea. Hamasien reached the final where it faced the mainly Italian club of Gejeret. Hamasien won the game 2–0. But there were protests from the Italians about the poor standard of refereeing, and a rematch was ordered. This time the Italians walked away with the cup. Protesting in their turn, Hamasien refused to play any future games against Italian teams and played only British teams. Without Hamasien, the enormous local support which would come to watch the games also disappeared. The gate receipts declined for the Italian clubs, and Hamasien was subsequently invited to rejoin the league.

Eritrean political consciousness, and the decline of Italian influence, was also starting to reveal itself. The indigenous local newspapers, encouraged by the British, had started to express the interest of Eritreans, not just in the debate about the future of the country and whether it should be independent or federated with Ethiopia, but also in the debate about independence in football matters.

In 1950, the Eritrean clubs met and decided to set up their own football federation. Three of the old Italian clubs – Eritrea, Asmara and Gejeret – joined the new league, which retained the stratification of Serie A, B and C. Around 30 clubs were registered with the new federation. Within 14 years of establishing the first indigenous teams, Eritreans had asserted their footballing independence. The Italian population of Eritrea, whilst still substantial, numbering around 15,000, was declining. The influence of CONI was diminished and it handed over its office to the Eritreans in

1954. However, the relationship between Italy and Eritrea did not end. Italians were involved in the running of the new federation. In Eritrea today, indeed, there is still large support for and connections with Italian teams, a legacy of the thousands of Eritreans who moved to Italy during the war of independence.

Meanwhile, new political developments were unfolding. In 1952, the United Nations implemented a decision that Eritrea would be federated with its southern neighbour Ethiopia, at that time headed by the Emperor Haile Selassie. In all areas of life, Ethiopia gradually tightened its grip on its new province; football was not immune. In 1953–54, Eritrean teams were told to register with the Ethiopian Football Federation. In doing so, Eritrean players would also be eligible to play for the Ethiopian national team. Each season, the Eritrean league champions would travel to the Ethiopian capital Addis Ababa to play in the King's Cup. Eritrean teams dominated the cup competition for the first few years: Hamasien won it in 1955 and 1957, and other Eritrean champions, Akula Gisae and Telecommunications, won in 1958 and 1959. The ultimate triumph was in 1963, when Eritreans made up nine of the eleven players on the Ethiopian team which won the third African Nations Cup. These were halcyon days for Eritrean football. Kiflum Araya, a defender in the team, recalled to journalist Martin Barclay in 1999 that 'on that day we all received a medal and 500 birr from the Emperor Haile Selassie' (*African Soccer* no. 43, March 1999). He added, '[W]e were pure amateur players and sometimes we had only enough time for a wash, a drink of tea and some break between our jobs and playing football. But we were hard workers on the pitch.'

Football and Italian–Eritrean–Ethiopean relations

The foregoing narrative told the story of the gradual emergence of Eritrean football from Italian domination. The development of football mirrored the gradual emergence of Eritrean political debate. Football thus provided an important forum for the expression of Eritrean indentity.

The massive turnout of support for the native club Hamasien represented an early expression of solidarity against the colonial rulers. Their subsequent non-attendance at the Italian league games during Hamasien's absence was a sign that support for the main indigenous team was more important than watching football per se. Identification with clubs like Hamasien was not difficult to achieve as it stood as the one superclub drawn from all the other indigenous teams.

Italian hostility to Hamasien as purely an Eritrean team was evident. One chant that was heard from some Italian spectators during the final of the Coppa Torino was 'You can't let the cup go to the slums of Aba Shaul',[3] a reference to a part of Asmara which had long been identified as a native area. Paradoxically, however, football also revealed Eritrean and Italian interaction. Not surprisingly, following decades of Italian presence in Eritrea, there were considerable numbers of half-Italian, half-Eritrean children, despite occasional fascist attempts to prevent mixed-race relationships. One club, called Junior Team, was reportedly dominated by mixed-race players. Two of the stars of Eritrean football in the 1950s and 1960s, the brothers Luciano and Itallo Vasalo, had an Italian father. The two players were in the Ethiopian team which won the African Nations Cup in 1963.

Football also provided a forum for Italians to show their dislike of the new British administrators. Historian Francesca Locatelli tells of a game between a British and Italian team during the Second World War which is revealing of Italian attitudes.[4] During the game, the largely Italian crowd would chant 'Ro–Ber–To'. The British naturally assumed that Roberto was a particularly good player on the Italian team. In reality, 'Ro–Ber–To', stood for 'Rome, Berlin, Tokyo', the capitals of the Axis powers who were fighting the Allies.

There would also be occasional displays of animosity as the Ethiopians tightened their grip on Eritrea. Yemane Dawit, current President of the Eritrean National Football Federation, described a match he attended:

> I remember Hamasien playing St George (an Ethiopian team), it was around 1966, and the Ethiopian soldiers were here [in Asmara], and the Ethiopian soldiers were for St George. Hamasien won but there was a fight between some players. There was some stone throwing, and some bullets, about 100 people had minor injuries.

Later on as the Eritrean war of independence was unfolding, the team supported by the Ethiopian army in Eritrea was called Walia. Eritreans would then voice their support for whoever was the opposing team.

As in other areas of Eritrean life, there is a danger that too much of the history of football has been politicized by what happened later. The 1950s and 1960s were, after all, the early days of the independence movement, characterized by strikes, boycotts and student protests at the encroachment of Ethiopian authority. Many Eritreans lived throughout the war in Ethiopia, and consider themselves Ethiopian as well as Eritrean. The Ethiopian victory in the 1963 African Nations Cup is still regarded as a moment of glory, not least because of the predominance of Eritrean players. It is difficult to say whether Eritrean players were overly concerned by playing with Ethiopian teams or for the Ethiopian national team. Politics may not have been on everyone's agenda. One ex-footballer who played in the 1960s confided that the opportunity to play football and travel around, even abroad, was too good to be true. The Ethiopian team, for example, went on tour and played teams from Yugoslavia, Czechoslovakia and Russia.

Football, war and liberation[5]

During the 1960s and early 1970s, Eritrean football teams continued to compete with each other. A sort of Super League was created in which the top three teams in Eritrea competed with teams in Ethiopia. It was perhaps an attempt to ease the integration of Eritrea into the Ethiopian empire.

Eritrea had been federated to Ethiopia in 1952 by the UN after a fierce, unresolved and largely ignored debate inside Eritrea on whether the country's future lay in independence or as part of a federation with Ethiopia.[6] The United States, Britain and Ethiopia backed federation, not least because Eritrea had a coastline and Ethiopia was landlocked. Parts of the two countries also shared a similar language and culture. Eritrea was supposed to have a large degree of autonomy – it had its own National Assembly. But over time, Ethiopia whittled away at this autonomy until it finally annexed the small nation to its north in 1962. Armed resistance to this Ethiopian annexation began to grow, evolving into the highly disciplined liberation movements fighting for an independent Eritrea.

In Eritrean football, there was increasing competition between the teams based around regions in Eritrea. Hamasien, in the highlands around the capital, Akula Gisae, the region south-east of the capital, and Seraye, the highland region south of the capital, were the biggest rivals. Over the years the rivalry grew. Occasionally, there would be violence, though usually between individuals rather than between groups. The regions shared the same language, Tigrinya, and largely shared the same religion, Christianity, but different regional identities started to be expressed most clearly during football matches.

To the Eritrean liberation fronts, the ELF (Eritrean Liberation Front) and the EPLF (Eritrean People's Liberation Front) who had taken control of much of Eritrea, division amongst the people was dangerous. They wanted unity above all to resist the Ethiopians. It was believed that the Ethiopian government was deliberately promoting the regional rivalry in a policy of divide and rule. Yemane Dawit, now the President of the Eritrean

Football Federation, was a member of the EPLF: 'People were attached to a certain name of a team, were so involved even if they did not know about football, but still they would feel it, if this region lost.' He added:

> People in high office were using these issues to divide the people. Not only in football, it started going on in day to day activities and government authorities, and the Ethiopians deliberately tried to play one against the other.

To counter this, in 1974, the liberation fronts sent a joint letter to the football clubs. The clubs were asked to stop playing because their presence at the game itself promoted regionalism. The clubs agreed and football was stopped in Eritrea; Eritrean teams withdrew from all competitions.

The same year saw political upheavals in Ethiopia as Haile Selassie was overthrown. Ultimately he was replaced by an army Colonel, Mengistu Haile Mariam. During the struggle for power in Ethiopia, Asmara, like parts of Ethiopia, was subject to the 'Red Terror' in which thousands were 'disappeared' as Mengistu eliminated opposition, real or imagined. This impinged on football, as Yemane recounts:

> All teams were disintegrated, not just because of the Front's order, but also because of the situation in Asmara. Half of Asmara went to join the fronts, or went outside, or went to Sudan as refugees.

Kiflum Areya, a national selector of the Ethiopian national team for 15 years, was quoted in *African Soccer* as saying:

> At that time many of our players went to fight in the field or, like the striker Mohammed Abdella, who went to play in Saudi Arabia, escaped to other countries. As the expert players left, the quality of the side decreased.

As the liberation forces surrounded the city Asmara itself was gradually cut off from the rest of the country. Under Haile Selassie, the United States and Israel had supported Ethiopia. However, when the Marxist dictator Mengistu Haile Mariam took power, newly communist Ethiopia was backed by the Soviet Union, Cuba and Yemen. The intervention by the Soviet Union was crucial as by 1977 the liberation forces had control of Eritrea, except for the capital Asmara and the two ports of Massawa and Assad. As billions of dollars of military hardware poured into Ethiopia from the Soviet Union, Eritrean liberation fighters were forced to retreat to the mountainous north of the country, a move known in Eritrea as the 'Strategic Withdrawal'. However, an underground resistance movement remained in areas under Ethiopian occupation.

After the Eritreans' Strategic Withdrawal, the Ethiopian government gradually restarted football in Asmara. Ironically, the promotion of regionalism through football, which had been feared by the liberation fronts, was not repeated by the new communist Ethiopian regime. The new football teams were to be attached to factories. Players would be given nominal jobs in the operations of the factory that sponsored the team to make it easier for them to train. Hence new teams were known as the Shoe Factory, Food Preparation, Sack Factory, Electric Authority, the Municipality. Many of the teams in today's Eritrea are still linked to these bastions of communist ideology.

Football and the forces of liberation

As the struggle for Eritrean independence intensified, the liberation fronts continued to use football to raise both awareness and funds for the fight for independence. It was also used as a way of keeping the communities of refugees in touch. The EPLF became the only liberation front in Eritrea, having fought a bitter civil war with the ELF. The ELF had organized teams from some of Eritrea's former soccer stars who had fled the country. Games were arranged in Sudan; there was even a series of games in Syria and Iraq. The Eritreans lost only once in ten matches during 1975–78 (*African Soccer* no. 43, March 1999). Indeed, there are still Eritrean soccer festivals in the US which are used by the diaspora community as another way of getting together.

In the north of Eritrea, the Liberation forces regrouped and held out against repeated onslaughts, having built trench lines stretching over a 100 kilometres, complete with underground hospitals, schools and workshops. Their weapons of control were captured from the Ethiopians and used against them. No other nation gave formal assistance, albeit various Arab states helped informally.

Football was played by the liberation forces when there was a lull in the fighting. Yemane Dawit, President of the Eritrean Football Federation, played whilst in the field. At the time he was in the Social Affairs department of the EPLF (the EPLF had developed a government in the field), stationed behind the front line in one of the EPLF base areas, in a place called Orota:

I was playing a lot. From 1979 there was some kind of regularity to games. To make a field was always dangerous because it was an easy target. It always stopped because of some battles, so it was not regular.

There were games between teams from different departments; the Department of Education would play against the Department of Health or Social Affairs, Yemane recalled. Astonishingly, there was even a team made up of Ethiopian prisoners of war that would play against the other EPLF teams in the Orota area in what might be considered an attempt at rapprochement, to show that Eritrea had no hard feelings towards individual Ethiopians. Yemane explains:

If there was a little peace we would travel to play each other. In 1987, there was a front-wide competition. Each division had a team. From my area of Orota we had a select team, we picked the best players from the different departments. We had different teams from three base areas then we had teams from around ten army divisions.

The football games were potentially dangerous, as Ethiopian bombers dominated the skies over Eritrea:

We usually played between 5.00 and 6.30 in the evening, the usual danger from aircraft was in the early morning. Sometimes in the final we had two or three thousand spectators because it was held near the Revolutionary School.

The Revolutionary School was made up of the children of liberation fighters or children orphaned by the war, known by the EPLF as the 'flowers of the revolution'. Over the years several thousand children passed through the school. Set up behind the front lines, it occasionally moved site to avoid being too close to the fighting. It was well camouflaged to avoid being a target from bombers. If the situation were safe enough, the children would play football.

Football matches were also shown in the field as part of entertainment for the troops. Videos of World Cup games, for example, were recorded in EPLF offices in Sudan and sent to Eritrea. Hundreds would gather round one small TV to watch. Following the liberation of the port of Massawa in 1990, access to televisions increased. A veteran remembers watching the World Cup on a portable TV hooked up to a generator just behind the front lines:

It was great, except one night, the light from the TV must have been noticed by a forward observer, because at dawn the next morning our position was bombed and the TV got hit by shrapnel.

Eritrean football into independence

Eritrean forces finally liberated the entire country in 1991 having fought their way from the mountains in the north where they had retreated in 1978. At the same time, an allied rebel movement in Ethiopia took power, as Mengistu fled to Zimbabwe. Around the time of Eritrean official independence in 1993, Eritrea and Ethiopia played a friendly game which Ethiopia won on penalties. Football was the sole way of rebuilding bridges after the years of war, and a recognition of Eritrea's status as an independent nation. The new Eritrean National Football Federation was accepted into both the Confederation of African Football in 1997 and the world governing body FIFA in 1998. In the same year, war between Eritrea and Ethiopia began again over a disputed border. Football matches between the two countries were halted. This war saw the mass expulsion of ethnic Eritreans from Ethiopia which included some ethnic Eritreans with Ethiopian nationality who had played for the Ethiopian national team. Their deportation only served to increase the footballing talent in the nation.

In 1999, Eritrea and Ethiopia were drawn to play each other in the preliminary round of the African Nations Cup. Ethiopia refused to play the match, so Eritrea went through on a bye. Since the July 2000 ceasefire between the two countries, neither country has sent a team to the other to play a match. If relations are to be normalized, such a fixture should be considered a move towards the thawing of hostilities.

The recent war damaged Eritrea's footballing prospects. The first division competition was maintained with each of the ten teams allowed to keep 18 players, whilst all men (and women) between the ages of 18 and 40 were eligible for national service which formed the bulk of the Eritrean army. At the height of the war, mass mobilization saw around 10 per cent of the entire population called up. The economy was badly hit, national servicemen and women would receive the equivalent of US$15 dollars a month pocket money, there were thus fewer people around to attend, and in reality who could afford to attend football matches?[7]

A further problem for aspiring young players was that only established players were kept away from national service to play and train. Development of young talent was focused on those still in school and therefore exempt from the call up. However, some of the military teams who were part of the league system did benefit, picking up talented young players who were technically on national service.

Moving on: the future for Eritrean football

The current teams are centred on Asmara. The old shoe factory team, Hensa, won the title last year. Some wealthy Eritreans who made their money abroad have taken an interest in football. The team Red Sea is the beneficiary of Tewolde Vaccaro, a rich businessman based in Italy.

There are gradual moves towards professionalism, but the lack of training facilities is a major problem. Others in the football world think that the education system and urbanization have damaged Eritrea's football future, arguing that the lack of a coherent sports programme at schools and the loss of open spaces due to urban expansion have removed the availability of football. One former player, a veteran of the 1960s, described a time long gone, when he used to train and improve his stamina by running through the muddy fields in and around Asmara. Many argue that Eritrean players have got physically smaller since the days of the 1950s and 1960s. Certainly, the team photos of old show tall, well built men, very different from today's tough but thin players.

Eritrea's footballing development is an interesting case. Born out of Italian colonialism, the game was to be shaped by an early degree of indigenous political awareness and independence, and moulded by war. The Italians' influence on football in Eritrea is still around, whether it is the presence of Juventus strips in the shops – though now matched in number by Manchester United tops – or the fact that most Eritreans shout '*Mano*' (Italian for 'hand ball') when anyone handles the ball. Football is not the only Italian sporting legacy. Cycling is probably more popular than football in Eritrea, at least in terms of spectators, where often 20,000 turn out to watch a cycling race. Still, on most street corners and in villages, children play football with anything they can find. In the African context, Eritrea's footballing history tells a tale of players with remarkable skill and determination. A story of football and a nation beset by the issue of nationalism, wherein football was at times above it all yet at other times part of the struggle for Eritrean identity. In the War of Independence, 65,000 soldiers were killed and an estimated 200,000 civilians lost their lives. In the more recent war, 20,000 soldiers were killed and an unknown number wounded. Hundreds of thousands have fled their homes or become refugees. Everyone and everything in Eritrea has been affected. Only prolonged peace might see a return to the glory days when Eritreans were part of the best team in Africa.

Eritrean footballing heroics have occurred in the last few years, such as a goalless home draw against Nigeria in a game which had to be played on a school pitch whilst the stadium turf was re-laid. Eritrea also drew with Cameroon at home in another goalless draw. There have been a few stunning victories, and even more stunning losses. The link between Eritrea's military past and football was again on display when an Eritrean government minister in 2000, upon hearing that Eritrea had lost to Sudan 5–0 in a friendly, was overheard remarking, 'We didn't lose; it was merely a strategic withdrawal.'

Acknowledgements

My thanks go to all informants, formal and informal, who helped with this chapter.

Notes

1. Much of the ensuing discussion is based on an unpublished manuscript written in 1995 by Dahab Tuku, who was working for the Sports Affairs department of the Eritrean government. The manuscript, written in Tigrinya, was collated from interviews with players and officials. It was donated to the Eritrean National Football Federation in 1995.
2. See Iyob (1995) for an overview.
3. Unpublished research manuscript, by Dahab Tuku, donated to Eritrean Football Federation, 1995.
4. I am deeply indebted to Francesca Locatelli for giving me this information whilst she was in Asmara researching her history PhD at the University of London.
5. For background information on the period, see Connell (1993); Pateman (1998); Negash (1997) and Iyob (1995).
6. For the political situation in Eritrea during this period see Negash (1997) and Iyob (1995).
7. The army organized games of football; however, it was volleyball that became most popular amongst the military, presumably because it was easy to fix a rudimentary net and it took up less space.

2
Football in Algeria: Between Violence and Politics

Youssef Fates

The political history of Algeria, as constructed and imposed by historians and political scientists, does not take into account certain phenomena. Only in literature – Camus in *Le Minotaure*, and the recent nostalgic works on Algeria – is a part reserved for football. Football indeed occupied a significant place in the everyday lives of French people and Muslims in Algeria during the colonial period. It is necessary for us to exceed the traditional approaches of historians, to formulate a largely open history, a total history that deals with all aspects of human activity, one that, by including football, serves to produce a history of Muslims and Europeans, of men and women in the everyday society.

In 1830, Algeria became a military conquest of the French and its populace was colonized. The indigenous Algerian culture was destroyed, and European culture was intended as a substitute at various levels including the imposition of new body techniques and sporting games. Thus, in this chapter, our historical approach addresses *la longue durée* by covering the two important periods of Algeria: the colonial times (130 years of French colonization), and the post-independence times (40 years since 1962) under a new, postcolonial state.

This approach permits us to address structural and conjunctural issues, to explore how football can become a medium for political action. Our perspective takes as its subject the politics, and through that the history, of Algeria. We explore the roots of the sport in colonial Algeria, considering the introduction of football and other sporting activities, examining the processes that made it emerge, to show above all the first uses made by the two communities, European and Muslim. Revisiting colonial times makes it possible to see the weight of history within the sociopolitical understanding of modern Algerian football. Through this genealogy we underline the continuities and changes between yesterday and today.

Algerian football: social genesis and cultural contact

There is no accurate record as to when football, the premier sport in Algeria, was introduced. However, some documents like sports magazines and the *Sports Record Book of 1908* show that football practice started at the start of the twentieth century, first mainly in the region of Oran. In 1901, two clubs, Sporting Club Oranais and the Club Athlétique, organized the games of *l'Assoce* (association football) in Algeria. Other clubs were created, such as Football Club Oranais in 1903 and Galia Club Oranais in 1906. In the region of Algiers, a year after football's emergence, the first clubs were founded: Sporting Club Algérois in 1902, Racing Club Algérien in 1903, the Football Club Blidéen in 1903, the Gallia Club Algérois in 1905. Many retained their Anglo-Saxon names. The first steps in North African football were taken in the region of Oran among the European community, some 70 years after France had established its colonial hold in Algeria.

According to the 'Cédéjistes d'Oran', Algerian football was born in 1897. In fact, the Club de Joyeusets d'Oran was the first club to play football in Algeria. The club was founded in Oran in 1894, on 'a June evening, by about 30 students, happy lads in search of a break from the rather tedious lectures in rhetorics, philosophy and mathematics' and where they would be able to re-create themselves as the 'Joyeux'.[1] Their club was multicultural and was comprised of Jews, Spaniards and Italians – but not a single Muslim. The founding members would meet in a building (in 'the Belleville'), next to the market of Kargentah from which unpleasant odours reportedly emanated. Following a loan from the Société des Courses de l'Hippodrome (a horse-racing association), they began with athletics and then introduced football.

Promoting football was very difficult at first: not only materially, at a time when players had to mark the pitch's lines using plaster powder, and when the same shoes would be bought and worn by three to four players; but also representatively as it would generate conflicts between parents and children.[2] The rules to which they were initiated, using the *Petit Français Illustré* as published in 1897, could not be applied to the letter.

With some difficulty, other teams were formed in large Algerian towns. They were comprised of students, bank employees and a few workers who played on poor pitches causing numerous minor injuries (such as sprained ankles) and sometimes very serious ones. At the outset, sport had been disliked by teachers but the increasing number of clubs shows the irreversible grip of football on the Algerian territory. Subsequently, the Algerian sport press that developed was controlled by the colonial authorities.

The *departmentaux* were administrative regions controlled by France, and their championships started in the early 1900s. The first official clubs formed between 1901 and 1903 contested the regional championships. In the Oran region, the first football championship was organized in 1902; in Algiers the first was contested in 1905; and 1908 in Constantine, after the relevant committee was formed in 1907.

A championship tournament was introduced and contested in 1904 in Algiers and in 1905 in Oran between the same teams (Sporting Club Oranais and the Stade Algérien). In 1904, the Football Club de Bône was defeated 3–1 by the Sporting Club Oranais in Algiers. It was this very match, 'a sensational encounter', that triggered football's rise.

From 23 April 1905, the Algerian championship was stopped and only restarted in 1908; the break was due to reorganization of the football committees. Moreover, football results in Algeria in 1910 show that independent clubs, non-members of the football association, also held a championship and a cup competition. All this demonstrates how football won over Algerians.

Furthermore, the territorial diffusion affected many more regions, notably North Algeria. In Medea, the Sporting Club Médéen put together a football team that contested fixtures in 1908. At the same time, Bône had a total of 200 players. In Kolea, the Union Sportive de Koléa played against the Football Vétéran de Koléa (*L'Algérie Sportive*, 29 February 1908). The Football Club d'Orléansville organized friendly matches and covered the expenses of visiting teams (*L'Algérie Sportive*, 11 January 1908). In Grande Kabylie at Fort National, and even in the villages of Petite Kabylie, football teams were put together and games were played wherever the ground allowed. Sometimes the young played against the 'Zouaus' (infantry) and army soldiers. In Kabylie they were supervised by Algerian veterans. In the early days, players in informal games often did not know football's rules, hence the referees implemented the laws according to circumstances and agreement with the players.

Football development in Algeria was helped by English sailors and tourists, the latter coming to Algeria to flee the English winter. In fact large ports like Algiers, Oran and Bône benefited from being situated on the world's main maritime routes. The English, the Dutch and the Swedish came to share their experience and technique, playing games against Algerian teams from 1902 onwards. At the same time, the local population had the chance to frequent football games for which they showed real enthusiasm.

In Algiers, the games took place at Champs de maneuvres, a military ground, every Sunday. Sometimes they served as opening events for meetings of international affairs. In 1906, an English team from the *Dreadnought* warship won a game against the Sporting Club d'El Biar before a crowd of 2000 people. After the game and in honour of the teams, a buffet was held in the guest-rooms of the pub, the Brassiere Lyonnaise. 'La Marseillaise' and 'God Save the King' were sung, so local players and Englishmen mixed happily, according to reports (*L'Algérie Sportive*, 28 January 1913). The Swedes from the Dristigheten who played against Algerian teams three times were thanked by the Sportmen Algérois in the presence of the Consul from Sweden, Mr Kohler, and Lieutenant Von Heidenstamm (*L'Illustration Algérienne, tunisienne et marocaine*, 30 November 1906). Further matches were played afterwards. In Oran in November 1913, the English sailors' team from the *Cumberland* and the combined team from the Oran region played out a draw. The following Sunday the officers and crew from the *Cumberland* won against the Gallia Club Oranais.

It is worth pointing out that the English not only played in the ports but also travelled inside the country to the more remote towns in the east where football was well established. On 19 March 1926 a team from the Association Sportive Bônoise beat an English team. In Philippeville, in their hometown, a select team won against the English sailors. In March 1933, in Guelma, the English took part in a match to raise money for the famous goalkeeper Larosa who had been injured in Constantine. The English squad, which had an excellent, athletic side, gave the ESG team a sound thrashing. A post-match reception was held in honour of the two teams' representatives and Mr Bowber, the British vice-consul in Bône (*L'Echo des Sports du département de Constantine*, 15–29 March 1933).

In January 1934, the English squad which had defeated Racing de Philippeville won against AS Constantine in the presence of General Kieffer and the main officers from the English squad. These matches had a ceremonial function and strengthened the friendship between the Algerians and the British. However, the football relationship between Algeria and France took longer to develop. In 1908 an Algerian select drew against a local team in Nice. In May 1908 a friendly match organized by the Festival Committee of Algiers saw Algiers play against Riviera from the South of France, and a team of sailors from the *St Louis* against the GS of Algiers (*L'Algérie Sportive*, 17 May 1908). In 1914, a Parisian team played against an Algerian team.

The Algerian Football Association was established in 1919, when the French association was founded in Paris. The regional leagues were established at around the same time: the Oran league in 1919, those in Algiers and Constantine in 1920. By 1923, the Algiers league had 36 clubs participating, while the Constantine league had 23 clubs. The Oran league was the strongest with more than 40 clubs.

With the growing popularity of football, several matches took place during the 1920s and 1930s between French and North African selects, or between French teams and teams from Constantine, Algiers and Oran. In 1923 the Red Star team from Paris met the Football Club Blidéen before the Governor General of Algeria. In December 1931 in Algiers, a match between the French national team and the Sélection d'Alger was played before 10,000 people. Another North African team of players from Oran and Morocco (due to geographical proximity) drew against the French team. The results showed that Algerian teams were competent.

At the international level, because of their proximity, teams from the Spanish Peninsula sometimes played in the region of Oran and Algiers. In 1930 the Futbol Club de Elche (Spanish) triumphed against the Algerians at a local stadium two days in a row (Saturday 5 and Sunday 6 September). Later on the Météor club from Prague drew against the Gallia d'Oran and FC Carthagène won against CDJ from Oran.

Before 1914, teams from Algiers, Oran, Constantine and Tunis contested a North African championship. Morocco entered the tournament in 1926, and Tunisia withdrew from 1927 to 1933. The Union of the North African Leagues (ULNA) was established and organized a cup tournament that began in 1930. In the nine times that it was contested up to 1939, Algerian teams won the cup six times (Club des Joyeuses d'Oran winning four times, Racing Universitaire Algérois winning twice).

At school level, football was very popular with secondary school pupils from an early date. In Algiers' secondary school, sports and particularly football were authorized by the deputy head in 1900. The pupils organized a football tournament to break up school's monotonous routine. Matches were played during the 4.00–5.00 p.m. break in the schoolyard that was far too small and full of trees to be suitable. The football itself was a small tennis ball that was actually well suited to the schoolyard's dimensions (*L'Algérie Sportive*, 20 May 1911). But the development of sports in schools was difficult due to the common law legislation, particularly Articles 1382, 2383, 1384 and the Penal Code legislation 320 that held teachers liable for any accidents that might occur. A new law, dating from 29 July 1889, did shift the state teachers' liability across to the state itself, but they remained legally bound by the Penal Code (*L'Algérie Sportive*, 17 May 1908).

In 1906–07 the secondary school pupils put together football teams. In Dellys at this time some students from colonial training school formed a football club and an athletics team. They organized rallies with the young students spending holidays with their families in Tizi Ouzan (*L'Algérie Sportive*, 18 January 1908). They played matches against the towns' clubs. In 1908 *L'Algérie Sportive* reported that the Union Sportive Bougiote (USB) was defeated by the young team of secondary school pupils who had been spending their holidays in Bougie (*L'Algérie Sportive*, 30 December 1908).[3] This suggested that, in the early days, the standard of play at official clubs for local Algerians was very low.

In 1910 in Batna, the ASB (Association Sportive de Batna) took up the challenge to play against (and defeat) a team of pupils from Constantine secondary school. In contrast, in Dellys, the pupils beat the locals. In Oran, the Buerere Oranaise, a Jewish club, drew against the marvellous Oran club consisting of secondary school pupils. These tournaments were played independently as some clubs were not registered with the football association (*L'Algérie Sportive*, 1 January 1910).

In the Constantine area, according to the owner of a sports daily,[4] a Mr Carbuccia, an influential member and official of the Constantine sporting community, football was apparently permitted in schools during the Great War (1914–18). He remembers the secondary school Union Sportive and the trainee teacher's Normale Sporting Club, a modest team from the upper primary school for whom he acted 'gloriously as goal referee' in Constantine. After the war when real physical education teachers took over from army monitors who had been available to work in schools, interschool football matches became ten a penny.[5]

The Constantine Football League organized an official schools' championship in which the following clubs were involved: Bône Colonial secondary school, Bône Upper Primary School, the Ecole F. Buisson in Philippeville, the Philippeville colonial secondary school, the Constantine Medersa, the Ecole Jules Ferry in Constantine, the Practical Industrial School in Constantine, the Upper Primary School in Batna, and the Complementary School in Souk Ahras (*L'Echo Sportif du département de Constantine*, 17 January 1934). Moreover, from the 1920s football associations were set up along ethnic and national lines. In Algiers mono-ethnic sports clubs of Spaniards and Italians were founded. The Cervantes Football Club, created on 9 June 1921,[6] aimed to 'spread and open up to young Spanish people in Algiers the love and practice of all sports in general and especially football and athletics' (Article 2 of its statutes). The club defined its colours as 'vertically striped blue and tobacco brown, with a yellow and red badge embroidered with the club's initials, white shorts, black stockings with brown tops and a Basque beret' (Article 4). This foreign club's president and insurance broker was Pascal Molina.

The Iberica Football Club was created on 21 November 1923 and headquartered in the basement of the Brasserie Algéroise. However, this club was open to other communities since Article 4 of its statutes states that it could admit as members any individuals of any nationality that could be regarded as honourable. In 1933, it showed no signs of activity. It may have disappeared without any winding-up declaration. Similarly, the Herrica Football Club, whose headquarters were in the basement of the Brasserie Algéroise, and the Boz Espagnola were to disappear at the start of the Second World War.

L'Union Sportive Italienne Pietro Cérésa, founded on 6 December 1928, had all sports as its aim. Its shirt bore the name 'USI Pietro Cérésa'. Its pennant bore the colours of the Italian national flag (Article 3 of the statutes). Its benefactor members were the Consul-General of His Majesty the King of Italy in Algiers and two Italian entrepreneurs in woodworking. This club also ceased activities at the outbreak of war.

In the Oran region, where a large Spanish community was to be found, there were football clubs formed by Oran Spaniards such as the Hijos d'España founded in 1927, and the Hispana Club d'Oran created in the 1930s. In the Constantine region, to be exact in Bône, we find another Italian mono-ethnic sports club. These mono-ethnic teams were heavily criticised by sports officials who talked of risks of violence.[7] In reality, mention must be made of the context: 1934 is the year the World Cup was organized by fascist Italy (*la Coppa de Duce*). Nevertheless, it was observed that different peoples lived side by side on Algerian soil, on good terms with one another, in brotherly understanding even. It was in everyone's interest for that to continue, and everybody had a duty to take care to eliminate causes of friction. For that reason the authorities had to prevent the foundation of certain teams with a national or racial character.

The establishment of football clubs in 1901 did not prevent teams from emerging with a strong ethnic or national identity. However, ethnic mixing was promoted by the colonial authorities, for example by having Muslim clubs define themselves as 'Franco-Muslim' or 'Franco-Arab'. In some small towns, inevitably, some clubs were multiethnic. In the Arab-Muslim community the first people to play football did so in European or mixed clubs. According to the foremost Algerian sports paper *L'Algérie Sportive*, the first 'informal' football club founded by Muslims was in 1910 in Dupéré (Ain Defla). It adopted green as its colour, as the symbolic colour of Islam, and was called L'Etoile Sportive de Dupéré (*L'Algérie Sportive*, 26 March 1910). It was not until 1921 that the greater Arab club was founded, the Mouloudia Club Algérois, the MCA.

From the 1930s football developed to become the most popular sport among indigenous Algerians. It attracted large crowds of spectators, and also large numbers of players outside organized clubs. Arab-Muslims were to turn it into a medium for affirmation of their identity and a means of struggle for nationhood. Violence in football was to become a mode of political expression.

Colonial Algeria, football, nationalism and violence

The Algerian people were to develop a new public form of political expression in a domain that was considered coarse and commonplace, thus putting an end to the pseudo-neutrality of sport. Political opposition through sport and in particular through football began in the earliest matches of the earliest Arab-Muslim mono-ethnic teams. It built up to a crescendo and took the shape of violence as if on a battlefield.[8] Arab animosities – usually kept hidden despite their revolutionary potential since the arrival of the colonizers[9] – were on intensive display during football matches between European and Arab clubs.

According to the political scientist Bruno Etienne, who devotes a passage to sport in his analysis of Algerian nationalism, football matches were for a long time used in the 'settling of scores as mediated through Arab and European teams' (Etienne 1977: 168). According to the Islamic specialist Jacques Berque (1962: 87), matches were 'a kind of compensatory response that was flung in the face of political misfortune'.

Three essential sources offer evidence of the frequency and intensity of football violence during the colonial period:

- the archives of the French police and of the different Governor-Generals
- the press of the period, where match reports are to be found, alongside literature with anecdotal and poetic accounts, but which raise problems of authenticity and truth
- the accounts by Arab club officials, players and supporters.

However, even if no statistics of incidents in sporting events exist that would allow us to establish a quantitative estimate (and thus reduce the subjectivity of conclusions), there do exist many traces of such incidents in the circumstantial reports made to the Governor-Generals of Algeria.

If we look at the archive of the colonial authorities, interethnic sports violence, especially football violence, was concentrated into three decades

(1930s to 1950s) when it reached breaking point. From the development of Arab clubs up to the end of hostilities in Algeria, sporting encounters between European and Arab were characterized by their hard physical confrontations, not only between players on the pitch but also between spectators on the terraces and, afterwards, outside the stadium.

The roots of this violence go back to the beginning of the earliest matches of team sports. Violence in sport appeared first in association football, from its inception, since it was to become the most popular game and the spectacle most likely to stoke up the enthusiasm or anger of crowds. And it began with the first matches of clubs created in Algeria. Many accounts can be found in the press. In an article entitled 'Just like the era of the barbarians', the newspaper *L'Algérie Sportive* (no. 5, 11 November 1906), reported incidents during the Sunday match between Sporting Club of Maison Carrée and Sporting Olympique of Maison Carrée, an authentic derby match. It recalled that two years before (thus 1904), following a ding-dong match between the two clubs, the referee was jeered. 'The maniacs from Maison Carrée, had it not been for the intervention of a number of sportsmen [players] would have laid hands on the referee.' It added, 'The exploits of these Apaches do enormous damage to sport.'

Of course this nascent violence involved Europeans first of all. It was sanctioned, and it was also vigorously criticized. The Europeans responsible for the violence were called 'Apaches', 'savages' and 'maniacs'.[10] This 'negative Indianization' of European supporters placed them outside civilization. On the other hand, those who opposed violence received the gratifying title of 'sportsmen', which had a positive connotation, a term that should be distinguished from 'sporting' (player) that was reserved for practitioners of a sport. In the same way, later, these names were applied to indigenous Algerians by journalists, the European population and the colonial authorities (this terminology can be found quite often in official administrative reports).

The violence continued without interruption. It was condemned by the sports press who stressed the sentimental and family aspects of fandom, the family being an important part of the culture of the European colonizer. The violence worsened because of the lack of security or barriers around the pitch in the early days of football. Spectators watched standing on earth banks around the pitch to get a better view. Others stood on chairs around the touchlines and could be hit in the face by the ball, making the game potentially more explosive. Moreover, they could easily invade the pitch at any moment. The violence was born of passion on strictly sporting grounds. International matches such as those against the British, Dutch and Swedish boat crews coming to Algeria were the only ones not to arouse sports violence, but were rather occasions to demonstrate friendships.

In colonial Algeria, in the football domain where more often than not it was more than a game, the violence generated was directed against the colonial state. During football matches, especially those between Arab-Muslim and European teams, the game was played out over three hours instead of the usual 90 minutes: an hour and a half on the pitch and an hour and a half on the terraces. Sometimes there was no link at all between what was happening on the pitch and what spectators were doing.[11]

Interethnic colonial matches were occasions for the crowds, attracted, divided into two camps, to confront each other, to hurl invective and insults, and to come to blows. The indigenous crowds, compact in their solidarity, were divided into two parts: those in the enclosure that may be called the paying stand[12] and those perched on whatever viewpoints they could find, however derisory – the smallest surface of a building near the stadium, trees, the walls surrounding the stadium, electric poles, or long roofs. These were the 'pirate stands' of the cheats, the unemployed, the poor who could not afford a ticket and who were as one with every reaction against the European side.

The stadium was the space and the match was the time for the dramatization of the struggle between colonized and colonizer. Analyses of football matches, veritable theatres of interethnic confrontation in the Algerian case, show that physical violence (inside and out) was frequent. Despite material protective measures (metal barriers) and police reinforcements, there were many such incidents at sporting encounters between European clubs and Arab-Muslim clubs. Indeed most football matches were often peppered with serious incidents between the two communities.

The first period covers the 1930s up to 1945 with an intermission during the Second World War. Reports established by the colonial authorities on incidents occurring in football matches illustrate that the Djidjelli Sports Club, the JSD, in the Constantine region, accounts, on its own, for the majority. Analysis of reports available from the Algerian Governor-General's office shows the JSD was the recipient of much repressive action. In fact, it was often convicted and fined. Its supporters manifested permanently bellicose attitudes towards Europeans. Other clubs were not free of this characteristic.

The Oran region comes in third position behind Constantine and Algiers in terms of frequency of incidents reported between Arab-Muslim teams and European teams received by the Governor-General of Algeria. The Oran region does not escape the general rule, but incidents are fewer.

The second period covers May 1945 until November 1954, from the events in the northern Constantine region to the start of the struggle for national liberation. The intensity of this violence increased noticeably from 1945 onwards. A report by General Henri Martin, commander of the 19th battalion, points out that a football match gave rise to a veritable nationalist demonstration.[13] The document recounts demonstrations by Arab-Muslim scouts, indigenous housewives demanding bread, agitation disrupting sports matches, seditious cries, slogans and various acts of aggression against representatives of the authorities. These were warning signs of a war in the making confirming the premonitory view of the chief of police.

The violence was to continue, and to increase. Even 'friendly matches' between Arab-Muslim teams (MCA) and European teams (Olympique d'Hussein Dey, OHD) or matches on the Muslim feast day of Achoura (the tenth day of the Muslim year), which drew thousands of spectators, mostly Arab-Muslim, contained incidents and fist-fights between players of rival teams who exchanged blows and political taunts.

In 1954, at the start of the struggle for national liberation, sports violence reached its height during the armed struggle. It copied revolutionary violence. From 1954 to 1956, the number of incidents increased.[14] Analysis of incidents occurring in different stadiums in Algeria shows that law and order was markedly deteriorating. The oldest Arab-Muslim club, Le Mouloudia, demanded the suspension of the League Championship in the 1955–56 season following serious incidents in its last three matches. Other incidents followed, notably on Sunday 6 March 1955 in various stadiums of the Algiers region. They were analysed by the colonial authorities only on the sporting level; any other aspects were brushed under the carpet. For the police authorities the incidents had no political significance. Their origin lay in the local chauvinism of supporters from Blida, unhappy at their club's defeat. Curiously, the authorities would not recognize the political nature of the incidents happening in the middle of the Algerian War. They tended to punish Muslim rather than European clubs, to strengthen the security arrangements at games, or to ban spectators from attending some fixtures. Nevertheless, the break between the communities had been consummated and the process would only amplify.

The press had a range of views on the situation, but attached no political significance to it either. The *Alger Sport* tried to identify those responsible for the incidents. It admits that matches between L'Union Sportive Musulmane Blideenne and ASSE, or RUA and Nasr Athlétique from Hussein Dey gave rise to 'regrettable incidents that had nothing to do with sport'. Furthermore stating that this was not a local problem and recalled occurrences in Latin America. But for this newspaper, responsibility lay with the organizations responsible for discipline within the stadiums: the police, the disciplinary committee and, in the final analysis, the League Executive.

In the published interpretations, some referees were blamed for their 'unbelievable largesse' in falsifying the results of matches and for annoying the players who then gave full vent to their bad temper. The press demanded that referees used both clear vision and authority in their sanctions. They criticized referees' benign attitudes towards players' actions that had nothing to do with sport, and their leniency that only encouraged players to commit the same acts again.

L'Echo d'Alger proposed that repression of such acts be taken out of the hands of the Football League and given to the public authorities. *Le Journal d'Alger* thought rather that there were insufficient police in the stadiums. Neither paper felt the problem could be solved by measures taken within the sport, but rather by the police and by political action. Ideally sport should be regulated by the public authorities, and unilaterally.

In 1955, sports violence broke out all over the country. The press reported serious incidents on football pitches. Knives were used, representatives of the law were struck, supporters were injured. One player suffered a serious head wound and died soon afterwards from his injuries (*Le Tell Sportif*, 30 March 1955).

The Oran region was shaken by the same troubles. On 28 March 1955 the Chief of Police in Saint Denis du Sig, in a report to the Prefect (government representative) of Oran, recounted an incident in a match between Sporting Club Sigois (a European club) and the Croissant Club Sigois (an Arab-Muslim club) where an Algerian lost an eye following the breaking-up of a crowd by the police.[15] Even the smallest of Algerian villages was not spared from intercommunity football violence.

The increasing number of such incidents in sports events seems to be a tangible sign of the progressive worsening of relations between the two ethnic groups. Picking up Bromberger's idea,[16] one argues here that the football match was no longer a festive interlude to everyday space and norms. In this way, by generating interethnic violence, football had a lasting impact on the ending of the artificial harmony between the

European and the Arab-Muslim communities that rubbed shoulders in the cafe and the stadium. Indeed, while they were in constant contact, there was rarely any exchange or mixing, except for some assimilated Arab-Muslims or marginalized people of the European underclass.[17]

If on the football pitch, inevitably, technical and tactical factors induced individual confrontations, in the stands it was impossible for people to ignore each other; the two communities were in close juxtaposition, and this explosive mixture would catch fire at the moment of and for the duration of a general brawl. The police would intervene but only to separate people and to return 'the ethnic mosaic' to square one. Some colonizers had a phobia about close contact with the indigenous people, matching indeed the fears of the indigenous Algerians who refused assimilation and closer contact with the European Other. This was motivated by fears of a loss of difference that might be exploited by the indigenous Algerian and turned against the colonizer, and came from a structured colonial mentality reinforced by ideology, culture and spatial organization which established real segregation.

Football condenses a number of modes of symbolic expression: the first category has as its direct medium material objects; the second is situated in the domain of language; and the third in the domain of behaviour and practices, in which the politics of nationalism, making great play of the symbolic, found an ideal terrain in Algeria. It was therefore reinforced and found succour through the sporting sign system that was offered, over the long term, by sports clubs and their material symbols and powerful accessories, colours, insignia, abbreviations and names. This conglomeration of signs was one of the markers (and modes of expression) of identity for Arab-Muslims, in a pre-political register. Football provokes visual decoration and a particular behaviour among supporters that is the equal of religion and outdoes politics. Political activity in the sporting domain was a locus of affect and a producer of emotion and violence; it generated new forms of action that enriched nationalists' traditional political activity (such as leafleting, newspapers, meetings and petitions).

Indeed, substantively in opposition and in the various conflicts born of sporting competition, football was far from being a means of bringing people closer to the European community. It was a phenomenon favouring differentiation and particularism that grew hand in hand with the increasing emancipation of Arab-Muslim youth, who used each example of organization and French concepts to escape from traditionalism, and particularly to move towards a nationalism of liberation that culminated in independence in 1962. During the period of French domination the activity of Arab-Muslim youth easily fitted the mould of Western forms introduced by colonization and French civilization, in their practice of a veritable 'homomorphism'. In the same way as the French language was an excellent natural means of expression of young people's struggle and their ideas, football, an object of the dominant community as a bodily and ludic style, was re-employed for their struggle's own end. The earliest pluri-ethnic sports clubs allowed players to gain experience that was put to use for Arab-Muslim sports clubs that supported the struggle for emancipation. Young Arab-Muslim sportsmen were using Western civilization to recover an Arab and Muslim identity as fundamental elements of being Algerian.

In this process, Arab-Muslim aggression in sport and the violence shown were channelled in positive directions by nationalist activists. This aggression and violence were charged into a form of combat, reinforcing awareness of the need for it to be used efficiently. This interethnic confrontation, that supported the nationalists' strategy of 'race against race' and generated violence in sport, was an intense method which effected an increase in the high political density of Arab-Muslim football clubs. It allowed the passage from negative, colonized individual to actor in history.

Postcolonial football and youth–state conflicts

In independent Algeria, football is being put to sociopolitical uses by young people and Islamic movements. In the past, the national football stadium was a space for 'nationalist discourse' through resistant actions, chants and *nachid* (patriotic songs). The stadium was a space for communal association, a privileged arena for learning how to challenge the social, cultural and political powers-that-be. In this sense, it was the equivalent of the Greek *agora*, and not the Roman *circenses* that the Algerian authorities wanted to construct. It became the only tolerated space for discharging the anger, frustrations and bitterness of young people. They expressed the full power of protest against the totalitarian state; football was their most effective vector of mass education. Football thus played a positive role in allowing Algerian society to kick-start a new signification of political engagement.

Through this citizens come to know, through a non-institutional participation that is founded on direct action, exactly how it was during the colonial period. The practices of young people within the football context serve to adapt and preserve their collective memory of protest.

The football match, in generating violence against the Algerian state, marks the end of civil peace and unity. It becomes a centre of political struggle and prefigures the civil war.

In addition, the analysis of violence's recurrence for 30 years shows that this disorder depends on the power of the state apparatus. It depends on the state's symbols, force and methods, and on the instability since October 1988 that accelerated brutally with the attempted takeover by Islamic forces in 1991.[18] Regressive impulses came to express themselves through the brutality of forced Islamic integration involving Algerian citizens.

Algerian religious fundamentalists, who were reformers during colonization, uphold the puritanism of religious doctrine. Morality is prioritized, to recover the health of the society through a system of immunity against dangers. It is presented as the only method that can allow the society to purify itself, to rediscover its power and its authenticity, to surpass the existential, identity and political crisis in which it is living.

The fight of the moral crusaders is directed against alcoholism, prostitution, games of chance and 'immoral spectacles'. They target youth and are interested in its problems. The reformists seek to generate a powerful nation-wide movement of youth through the creation of cultural circles and scouting associations with an educational mission and social purpose that diverts young Muslims from immoral temptations. This includes investment in the management committees of sports clubs. But they have not managed to obtain appreciable results in sport.

The sporting domain, crystallizing a number of primordial social problems, is also a terrain of struggle over an Islamic society. Female practices are condemned without reservation or respite. With re-Islamicization rampant, it is especially sport – that is to say male sport – that faces Islamic criticism.

Since November 1963, explosive incidents and condemnation from Islamic spiritual leaders have affected the renewal of Algerian sport. The first victims were female athletes encouraged by the first populist movement to refrain from participation. During the 1990s, the Front Islamique du Salut (FIS) was not satisfied with its victories over women's sport and so turned to young people. Half of the Algerian national football team enter the field of play with beards. During a break in Italy in preparation for the World Cup fixture against Egypt in November 1989, the players listened ostentatiously to cassettes playing prayers by the Imam of the FIS, Ali Belhadj. They conducted Islamic prayer at Venice airport. In 1990, at a match in his presence, Ali Belhadj decreed that applause was illicit (*haram*) and thus outlawed. He based this on the preachings of the prophet, that in meetings there is no applause but cries of '*Allah Akbar*' ('God is Great').

It was the first time in the history of Algerian football that the spectators, terrorized by Islamist injunctions, could neither express their joy at beautiful moments during play, nor support their team. From 1992, the activities of the integrationist Islamic army did not save Algerian football. The president of a club in Kabylie (JSBM) was killed in 1994, so too the President of the Algerian Football Federation (the FAF) in 1995. The Groupe Islamique Algérien (GIA) is also known to have deposited bombs in the stadium. Despite all this terror and violence, the power of Algerians' engagement with football did not diminish.

The historical analysis of a 'small object' (in this instance, football) in Algeria provides us with a fresh view on the colonial history of French Algeria. The colonial authorities set up a series of obstacles to control the meetings between Muslim and European associations. Financial segregation in the distribution of the subsidies, and general ostracism within the structures of framing and management, reinforced the daily humiliation of Muslims. The French governor of Algeria, though he lacked the legislative power, still introduced several coercive rulings that severely regulated matches between Muslim and European teams.[19] These obliged Muslim teams to have between three and five European players. Thus football helps us to analyse, while also reflecting, the patterns of domination experienced by colonized people.

The analysis presented here contributes to the study of social policy and allows a new approach for explaining Algerian nationalism. Other, more apologetic studies of Algerian nationalism, and official historiography, combine to render sacred the political facts of the Algerian revolution, its major figures and its social genesis. Such an approach tends to marginalize, or to omit, other forms of struggle, including that within sport. Nationalist figures made significant sociopolitical usage of football during the colonial period. In postcolonial times, it is the oppressed Algerian youth that explores football's political possibilities. The youth of Kabylie, in particular, have been astute in using the Sporting Youth of Kabylie (JSK), a large club, in their struggle to gain recognition. These examples definitively negate one of the theses defended by some neo-Marxists regarding football's role as the 'opium of the people', as 'alienating' and 'depoliticizing'. In Algeria, an 'authoritarian pluralist country', where real democracy does not arise, where youth is very significant (70 per cent of the population are below 30 years of age), football remains subversive. The stadium becomes a new paradigm for the redeployment of young people's political expression. Football and politics in Algeria remain a strong coupling.

Notes

1. From the French word '*joyeux*' meaning '*happy*' and referring to the club's name, the 'Club des *Joyeuses* d'Oran' which underlines their desire to reinvent themselves.
2. The parents were concerned that the game would distract their children from studying.
3. Two hundred people were at the match.
4. The *L'Echo Sportif du département de Constantine*, nicknamed 'the Pink' ('*le Rose*') because of its colour, was founded by Carbuccia in 1932 and disappeared in 1939, when war was declared, after 402 issues.
5. L'Amicale des Anciens instituteurs et instructeurs d'Algérie et le cerde algérianiste [the Algerian former primary teachers and instructors club and the Algerian Circle] 1830–1962. *Des enseignants d'Algérie se souviennent de ce qu'y fut l'enseignement primaire*, p. 379.
6. Registration number 844, headquarters 31 rue des Consuls, Algiers.
7. In an article entitled 'Note du jour: Pour le bien common', *L'Echoes sports du département de Constantine*, 30 May 1934.
8. Even if, on the surface, the majority of indigenous Algerians seemed submissive and obedient through habit and a spirit of resignation, there developed a strategy of dissimulation. The majority accepted domination with a conviction that it was only ephemeral. Conquerors have come and gone in this part of Africa, and only indigenous Arabs and Berbers have lasted. The French would disappear like all the others. This was the dominant school of thought among the indigenous peoples who based their passive resistance (on that), or as Jacques Berque says: 'The Algerian may have been politically defeated, but refused to be defeated existentially.'
9. Throughout the year football matches were organized with great frequency.
10. The term '*énergumène*' ('maniac') was used constantly up to and including the 1960s to describe indigenous Algerians responsible for sporting incidents. Other derogative expressions for Arab-Muslims were to enrich the list of terms, increasing the racial distance from Arab-Muslims and adding to allegorical humiliations.
11. Football matches also generated street demonstrations, on which we have, unfortunately, little information.
12. A sizeable number of young people gained access to the stadium by carrying the players' kit, acting as young 'body guards'.
13. Annex 3 of a report beginning 1 March 1945. SHAT 1H2812.
14. It should be stressed that two requests have been made of the National Archives in Paris to consult books concerning this period. They have been refused, since these archives are not open to the public.
15. CAOM Departement d'Oran 5258.
16. Christian Bromberger (1995: 120ff.) argues that a team's style is the affirmation of an imagined identity. He devotes long passages to showing the affinities

between way of playing and way of life, and people's representations and conceptions of their own lives.

17. In certain places: brothels (that were officially tolerated) and some cafes in the Algiers Casbah, as admirably described in the film *Pépé le Moko*, shot in Algiers in 1936.

18. Editors' note: In 1988, at least 500 young people were killed during violent clashes in Algiers. In 1990, the Front Islamique du Salut (FIS) defeated the ruling Front Libération Nationale (FLN) by a huge margin in the provincial and municipal election. The FIS won the 1992 national election but the ruling elite declared a state of emergency, remaining in power.

19. See in particular la circulaire Bordes no. 1513 du 20 janvier 1928, la circulaire Carde, la circulaire du gouverneur général Le Beau no. 1599 du 12 mars 1936, la circulaire no. 5599 du 8 septembre 1936.

3
A Story of Heroes, of Epics: The Rise of Football in Nigeria

Wiebe Boer

At the start of the new millennium, one of the major problems facing Nigeria's new democracy was the conflict between the legislative and executive branches of government. As a means towards resolving the rift, a novelty football match was played between the two branches in September 2000. The executive won 1–0 with the goal predictably being scored by President Olusegun Obasanjo before rain prematurely halted play (*This Day*, 4 September 2000: 1, 54). Several state legislative and executive branches later followed suit with 'peace' matches of their own.

The fact that such a match was proposed and played certainly exhibits football's importance in Nigeria. That the un-athletic looking President would himself don a national team jersey not just to watch a match, but to actually play one, further accentuates the point. As this and many similar stories testify, football in Nigeria, as in most African countries, is far more than a sport. National teams and star players are considered great sources of international prestige. The observable football passion among fans and players provides Nigerians, mostly male but increasingly female as well, with a rare bond transcending religion, class, ethnicity, region and age (Odegbami 1993: 11).

Soccer contributes to constructing and reproducing identities in Nigeria on three levels. First, through ethnically associated clubs, local level ethnic identities are strengthened; yet, through participation in national leagues and tournaments, these clubs contribute to national integration (cf. Lever 1983: 5).[1] Secondly, on the national level, national teams represent rare foci for collective identity throughout Nigeria. Soccer is key to nation-building and the development of the 'imagined community' of Nigerians.[2] Finally, through participation in international tournaments and Nigerians playing in foreign leagues, soccer integrates Nigeria within the international system with a level of respect hardly matched in any other arena. On this level soccer has been used as an instrument of Nigerian foreign policy and diplomacy.[3]

Considering all this, one might expect a booming trade in books and articles concerning football's development in Nigeria. Indeed, back in 1960, Father Fitzgibbon, one of the many Catholic missionary Fathers who have contributed to football's development in Nigeria, wrote: 'A good book must be written about the story of football in Nigeria. It will be *a story of heroes, of epics* that are now fading gently into the distant past ...' (Fitzgibbon 1960: 7). Unfortunately, those memories have continued to fade, and as yet no truly comprehensive history of the game in Nigeria has been written. The Nigerian Football Association (NFA) has almost no archives and a historical library with less than five different titles. The NFA knows so little about the history of the game in Nigeria, that it even incorrectly states its own founding date as 1945, twelve years after the first meeting of the original NFA in Lagos (see *Nigerian Daily Times*, 21 August 1933: 6, 25 August 1933: 6).

In its brief history of football in Nigeria included in an NFA brochure, the following is stated:

The history of football in Nigeria is dependent on who writes it. No one can precisely tell when it all began. It is a popular belief that the game of football was introduced to Nigeria by former British colonial masters. The game was first implanted in schools run by the colonial administration.

From the schools the game flourished and acquired more popularity and later on led to the formation of amateur football clubs. History also tells us that as far back as 1914 when Nigeria was amalgamated, football had started being played by Nigerians but on a recreational and relaxation basis.

The man behind these early football games is no other person than Baron Mulford, a Briton whom we are made to understand used to organize weekly matches between Europeans and Nigerian youths. From this point people began to take an interest in the game.

By 1949, Nigerians have learned the tricks of the game leading to the establishment of a national team that toured Britain that same year. It will be pertinent to note that the formation of a national team for Nigeria was carefully nurtured by Mulford. This was confirmed by yet another Briton, P.A. Courtney, who was a one-time colonial chairman of the Lagos District Amateur Football Club.

In a dinner organized for the team that was preparing to tour Britain Courtney said, just before the departure of the team, that 'this team is a revolution in the development of football brewed by Mulford in the early 1930s'.

With this affirmation one can attribute 1931 to be the birth date of organized football in Nigeria. Another thing to note here is that nobody can pinpoint where football was first played in Nigeria. Some people are of the opinion that football was born in Calabar, while others claim Lagos ... (NFA 1999: 2)

That, then, is as complete an official history of football in Nigeria as one can find. So little is known about the history of something that is so important to Nigeria's national identity and character as football. In some ways, such a rudimentary history is symbolic of a major problem facing Nigeria: the lack of any kind of national identity, the kind of identity that other nations have carefully forged through remembering their glory and forgetting the inglorious (cf. Anderson 1983).

Like many African states, Nigeria's nationhood has a brief and necessarily fragile genealogy. The entity that is now the Federal Republic of Nigeria was not formed that way from the beginning. The British occupation began with a presence in Lagos in 1861 followed by expansion through trade in the Niger Delta region that led to the formation of the Oil Rivers Protectorate with headquarters in Calabar. The Oil Rivers Protectorate was then expanded to include all of Southern Nigeria minus Lagos, which remained a colony. In 1900, the British government purchased Northern Nigeria from the Royal Niger Company for £865,000 and declared a protectorate with its capital at Lokoja. The capital later moved to Zungeru and then to Kaduna. In 1906, Lagos, still a colony, became capital of the Protectorate of Southern Nigeria. In 1914, the Lagos colony, the Protectorate of Southern Nigeria and the Protectorate of Northern Nigeria were amalgamated to form what is now Nigeria.[4]

Although joined into one political entity, the North and the South were treated in very different ways because of the strong presence of an Islamic aristocracy that had ruled parts of the Northern region for a century. The British governed indirectly through these Islamic rulers, even placing Muslim rulers over people they had never previously conquered. Furthermore, the British colonial government made it difficult for Christian missionaries to enter the region, entailing that most education in the North was accomplished through government schools while in the South it was carried out by missionaries. The influence of the public school and Oxbridge-educated colonial school administrators entailed that the relatively few Northerners who did receive Western education were inculcated with a higher respect for the recreational activities of the British elite – cricket and polo, rather than football. This would have a great impact on the slower adoption of the game in the North than the South where the largely working-class, football-playing missionaries did most of the educating.

For Nigeria, football is a rare avenue for telling the history of a territory with such a piecemeal and externally motivated development, but even that opportunity has been neglected. In the following pages, we attempt to begin telling the story of football in Nigeria, a story that all Nigerians can share.

In the beginning

In precolonial times there was nothing remotely similar to the colonial game of football that was played by Africans. None of Nigeria's major indigenous languages have precolonial words for the game of football or even for a ball.[5] No one knows for sure where modern football was first played in Nigeria. Probably, early British traders and colonial officers and soldiers played games on the shores of Nigerian ports as they did elsewhere in the world during the late nineteenth century (cf. Mason 1995). It is hard to imagine that no Nigerians at all would have watched, if not participated, in such games.

'The road to Calabar lies through the Island of Jamaica', wrote the Rev. James Luke (1929: 11) in his missionary memoir. The same is true for the road to Nigeria's international football success. Allow us to explain. Following the abolition of slavery in the British Empire in 1834, Jamaican Presbyterians who had formerly been enslaved were inspired both by the interest of free Africans in the diaspora to return to their ancestral continent, and by the call of anti-slavery activist Thomas Fowell Buxton to evangelize Africa. Along with the support of European missionaries, the Jamaicans proposed a Christian mission to West Africa. Uninhibited by lacklustre support from Presbyterianism's Scottish home, an Irishman serving in Jamaica named Hope Waddell led the effort. The prospective mission group finally received an invitation in 1844 to come to the Cross river (in the south-east of modern Nigeria) from Obong Eyamba, the area's traditional ruler (Kalu 1996: 216).

In 1846, a group of Presbyterian Church elders – both Jamaican ex-slaves and European missionaries – met in St Ann's, Jamaica, the birthplace of Bob Marley a century later, and decided to launch the mission effort to Africa. Pursuant to Obong Eyamba's invitation, they picked Calabar as the mission's site – a town on the Cross river that had for centuries been in trading contact with Europe. Hope Waddell subsequently embarked with a small team.[6] After almost a half-century of mission work in Calabar, the Presbyterians started a school there in 1894 called the Hope Waddell Training Institution, which remains one of the best in Nigeria. In 1902, Rev. James Luke became school principal. Rev. Luke had been a missionary in Calabar previously, but was invalided to Jamaica in the 1890s. After seven years, he returned to Calabar, bringing with him the game of football.

In 1903, reference was made to a football game that was to be played during the festivities celebrating the twenty-fifth anniversary of Wesleyan High School in Lagos (*Lagos Standard*, 20 May 1903). A cricket match was played instead, but this mere mention implies that people in Lagos were already playing football (*Lagos Standard*, 20 May 1903).[7] The first recorded game of organized football in Nigeria, however, took place on 15 June 1904 at Hope Waddell Training Institution. A team of Nigerian students and expatriate teachers defeated a team from HMS *Thistle*, a British ship docked at the port, by the score 3–2 (Aye 1967: 146–7; Aye 1986: 23).[8] Right from the beginning, therefore, football in Nigeria had an interracial character. The casual reference in the school's log book to that first recorded match: 'June 15th, 1904: Football played. Institute won (3 to 2). Institute v. Thistle' (Hope Waddell Training Institution 1894–1908: 415)[9] implies, however, that the game was likely already well known there. In addition, if a team composed largely of Nigerian schoolboys could already beat a team of working-class British sailors, one has to imagine that the boys were already well acquainted with the game.

Of course football would not progress in Nigeria if only one school played the game. A football enthusiast in the Intelligence Department of the Southern Nigeria Regiment, Captain Beverley, organized Nigeria's first cup competition. The trophy became greatly prized by Calabar teams; its first winners were the Southern Nigeria Regiment in 1906 and 1907, followed by Duke Town School in 1908, and Hope Waddell in 1909 (Aye 1986: 22).[10] Military participation suggests how football spread into Northern Nigeria beyond the reach of mission schools.[11] A large percentage of early colonial soldiers and police officers were ex-slaves from throughout the Northern Region; it is likely that they took the new game with them to different parts of the North upon retirement (Clayton and Killingray 1989; Baker and Mangan 1987).[12] Nevertheless, football was still known as the 'Calabar game' in the 1920s. Football's popularity quickly spread to Lagos both through mission and colonial schools and through the young educated Calabar men who moved to Lagos when it replaced Calabar as the colonial capital of Southern Nigeria in 1906. In the same year, Frederick Baron Mulford arrived to work for the Lagos

Stores to begin playing his central role in the popularization and organization of football in Lagos and Nigeria.

The game spreads

Boys who attended both mission and government schools across the territory played football in a more organized way. They then took the game to the streets and villages where it became a Nigerian game. Nnamdi Azikiwe, a future leader of Nigeria's colonial struggle and Nigeria's first president, remembered playing football on Lagos streets back in 1916. His description of boys' football then sounds similar to the childhood memories of great footballers today:

> When I arrived in Lagos at the age of eleven I found the open spaces in front of King's College, to our neighbourhood boys known as 'Toronto', a mecca for juvenile sports. We played football there with mango seeds, limes or oranges or old tennis balls. Any collection of boys would be divided into two sides and a spirited game would ensue. We made and altered our rules to suit each game and so we emerged to become self-made soccerists. (Azikiwe 1970: 402)

Obefemi Awolowo, another Nigerian nationalist, has similar memories of football in Lagos as a child during the 1920s (Awolowo 1960: 42).[13]

Azikiwe, a Hope Waddell Training Institution student in the early 1920s, subsequently joined the Diamond Football Club in Lagos, winning the Lagos league in 1923. He went on to captain the Lincoln University team in Pennsylvania in the early 1930s where he earned his first degree.[14] He included sports clubs – founded in rejection of racially exclusive colonial sports clubs, known as Zik Athletic Clubs (ZAC), among his numerous business, political and social ventures across Nigeria. His tours of the Eastern, Western and Northern Regions from 1941 to 1943 with the Zik Athletic Club's senior football team in Lagos were early examples of football's use as a tool of political mobilization. The two tours took Azikiwe and his footballers to Benin, Sapele, Warri, Burutu, Asaba, Onitsha, Enugu, Aba, Port Harcourt, Ibadan, Kaduna, Jos, Makurdi and Calabar with combined crowds of some 50,000 spectators. Organized under the auspices of raising funds for the war effort – forcing colonial officials to show support – Azikiwe would use post-match events to give speeches openly criticizing British colonial policy, exhibiting football's early use as a tool of political mobilization.[15] At his installation as the first indigenous Governor-General of Nigeria in November 1960, numerous matches were played in Azikiwe's honour, including a Nigerian victory over the Egyptian national team. By this time, both Azikiwe and the sport he supported so extensively had become the star attractions of Nigerian society.

Football in the North

Although football was popular in places like Jos, Kaduna and Kano, players and supporters in the North remained largely Southerners who had migrated for reasons of employment or trade. Interracial football was played by colonial officers and indigenes in places as far into the North as Yola, Maidugari, Bauchi, Gombe and Biu as far back as the early 1930s.[16] However, those associated with the Northern Islamic elite mentioned above preferred more 'dignified' games like cricket, field hockey and especially polo, which remains the favoured sport of Northern aristocrats (Skinner 1996: 77). Some members of the rising young Northern elite played football anyway, and D.H.E. Vesey, a colonial education officer, remembers playing in Gombe in 1930 with two mallams (teachers) who were kitted out in 'rather a lot of flowing robes'.[17] For students from the 'pagan' (non-Islamic) North, now known as the Middle Belt Region, football was more acceptable; by 1927, it was declared to be 'the most useful' of the 'standard games' for physical exercise.[18]

It was not until the 1950s that Northern elites began identifying with football, just as their Southern counterparts had done decades earlier. The aristocratic Ahmadu Bello, the Sardauna of Sokoto, and the leading politician from Northern Nigeria in the 1950s and 1960s, played football while schooling at Katsina College, the oldest secondary school in Northern Nigeria. Like Azikiwe and Awolowo, he participated in numerous other sports, showing that football was certainly not promoted above other sports by British colonialists. Sardauna's favourite game was 'Eton Fives' (Bello: 1962: 29); to work with him, it was said one had to know how to play.[19] Although a limited player himself, the Sardauna did recognize football's appeal and sponsored numerous tournaments throughout the North, including interschool matches and for teams from Public Works Departments when he was Northern Regional Minister of Works in 1953 (*West African Pilot*, 23 February 1953: 4). Other Northern politicians also recognized the importance of the game. For instance, Alhaji Usman Nagogo, the Emir of Katsina – a leading Northern traditional ruler – and a world renowned polo fanatic, attended the Governor's Cup final (first played in 1945) between Calabar and Kano at the King George V Stadium in Lagos in 1954 (*West African Pilot*, 4 October 1954: 4). The

Emir of Kano, Alhaji Muhammadu Sanusi, sponsored a tournament for senior teams of Kano's Social Welfare Clubs. Finally, Alhaji Tafawa Balewa, Nigeria's first prime minister, became patron of the Nigeria Referees Association, an affiliate body of the NFA, in 1958 (*West African Pilot*, 16 January 1958: 4). By independence, therefore, football had spread sufficiently so that even elite Northerners more inclined to cricket and polo found football important enough that they gave it their patronage and attention.

Early organized football

Football was never fully organized in Nigeria until a handful of Europeans formed the Lagos and District Amateur Football Association (LDAFA) in 1932. The LDAFA organized the War Memorial Cup competition (later renamed the Mulford Cup) as well as the separate African and European Leagues. At its inception in 1933, the NFA was affiliated to the Football Association of England. The association did little until the 1940s, and even then it was restricted to the Governor's Cup (later Challenge Cup) and the annual intercolonial duel with the Gold Coast inaugurated in 1951.

Football was first popularized in the great early secondary schools around Nigeria like Hope Waddell. Later, amateur clubs emerged often out of teams formed by government agencies and local trading firms who would hire great players as employees from around the country and bring them to Lagos. These clubs and their leagues first developed in Lagos before spreading across Nigeria. The oldest organized football club is believed to be the Public Works Department (PWD) formed in 1929. The club of H.A. Porter, founding president of the NFA, the PWD never won a major honour, but had an interdepartmental league of 13 teams even three years before the Lagos Amateur League began. Another club in Lagos, Railway, was officially launched in 1942 although it had existed since 1937 when it was formed through the incorporation of two clubs that were already in existence. One of them, the Railway Institute, was a parent club of the NFA in 1933. Railway became the most successful club of the 1940s and 1950s, winning numerous Lagos League and Governor's Cup trophies.

In the North, Plateau Province was the first major hotbed of football, but it was only in 1946 that the Plateau Amateur Football Association was inaugurated. Within a year, the Plateau team had won the Northern final and reached the national semi-finals of the Governor's Cup. Plateau football was heavily influenced by tin mining and affiliated companies. European miners had their own club, called the Yelwa Club, where cricket was played while African miners had separate facilities and a football stadium in Bukuru sponsored by the mining company. A similar division existed between European and African clubs in Jos town and other provincial capitals.[20] Most small mining camps in the bush had social clubs and football fields for African workers, as did the National Electric Supply Company (NESCO) that powered the mines. Mahmoud Hassan, a mine labourer during the Second World War, recalled his European bosses organizing football matches on Saturdays between African labourers and African clerical staff.[21] It was from mining company-supported football that John Dankaro, the first Northern football star, emerged as a member of the national team in 1949. Unsurprisingly, Plateau teams became the first to challenge the national supremacy of Southern teams. Elsewhere, the Ibadan District Football Association (IDAFA) was formed in 1937. Also, the Abeokuta District Amateur Football Association was officially founded on 26 September 1947, but had its origins in the 1930s with a league featuring several teams. By the mid-1940s, provincial capitals even as far from Lagos as Yola had organized football leagues, although still largely dominated by Southern players.

Going national and international: late colonial soccer

In 1945, the Governor's Cup, renamed the Challenge Cup in the 1950s, was inaugurated with a trophy donated by Governor Richards. This enabled organized football at a truly nationwide level and confirmed government support for expansion. The tournament began as an all-Lagos affair and was launched with little fanfare or national attention.[22] But from 13 entries in 1945, it rose to 32 in 1950 and 87 in 1959. Entries have since crossed the 100 mark, especially growing after 1971 when the competition was played nationwide on a club basis instead of along the lines of township selections. An added attraction was the introduction of regional qualifying series, which gave way to separate Challenge Cup competitions within each state of the Federation.[23] The Challenge Cup's appeal led to agitations for a national league that did not finally kick off until 8 January 1972.

Intercolonial matches between Europeans in Lagos and their counterparts in the Gold Coast began as early as 1903. Gold Coast cricket, polo and tennis teams came to Lagos to launch a historic series of 'intercolo' competitions between Nigerians and Gold Coasters (now Ghanaians) that continue today (*Lagos Weekly Record*, 11 April 1903: 3, 18 April 1903: 3, 25 April 1903: 3; *Lagos Standard*, 15 April 1903).[24] Other sports were introduced, including swimming, athletics, rugby, table tennis, field hockey, basketball and, starting in 1937, football. While the first intercolonial matches were all European, by 1910 African players from the two colonies also had their own parallel contests. Eventually mixed teams competed and by the time of the first genuine football international in 1951, it was an all-African affair. Although Nigerians serving in India and Burma in the Second World War excelled in games against soldiers from other parts of the world, these matches could not really be considered true international fixtures (*West African Pilot*, 12 January 1946: 4, 6 February 1946: 4, 10 May 1946: 4). The first real international exposure of Nigeria's players was the 1949 UK tour by an NFA select side, as part of a series of UK tours by Nigeria's athletes that started with athletics in 1948. The team played several English amateur clubs, winning two games, drawing two and losing five. They usually played barefoot and were very popular with English crowds amazed at how good African players were.[25] In turn, in 1958 an English Football Association XI (not the national team) toured Nigeria. Although there were some encounters between Lagos selected sides and the selections from former Gold Coast, Nigeria did not play a full international until 1949 when the team returning from the tour of the UK played Sierra Leone on 8 October, winning the game 2–1. Two years later, an annual competition between Nigeria and Gold Coast/Ghana was initiated. Matches for the series alternated between Lagos and Accra until 1959. By then, qualifying fixtures for the Olympic Games and the World Cup had assumed priority, although Nigeria's record against Ghana was poor.

At independence in 1960, football was truly the dominant sport in the South and its appeal was fast spreading even among indigenes of the North. By then, Nigerian teams had played national or club teams from England, Germany, Ghana, Sierra Leone, Togo, Cameroon, Egypt, Dahomey (Benin), Côte D'Ivoire and even Lebanon. Football was drawing Nigeria into the international community; Nigeria became a provisional member of FIFA in 1959 and a full member on 22 August 1960, before the country gained its political independence from the UK on 1 October 1960.

After independence: an inauspicious beginning

During the heady days of independence, there was a busy soccer schedule centred largely on Lagos. Nigeria lost to Ghana in a World Cup qualifier in Accra at the end of August. The next day, Prime Minister Alhaji Sir Tafawa Balewa officially opened the new 30,000-seat National Stadium in Surulere, Lagos, for use during independence celebrations, and in future, as the centrepiece of Nigeria's sporting spectacles. Balewa congratulated the builders for 'getting the stadium ready on time both for the Independence Celebrations and the West African Games and possibly the next Olympics in which Nigeria shall be the host country' (*West African Pilot*, 3 September 1960: 2). Meanwhile, the National Secretariat of the National Council of Nigeria and the Cameroons (NCNC – the political party of Nnamdi Azikiwe) issued a statement formally deploring the loss to Ghana. Evidently, the strategy of pursuing huge and rather untenable sporting ambitions, and football's role in Nigeria's foreign policy, were already being outlined before the country had joined the league of free nations.

Nigeria then hosted the four-nation Nkrumah Gold Cup, but lost the final to Ghana. While controversy raged over another football failure, touring parties from England's Middlesex Wanderers and the Ivoirian national team arrived. To highlight Nigeria's integration within the dynamics of Cold War sporting diplomacy, a tour by Moscow Dynamo, 'one of the world's leading soccer clubs' (*West African Pilot*, 12 October 1960: 8), was also planned. However, Nigeria's first participation in an international tournament, the 1963 African Nations Cup, did not bode well when they lost 6–3 and 4–0 to Egypt and Sudan respectively. A few years later, Nigeria was thrust into a bloody civil war, during which a team actually qualified to represent the country at the 1968 Olympics where they lost their first two games and drew their final one 3–3 with Brazil.

Postcolonial club football

Following the continued failures of the national team in the 1960s, the question of a national league re-emerged. After several false starts and to little fanfare the Nigerian national league featuring eight teams kicked off on 8 January 1972. The league reverted to a knockout format from 1975 to 1978, but in 1979 Division Two was introduced and in 1983 the third division was added. The league turned professional in 1990. Shooting Stars of Ibadan won the African Cup Winners Cup in 1976, a feat matched by Enugu Rangers the following year. In 1990, BCC Lions of Gboko, one of the newer generation clubs, won it again. Other than these, no Nigerian club has won any continental tournament and, after 40 years of trying, the African Champions Cup continues to elude Nigeria.

Oil boom and beyond: the slow rise to international prominence

It is said that when Pelé's club Santos came to play in Nigeria in 1969 a ceasefire was called in the Biafran War (the Nigerian Civil War) (Murray

1996: 122). Soon after the war, in January 1970, General Gowon, the head of state since 1966 and a football star in his secondary school days (Elaigwu 1986: 31), commissioned the refurbishment of the National Stadium, to house 60,000 fans and to host the 2nd All Africa Games in January 1973.

At the final football match of the multisports event, Nigeria, captained by an Igbo player, beat Guinea 2–0 in a spectacle designed to show Nigeria's emerging power in sports and beyond. It also exhibited Nigeria's full reunification after the terrible war where players from all parts of the country, including the defunct Biafra, brought the nation glory.[26] Despite the government's hype, winning football gold was not particularly prestigious, although it was Nigeria's first international trophy. On a broader level, the victory was part of a complete overhaul of Nigeria's postwar image and infrastructure as facilitated by the oil boom.

Aided by the growing national league, Nigeria became an African football power through qualifications for the African Nations Cup, and an Olympic berth in 1976 that they boycotted for political reasons related to the apartheid regime in South Africa (Baker 1987: 288). Football and the National Stadium were important to the remaking of Nigeria as an emerging leader of the black and African world, as reflected too in the 1977 Festival of Black and African Arts and Culture (FESTAC '77) (Apter 1996).

Before the 1980 African Nations Cup hosted by Nigeria, recently inaugurated democratic president Shehu Shagari charged the Nigerian team (the Green Eagles), saying, 'A victory for Nigeria would further make her stand above other African countries and also justify her claim to be Africa's leader in all aspects of life including sports' (*New Nigerian*, 8 March 1980: 14). That Nigerian politicians are not interested in soccer just for political reasons, but also as genuine fans, Shehu Shagari, 'a man who keeps his emotions under control in public', let down his guard and, during Nigeria's demolition of Algeria in the final, 'he stood up to wave his rattle gleefully like a schoolboy with joy written all over his honest face' (Akpabot 1985: 49). As a member of the Northern aristocracy that once viewed football as undignified, Shagari's excitement symbolized football's meaning to people throughout the country. And he did not stop there. After the match he hugged Segun Odegbami, the scorer of two of Nigeria's three goals. 'Eagles to Get National Honours', shouted the headlines the following Monday, and cash prizes were certain to follow (*New Nigerian*, 24 March 1980: 1). The Eagles were discussed on the Senate floor following their victory, with calls to give them all houses and for them to be sent 'anywhere in the world to acquire more knowledge on soccer' (*New Nigerian*, 26 March 1980: 23).

Things fall apart: senior failures, youth triumphs and the opening of the export market

Just as corruption cut short Nigeria's economic dream during the 1980s, so the national team did not sustain their early promise, continually missing another African Nations Cup victory, a World Cup berth, and managing only a dismal performance at the 1988 Olympics. The highlight of the rest of the decade was Nigeria's victory in the 1985 Under-16 World Cup in China, Africa's first football world champions. In the mid-1980s, another development began which would eventually transform Nigerian football – the 'export' of players to European leagues. This exodus is not, however, a recent trend but had begun with Nigerian students studying abroad who excelled at many sports in British universities as early as the 1940s (*West African Pilot*, 28 February 1945: 4).[27] In the 1950s, boxers like Dick Tiger and Hogan Bassey migrated to fight in British rings, returning to Nigeria as national heroes after winning Empire and World titles under the British flag. In football, the trickle began in the 1950s when international players such as Tesilimi 'Thunderbolt' Balogun, John Dankaro, Dan Anyiam and Titus Okere left to play and study in England.

Domestic economic decline in the 1980s and increasing revenues in European football inspired ever-greater numbers to play professionally abroad. The effects were twofold. First, the Nigerian national league was increasingly impoverished and is now basically a farm league for clubs in Europe and elsewhere, losing rising stars long before they peak. Secondly, Nigerian players abroad gained training and vital experience at a far higher competitive level than any African league could offer. This would eventually be the catalyst for Nigeria's rise to the status of football superpower. The same mismanagement that cut short Nigeria's progress towards the status of economic superpower ironically aided indirectly in bringing Nigeria football glory. Now, Nigerian players are abroad as early as age 13, and nearly the entire national team plays outside the country.[28] In short, one of the foundations on which the country's frail unity is built – the national teams – are themselves increasingly disconnected from the country whose hopes they carry.

Journey to the top: women lead the way

In 1939, a football enthusiast wrote to the *West African Pilot*, asking: 'Do you approve of a women's football team? If not please say why women shouldn't play football.' The sports editor responded positively, saying there was no reason why women should not play football (*West African Pilot*, 17 February 1939: 8). Although women's football was not recognized as an official sport in Nigeria for another 50 years, women did play the game. Over the ensuing decades, there were numerous reports of novelty or charity matches between teams of men and women, with women almost always winning. One interesting match was a charity event in Lagos between middle-aged Igbo men and a team of Igbo ladies in which Nnamdi Azikiwe himself was billed to play. Instead, he was only permitted to serve as a referee in the match that the women won 4–1. The catch was that the entire eleven of the women's team from the first half were replaced in the second since women were supposedly unable to play an entire match (*West African Pilot*, 16 May 1950: 4).

In 1950, following orders from the English Football Association, the NFA declared that women's football should not be encouraged, and that NFA grounds or referees should not be used for women's games (*West African Pilot*, 2 June 1950: 4). Novelty matches continued, but any plans for organized women's football had to be shelved. Indeed, a report from the late 1950s decreed that football, alongside basketball, boxing, cricket, water polo and wrestling, were to remain male domains (Powell [1963?]: 2).[29] Although played by schoolgirls, only in 1989 did football for women become officially recognized when it was first included at the National Sports Festival (Abdullahi 2000: 90). Two years later, Nigeria's women were playing in the World Cup. While it only took them two years to make the top, it took Nigeria's men 61 years from the launching of men's nationally organized football to accomplish the same feat.

Nigeria's dominance of women's football, however, is still limited to Africa. In 1991, they finished tenth of twelve at the inaugural FIFA World Championship in China; at Sweden '95 the results were similar. The women's national team, named the Super Falcons, qualified for their third World Cup by winning the inaugural African Women's Nations Cup hosted by Nigeria in 1998. Little hype surrounded the championship, but large crowds and amazing team performances ended with a 2–0 victory over Ghana before a 30,000 capacity crowd in Abeokuta (*Complete Football International*, December 1998: 6–9).

Despite great popular support and the emphatic victory, the government made little political capital from the tournament or the victory. The players were not even granted the usual invitation to meet the head of state after their triumph. It was not until a year later, when Nigeria surprised the world with a fifth-place finish in the 1999 Women's World Cup, that the government paid them attention. Although their poor performance at the Sydney Olympics was a setback, Nigeria's women remain unbeaten in Africa after winning the second African Women's Nations Cup held in South Africa.[30]

A light in the darkness: football success under Abacha

In 1993, Nigeria's Golden Eaglets won their second junior world title, and in 1994 the senior team won their second African Nations Cup title. Also in 1994, Nigeria competed in their first men's World Cup, the true test of football greatness, duly impressing the world.[31] In 1996, Nigeria won Olympic gold, an event that will forever be enshrined in people's memory as a great day in Nigerian and African sporting history. Many would agree that the 1994 and 1996 victories were the only shining moments during the dark days of General Abacha's leadership. Even Abacha's supporters listed these 'great' accomplishments when promoting his candidacy as a civilian president, exhibiting the importance of football and the dearth of redeemable political aspects to his regime.

Nigerian football has been behind not only Nigerian pride in the international arena, but black and African pride generally. When Jamaica hosted Nigeria in a friendly in 1998, they did so partly to prove themselves as a great *black* soccer power. Nigeria returned to the World Cup in 1998 as a highly rated team, beating Spain dramatically in their opening game less than a week after the death of dictator Sani Abacha in June 1998. After their stellar early performances at France '98, the Nigerian players were hailed as the 'Pride of Africa' in a South African soccer magazine (*Kickoff*, 13 July 1998) while the Brazilians began calling themselves the 'Nigeria of South America'.[32] Before the disastrous Nigeria–Denmark match where Nigeria lost 4–1, and was the only African nation left in the tournament (and the only black nation, unless one characterizes Brazil in those terms), Nigerian defender Taribo West said: 'This is for all Africans. It is about black pride.'[33] As Nigeria had been culturally and economically for the black and African world in the 1970s, in the 1990s Nigeria emerged as the centre of black and African football pride – a huge burden for Nigeria's stars to bare.

'Hosting the world amid poverty': soccer and the rebirth of the nation

Abacha's death in 1998 allowed General Abdulsalami Abubakar to reinvent the nation, partly through his return to democracy programme, but also predictably through football. After earlier youth level successes, Nigeria were granted the right to host the 1999 FIFA World Youth Cup, after the privilege had been withdrawn in 1995 on spurious health grounds. Abacha's passing eased FIFA's qualms about Nigeria's role, although repressive dictators and FIFA have often gotten along quite well (e.g. Argentina '78). The tournament was wedged between presidential elections and the writing of the 1999 Constitution, so it inevitably became part of the nation's rebirth. Abubakar wrote:

> [S]ince the present administration took over, the country has witnessed gradual integration into the international community. It is only most cherished that the game of football which has remained a big symbol of unity and peace in Nigeria will also finally open up the country to the rest of the world. (Abubakar 1999: 3)

Much effort went into whitewashing Nigeria's image and cleaning up the streets through what the organizers called 'Operation Keep Beggars and Destitutes Off Major Roads'. Nigeria is now a terribly poor country and to spend $110 million on improving facilities for the youth tournament seemed to many a waste of money, but certainly not to Abubakar ('Nigeria's investment in Youth Championship will pay off', *Nando Media*, 11 April 1999). However, in contrast to the equally ambitious Festival of Black and African Arts and Culture hosted in 1977 (FESTAC '77 – hosted when the stronger economy enabled popular participation), the 1999 tournament was a spectacle remarkable in scale that average Nigerians could barely afford to attend.[34] Some commentators claimed the fans' absence was a form of political protest. Indeed, soccer has been a site of resistance in Nigeria when more overt protest could invite severe repression.[35] An organizational success, but a failed spectacle, the tournament also saw Nigeria endure a 'national disgrace' once again when losing to lowly Mali 3–1 in the quarter-finals (*Nigeria NewsNetwork*, 21 April 1999).

22nd African Nations Cup, Nigeria and Ghana, 2000

In co-hosting the African Nations Cup with Ghana in 2000, the experiences of Nigeria '99 were reversed. President Obasanjo, elected only weeks before Nigeria '99, never identified himself with the tournament. In an unprecedented move, he was not even in the country when the tournament began, but had gone to France on a trade mission. Ignoring this ambivalence, however, Nigerian soccer fans went to the stadia en masse, often filling them to double the official capacity. When

Nigeria only managed a draw with Congo, fans attacked the NFA office in Lagos and the Super Eagles' team bus.

When compared to the interethnic and interreligious conflicts before the tournament that were threatening to tear Nigeria apart, the tournament proved yet again how central football is to Nigerian identity and unity. Suleyol Mngerem of the *Nigerian Guardian* wrote during the tournament: 'Truth be told, the unity you see in our faces, the hope you feel in the air, the oneness of spirit which is so thick you can cut with a knife is beautiful. I don't care much for football but I just have a good feeling when it's football season' (*Nigerian Guardian*, 5 February 2000). After the semi-final victory, former Super Eagles coach Paul Hamilton commented: 'Wherever an organized match is being played anywhere in this country, people from the different ethnic groups come together. When the victory they hope for comes they are united, as if they are from the same womb' ('Semi-final success unites Nigeria', *BBC News Online*, 11 February 2000).

Throughout the tournament, hyper-Nigerian nationalism was apparent, reaching a peak before the game against South Africa with fans from both countries exhibiting xenophobic attitudes. Creditably, the Obasanjo government did not exploit these sentiments to bolster Nigeria's fragile unity. After losing the final to Cameroon, the Nigerian captain, press and fans were bitter because of the controversial finish.[36] The Cameroonian government was so concerned for their team's safety that they sent Presidential guards to escort them home ('Cameroon Protects Lions', *CNNSI.com*, 14 February 2000). Again to his credit, Obasanjo accepted the loss as 'the verdict of God' and thanked the team for doing Nigeria proud.[37]

The tournament is now all but forgotten, and Nigerians are back to dangerous discussions about dividing the country. Soccer helps to unite Nigeria but, as Obasanjo appeared to understand, it is too shallow a force to contend with very real problems. He has come a long way from some of the unrealistic demands, claims, expectations and rhetoric regarding soccer of earlier Nigerian leaders.

The development of football in Nigeria constitutes a remarkable social phenomenon. That something so foreign would take the hearts and minds of more Nigerians in more places around the country than any other aspect of colonial culture would have been completely unpredictable in the 1890s, 1920s, or probably even the 1950s. As football spread from the coast to attract attention and devotion from people across Nigeria, so too spread an increasing understanding of what it was to live within those randomly created borders, that it meant one was 'Nigerian' and not something else. As people indigenous to Nigeria increasingly made the term 'Nigerian' their own, so too did they make football Nigerian, at the expense of sports like cricket, polo or field hockey, that had been considered more 'dignified' and 'cultured' by Nigeria's uninvited rulers.

So what makes football increasingly popular in the postcolonial era? Perhaps it is because football is almost the only arena in which the country has visibly and continually improved, albeit not as far as the rhetoric would have one believe. Or maybe it is simply because, as the late sports writer Sam Akpabot wrote, the Nigerian game is so dynamic and exciting that their performances can cause 'young men to faint, holy men to swear and strong men to become impotent for a day' (Akpabot 1985: 67).

Notes

1. For example, the contest between IICC of Ibadan and Enugu Rangers, two of Nigeria's historically dominant club sides, was described as 'a battle between the East and West of Nigeria' ('Interviews: Segun Odegbami', *Cyber Eagles*, September 1999: 2). But even while these two clubs symbolized Nigeria's subnational identities, the fact that they played each other within the same national league shows an acknowledgement of a larger, more national, identity.
2. Prior to the 1998 World Cup Nigeria was still in the dark days of the regime of the late dictator General Sani Abacha. During Abacha's tenure, repression in Nigeria reached levels previously unknown, leading to much despair about the future of Nigeria. Nigerians would often say then that the only reason for national unity was to promote a strong national team and a good 1998 World Cup performance.
3. For example, military dictator Sani Abacha's withdrawal of the national team from the 1996 African Nations Cup in South Africa due to Nelson Mandela's outspoken criticism of the execution of Ken Saro-Wiwa. Saro-Wiwa was a minority rights and environmental activist bringing attention to the injustices caused by the Nigerian government in the oil-producing Niger Delta region. He was executed by the Abacha junta in November 1995 and an international outcry followed. Abacha's official excuse for the team's withdrawal was that South African authorities would not be able to ensure the safety of the Nigerian team.
4. The only addition was a piece of Cameroon that was administered by the colonial government in Nigeria after the First World War and became an official part of independent Nigeria in the 1960s. The southern portion of English Cameroon voted to join the French portion of Cameroon, although it was administered as part of Nigeria from the end of the First World War until Nigeria's independence in 1960.
5. This contradicts Akindutire's (1991) claim that something like football, albeit in an unorganized fashion, existed in parts of precolonial Nigeria. He has no references to authenticate his claim, so it seems quite hard to accept.
6. Although Hope Waddell and Mary Slessor, the most famous of Calabar's Presbyterian missionaries, were indeed European, a good portion of the

missionaries there were Jamaicans of African descent, a fact of which few Presbyterians in present day Nigeria are aware.

7. Cricket not only predates football in Nigeria, but also remained hugely popular in places like Lagos well into the mid-1900s for Europeans and Africans alike.

8. In the advertisement to enthusiasts planning to visit Calabar for Nigeria '99, the FIFA Under-20 World Cup, we are told: 'Football comes home! It all started in Calabar almost a century ago' (*Complete Football International*, Special Edition, April 1999: 47).

9. Thanks to Rev. Nsa Eyo, Principal of Hope Waddell Training Institution, who allowed me access to the Institution's log book during my visit in May 2001. According to Eyo, the fact that the log book still exists is a miracle. After capturing Calabar during the Biafran War, federal troops camped at the school and destroyed most of the Institute's literature when they used the books for firewood.

10. Confirmed in Awoyinfa (1957: 4).

11. Many of the early educational institutions in Nigeria were started by missionary organizations. Since the colonial government did not allow missionary activity in the heavily Islamic 'Holy' north, there were much fewer educational institutions there at which sports like football would have been played.

12. Sports were an active part of life for the British and Nigerian members of the West African Frontier Force, polo being almost an obsession. For sports like field hockey, athletics and football, there were organized leagues within and between separate battalions. For details on sports in the colonial Nigerian military, see *The Regimental Journal of the Nigerian Regiment*, which began in 1926, and its 1950s successor *Nigerian Military Forces Magazine*.

13. Shortly after joining Arsenal of England in January 1999, Kanu Nwankwo, the captain of Nigeria's gold-medal-winning team at the Atlanta Olympics, said: 'When you are growing up there, sometimes you play without boots, in bare feet, and you just go out and kick the ball around after school until it is dark. I played all the time, only returning home when it was time to sleep' (*Arsenal Magazine*, March 1999: 34).

14. Azikiwe's half-brother Ernest captained Lincoln University's soccer team in 1963 and his son Nwachukwu captained Harvard in 1967 (Azikiwe 1970: 152).

15. See *West African Pilot* (Zik's newspaper) from 3 December 1942 to 21 February 1942 for the Eastern and Western tour. For the Northern tour, see editions from 2 November 1942 to 16 January 1943.

16. Randal E. Ellison, 'Papers, Education Department, Maidugari', Rhodes House Archives, Oxford, *Mss. Afr. S. 421*, 27 December 1931, pp. 2b and 3a; D.H.E. Vesey, 'Letters to Father and Others', Rhodes House Archives, Oxford, *Mss. Afr. S. 644*, 17 September 1930, p. 1; 11 October 1931, p. 4; 6 December 1931, p. 4.

17. D.H.E. Vesey, 'Letters to Father and Others', Rhodes House Archives, Oxford, *Mss. Afr. S. 644*, 17 September 1930, p. 1.

18. Stanley A. Hammond, *Pagan Schools: The Training of Teachers*, 1927, Rhodes House Archives, Oxford, *Mss. Afr. S. 1325*, p. 21.

19. Anthony Kirk-Greene, interviewed by Wiebe Boer, St Antony's College, Oxford, 22 February 2001.

20. Pa Raphael Shonekan, interviewed by Wiebe Boer, Jos, Plateau State, 18 March 2001.
21. Mahmoud Hassan, interviewed by Wiebe Boer, Sabon Gida Kanar mining camp, Plateau State, 15 March 2001. Hassan said that the labourers always won and that he was a striker. He showed me a bump on his foot that he claimed came from playing football in the 1940s.
22. The 1945 Governor's Cup final that Marine won against Corinthians was barely noted even in the usually soccer-mad *West African Pilot* (8 November 1945: 4).
23. Before independence, Nigeria was administered in four separate units – the Northern region with twelve provinces, the Eastern region with five, the Western region with six provinces, and the Lagos colony. Each region had a governor, and Lagos had a commissioner. The colony as a whole was administered by a Governor-General with his capital in Lagos. Following independence, an additional province was created called the Mid-West Province, and each was administered by a regional premier. The structure changed with the creation of twelve states in 1967. There are 36 states now, each with its own governor.
24. In early colonial times, 'Nigerian' and 'Gold Coaster' meant a European colonial officer who worked in those territories, not an indigene. Later, terms such as 'Nigerian African' and 'Nigerian European' were used to delineate what race of 'Nigerian' was being referred to. It was not until the late 1940s that 'Nigerian' was finally used to mean what it does now – a person with origins within the boundaries of the Nigerian state.
25. Pa Raphael Shonekan, interviewed by Wiebe Boer, Jos, Plateau State, 18 March 2001. Shonekan was a spectator at one of the matches in England. He was surprised that the Nigerians played barefoot since he and other students at King's College were already wearing shoes to play football in the 1930s.
26. The event was designed to help Nigerians 'forget' about Biafra. See Coronil (1997: 67).
27. One athlete was Godfrey Amachree, captain of the combined University College and London School of Economics football team. He later became the first indigenous chairman of the NFA in 1959.
28. In fact, a number of Nigerians have played or are playing for the national teams of other countries, including England, the United States, Malta, Hungary and Poland.
29. It is impossible to ascertain the exact date of the report to any further detail.
30. For a brief introduction to women's soccer in Nigeria, see Abisuga and Awurumibe (1991). The final match ended before full time (with Nigeria leading South Africa 2–0) because of fan violence in the stadium. The disorder indicates how much the popularity of women's football has risen over the last decade.
31. They lost out to Morocco by a mere coin toss to be the African representative in 1970, and lost out to Tunisia for the 1978 World Cup through an own goal!
32. Seamus Malin, ABC Sports, 28 June 1998, Nigeria v. Denmark sportscast.
33. Bob Ley, ABC Sports, 28 June 1998, Nigeria v. Denmark sportscast.
34. The average ticket price was roughly equal to an average day's pay.

35. For example, during the confusing and tense political climate between the annulment of the 12 June 1993 elections and the Abacha coup of 17 November, any protest was dangerous. Sonny Okosuns, one of Nigeria's most popular musicians, recorded a song entitled 'Political Game' in which he commentated upon (over a fresh background beat) a soccer match between 'Democracy United' and 'Interim Bombers FC'. Elsewhere, when the unpopular military governor Habibu Shuaibu Idris arrived at the Jos Township Stadium for the Plateau State Challenge Cup Final in July 1998, the crowd began cheering 'Barawo, barawo' meaning 'Thief, thief'. Two weeks later, he was removed.

36. Cameroon won when Nigeria's Victor Ikpeba's penalty kick was mistakenly ruled as a miss. Ironically, in the first match between Nigeria and Cameroon, held in Lomé as part of Togo's independence celebrations, Nigeria was awarded a controversial penalty in the second half after which the Cameroonian team walked out in protest ('Kameroun Team Walk Out to Avoid Defeat', *West African Pilot*, 28 April 1960: 7).

37. Cited in 'African Nations Cup: Nigeria accepts result as "God's verdict"', Agence France-Press, 21 February 2000.

4
Between Colonialism, Independence and Globalization: Football in Zimbabwe

Richard Giulianotti

To domestic and international observers alike, Zimbabwean football is an enigma. The game has a particularly long history throughout the country and is the dominant sport among Africans. Yet Zimbabwe's impact on the international stage has been very minor, the national team having qualified for one African Nations Cup finals and no World Cup finals, while the club teams have had little impact in continental tournaments.

In this chapter, I provide a concise sociological analysis of the social history and contemporary structural condition of Zimbabwean football. The chapter is divided into two general sections. First, I examine Zimbabwe's modern football history through an analysis of the nation as a venue of British imperial expansion, revolutionary struggle and subsequent independence. Second, I discuss in more detail the most recent period regarding Zimbabwean football and the wider society, from 1990 onwards. The analysis is principally a political-economic one, and concentrates on how football's social history has been heavily influenced by elites at the epicentre of three critical social processes in Zimbabwe: colonization, nationalism and globalization.

The township game: a brief social history of Zimbabwe and its football

Zimbabwe is a landlocked country in the southern Africa region, bordered by South Africa (in the south), and by Botswana (west), Zambia (north-west) and Mozambique (east). Zimbabwe's 12.2 million citizens are commonly distinguished in ethnic terms by linguistic tradition. Shona-speakers comprise around 80 per cent of the population and predominate in the northern provinces (especially Mashonaland) and the Midlands. Sindebele-speakers comprise around 16 per cent, are primarily of Ndebele cultural extraction and most numerous in the south (notably Matabeleland provinces). Whites or 'Europeans', who had numbered over 250,000 at the height of colonial powers, make up less than 1 per cent. However, this ethno-linguistic triangle is something of a colonial construction, and disguises the cultural diversity and linguistic complex of Zimbabwe, notably within the relatively heterogeneous 'Shona-speaking' category (cf. Worby 1994).

The modern social history of these peoples may be divided into four broad periods. The first, precolonial period is most remarkable for the creation of what is now known as the city of 'Great Zimbabwe' from around 1100 AD, housing the leaders of up to 10,000 Shona-speaking people who themselves lived and worked around its perimeters (cf. Beach 1994: 68–71). The city-state declined mysteriously through the seventeenth century, but Shona-speaking peoples continued to build settlements in more northern areas. In the 1840s, the south-western areas were taken over by King Mzilikazi, who led his peoples north from the Cape to create a powerful, Ndebele-speaking tributary state with its base at Bulawayo. Mzilikazi was succeeded, upon his death, by his son Lobengula in 1870.

The second colonization period began in 1890 with the Pioneer Column, drawn from Cecil Rhodes' British South African Company (BSAC), crossing north into current-day Zimbabwe. Reflecting Rhodes' imperialist maxim that he would colonize the planets if he could, the prospectors annexed the north while manufacturing a war in 1893 against the Ndebele in the south. Lobengula was promptly defeated and driven into the bush where he disappeared, presumed dead, a year later. The BSAC and white settlers from South Africa and Britain then established the new military-industrial complex of Rhodesia. A joint Shona-Ndebele uprising (the First Chimurenga) was put down in 1896, and the BSAC and white settlers from South Africa and Britain set about founding the new province of Rhodesia. Indigenous peoples were collectivized to work on white-owned farms; an African urban proletariat was forged to work in the mines or industries and services in larger conurbations (Phimister 1988). The BSAC scaled down its operations and ceded power to the white populace in 1923 to found the new state of Southern Rhodesia, with Bulawayo the main centre, and Salisbury (renamed as Harare in 1982) the major northern conurbation.

During this period, the settlers had invented categories of tribal identification and tradition, to know and control the diverse African populations (Worby 1998: 566; Jeater 1995). As a study in Foucauldian 'governmentality', these 'colonial fictions' of tribal category served to inculcate systems of self-knowledge and collective identity across local peoples (cf. Foucault 1982). Tribal taxonomies ignored the genuine diversity of linguistic and cultural influence across Rhodesia, but their effects upon African practices and identities were multifarious. In Bulawayo, feuds, rivalries and eruptions of violence ensued in the late 1920s, especially involving widespread fears among African residents regarding migrant gangs from Mashonaland. Through the prism of tribalism, the British respected the Ndebeles' military resolve, political prowess and awareness of hierarchy, whereas the Shona were dismissed as 'a miserable cowardly lot' and too keen to enter an *indaba* (discussions) rather than make decisions (cf. Beach 1994: 11). Later, from the late 1940s onwards, the Ndebele were granted greater administrative and political influence in Bulawayo, unlike their fellow Africans in Salisbury.

Sport's social texture was underpinned by this unfolding of colonial hegemony. The Pioneer Column's men were almost definitely the first players of football and rugby in the region (cf. Thompson 1935). By 1900, several sports clubs had been founded in the emerging towns, thus establishing competitions in football and other team sports. Organized sport was the exclusive preserve of whites, although internal gradations are noteworthy. Football was particularly popular with new arrivals from 'Home' (including soldiers) but most Rhodesian schools followed the British model by educating boys in the more imperial sports of rugby and cricket (ibid.: 105). Africans in Southern Rhodesia were probably introduced to football when, from 1923 onwards, black mineworkers from the Transvaal migrated north to arrive in Bulawayo and the Midlands towns, seeking work and playing games in their spare time. Local Africans quickly favoured football – a game that required little economic and cultural capital from those with no resources for equipment or proper pedagogy in sports practice. Township clubs sprung up through the 1920s and 1930s, one of the oldest and most successful being the Lions Club of Bulawayo (renamed the Matabeleland Highlanders in 1937) which was formed by the grandchildren of Lobengula, the last Ndebele king.

Ethnic affiliations acquired prominence within specific sporting institutions and the social relations of competition, but at bottom the collective and 'intertribal' organization of township sport was more potent in its vindication of African cultural autonomy. In Salisbury, colonial obsession with ethnic categorization induced white fears that township boxing clubs might be organized by Africans along potentially explosive tribal lines. In reality, boxing held a 'supratribal' attraction that encouraged African cultural autonomy and thus appeared more potentially injurious to white interests (Parry 1999: 76). Football (like boxing) was a venue for expressions of ethnic pride and intercultural rivalry, notably between Ndebele and Shona peoples within clubs (Stuart 1989: 102–3; Ranger 1987; Beach 1994: 186). Soon, the Ndebele origins of the Lions were most apparent, as its other peoples left to join other clubs forming in the 1930s, such as Mashonaland Saints (now Zimbabwe Saints) and 'North Rhodesia' (for peoples from today's Zambia). In 1936, the Osborne Cup competition came into existence for African teams, following the donation of a trophy by a white social worker in Bulawayo, and similar tournaments were soon established. In Salisbury, by 1938, there were 19 township teams in two divisions under colonial auspices (Parry 1999: 77). Most notably, the Bulawayo African Football Association (BAFA) was formed in the mid-1930s to administer African football affairs, under the paternalist gaze of the white-controlled African Welfare Society (Stuart 1996: 170, 176).

African football reflected the systematically enforced cultural and economic dependency of Africans under Europeans. In Bulawayo, profits from the African townships' beer gardens were diverted into the construction of various stadiums and sports facilities from the 1930s onwards. Such projects redoubled the material, social and cultural divisions between white elites and African township residents. They were effectively self-financed by the African communities, absolving Europeans of major financial burdens regarding township development (Kaarsholm 1999: 233). Meanwhile, equipped with some local facilities, the African population remained categorically excluded from the kind of sport-related development – in pedagogy, facilities and competitive exposure – that whites enjoyed. Attempts by African clubs to join the white-controlled Southern Rhodesia Football Association were brusquely rejected. Even African control over fixtures was not possible, as white social workers took on the crucial rational and normative function of refereeing games until 1941. In Salisbury at least, one consequence was that Africans broadly preferred, from the European viewpoint, more hedonistic and less hygienic recreation, notably in drinking and dancing (Parry 1999: 77).

The third period of Zimbabwe's modern history begins in the 1940s and covers the years of more overt and militant struggle against white domination. Political resistance was manifested through industrial action and public protests seeking African suffrage and better working, educational and living conditions. In 1945 and 1948, strikes were organized by African workers, seeking recognition for labour movements and increased wages, but with only limited success. Significant divisions within the urban African population became established, notably between migrant and resident workers, and less clearly between ethnic groups (Lunn 1999: 173–7). Following 1948, the key to the anti-colonial struggle lay in winning the peasant struggle within the countryside. Social conditions did improve for long-term residents in Bulawayo through the 1940s and 1950s, particularly when the liberal modernization approach of Dr Hugh Ashton, of the Native Administration Department, came into effect. Africans acquired greater control over local associations and trading, but more fundamental forms of emancipation remained intangible. By the early 1960s, the mass movements of Africans were underpinned by nationalist ideologies, reflecting heightened senses of African historical and cultural identity. Joshua Nkomo emerged as the key political leader, first through the African National Congress (ANC) and finally, following the ANC's banning, by the Zimbabwe African People's Union (ZAPU) in 1961 (Ranger 1968: 239, 241).

The colonial government had struggled to establish an effective framework for governance across the region. Southern Rhodesia's 'Federation' with Nysaland (now Malawi) and Northern Rhodesia (Zambia) had been established in 1953 but independence was granted to these states a decade later. After ZAPU's banning and the exile of its leadership, regional and tactical disagreements ensured the nationalist movement became dichotomous in structure and culture from 1963 onwards. The breakaway Zimbabwe African National Union (ZANU) was primarily Shona-speaking and (following the deaths of other leaders) increasingly controlled by Robert Mugabe. ZAPU became more characteristically Ndebele-speaking and remained under Nkomo's leadership. In 1965, the more reactionary policies of the colonial government crystallized when Prime Minister Ian Smith made his Unilateral Declaration of Independence from the UK. UN sanctions and UK diplomatic interventions ensued. The rival African nationalist parties united again as the 'Patriotic Front' and, in 1966, the Second Chimurenga (liberation war) became a reality. The conflict intensified from 1972 onwards, as ZANU's military wing (ZANLA) spread its influence among rural African communities; in 1977, ZAPU's military wing (ZIPRA) became more active. In full, the war produced 80,000 dead (around 1000 of them whites); nearly half a million wounded, and quarter of a million refugees (De Waal 1990: 80–1). By the late 1970s, the war had crippled Rhodesia's economy and public services while approaching half of the country was under guerrilla control. A settlement – the Lancaster Agreement – was negotiated in 1979, finally granting Africans the vote while placating white farmers that there would be no uncompensated land seizures. The Popular Front (PF) movement split once more so that, in March 1980, the new electorate voted in 57 ZANU-PF candidates, with Nkomo's ZAPU-PF party winning 20 seats out of 80 constituencies. The Republic of Zimbabwe came into force one month later.

Football and other sports contributed significantly to the liberation struggle, but structurally these realms of popular culture were not purely determined by political or economic predicates. After the Second World War, the expanding football system continued to be organized along racial lines, with separate football leagues for Europeans, Coloureds and Asians, and Africans. The first multiracial fixture in Southern Rhodesia took place between Matabeleland Highlanders and an Asian Select in 1948, but integrated matches remained rare. African resistance to tightening white hegemony over social affairs saw football become a venue of open struggle. When the municipality threatened to annex African football, the local populace rebelled. In 1947–48, the Africans' football boycott in Bulawayo lasted longer than the general strike in the city, and was successful in preserving African control (Stuart 1989: 10). Cultural politics fed into the labour and nationalist struggles as some local African leaders owed their charismatic influence across townships to prior involvement in top-level football. African administration of football was demonstrably sophisticated and created an effective, parallel football system to rival the European one which had struggled to rebuild itself after the ravages of global war. Inter-African competition had become more advanced, while the rise of a black middle class promoted the organizational capacities of the African game. In the early 1940s, provincial select teams were formed in Salisbury (Yellow Peril) and Bulawayo (Red Army) and entered into popular competition. In 1953, the African football community created its first national league competition, under the aegis of the new Southern Rhodesia African Football Association, which distributed teams into geographically defined competitive levels. A year later, a national referees' body for African football was established. 'International' friendly matches between various African select sides and teams from bordering nations were occasionally contested from 1951 onwards.

Through the 1960s, while Southern Rhodesia's government adopted a harsher stance on African emancipation, the football organizations appeared better able to assimilate African interests and thus sustain Rhodesian membership of world society. In the early 1960s, African players began to be selected for the Rhodesian national team and the first 'multiracial' national league tournament took place in 1963. In that same year, black players from two other Salisbury teams left to form the Dynamos club, based in the Mbare township, and went on to win the

Austin Cup, the major Rhodesian cup competition which had previously been a whites-only tournament. Under pressure from FIFA President Sir Stanley Rous, the first multiracial football body – the Football Association of Rhodesia (FAR) – was established two years later, and so Rhodesia became a fully-fledged FIFA member in 1965. Rous had sought to harmonize 'racial' differences in Rhodesian football by inserting a clause into the FAR's constitution, decreeing that the three vice-presidents of the body should be of European, Coloured and African category respectively. Most African football came increasingly under the auspices of 'soccerboss' John Madzima at the Rhodesia National Football League (RNFL). Rhodesia's last international fixture was a defeat against Australia in a replayed World Cup qualifying match in 1969; in 1971, following pressure from independent African nations, FIFA suspended Rhodesia's membership. The FAR's powers were also compromised by rival associations which ran their own tournaments, notably the 'non-racial' NFAR which joined with the South African league in 1975 to run its own tournaments.

According to Lunn (1999: 178), Zimbabwean nationalism had become 'steadily more estranged from the concerns of the mass of urban Africans after 1948'. This indirectly assisted African males in the formation of township football clubs as member associations or supporters groups. Other associations included sports societies, dancing clubs, a multitude of religious groups, and burial societies that fulfilled numerous social functions (Bourdillon 1987: 322).

The Smith government and South Africa's apartheid regime talked up the dangers of intertribal violence in any post-independence Rhodesia. In football, violent rivalries became more prominent between supporter groups throughout the 1970s. In Bulawayo, Highlanders and Mashonaland United fans were known for fighting battles in the week running up to fixtures between the teams. Under pressure from Joshua Nkomo, football clubs removed their 'tribal' name affiliations, hence the Matabeleland Highlanders became known as the Highlanders and Mashonaland United were renamed the Zimbabwe Saints. Nevertheless, the linguistic and ethnic associations of these clubs remained.

The liberation war did impact upon football's infrastructure with some league tournaments reverting to a regional basis due to travel problems through zones of conflict. The banning of informal public meetings since the 1960s had turned football into one of the few arenas in which Africans could gather legally in large numbers, and so political dialogue inevitably resulted. Nevertheless, reflecting the everyday relative autonomy of football (*qua* popular cultural superstructure) from core conflicts within other spheres, some African clubs did accept (and ultimately embraced) some white players and officials while disputes involving clubs and football officialdom reflected senses of civic and 'ethnic' rivalry within the African community. For example, the Highlanders club from Bulawayo recruited white players such as Bruce Grobbelaar and Boet Van As during the 1970s while other whites became supporters and latterly club officials. More broadly, football provided a rare leisure space in which whites were permitted by an increasingly repressive security system to interact with Africans. Highlanders withdrew from the national league tournament in 1976 in dispute over a crucial ruling by the governing body that favoured the Dynamos club based in Salisbury. By 1979, most leading African clubs had also quit the RNFL to form the National Professional Soccer League (NPSL). As the liberation war came to a close, significant political repositioning occurred. John Madzima submitted a successful application to FIFA to create the Zimbabwe Football Association (ZIFA). Rothmans, the transnational tobacco corporation, secured a crucial sponsorship deal with the NPSL. Thus, in anticipating Zimbabwe's future political economy, football's institutional independence was recognized, but reliance on foreign capital and transnational corporations allowed for its survival.

The fourth period of Zimbabwe's history spans the first decade of full independence. The ZANU-PF government inherited a fractured nation in human terms, but a relatively strong economy and good infrastructure. The government was conciliatory towards former enemies, and some whites were included in the cabinet. Social and industrial reform was particularly beneficial to farm employees, but whites retained control of farms and many transnational enterprises, in part due to the lack of well trained Africans. The government held control of 'parastatal' institutions crucial to Zimbabwe's infrastructure and health, including grain and electricity boards and the national airline. South Africa's apartheid system retained a strong influence over Zimbabwe's financial sector, trade routes and national security: border raids and assassination attempts were continuing hazards for the new regime (Dzimba 1998).

A new semiology of national identity was articulated to bind the new citizenry. The mass media and education system were brought under ZANU-PF hegemony, to disseminate nationalist myths and political information. The new Zimbabwe had the national capital, Salisbury, renamed as Harare; many other towns and cities acquired Africanized names while streets were renamed to commemorate nationalist leaders and revolutionary events. Landscape was again crucial to the new nationalist conjunction of knowledge and power. Great Zimbabwe's ruins were redefined as evidence of an historic Zimbabwean destiny. Heroes' Acre was constructed on Harare's outskirts to become the burial site of Zimbabwe's architects; its immense murals portrayed Robert Mugabe, in true socialist realist style, literally heading the forces of Zimbabwean independence.

The most intense post-independence violence was directed by the ZANU-PF state against its imagined enemies among fellow Africans in the ZAPU-led regime of Matabeleleland. Werbner (1999: 92) explains how the violence of 'quasi-nationalism' against fellow citizens was pivotal to this nation-building process. Quasi-nationalism is rooted in myths of 'ancient hostility' between ethnic groupings that share opposition to colonial rule. At the postcolonial moment, the state is captured, and its most powerful incumbents 'bring authorised violence down ruthlessly against marginalised antagonists who are in the nation yet for terrible moments not entirely of it'. That violence resulted from the disintegrating alliance between ZANU-PF and ZAPU. Attempts to integrate both movements within the new Zimbabwean state failed, particularly as ZAPU leaders were critical of Mugabe's one-party state doctrines and ZIPRA (ZAPU's military wing) lost ground within the new state army. Following the alleged discovery of arms on ZAPU-controlled farms, ZAPU figures were dropped from government and ZIPRA guerrillas returned south where some disparate groups launched occasional attacks on whites. Mugabe's response was hawkish in the extreme, sending south the notorious Fifth Brigade, trained in North Korea, to flush out and eliminate 'dissidents' and 'terrorists'. Under a legislative smokescreen that declared a virtual state of emergency in Matabeleland, the Fifth Brigade wreaked havoc throughout the region between 1983 and 1987, systematically exterminating local elites and terrorizing those suspected of anti-ZANU sentiments (Werbner 1999: 93). Language was the arbiter of individual fate: 'To speak any variant of Shona was salvation. To speak Sindebele was to risk annihilation, both as a legitimate citizen and as a human subject' (Worby 1998: 566). One independent inquiry into the period estimated perhaps over 6000 people died, over 10,000 were detained and perhaps 10,000 again were tortured (CCJP 1997); other estimates suggest over 20,000 deaths. Undoubtedly, the massacres have left a deep and painful legacy throughout the region (Werbner 1995, 1999). ZAPU support failed to dissolve in Matabeleland, so unity talks began in 1985, concluding two years later in the Unity Accord and ZAPU's effective assimilation within ZANU-PF at national level (cf. Jenkins 1997: 591–2). ZAPU's great leader Joshua Nkomo returned to government and campaigned against any inquests into the terror in Matabeleland, to preserve national unity and reflecting his own 'pyramid' identity that placed the nation above regional or 'tribal' identification. But enforced political unity could not disguise the rising economic and administrative problems within Zimbabwe. Sustained allegations arose of corruption inside the parastatals while key public sector workers and students held demonstrations seeking reforms and better administration. Similarly, as economic globalization took hold in Zimbabwe, the nation's finances and social infrastructure were increasingly dependent upon foreign transnational corporations and fragile global prices in key export commodities such as tobacco.

Where did football stand in the midst of this structural reinvention and social division? The arrival of majority rule enabled Zimbabwe to compete in the African Nations' Cup and the World Cup, but they failed to qualify for either tournament's final stages and thus struggled to raise significant revenues. Government influence within ZIFA was effected through the election of President Canaan Banana (latterly imprisoned for male rape) as patron; Banana also ran his own football team, the State House Tornadoes. Later, Leo Mugabe – a qualified engineer, small businessman and nephew of the Prime Minister – was appointed ZIFA Chairman in 1993. The Independence Trophy, contested by two top clubs (usually Highlanders and Dynamos) became an integral feature of the Independence Day national holiday, particularly following the opening of the 60,000 seat National Sports Stadium in Harare in 1987. Later, as anti-ZANU sentiments began to rise, capacity attendances at these fixtures were presented by state media as a reflection of mass support for the government. However, ZIFA's poor administration and chronic financial problems were notorious, and threatened to provide metaphorical spaces for coded discussion, across the public sphere, about nepotism and corruption throughout the new state. In 1987, after accumulating crippling debts of ZIM$700,000 (around US$421,700 at the official exchange rate), the ZIFA executive was forcibly dissolved by the Ministry of Youth, Sport and Culture. Constant administrative squabbles surfaced between ZIFA and the NPSL, leading the clubs to secede again in 1993.

Zimbabwean dependence upon richer nations was reflected in football in two key structural ways. First, financially, the club system was heavily reliant upon sponsorship from transnational corporations (TNCs) that had established themselves in the old Rhodesia. Key TNCs were the brewers Natbrew (based in South Africa) and the cigarette companies Rothmans and BAT, the latter having invested in the Osborne Trophy's development in 1936. Second, technically, due to the lack of qualified African instructors and administrators, Zimbabwe's football system was still strongly influenced by white coaches and playing styles. The more physical, long-ball aspects of British football were obdurate, residual features of Zimbabwe's colonial sporting inheritance, and at some odds with the growing hegemony of continental playing systems and technical styles that were to be found elsewhere in Africa due to the influx of European coaches. Clubs such as Dynamos and the national side are still regarded as having traditionally British playing styles.

The most popular football clubs continue to hail from high-density suburbs (townships), notably Dynamos from Mbare in Harare (the 'Glamour Boys' or the 'seven million fans' club, in popular mythology) and Highlanders from the Makokobo and Mzilikazi townships in Bulawayo. Like the NPSL, both clubs (notably Dynamos) were dogged by constant political struggles and wrangling over supporter allegations regarding misappropriated finances. Another successful club between 1980 and 1990 was a company team, CAPS United (the 'Cup Kings'), while other notable sides included the new army outfit, Black Rhinos, based in Mutare (near the Mozambique border) and formed after numerous top Harare players were attracted in 1983.

Club football was a significant space in which senses of regional difference, with strong ethnic inflections, came to be expressed. Kaarsholm (1997: 247) has noted how, following the collapse of the Ndebele state, 'culture ... became the medium through which Ndebele identity and autonomy was able to hibernate and survive until such times when the cultural agenda might again be turned into a political one'. That sense of identity was certainly enhanced by the close geographical, demographic and historical ties between Bulawayo and South African towns, notably Johannesburg, allowing cultural exchanges to occur involving dancers, musicians and athletes (including football players). Today, the Highlanders club has a close institutional friendship with the Orlando Pirates club from Johannesburg; the ground section at Bulawayo's Barbourfields Stadium favoured by Highlanders fans is popularly known as 'Soweto' (after the South African township); and many Highlanders fans wear Orlando Pirates symbols and colours.

While the terror in Matabeleland is examined with difficulty and rarity inside formal politics, popular culture has been more accommodating. There were no notable incidents of violence between Highlanders fans and rivals from Harare during this period – the Ndebele people recognize that the atrocities were instigated by the ZANU-PF state, not Shona-speakers *in toto*. However, Highlanders supporters have created songs and chants that commemorate the atrocities of the 1980s and which are intended to give strength to players during fixtures. That collectivism is also expressed through the intense suspicions of many supporters and players towards Zimbabwe's football authorities and the police force at football matches, on the grounds of their perceived leniency towards Harare-based clubs, players and supporters.[1]

1990–present: globalization and structural decline

The final period of national history discussed here runs from 1990 to 2003 (period of writing), during which Zimbabwe has fallen into a startling and apparently irreversible structural decline. In 1990, faced with a declining economy and pressure from global financial institutions, the Zimbabwe government introduced the first of a series of neoliberal structural adjustment programmes (SAPs). Droughts and a very poor crop harvest in 1991 provided a disastrous social context for the imposition of neoliberal reforms. Only the financial sector, landed gentry, and some elements of the growing capitalist class benefited from SAPs. Public services were reduced severely, placing a greater onus on international NGOs to make what Appadurai (2000) terms 'globalization from below' a viable project, in part by propping up essential services such as education and health care. On the evidence of the SAPs, one group of social analysts concluded that, for Zimbabwe, 'neo-liberal globalization is a programme of social exclusion of the majority of the people to the benefit of a few' (*ZHDR* 1999: 67).

Entering the new millennium, Zimbabwe's economic and social conditions deteriorated ceaselessly. The chaotic and often illegal state seizure of white-controlled farms, coupled with regional droughts, left up to 7 million people facing starvation in late 2002. The Zimbabwean economy contracted 20 per cent over three years and continued to shrink. Unemployment stood at around 70 per cent, pushing workers into the desperate 'informal economy' (such as street hustling, selling vegetables on street corners, petty crime). Hyperinflation ballooned to over 150 per cent and foreign currency reserves were virtually emptied. Recurring shortages of fuel and other essential imports were partly alleviated by trade deals with the pariah international state of Libya. The Zimbabwean dollar lost 95 per cent of its value within a dozen years; its exchange rate was fixed by the government, but the more realistic, unofficial 'parallel market' marked the 'Zim' at ten times lower than its official value. The social consequences of economic collapse have been disastrous. Crime rates in urban areas have spiralled, notably in Harare's townships and in Chitungwiza, the capital's high-density satellite city. Zimbabwe's renowned education system has buckled as parents struggle to pay fees and hungry children lack the energy to attend. Over 3 million

Zimbabweans have migrated to South Africa or the UK, despite more stringent border controls and visa restrictions. Middle-class Zimbabweans are particularly keen to emigrate, thus further deskilling and destabilizing the nation.

With up to 75 per cent of the population living below the poverty line, a medical catastrophe continues to thrive. Conservative estimates indicate one in four of the active adult population is HIV positive, with people aged 15–35 particularly vulnerable to transmission by heterosexual sex. Entering the new millennium, around 2000 Zimbabweans were dying each week from AIDS or AIDS-related illnesses. Adult life expectancy stood at 37.8 years, hence the population is moving into decline numerically. The pandemic has devastated kinship networks, removing wage earners within families, and placing impossible care burdens on senior citizens and depleted local health services. Over 600,000 children have been orphaned, contributing in part to the growing numbers of 'street children' in urban centres (Bourdillon 1994). Urbanization, population mobility and poor public health information were the major initial catalysts for the social spread of HIV; poverty is undoubtedly relevant too, although the disease is also entrenched among white families and communities.

Although ZANU-PF retained strategic control of much of Zimbabwe's public sphere (notably the state-owned media), political dissent has been expressed through the independent and highly critical *Daily News* newspaper, founded in 1999. The opposition party, the Movement for Democratic Change (MDC), won 57 out of 120 seats at the 2000 general election, following a campaign of violence and intimidation orchestrated by ZANU-PF in which over 30 people died. Notably, the MDC swept all seats in the major cities and in much of Matabeleland; ZANU-PF's strength remains in rural areas, notably through the influence of village patriarchs (Alexander 2000; Compagnon 2000). Continuing, unhindered attacks on MDC supporters, and the government's ousting of critical judges, suggest that the justice system and the wider civil society are now dominated by a distinctive political class. The EU and US introduced trade and travel sanctions against Zimbabwe's political leadership, but undeterred, the Zimbabwean parliament passed further legislation in 2002 to muzzle the independent media. Inevitably, Zimbabwe's spectacular decline has seriously damaged public psychology: a 2002 international Gallup Poll found Zimbabweans to be the most pessimistic people on earth.

Three key aspects of Zimbabwean football have reflected this deteriorating national condition through the 1990s and beyond. First,

Zimbabwean football has continued to be bedevilled by chronic financial problems and domestic institutional feuding. ZIFA constantly struggles to finance the national team and its flagship tournament – the ZIFA Cup – was suspended from 1996 to 2001 due to lack of sponsorship. Revenues within football have also been reduced, as midweek matches were stopped in 2001 due to the high cost of floodlighting and low attendances. Meanwhile, ZIFA, the NPSL, the Sports Commission and the government's sport departments have regularly fought out their squabbles in the civil courts. Both football organizations have been embroiled in damaging corruption scandals. In February 1996, independent auditors declared ZIFA insolvent. Four months later, the Minister of Sport, Recreation and Culture appointed an independent Commission of Inquiry to examine the 'serious problems' affecting football in Zimbabwe.

After collating evidence from open meetings across Zimbabwe, the Commission published a highly critical 150-page report in March 1997. ZIFA was criticized for failing to provide constitutionally for the interests of the professional league and its member clubs (CEMFZ 1997: 20). Strong implicit criticism was directed at Leo Mugabe through the recommendation that the ZIFA Chairman should possess significant administrative experience and thus understand 'the various problems faced in soccer' (ibid.: 17). ZIFA's daily administration, the Commissioners asserted, should be controlled by a CEO, not the Chairman and his Executive. The new CEO should be a 'high calibre football administrator', and so would probably come from abroad (ibid.: 103). Exploitation of players and general corruption were also highlighted. The national team and domestic clubs are heavily reliant on gate-money, but the Commission estimated that around one-third is skimmed illegally by various employees and officials. Potential corporate sponsors expressed reluctance to invest due to fears of ZIFA's mismanagement (ibid.: 68–9).

Continuing corruption and intermittent reform followed the report. A year later, the NPSL's Secretary-General, Chris Sibanda, was deposed amid accusations of massive fraud. Corruption scandals involving directors have also beset several clubs. In 1999, Dynamos were placed under ZIFA-appointed control after the elected executive had failed to pay players and allowed the club to slip into bankruptcy. ZIFA's involvement generated wider criticisms that administrative rules were being bent or broken to help Dynamos. ZIFA's executive eventually voted Leo Mugabe out of office in December 2002 after US$61,500 of FIFA grant money had disappeared.

Corrupt practices inside football must be understood within a broader societal context at three levels. In lower administration, unemployment, poverty, inflation and the rise of the informal economy promote irregular financial dealings as a self-help strategy within a neoliberal moral and financial climate. At the middle level, among higher football officers, corrupt practices represent a response to growing income differentials between a public sector squeezed by inflation and retrenchment, and the more affluent business middle classes (*African Development Report* 2001: 123). At the upper level, football corruption reflects the insulation of elite state employees from financial accountability: though their term in office may be terminated occasionally, imprisonment is almost never a serious risk.

Second, Zimbabwean football connects in complex but not predetermined ways to nation-building and arising political conflicts. Football's overt exploitation for political and ideological purposes has been relatively restricted. In 2000, Zimbabwe was stripped of the right to host the African Nations Cup finals after the government failed to guarantee any debts incurred by the tournament. Belatedly, the government then announced that it would underwrite any such future tournament, although such a prospect has become remote. More recently, ZIFA stated that the government would contribute ZIM$10 million towards the refashioned 'ZIFA Unity Cup'. Independent media and opposition politicians criticized ZIFA's willingness to accept ZANU-PF backing, while FIFA warned against political interference in football (*Daily News*, 21 and 22 August 2001). Indeed, it is only in the new millennium that ZANU-PF interference within sport has become systematic. The national cricket organization, the Zimbabwe Cricket Union (ZCU), has come under strong ZANU-PF influence. In football, the government has intervened to halt elections within ZIFA that FIFA had insisted should go ahead.

ZANU-PF's dwindling support in the cities has encouraged the state and its officials to view public gatherings at football fixtures with anxiety or hostility. A political subtext lurked behind Zimbabwe's worst football-related disaster when 13 fans died and scores were injured at the Zimbabwe–South Africa fixture in July 2000, held at the National Sports Stadium. South Africa had been leading 2–0 when supporters began throwing some missiles onto the field of play. Other supporters had been making the open-palm greeting that was the MDC's main symbol during general elections the previous month. Police responded to this perceived political provocation by closing exit gates and firing tear-gas canisters over perimeter fencing into the packed stands. While a fatal stampede ensued among trapped fans, several players were overcome by tear-gas fumes and collapsed on the pitch. FIFA awarded the victims' families US$10,000 each and temporarily closed the ground. ZIFA organized a benefit fixture for the victims, and followed state media in refusing to blame police actions for the disaster, although evidence at a public inquiry over two years later left little room for doubt.[2]

One may speculate that a latent political meaning – centring on social alienation and senses of personal disenfranchisement – emerges from increasingly common, match-related forms of fan disorder. At one incident, Highlanders were losing a cup final to Dynamos in December 2000 when their fans bombarded the pitch with missiles, forcing the game to be abandoned; fighting and vandalism occurred outside the stadium, resulting in a police van containing patrol dogs being overturned and set alight. Five months later, missile-throwing fans forced the abandonment of an African Champions League tie as Highlanders trailed Young Africans of Tanzania. A more overtly political form of disorder has occurred through supporters protesting or rioting when they are confronted by inflated admission charges to fixtures. In March 2001, violent confrontations were reported at two grounds following the NPSL's decision to double admission charges in line with inflation. At Rufaro Stadium in Harare's Mbare township, scores of fans fought with police who responded by firing tear gas (*Herald*, 6 March 2001).

Third, neoliberal reforms have had harsh consequences for Zimbabwean football. At grassroots level, there are fewer resources for playing organized football; many of the townships' youth or community centres, for example, have closed due to local authority budget cuts, or they struggle to secure long-term NGO financing. Some clubs set up by local projects for street children have prospered, reflecting both the institutionalization and remarkable self-determination of a young African underclass. Attendances at top club matches are still relatively high, but basic lack of disposable income ensures that attempts to chase inflation through admission rises, particularly by ZIFA for national team games, can produce paltry crowds. Fuel shortages prevent football teams from travelling to fulfil fixtures in the lower divisions. Similarly, off-field earnings for the clubs or national association are very restricted: the market for merchandise is negligible, and the social clubs attached to the football clubs struggle to retain patrons.

Neoliberalism has squeezed the traditional corporate structures and institutional financing of Zimbabwean clubs. Clubs owned by corporations (such as CAPS United or Lancashire Steel) and those controlled by the military (such as Black Rhinos and Chapungu) have had to endure reduced internal support or the reality of liquidation. Clubs owned by supporter associations (such as Highlanders, Dynamos and Zimbabwe Saints) have faced declining memberships and relatively lower annual subscriptions. More secure clubs tend to be patronised by wealthy owners or shareholders. For example, the AmaZulu club of Bulawayo is owned by Delma Lupepe, one of Zimbabwe's richest entrepreneurs who made his fortune in the communications sector. Lupepe is originally a Highlanders supporter; his initial attempts to invest in that club were rebuffed by local officials keen to display their continuing political control. Upon forming AmaZulu, he set about buying up the most talented local players and paying football staff the highest salaries nationally. Lupepe has expressed his desire to dilute his ownership through a share issue scheme, but the club currently struggles to draw sufficient supporters locally due to the traditional ties of Highlanders with Bulawayo's high-density suburbs. AmaZulu is typically viewed as the most professionally administered club, and a range of sportswriters and football officers have pointed to the neoliberal corporate route (that is, the creation of private ownership by rich patrons or shareholders) as the most effective way ahead for the nation's club system (see, for example, *The Mirror*, 12 January 2001; *Daily News*, 20 November 2001). Such a proposal reflects the pervasive hegemony of neoliberal thinking and policies, but it faces the practical problem of finding enough financial investment from the open market while threatening in theory the democratic structures of clubs. Lupepe himself has recognised the importance of club–community ties by gifting money and equipment to several rival clubs.

Within a directly global context, Zimbabwean football faces deeply interrelated problems in terms of elite labour (enskilling and mobility), external media revenues, and consumer identification. Zimbabwean football is not the worst placed economically in southern Africa, hence local clubs recruit top players from neighbouring Botswana, Malawi and Zambia. However, Zimbabwe's top few players can earn only a lower-middle-class wage that is tied heavily to win bonuses and match appearances. For all clubs, with the recent possible exception of AmaZulu, player sales are the main source of external revenues. Selling television rights to the state broadcaster, ZBC, offers virtually no income. All players target the 'great trek south' to South Africa for far stronger financial security, or the less viable dream of joining the European leagues. Star players are sold for a small fraction of their true global market value: for example, the national team's captain, Peter Ndlovu, was sold in 1991 by Highlanders to Coventry City for around £20,000. European coaches and agents have established clubs and football schools in Zimbabwe's suburbs, to identify and develop talented players, in theory to sell them on to foreign clubs for substantial personal profit. African coaches act as underpaid local scouts and foremen, in locating and partially refining raw talent. Thus, Zimbabwe's player development system can resemble neocolonialism with the best African 'cash crops' destined for richer markets. Meanwhile, the geographical mobility and continuing township culture of most players has contributed substantially to HIV infections; at least four players from one specific championship-winning squad from the 1990s have contracted AIDS-related illnesses.

The shallow commercial revenue streams in Zimbabwean football contrast markedly with the international financial sources (notably in media) that have been tapped by the more colonial, white-dominated sport of cricket. Wealthy South African television stations have little interest in the Zimbabwean game aside from helping to finance club and national tournaments in southern Africa. Conversely, after gaining full international Test status in 1992, the ZCU has gained most income from foreign television fees and related sponsorship. For example, some US$10 million accrued from tours by India and West Indies alone in 2001, of which around US$1.5 million was paid to players and much of the remainder went on administration, travel expenses, facilities and renovations, and the expanding township development schemes. To earn that same sum, Zimbabwe would need to overturn its football history by qualifying for the World Cup finals. In the meantime, like many other cultural institutions within Zimbabwean civil society, ZIFA is financially dependent upon the philanthropy of international NGOs (including FIFA) to fund sports development programmes.

International media systems present other challenges to Zimbabwean football. The African population has long engaged with Western consumer culture (Burke 1996), but globalization of popular cultural forms has intensified to create new forms of social division and identity through new patterns of cultural consumption. The young African middle classes – equipped with varying balances of economic, cultural and educational capital – are known locally as the 'nose brigade', for their highly symbolic preference for the English language and its distinctive colonial vowels, and their apparent alienation from local languages and forms of popular culture. The 'nose brigade' habitus is closely associated with global cultural consumption, particularly the commodified black American 'ghetto' clothing style, the embracing of TNC merchandise signifiers (notably Nike or Adidas), MTV music, and global sports such as football and basketball. Local football affiliations are superseded by interest in richer football leagues, notably in England and South Africa, which are given blanket coverage by the South African satellite stations and beamed into urban sports bars, hotel rooms or high-walled residences in the low-density suburbs. (Some have argued that African football officials and journalists also parade their support for international teams because local football is considered 'too backward'.) The commodification of global football-related media products means that Zimbabwean state media, which had televised English football highlights in the past, can no longer afford the fees for radio commentaries from the English Premier League (*The Mirror*, 12 January 2001).

Evidently, Zimbabwe's political economy, and its location with regard to global economic and cultural flows, has a major impact in shaping the social history and contemporary condition of football within the country. As we have seen, three historical forces with a global dimension, and relating specifically to the political economy of modern Africa, have had a dominant impact upon Zimbabwean society in general and football in particular. First, colonialism constructed Zimbabwe *qua* Southern Rhodesia, as an economic servant and political satellite of Britain's imperial project. Football was introduced by the white settlers; its adoption by Africans and the game's subsequent organization in the colony reflected the political struggles and ideological contradictions of white governance and cultural hegemony. Second, during the independence struggles, football reflected (without being determined by) many of the conflicts that shaped the new state. Third, Zimbabwe's structural decay and social decline have been precipitated by neoliberal economic and social reforms ushered in by greater globalization, and by mismanagement and corrupt practices at key locations within the Zimbabwean state. Football remains Zimbabwe's most popular sport, but domestically the game is bedevilled by an impoverished infrastructure and poor administration, while foreign football leagues and rival sports have more advantageous commercial positions with regard to global revenue streams and the positive symbolism of international cultural products.

It is difficult to envisage Zimbabwean football making a spectacular economic and political break from the difficult circumstances of the nation-state as a whole. For the next decade at least, the vast majority of Zimbabweans will continue to live with the interrelated material and medical risks to their personal survival. In such harsh circumstances, there are very limited physical and economic resources for participation or investment within sporting pastimes. Zimbabwe's football system will continue to be relatively dependent upon both the core regional nation (South Africa) and, to a lesser extent, European nations, in terms of transfer fees, sponsorships, and the dissemination of media images of the global game. A new post-Mugabe government will be better placed to attract Western capital and NGO assistance which, if corrupt filtering of monies can be minimized, should feed through to the game's grassroots to help organized sport within the old townships. However, given the imposed global orthodoxy of neoliberal policies in the developing world, and the continuation of Africa's dependency upon the northern hemisphere, football's club system may be transformed in ways analogous to Europe and South America. In an era in which borders are being broken down, one possibility is that the top Zimbabwean club teams could be drawn into more systematic competitions alongside top South African clubs and others across the southern African region, with South African television stations funding the new venture.

Acknowledgements

My thanks to numerous contacts within the Zimbabwean football system for their insights and advice during interviews. In academic circles, I am particularly indebted to Brian Raftopoulos, Terence Ranger and Blair Rutherford. The research for this chapter was financed by the University of Aberdeen.

Notes

1. The crowd disorder surrounding a Highlanders–Dynamo fixture in November 1989 might be cited as evidence of this general perception. Midway through the second half, a Highlanders player, Mercedes Sibanda, was shown the red card for an innocuous challenge on an opponent. As he protested, a senior police officer took the extraordinary step of grabbing the player and dragging him from the field. Crowd missiles and fighting then followed, the referee abandoned the match, and several police officers were injured in the concluding mêlée (*Bulawayo Chronicle*, 26 November 1989).
2. Two years earlier, the Zimbabwean police force had been blamed by independent media for triggering a stampede that killed five supporters inside the National Sports Stadium at the Dynamos–Highlanders fixture on Independence Day. The police had allowed 80,000 fans to enter a 60,000 capacity stadium and, it was alleged, failed to monitor crowd safety and security (*Zimbabwe Mirror*, 24 April 1998).

Part Two
Footballing Colours

5
Ngoma Reverberations: Swahili Music Culture and the Making of Football Aesthetics in Early Twentieth-Century Zanzibar

Laura Fair

Music, dance and other forms of expressive culture have long played central roles in coastal East African societies, providing opportunities for leisure and relaxation as well as platforms for debating individual and collective standing within the larger community (Strobel 1979; Glassman 1995; Fair 2001; Askew 1999). Although football, introduced into coastal Swahili societies during the early colonial era, was a foreign cultural form, the Swahili men who began playing it quickly infused this European game with meanings that expressed their own cultural heritage. In the case of urban Zanzibar, men transformed the football pitch into a new venue for the expression of communal solidarity and rivalry while simultaneously infusing the playing and watching of the game with aesthetic elements from existing drum and dance competitions (*ngoma*). Much like Trobriand Islanders, who creatively adapted the British game of cricket to make it their own (Leach and Kildea 1975), Zanzibari men brought cultural components from existing leisure pursuits to football, thus helping to enhance football's popularity during the early twentieth century.

Rational recreation, empire and the beginnings of football in Zanzibar

Football, field hockey and cricket were first introduced into the islands of Zanzibar, in the late 1870s, by workers employed by the British-based Eastern Telegraph Company (ETC) who came to the isles to lay the cable linking Zanzibar to Aden and England (Lyne 1905: 71; Kamati Maalum 1981: 2). The twenty Europeans and eight Asians who comprised the permanent crew of ETC on Zanzibar regularly divided themselves into teams and passed their evening hours playing one of these three games. During this same decade, the Universities' Mission to Central Africa (UMCA) opened its St Andrew's College, just outside of Zanzibar town. St Andrew's was intended as a training post for African teachers and clergy who were then sent throughout East and Central Africa to open churches and schools and spread Christianity. Football and cricket were widely incorporated into the curriculum at St Andrew's and graduates of the college have been credited with spreading these games in East Africa (Anthony 1983). The introduction of European sport and games was thus closely linked with key imperial institutions, including missions, the military and business concerns, the leaders of which firmly believed in the educative and moralizing impact of sport (Clayton 1987; Mangan 1987).

During the industrial revolution in England, industrialists, Members of Parliament and moral reformers came together to transform popular recreation and leisure pursuits in an attempt to 'civilize' and 'stabilize' the working class and urban poor. Leisure activities such as drinking, gambling, racing and cock-fighting were increasingly subjected to state control, while moral reformers attempted to modify the recreational tastes of British men in order to make them more 'suitable' to the 'modern' capitalist era. In the nineteenth century, football was appropriated by the middle and upper classes and gradually transformed into a more 'rational' form of recreation (Thompson 1966: 401–47; Thompson 1967: 59–96; Cross 1990: 86–104; Reid 1976: 76–101; Henry 1993: 6–12; Delves 1981: 89–127). The guiding philosophy of the rational recreation movement was that the new values necessary for industrial life could be subconsciously developed within the working classes by reforming leisure, including sport. Football and cricket had long been played by rural working men, but football matches typically involved innumerable players in a village, who drank, played, ate, drank and then played some more in the course of a game. Now, however, contests no longer lasted until men were either too drunk or too sore to play, they went on for a specific period of clock-measured time. Games that were organized around a clock and divided into halves and quarters were believed by the advocates of rational recreation to instil respect for clock-measured time, to teach men to 'make the most' of their time, as well as the necessary discipline of being on time. The codification of game rules was also believed to instil the type of discipline necessary for factory work, while the policing of games by a referee was intended to instil respect for authority in all areas of life. Exercise, or what widely came to be known as 'muscular Christianity', was said to contain and safely expel pent-up sexual energy, which might otherwise be turned to anti-social or un-

Christian ends. Even the establishment of organized teams was said by philosophers of the era to be of value to society, teaching young men of the need to suppress their personal goals and desire for the greater good of the team, factory and nation.

These philosophies of 'rational recreation' and 'muscular Christianity' were transported across the globe during the colonial era. During the early twentieth century, colonizers across the African continent began laying increasing emphasis on the development of sport within the colonies, in hopes of moulding a 'disciplined' working class from the mixed assortment of individuals living in urban Africa (Couzens 1983; Clayton 1987; Mangan 1987; Martin 1991: 56–71; Badenhorst and Mather 1997: 56–71). Colonial administrators in Zanzibar saw the expansion of team sports as an important means of ridding the island's men of what the British perceived as their 'sloth' and 'lack of initiative'. As the publishers of Zanzibar's *Official Gazette* commented, 'the health of young Zanzibar cannot fail to benefit by increased inducement to enjoy vigorous exercise during the afternoon leisure instead of loafing in the stuffy bazaars' (supplement to the *Zanzibar Official Gazette*, 7 February 1920). Sport, it was hoped, would transform the 'lazy' African into a disciplined man working hard in the interests of empire. Members of the mission community and colonial service played an important role in the formation of some of the earliest teams in the isles. Three of the earliest African teams to organize in Zanzibar were the St Andrew's (Kiungani) College Boys, the Universities' Mission to Central Africa school and the team of the government school. The UMCA incorporated the 'lessons' of sport into the curriculum not only at its primary and secondary schools, but also at the 'Boys' Club' that it ran for urban youth. The aim of the club was to catch homeless and uncared-for youth at an early age, 'before they began a life of crime and developed into hardened old criminals', and to teach them about the dignity of labour, the value of authority and the manners of good citizens (Watoto Club 1936). Boys who attended the club were given neither food nor clothing, as this would run counter to the goal of teaching them the value of waged labour, but were helped in finding jobs around town, primarily as runners and porters at the bus stand. Boys were also required to participate in the 'healthy recreation' offered by the club, such as football, boxing and ping-pong, which club organizers believed would 'instill in them the club spirit ... and a sense of good citizenship'. Until the end of the colonial era, participation in sport remained a central component of the 'educational experience' of urban island men. Juma Aley, who later captained the Zanzibar national cricket team for over a decade, recalled how sport was used to instil respect for law and authority amongst the students at the Boys' Secondary School, where he attended as a child and later taught as an adult:

> Sports did a great deal of good not only from a physical angle, but in inculcating discipline which had many great and lasting impacts on character training. The referee's word is final and the umpire's decision is final went into the head of every [student] ... There were no appeals of the referee's decision and you could not play unless you were prepared to follow the rules! Back then, young men learned to obey authority. (Aley 1992)

Through such school clubs young men were also unconsciously groomed to accept their relative 'place' within the colony. Young Arab and Asian men who were being prepared for positions of authority or supervision within the colonial administration were encouraged to develop a taste for the refinements of cricket, and Juma Aley himself went on to occupy key posts in the colonial administration during the period immediately prior to independence. Young men who were deemed more suited for jobs as junior level clerks were directed towards field hockey, while football and boxing were the sports that were considered most 'appropriate' for the African working class.

Watching students at the various schools or British employees of the empire play these games became an increasingly popular urban pastime in and of itself and gradually the young men of Zanzibar town began to take up football themselves. During the 1910s, football took off with lightning speed and continued to expand in popularity throughout the 1920s. According to men who grew up in town during these years, by the 1920s 'everyone' was playing football (Aley 1992; Said 1991; Makame 1991; Othman 1991). The publishers of Zanzibar's *Official Gazette* were utterly amazed at the speed with which football had taken off during the First World War. The small, unobtrusive sports column that focused on write-ups of European golf and cricket matches in the 1910s, grew to several pages dominated by coverage of football by 1921. By as early as 1920 the editors of Zanzibar's *Official Gazette* were reporting their astonishment at how popular football had become, declaring 'the enthusiasm for football amongst the natives shows no sign of diminishing. New teams are constantly forming and we have difficulty accommodating all the teams on the playing field' (*Official Gazette*, 7 February 1920). By the mid-1920s matches were regularly drawing crowds of 3000–4000 spectators, and it was not uncommon for particularly important matches to bring as many as 10,000 fans down to the central football field to cheer their teams on (*Official Gazette*, 5 January 1925, 22 August 1925, 17 October 1925, 3 April 1926, 17 April 1926, 29 November 1927, 3 November 1928). By the late 1920s the editors of the *Zanzibar Official Gazette* were proclaiming football 'the national game'. However, the young men who took up football and transformed it into the new national game did so not because they were overwhelmed with desires to 'improve' their industrial character or Christian morality (most were in fact Muslim), but because they were able to infuse football with elements of indigenous recreation and leisure aesthetics and thus transform football into a game that had important local meanings.

Ngoma reverberations

Although the form of football was new to the isles, the principles of organization and competition resonated with existing forms of recreation that were widely popular in nineteenth- and twentieth-century urban Zanzibar, expressed most prominently through *ngoma* – drum, dance and poetry competitions. Competitive *ngoma* were held on a daily basis in nineteenth- and early twentieth-century urban Zanzibar and these popular urban pastimes served as important vehicles for reflecting and contesting the numerous class, ethnic, status and neighbourhood divisions within urban society. In the nineteenth century, Zanzibar served as the entrepôt linking producers of slaves, ivory and other commodities from East and East Central Africa with markets in the Persian Gulf, Europe, Asia and the Americas, while the islands of Zanzibar also became a major slave-based plantation society (Sheriff 1987). Island society thus had the potential to be highly divisive, and urban popular culture and leisure activities often served to articulate as well as ameliorate class, race and ethnic antagonisms rooted in slavery. As a new form of popular leisure, football gave expression both to new social divisions brought about by colonialism, as well as the desires of many former slaves and slave owners to distance themselves from the past.

In the 1910s and 1920s, numerous new forms of urban leisure were created as expressions of a will amongst certain segments of the urban community to bridge earlier divides rooted in slavery. Two of the earliest independent football clubs formed during this period were known as New Kings and New Generation, their very names thus seeming to articulate desires to move beyond the islands' nineteenth-century history rooted in slavery. The composition of these clubs also indicates that such desires were not unique to the former servile classes, as both teams also included amongst their members men whose families' wealth was based in their ownership of slaves. Football clubs were not the only forms of popular leisure to express such desires, as new dance clubs and *ngoma* troupes similarly emerged during this era, including two *ngoma* known by the names Changani and Kunguiya. While these football and dance clubs were often financed and supported by the wealthiest members of the clubs, their stars and captains were typically from poor, slave or working-class backgrounds (Feruz 1991; Othman 1991, 1991b; Hilal 1992; Othman 1995). Thus for members of this 'New Generation' who participated in urban leisure activities it was possible for individuals from poor and servile backgrounds to become the 'New Kings'.

One important characteristic of Swahili music and dance troupes was that they provided individuals from poor and socially marginal backgrounds with opportunities for achieving status, titles and positions of authority within their clubs that were often unavailable in wider society. Because these clubs often incorporated members from a range of class and status positions, or alternatively pitted clubs of class and political rivals against each other, they provided a ritualized atmosphere in which the poor and socially marginal could temporarily upset the existing social order (Glassman 1995; Strobel 1979; Fair 1997a; Suleiman 1969; Franken 1986; Mtoro 1903). In the context of *ngoma*, slaves and poorer members of society could publicly display their skills as dancers, drummers and poets, and in the process earn respect for themselves and their abilities. Like the football clubs New Kings and New Generation, it was not uncommon for poor men and women to become the leaders of clubs whose membership incorporated the economic and political elite. Yet, while participation in *ngoma* provided opportunities to improve one's status and social position, most dancers and participants in these popular leisure activities were women. When football was introduced, however, it provided a similar competitive and ritualized venue for men to develop and display their skills. For instance, Hamidi Feruz, the child of former slaves, not only captained New Kings, he also became widely known and respected amongst men of all class and status backgrounds because of his skilful ability to move the ball and direct the game from his position at centre-half. His control over the ball and impressive talent at cutting through players on the opposing team, as he frequently drove the ball towards the goal, also earned him the nick-name 'Mapanga' ('machete'), after the big, sharp knives wielded by island men. By the time he was 20, 'Mapanga' had become a household name in urban Zanzibar. While Europeans rarely took notice of individual island men from slave and working-class backgrounds, Mapanga's skill as a footballer also made many members of the island's colonial service sit up and take notice of him. Glowing reports of his latest football feats were also regularly reported in the *Official Gazette*, a paper which again rarely took notice of events and persons from the islands' African community. According to many participants, football became the male equivalent of women's dance associations, competitive clubs in which every participant stood a chance of emerging as a star known throughout the town (Hilal 1992; Othman 1991; Feruz 1991; Ali 1991; Aley 1992; Said 1991; Seif 1992; Said 1992).

Another parallel between *ngoma* and football was that clubs were often organized in paired rivalries (Bakari 1995; Othman 1995; Askew 1999; Othman 1991; Feruz 1991; Ali 1991). Although each club played all of the others in their particular league, matches that pitched known rivals against each other were always the most intense. The basis for these rivalries varied from expressions of extreme antagonisms based on class, status and ethnicity to splits in clubs arising out of personal arguments amongst important members. Regardless of the reason, having a defined rival was widely regarded as a necessity if a team hoped to develop the skills of their players or establish any lasting impression upon fans. Clubs that failed to establish such competitive rivalries rarely lasted for very long. Some of the most important football rivalries to develop during the early twentieth century expressed class-based antagonisms that were based in social and economic transformations introduced by colonialism. For instance, matches that pitted the casual labourers, boatmen and domestic servants who largely comprised New Generation against young men who were training to become colonial clerks at the government school regularly drew large and enthusiastic crowds. The wealthy and prestigious local allies of the British regularly sponsored sports clubs organized along ethnic lines and these too had key rivals drawn from among the poor and working-class members of their ethnic communities. One key match in 1928, which pitted the working-class members of the Comorian community against the club sponsored by the elite of the community drew an estimated 10,000 spectators to the field (*Official Gazette*, 3 November 1928). To paraphrase one participant in these events, competition – particularly that centred on paired rivalries – was the fuel that drove urban football and *ngoma* culture.

Like earlier drum and dance competitions, football also provided participants with a ritualized atmosphere in which it was safe and acceptable to challenge their social and political superiors. Although Europeans in most African colonies refused to participate in competitive games with Africans (Martin 1991: 61; Jarvie 1985; Couzens 1983: 202–12), in Zanzibar, perhaps because it was such a small colonial outpost,

Europeans regularly competed both with and against local sports teams. Not surprisingly, matches between European and Zanzibari teams also regularly drew large and excited crowds. During the First World War, the men who worked as caddies on the European golf course formed a team, United Service, more commonly referred to as 'Caddies'. Although these men were not so affectionately referred to as 'wretched little golf *totos* [children]' by some of the Europeans for whom they worked on the golf course (Younghusband 1908: 218), the Caddies' players challenged colonial discourses of African infantilization by trouncing the team of European men on the football field in full view of thousands of spectators (supplement to the *Zanzibar Official Gazette*, 5 January 1925, 22 August 1925). In 1925, the Caddies faced off against the European team, known as Mnazi Moja, in the finals for the first cup match ever played in the isles. After 90 minutes of play the score was 0–0, so the match went into overtime, yet still there was no score. This was in the days before penalty kicks had the power to determine the outcome of key cup matches, so several days later the players and fans returned to the pitch for a rematch. Although the European team ended up defeating the Caddies 1–0, the final score was less important to the African working-class crowd than the skilful way the Caddies outplayed Mnazi Moja and the sheer fact that they were able to 'take on' the men whose bags they carried on the golf course and hold their own (Feruz 1991; Said 1991). The Caddies demonstrated their ability to beat the Europeans at their own game later in the year, when they met again for another cup match. Yet again, the initial match ended in a draw. But in the rematch it was the Caddies who emerged victorious amid great cheers from the crowd (supplement to the *Zanzibar Official Gazette*, 22 August 1925). Outmanoeuvring European players, especially members of the colonial service, enhanced island men's sense of manhood and symbolically undermined colonial hierarchies that placed Europeans on the top of the social scale. As C.L.R. James explained the temporarily equalizing effect of sport in the colonial West Indies, 'here on the … field if nowhere else, all men in the island are equal' (James 1963: 55).

Island men were attracted to football not because it imbued them with a respect for British authority or a sense of their position within the empire, but because it resonated with aspects of competitive coastal culture and indigenous leisure pursuits. Members of Zanzibar's colonial administration had very little respect for one of the most popular existing forms of leisure in the isles: gathering in courtyards and on *baraza* (stone seats built along the front of Swahili homes) to dissect and disseminate the latest local gossip. British perceptions of these activities as 'loafing' illustrates that definitions of what constitutes 'constructive use' of leisure are culturally bound (Martin 1995; Ambler 1996; Ambler 2002). For many island residents, this practice of gathering in their neighbourhoods to socialize and disseminate news was and still is a highly enjoyable and valued leisure activity as well as an essential element of community membership (Myers 1994; Fair 2001). As increasing numbers of Zanzibari men began to play football, they adapted football to meet their own local needs, combining the 'vigour' of football with pre-existing leisure pursuits; turning football grounds, practise sessions and clubhouses into the some of the principal sites where men would meet to exchange and debate local and international news (Othman 1991; Feruz 1991; Said 1992; Ali 1991; Salum 1991; Seif 1992). Playing or watching football and gossiping on *baraza* were not mutually exclusive leisure activities. Men gossiped about local issues and events while attending football practices and matches, between 4.00 p.m. and 6.00 p.m., and then continued their discussions on the *baraza* late into the evening, adding analysis of the latest match and debates about referees to their other topics of conversation. Although discussions and debates about teams, matches and referees were necessarily animated, and at times erupted into full-blown arguments, there is no evidence that anything resembling football hooliganism ever emerged as part of the game in Zanzibar (Wilson 1991).

During the period between the two world wars, football became an exceptionally popular pastime not only for players but for spectators as well. The size of the crowd was one criterion used to determine who won certain *ngoma* competitions and this tradition of incorporating spectators as a central part of the competition was continued in sport. A club's importance within the community was directly linked to its ability to turn out a large and enthusiastic crowd for a match or performance (Othman 1995; Bakari 1995; Hilal 1992; Ali 1991; Fereji 1991; Feruz 1991). Important teams, like large and important Swahili families, evaluated each other's social power by their ability to draw in supporters, be it at weddings, funerals or football matches. In the 1920s, being a member of the crowd at important matches became yet another venue where men went to see and to be seen. Like the crowds who came to watch dance and music contests, observers of football matches also played a decisive role in proclaiming victory for one team over another, particularly in the years before matches were refereed or in the street matches played by young men. Regardless of a referee's presence or the final score of the match, it was the men on the sidelines who determined the 'winners' through their endless analysis of players, strategy and style

(Othman 1991; Said 1991; Mirza 1991). Gathering at *baraza* to debate the relative worth of players and the nuances of their individual styles became an exciting nightly pastime in and of itself. Talking about strategy, style, teams, players and matches was also a pastime that could be thoroughly enjoyed even by those too old or immobile to play.

In terms of the aesthetics of play, island players and fans found bold, fast individual moves to be much more appealing than slow, collective moves down the field. Whereas British theories of the game taught in school emphasized 'teamwork', passing, and the execution of plays, fans and players in the isles held a definite preference for daring and unconventional moves by individual players, an emphasis that remains a defining feature of the 'island style' to this day. What defined a good and impressive team, both in the context of football and *ngoma*, was not necessarily their ability to play well together, but the innovative style and speed of the 'stars' who played. In the context of both *ngoma* and football, the addition or loss of one or two stars could utterly transform a club's standing amongst fans. In such a context the actual score was relatively unimportant to the fans and a team that lost in terms of points might well be judged the winner by spectators and fans whose interest was in innovative, individual expressions of style.

Spectator aesthetics not only echoed critical elements of *ngoma* culture, in many cases *ngoma* bands themselves were incorporated into sports events to make them more festive occasions. The jubilation of fans whose team had won often erupted into spontaneous parades as supporters gleefully escorted their team back home or proudly circled around town to the accompaniment of loud and triumphant music played by musicians who were amongst a team's fans. After particularly important matches the clubhouse often became the centre of a celebration that drew scores of men, women and children into the festivities. *Beni* bands, a form of African *ngoma* modelled on military marching bands, but which parodies Europeans, with their uniforms, side-drums, bugles and trombones, often accompanied teams from the field back home, adding to the air of jubilation (Seif 1992; Mzee 1992; Juma 1992; Ranger 1975; Martin 1991: 72–81). Beginning in 1926, annual competitions during the August bank holidays were held between football, cricket and hockey teams from Zanzibar and the Tanganyikan capital, Dar es Salaam. Fares on the government steamers were cut in half so that fans and well-wishers could accompany their favourite players and teams. According to men who remember these years, work in the town came to a virtual standstill when the ships returned, as 'everyone' converged on the port to greet the teams as they came off the boat with their newly won trophies. The streets again were filled with the sounds of revellers, *ngoma* and *beni* bands as thousands of spectators proudly escorted the teams back to their clubhouses, where they spent the remainder of the day and half of the night listening to tales of the matches in Dar es Salaam and soaking up news from the mainland (Aley 1992).

Enthusiasm for football amongst both players and fans in urban Zanzibar grew at an astonishing rate during the 1910s and 1920s. What dancing certain *ngoma* did to enhance women's sense of autonomy, respectworthiness and belonging within the urban citizenry, football clubs and competitions did for men. Urban men were drawn together in this new game, a game in which individual physical and mental skills were far more important determinants of status and potential than pedigree or property. Building on the traditions of competitive *ngoma*, football players and spectators took a European game and transformed it into a highly popular form of recreation that resonated with the rivalry and revelry that were and remain a central part of Zanzibar society. In many regards these early island footballers eschewed the games ethic as taught in British schools, preferring an aesthetic that resonated with their own Swahili dance and music culture.

6
Football and Apartheid Society: The South African Soccer League, 1960–1966

Peter Alegi

On Saturday, 6 April 1963, thousands of soccer fans gathered outside the Natalspruit Indian Sports Ground in central Johannesburg to attend matches of the South African Soccer League (SASL). But the gates were closed. A posted handwritten notice of the Johannesburg City Council's Non-European Affairs Department announced the cancellation of the games (*World*, 8 April 1963). Intrepid fans and organizers climbed over the corrugated iron fence only to discover that the prescient municipal authorities had removed the goalposts from the playing field! A group of supporters transported a set of goalposts from a nearby ground and lifted them over the perimeter fence at Natalspruit. SASL vice-president Dan Twala exclaimed in a defiant tone: '[W]e told the council we would play on our ground' (ibid.). That afternoon, over 15,000 people watched Alexandra's Real Fighters defeat Transvaal United 1–0 and Moroka Swallows crush Blackpool United 6–1. Why did the City Council shut out the predominantly black[1] crowd from Johannesburg's most popular football venue in April 1963? What was the defiant – and that day successful – SASL, who backed it, and what can an investigation of its history reveal about sport, politics, and society in apartheid South Africa?

The SASL radically transformed local football. The league marked the transition from amateurism to professionalism and consolidated football's vanguard role in black popular culture. The SASL revolutionized how South Africans played, coached, managed and followed the game. Known as the People's League to township fans in the 1960s, the SASL captured the imagination of South Africans longing for racially integrated competitions (letter to the editor, *World*, 15 May 1964). The expanding black press provided extensive coverage of the SASL's entertaining games, helping to entrench football in South African popular culture before the advent of state television in 1976. Broader support produced new forms of fan participation as seen in the founding of official supporters clubs. These new groups functioned as small-scale participatory democracies, acting as powerful expressions of popular culture's opposition to apartheid society. The league's meritocratic ideals crystallized the inextricably intertwined nature of sport and politics. After the banning of the liberation movements in 1960, sport became the site of virulent conflict on the domestic front and in the global arena (Nauright 1997; Booth 1998). The SASL's struggle for survival influenced the decision by FIFA, soccer's world governing body, to suspend the white Football Association of South Africa (FASA) from international football in 1961 (Darby 2000a; Sugden and Tomlinson 1998: 133–8). A collective life-blood in the grim context of Grand apartheid's bantustans, labour bureaux and internal security machinery, football delivered one of the first international indictments of the apartheid regime.

The formation of the people's league

The possibility of organizing football on a professional basis in South Africa had been the subject of debate since the 1930s (*Bantu World*, 30 November 1935). Money was no stranger to black football. In the 1920s slumyard teams in Johannesburg competed for cash prizes and, since the early 1930s, mines, factories and local associations offered employment and preferential treatment to workers who exhibited outstanding footballing skills (interview by the author with Peter Sitsila, Langa, 27 July 1995; Couzens 1983: 204). It was common knowledge that in the 1950s top clubs like Orlando Pirates and Moroka Swallows in Johannesburg and Durban Bush Bucks paid their best players 'under the table', distributing portions of the club's share of gate takings at big matches (Minutes of the Meetings of Orlando Pirates, 23 June 1949). Patron-managers and administrators reaped the lion's share of the direct and indirect material profits trickling out of the game, not least because amateur players, by definition, had no right to claim compensation for their sporting performances (Jeffrey 1992). Black soccer entrepreneurs in the Vereeniging area such as N. Molafo rose to fame in the 1950s by organizing 'ox competitions' (*Post*, 12 July 1959, 27 September 1959). The winners received a beast they either sold at the grounds for cash or carried back home in the back of a lorry for a fundraising function or a neighbourhood feast (*World*, 1 April 1961). This kind of communal consumption in the industrial urban milieu showed the continuing importance of established, agrarian values of solidarity and reciprocity.

The main consequences of hidden professionalism were inefficient administration, low standards of play, unequal distribution of financial rewards and seemingly hopeless segmentation of black football along racial and ethnic lines. Then, the founding of the whites-only professional league proved to be a catalyst for the black football world in South Africa. In June 1959, journalist Vivian Granger, businessman Lubbe Snooyman, Johannesburg councillor Dave Marais and others, mostly English-speaking whites linked to the United Party, launched the National Football League (Granger 1961; Litchfield 1963, 1965). The white league (NFL) secured financial support from crucial corporate sponsors, most notably British Petroleum, South African Breweries, and the United Tobacco Company. With the full support of municipal authorities, big business and the media, the NFL attracted sizeable crowds in Durban, Johannesburg and, years later, in Cape Town. South African Breweries linked the white FA Cup final to its popular Castle brand by naming it the Castle Cup. Because white soccer games rarely generated widespread enthusiasm, whites and blacks were surprised when Castle Cup finals between Johannesburg Rangers and Germiston Callies in 1959, and Durban City and Johannesburg Ramblers in 1960, drew 16,238 and 22,524 spectators respectively at the City Council-owned Rand Stadium (Litchfield 1965: 122). *Drum* magazine, the leading black periodical, picked up on the achievements of the NFL and publicly raised the question many were now discussing in private: what might happen if there were a nonracial, professional league run by black people?

> Remember that soccer is just another game to the whites. Rugby gets the crowds. Soccer gets what is left. Now, for non-white South Africans, soccer is the National Game ... Why shouldn't WE start our own professional inter-racial Soccer League? ... We've asked these questions the past few weeks, and, from clubmen and sports officials, the answer every time has been, 'Yes, let's try'. (*Drum*, August 1959)

Theo Mthembu, a leading sports reporter for the *Golden City Post* in the 1950s and 1960s, explained in an interview that another critical factor driving popular demand for a nonracial, professional soccer league was the migration of some leading black South Africans to European leagues. 'Players and officials were very much in favour [of pro soccer],' said Mthembu, 'it had been done in many parts of the world, they had their own players going out of the country [pauses] Dhlomo, Zuma, Mokone, they had been successful' (interview by Richard Maguire with Theo Mthembu, August 1991). Pretoria's Stephen 'Kalamazoo' Mokone was the first black South African footballer to play professionally in Europe when he signed a contract with Welsh club Cardiff City in the English Third Division in 1956 (Mokone 1980). Mokone joined Dutch second division club Heracles in 1958 and persuaded the club to sign Durban heroes Darius Dhlomo and Herbert 'Shordex' Zuma for the 1959–60 season. Early in 1961, top English club Leeds United signed Albert 'Hurry-Hurry' Johanneson, an exceptionally fast winger who had caught the eye of English scouts when he led the coloured 'national' team to Kajee Cup triumphs in 1956 and 1960.[2] Players' international experiences inspired fans; in Mthembu's words, 'those things made them feel that they had to do something to get up; but it wasn't everybody who could go overseas so why not start it at home? Let's play professional soccer right here!' (interview by Maguire with Mthembu). The SASL aimed to satisfy a voracious social appetite for top-class football in black communities across the country.

African, Indian, and coloured soccer officials from Johannesburg and Durban founded the pioneering SASL soon after the killing of black protesters by white security forces in Sharpeville and Langa townships and in rural Pondoland in 1960. In February 1961, ten African, Indian and coloured football administrators broke away from the anti-apartheid South African Soccer Federation (SASF), the leading amateur body that had amalgamated the South Africa African Football Association, the South African Indian Football Association, and the South African Coloured Football Association in 1951.[3] The 'rebels,' a group of educated, businessmen and white-collar professionals, established the South African Soccer League at a meeting held at the home of Lucas Khoza, at 67 Second Avenue in Alexandra township, Johannesburg (*The Sowetan*, 29 May 1991; *Drum*, May 1961). The professional soccer elders appointed R.K. Naidoo (Durban Indian Football Association, DIFA) as president, Twala (Johannesburg African Football Association, JAFA) as vice-president, Lutchman (DIFA) as secretary, and Alfred Thango (Durban & County African Football Association) as treasurer. The men established a 'Working Committee' whose members were I.J. Motholo (Durban & County), Louis Nelson (DIFA), Lucas Khoza (JAFA), E.I. Haffejee (DIFA), Louis Tangee (Blackpool United Football Club) and R. Mannar (Transvaal United Football Club) (*Official Program of the SASL Knock-Out Cup Final*).[4] The executive tightly controlled league affairs, its power unchecked by a constitution that awarded individual executive members ten electoral votes while giving each club only one vote. While the fledgling 'People's League' was not a democratic organization, its leadership elicited widespread support for nonracial sport, ably tackling gargantuan financial difficulties and intensifying opposition from the apartheid state and white sport.

A new game

The league's perpetual struggle to secure playing grounds and financial capital underlines the inextricable connection between sport and the political economy of apartheid. From its inception, the SASL fought to keep sporting dreams and financial investments alive by challenging racial segregation in sport. SASL's consistent commitment to nonracialism, a stance motivated by a combination of moral principle, political consciousness and market-driven interests, represented a direct challenge to Pretoria's masterplan of separate development. As a result, the organization entered into conflict with white sporting officials, municipal authorities and the apartheid state.

Carving out a nonracial sporting space at a time of unprecedented state repression required a pragmatic approach, and so the oppositional SASL did comply with some apartheid regulations. Most notably, in order to gain access to municipal stadiums the SASL regularly applied to local Group Areas Boards (GABs) for permits.[5] Initially, white authorities allowed SASL matches because the league was perceived as a 'non-European' affair. Only a few whites were involved, usually assuming positions of authority as coaches and referees. An important incentive for the state and its agents was the weekly collection of entertainment taxes at rates of 15–20 per cent which provided much-needed revenue. Faced with the serious political and social unrest of the early 1960s, the central state initially disregarded the operations of an upstart, black-dominated football league with scarce resources.[6]

Economic hardships and consumerization

Nascent professional clubs grappled with serious financial insecurity. Investments by Durban entrepreneurial groups, including Indian textile manufacturers, retailers in the Central Business District, organized crime syndicates and boxing promoters provided an initial injection of capital for individual clubs. Durban Aces United, for example, received the financial and technical support of Daddy Naidoo, a boss in the notorious Crimson League gang, as well as a promoter of professional boxing fights at Durban City Hall (Blades 1998: 58–9). In Cape Town, Bennie Katz, a Jewish businessman who owned several night clubs and racehorses, provided financial backing for the formation of the Cape Ramblers

Football Club (interview by the author with Conrad Stuurman, 9 February 1998, and Basil Jansen, 18 May 1998). The capital provided by powerful men such as Naidoo and Katz covered neither the operational costs for individual clubs nor those of the League itself. And so the meagre resources available to black entrepreneurs meant that the SASL also needed corporate sponsorships to survive.

Dan Twala approached the United Tobacco Company (UTC, now British American Tobacco) which had sponsored competitions of the Johannesburg African Football Association since the 1940s and also employed well-known black footballers as cigarette salesmen in black areas. The most famous among the UTC men was dribbling maestro Difference 'City Council' Mbanya (interview by Maguire with Mthembu). Since several of Mbanya's Moroka Swallows teammates were also UTC employees, the Soweto side was sometimes referred to as a UTC 'company team' (interviews by Richard Maguire with Sam Shabangu, Sydney Mabuza, Willard Msomi, Elliott Buthelezi, August 1991). As UTC salesmen, these footballers were better able to devote themselves to training than workers employed in secondary industry. Players-cum-tobacco salesmen travelled by company car from township to township, making deliveries to general stores and shebeens where they socialized, talked about club affairs, weekend matches and the game in general. Tobacco companies marketed their products to black people by advertising on billboards and posters located in frequently travelled areas in the townships, as well as on the radio and in newspapers and magazines. Famous players like Stephen 'Kalamazoo' Mokone endorsed UTC products, projecting an image of cigarette smoking as the glamorous, invigorating pastime of prominent black cultural icons (see advertisement in *Drum*, June 1958). Eager to attract more black consumers, UTC agreed to a sponsorship deal with the SASL worth R2000 in 1961, a partnership renewed each season during the league's existence. The UTC–SASL deal was mutually beneficial. The tobacco company gained access to vast township markets and the league obtained prize money for its competitions.

The league's early success

The SASL competition that kicked off on 9 April 1961 ushered in a new era in the history of South African football. Avalon Athletic, Berea and Aces United from Durban; Moroka Swallows, Transvaal United and Blackpool United from Johannesburg competed in the first SASL season (*Drum*, November 1961). These racially diverse teams produced an enormous improvement in the standard of domestic football compared to the 'hidden professionalism' of the 1950s (interview by the author with Vince Belgeums, Factreton, 27 March 1998). SASL clubs brought together the country's best African, coloured, Indian and, in exceptional cases, white talents. Regular training, specialized coaching, and legal financial retributions were introduced to black football. In the process, blue-collar black players performed tantalizing soccer that lured thousands of fans to games in South Africa's major cities. The excitement and unprecedented quality of the nonracial, professional league provided cultural spaces in which black South Africans forged new identities and networks, and enjoyed relief from the hardships of police repression and low-paying work.

A dazzling performance by 23-year-old left-winger Joseph 'Excellent' Mthembu of Pietermaritzburg, *World*'s unofficial Footballer of the Year in 1959, highlighted the league's explosive debut. Mthembu scored four goals in Durban Aces United's 6–1 rout of Blackpool United at Curries Fountain. A paying crowd estimated at between 7000 and 8000 people watched the inaugural contest for a reported gate-taking of R1240 (*The Leader*, 14 April 1961). Transvaal United from Noordgesig, the coloured township in Soweto, won the League championship in 1961, but fell short of the 'double' by losing the UTC Cup final to Cape Town Ramblers (2–4) in a memorable match witnessed by more than 20,000 spectators at the Green Point Track in Cape Town (*New Age*, 19 October 1961; *World*, 21 October 1961; *Drum*, November 1961).[7] Impressive crowds bear out the league's extraordinary success. The average paid attendance in 1961 was 6598 providing for R45,335 in gate takings at Durban's Curries Fountain, Johannesburg's Natalspruit Indian Sports Ground and Cape Town's Green Point Track (*The Leader*, 1 February 1963). However, contemporary newspaper reports and interviews with many former players, club directors and league officials pointed out that crowds at most matches were usually double the official figures. In Johannesburg, for example, thousands of fans scaled the fence or watched games from surrounding mine dumps. Tax evasion also encouraged the underreporting of match attendance. In light of this reliable evidence, it is reasonable to conclude that average crowds at SASL games approached 11,000 people.

Despite meagre financial resources and limited access to playing grounds, the SASL overcame government opposition and rose to national prominence. Teams joined the league for a range of reasons. After a successful first season, the SASL added Soweto's Orlando Pirates, Maritzburg City and Lincoln City from Pietermaritzburg, and Durban Hearts, and formed three provincial Second Division leagues with 46 clubs in the Transvaal, Natal, and the Cape. The promise of financial gain clearly appealed to people denied economic opportunities. The league's integrationist policies also garnered political support. Orlando Pirates, the Soweto team known as the 'People's Club', affiliated to the SASL largely through the efforts of their charismatic captain, the late Eric 'Scara' Sono, an ardent opponent of racism and segregation (Alegi 2000a).

For other participants the human desire to compete at the highest possible level superseded political concerns. Doug Lomberg, former captain and secretary of Cape Ramblers, described his involvement in the following way:

> The fact that I knew so little of the underlying political turmoil is of no surprise to me, simply because I chose to dedicate myself to promoting the game of soccer, to the success of the Cape Ramblers organization, to those wonderful team-mates of mine who sacrificed so much to elevate soccer to the relatively great heights we accomplished. (letter to the author, 19 February 1999)

Lomberg remembered with pride how fans appreciated Ramblers' 'entertaining and exciting brand of soccer'. Crowd figures demonstrate the league's tremendous popularity: total attendance in 1962 increased by 177 per cent from the previous year (*The Leader*, 1 February 1963). According to available data, the attraction of integrated professional football was such that (without taking into account returning fans) about 17 per cent of the black population living in urban areas attended SASL contests.[8]

Early scientific football and the black working-class street game

Professionalism improved playing standards so that the popularity of SASL matches owed a great deal to the exciting quality of the football on display. The fitness and tactical aspects of the game saw the most dramatic advancement. In an interview with *Drum* magazine, Lomberg explained the impact of professional training on amateur footballers in unambiguous terms:

> When we trotted out on the pitch for our first training spell, I thought we were a pretty slick bunch of soccer players. Brother! Did I have a lot to learn. An hour with a pro trainer [Samuels] and we were breathing like a lot of cart-horses. When I look back and see what he's done for our game I realize what a long way it is from amateur to pro. Our game

is unrecognizable. We're rippling fit, and our whole approach to the game is more serious. (*Drum*, May 1961)

This new emphasis on fitness turned physical conditioning from a weekly into a daily affair. With few training facilities available, a growing number of footballers worked out with professional boxers who willingly shared their knowledge and experience in maintaining rigorous, regimented fitness training routines. Footballers and boxers, the black working-class athletes par excellence, ran together through township streets in the early morning and evening, and trained in gyms lifting weights and strengthening both the upper and lower body (interview by the author with Bernard Hartze, Cape Town, 25 January 1998). Sparring was kept to a minimum, probably not at the boxers' insistence.

By the 1963 season, almost every SASL club employed a physical trainer, typically an individual borrowed from bodybuilding or boxing circles. Many teams were coached by whites, among them R.F. Young at Maritzburg City, Koos Brandsma at Lincoln City, Bobby Reed at Berea, and Norman 'Jock' Samuels at Cape Ramblers. Clive Barker, future coach of the South African team that won the 1996 African Nations Cup and qualified for the 1998 World Cup finals for the first time, took his first steps in the coaching profession at the age of 22 with Coastals Football Club based in the Clairwood section of Durban. Coastals competed in the Natal Second Division of the SASL and were later promoted to the First Division. White coaches brought different experiences and approaches to SASL clubs, but they all shared an emphasis on fitness and discipline.

Many black athletes shared white coaches' enthusiasm for physical conditioning. Napoleon 'Kallie' Page of Blackpool and Eric 'Scara' Sono of Orlando Pirates were among the athletes who worked out five times a week, alternating days with weights in the gym, to morning 'roadwork' (running) and late afternoon practice with the ball (*Drum*, July 1962, April 1963). Some players, however, criticized the approach of white coaches. One player argued that, 'apart from ordinary physical training routines they [whites] don't seem to teach us much theory. I feel they're holding back on us' (*The Leader*, 6 July 1962). The unwillingness (or inability) of some whites to modify European coaching methods and philosophies to suit the strengths of black players stunted the development of a creolized South African style of play.

Due to the difficulties in dealing with white coaches, black professionals said they usually 'learned more about football through reading overseas magazines' (*The Leader*, 6 July 1962). Without access both to formally trained coaches in the townships and to televised matches, black players educated themselves by reading and circulating British football magazines and coaching manuals. Edward 'Fish' Neku of Moroka Swallows, one of the top black goalkeepers in the 1950s and early 1960s, told journalist Sy Mogapi that he 'read a lot about the techniques of 'keeping from books written by well-known goalies' (*Golden City Post*, 23 September 1956). The distribution of European football films also influenced the adoption of new methods of play among black players and coaches. For 25 cents, an overflowing crowd at the Kings Theatre in Alexandra township in August 1962 were treated to Real Madrid's legendary 7–3 victory over Eintracht Frankfurt in the 1960 European Cup final (*World*, 9 August 1962).

The SASL produced a tactical revolution in the local game. The introduction of the attacking 4–2–4 system, popularized by Brazil in Pelé's first World Cup triumph in Sweden in 1958, was, perhaps, the most important change. Keeping pace with changes occurring internationally, the arrival of the 4–2–4 scheme in South Africa attenuated the 60-year dominance of the 2–3–5 'pyramid', the Italian *metodo* and the 'WM' formation (Giulianotti 1999a: 127–45). Avalon Athletic was one of the first clubs in the country to use the new attacking but physically taxing approach. Employing the 4–2–4 with stunning consistency and mechanical efficiency, Avalon became the league's most successful club. Avalon's goalkeeper Denzil Easthorpe, midfielder Cedric 'Sugar Ray' Xulu, former Leeds United trialist George Francis and striker Dharam Mohan spearheaded the Durban side to SASL championships in 1962 (shared with Aces United), 1963 and 1964, and to UTC Cup titles in 1963, 1964 and 1965.

The structural neglect of sport in black townships complicated the adoption of new tactics. SASL players developed their skills as youths in the narrow and uneven spaces characteristic of fluid, flexible street football. In the streets and patches of open ground in schools and townships, ball control, individualism, toughness and improvization far outweighed the importance of moving without the ball, creating and using space, combination passing and field vision. Former SASL star Conrad Stuurman pointed out how black youth began playing barefoot with a tennis ball in the streets

> When I had the ball and I wanted to beat somebody, I played the ball against the pavement on the other side so I'd get the ball back again. That's how we came to know the 'wall pass'. I didn't even know there was a name like 'wall pass' [laughs]! (interview by the author with Stuurman, Factreton, 25 February 1998)

Lack of youth coaching and development led one observer to comment on the lack of sound fundamentals in professional matches:

> positioning, defensive play, how to finish off forward moves, what to do with the ball when hard pressed, how to tackle properly and how to beat a man were all elementary points that were sadly neglected by our top teams. (*Drum*, December 1961).

These structural factors militated against the development of early versions of 'scientific football'. The street game's enduring ethos partly explains why the league's 5.11 goals per match average in the 1961–65 period was nearly twice that of leading contemporary European professional leagues and the World Cup.[9]

Economic deprivation hindered the organic development of the SASL in other ways. For example, contracted players could not afford to live by football wages alone. Most footballers earned R8 (£4) per match *played*; team members who trained regularly but did not play in official matches received no money at all. Some enterprising owners also offered incentive bonuses of R2 for a draw and R4 for a win (interviews with Jansen and Stuurman; *Drum*, January 1962). Low wages and non-salaried contracts meant that football emoluments could only supplement wages from regular employment as artisans, factory workers, clerks, teachers, messengers, drivers and manual labourers. Work commitments limited the amount of time athletes could devote to training. Training sessions were held after work, as players scrambled to reach the designated ground in the late afternoon, paying for transport costs out of their meagre wage packets. If players earned little more than pocket money, then club directors and investors hardly fared better. The case of Transvaal United in 1961 synthesized the gargantuan financial difficulties facing early professional football clubs. Despite winning the league championship and reaching the UTC Cup Final, Transvaal United barely covered its expenses at the end of the 1961 season. Players who participated in each of the club's 13 matches earned a grand total of R104 (£52). In 1975, the average monthly wage of Indian workers was R246, while coloured and African labourers earned R172 and R105 respectively (Archer and Bouillon 1982: 161).

The shared experience of underemployment, institutional racism and an irrepressible passion for football meant that supporters identified closely with players. Football heroes and favourite clubs brought joy and excitement to disenfranchised fans. Eric 'Scara' Sono of Orlando Pirates and Difference 'City Council' Mbanya of Moroka Swallows were among the most acclaimed stars. Scara Sono's popularity was such that, despite breaking his leg in August 1962 and missing the last three months of the season, *Post* and *Drum*, the two most widely circulated black periodicals, crowned him respectively 'Sportsman of the Year' and 'Footballer of the Year' (*Drum*, April 1963). Scara's physical strength, exquisite ball control, determination and anticipation made him the consummate township football artist. Thanks to his football skills and personal charisma Scara developed an intimate relationship with Pirates fans across the country (Alegi 2000a). 'What a marvellous player man. I get goose bumps thinking about that player, what a clever player', remembered the Capetonian defender Vince Belgeums who played against Sono many times. 'The man had flair, flair. A pleasure to watch at all times. It's difficult to mark this man. He plays off the ball, he's fantastic. He's all over; he's on the left hand side, he switches to the right side, he comes through the centre, he was a terror!' (interview with Belgeums). Scara's national popularity and his crafty style of play personified SASL's success.

Professional football's ritual spectacles challenged the drudgery and routine oppression of Verwoerdian apartheid (Magubane 1963; Evans 1997). Partly as a result of the economic boom's trickle-down effect, and partly because of the entertaining brand of football on display, more and more African, coloured and Indian women, youths and nuclear families attended football matches. As crowds became increasingly diverse during the SASL years, official supporters clubs appeared. These voluntary civic organizations spawned social networks of their own and stood as unmistakable examples of the 'festivity, friendship and community', and the sociability of soccer (Holt 1989a). Fan groups in the 1960s were, for good or ill, powerful expressions of popular culture formulating political critiques of apartheid society by aligning themselves with nonracial sport.

Supporters democracy

Supporters clubs provided moral support for teams and transportation of fans to away matches, but they also organized social events in the tradition of African mutual aid societies like *stokfels* (rotating credit associations), *manyano* (prayer groups) and burial societies (Gaitskell 1982; Cobley 1997). In this way, soccer paralleled music by providing a meeting space for common social and cultural experiences that sliced through class, race, ethnic and gender distinctions (Coplan 1985; Erlmann 1991). Through the activities of supporters clubs, South Africans of different ages, classes, occupations, regions, ethnicity and religion forged and maintained new individual identities and social networks.

The first organization to be launched was the Berea Supporters Club in Durban in 1961, followed by partisan fan groups supporting Orlando Pirates, Moroka Swallows, Blackpool, Real Fighters, Durban Aces and Maritzburg City.[10] Swallows boasted supporters clubs as far away as Durban and Mbabane (Swaziland), as the team's success in the SASL provided a key impetus to the nationalization of their support base. In January 1963, members of the SASL's numerous fan clubs formed a 'federation of soccer supporters clubs of South Africa ... [for the] promotion of true sportsmanship, friendship, and better understanding among its members ... and to protect [them] from abuse' (*The Leader*, 1 February 1963).

Women were important actors in the daily activities of supporters clubs, filling both conservative and progressive roles. The executive board of the Durban Berea Supporters Club was dominated by a group of Indian women (*The Leader*, 25 August 1961) who frequently travelled to away matches. Jeanne Pottier, who worked in the SASL's Durban office, became the first South African woman to be certified by the National Referees' Examination Board in 1963 (*Cape Herald*, 15 March 1963), although it is not clear whether she ever refereed an official league match. Urban African women had also involved themselves more directly in football. Orlando Pirates female fans '[c]lad in black and white uniforms ... became renowned for their fierce loyalty and inspirational singing and sloganeering at matches' (Maguire 1991: 90).

Fan clubs were so popular that meetings of the Maritzburg City supporters attracted over 400 people, while Orlando Pirates fans congregated regularly in the township's largest indoor hall at the Donaldson Orlando Community Centre (*The Leader*, 23 March 1963; *World*, 30 January 1964). Club meetings ostensibly functioned as forums for conversation, dissemination of news and discussions about the team's performances. An important feature was the promulgation of travel plans for an upcoming away game. Durban-bound buses left Johannesburg on Friday evenings or Saturday mornings and returned immediately after the match on Sunday nights (*World*, 12 July 1962, 30 October 1962). Apartheid laws required supporters to obtain travel permits before making the trip.

Supporter clubs served a social purpose in black communities. Saturday evening soccer parties, dances, *braais* (barbecues), and beauty pageants organized by and featuring women supporters, sustained the social and cultural lives of urban black people. These festive events enhanced the status and prestige of football teams. Fundraising draws such as the one held in Alexandra by Real Fighters supporters in May 1963 offered a portable radio, a case of beer and a half-bag of sugar as top prizes (*World*,

23 May 1963). Individual objectives complemented collective ones since ambitious members sought personal prestige and visibility within their communities. Functions hosted by Pirates and Swallows followers in Soweto were important dates in the social calendar of black Johannesburg, not least because they offered a chance to make or rekindle relationships, and to 'be seen' in the company of glamorous athletes, singers, writers, gangsters, shebeen owners and other socialites. These festive occasions featured catering by women supporters, speeches by prominent members of the African community, musical entertainment by live jazz, swing, dixie, or *mbaqanga* bands, and dancing into the night. Unlike the *stokfel marabi* parties David Coplan described (1985: 104), rivalries between clubs seemed to hinder cooperation in planning soccer socials and sharing the revenue. And yet the unwavering loyalties and intense competition engendered by football did not prevent people from cooperating in extraordinary circumstances. For example, Soweto rivals Moroka Swallows and Orlando Pirates established a Jeppe Tragedy Fund together with the SASL to assist families of eleven victims killed in a stampede at the Jeppe train station following a Swallows–Pirates match staged at Natalspruit (*World*, 1 November 1962).

Organized fan groups served a democratizing function for disenfranchised South Africans caught in the heightened repression of the post-Sharpeville period.[11] The serious dangers associated with joining banned political organizations led black people to channel their aspirations for power, status and prestige into social and cultural organizations, especially sports clubs and associations (Wilson and Mafeje 1963: 145; Kuper 1965: 309–64). By paying small annual dues, fans received a membership card granting them the right to vote and to present themselves as candidates in elections for sought-after offices in the executive board. In this way we can see how participation in the cultural production of professional football carried political implications. Supporters clubs partially filled the vacuum left by the apartheid state's draconian repression of mass political movements after April 1960.

The SASL's unwavering ideological commitment to nonracial sport strengthened its democratizing influence. Club members became political actors because supporting the 'People's League' meant taking a stance against institutionalized racial discrimination. When the South African Sports Association (SASA), the vanguard of the domestic sport boycott movement, launched Operation Support Only Non-Racial Events In Sport (SONREIS) in June 1961, the SASL and the overwhelming majority of its fans enthusiastically backed the campaign (*New Age*, 7 June 1961).

SONREIS had two main objectives: to curtail black people's attendance at white sporting events, especially Indians' support of NFL matches in Durban, and to boycott racialized associations set up by the apartheid establishment.[12] In 1961–62, for example, people on the Rand deserted matches of the National Professional Soccer League (NPSL), an organization created by white authorities with the help of cooperative African officials such as Seth Mzizi, Sydney Sepanya and Willy Baqwa. The SONREIS boycott was successful. The majority of black fans rejected racially segregated football, forcing the rapid (though temporary) demise of the pro-apartheid NPSL.

Physical confrontations

SASL's popularity had its costs. Burgeoning crowds were difficult to control in overcrowded sport grounds inadequately policed and without fences, walls or moats. High-stakes gambling, liquor consumption and poor officiating led to an increasing number of pitch invasions, brawls and riots. Crowd hooliganism was also linked to rivalries between groups of hard-core fans, usually comprised of *tsotsis* (young urban toughs) and street-wise city slickers (Glaser 2000). Youth gangs associated with Orlando Pirates, for example, staked out territorial claims behind one of the goals at Natalspruit, carving out an autonomous 'Pirates-only' area they called 'Congo'. Natalspruit ground became the source of a potent, inebriating sense of belonging and identity for hard-core Pirates supporters like Boy Shogwe: 'The Mecca of Soccer! Oh my God, I got married there! You know, it was the "in-thing." Man, it was my life.' Shogwe remembered with distinct pride his devotion for Pirates: 'There was a place we called the Congo, after the Belgian Congo you know, it was the roughest place because it was *Ours*. Pirates, Pirates, Pirates.' He went on to clarify the meaning of 'rough', saying:

> we would sneak in beer bottles and once we got drunk we would fill the bottles with urine – hey, it was a rough place. Congo, at Indian Sports Ground, it was the only pavilion that was *Ours*. If you sit there by mistake, conform or [silence] ... We fuck you up! (Alegi 2000a: 14)

With the advent of professionalism, betting on matches became more frequent. Although much more research into football gambling needs to be done, some preliminary evidence indicates that it was widespread and highly visible. For example, the Durban Indian newspaper *The Leader* reported that 'armed non-white policemen at the [Royal Agricultural]

Showgrounds [in Pietermaritzburg] last Sunday ... turned a blind eye to an Orlando Pirates official waving bank notes as he shouted odds against a Lincoln City victory' (*The Leader*, 13 March 1964). After Pirates defeated Aces 2–0 at Natalspruit in July 1964, the *World* reported that it 'was a great win for Pirates but the happiest man in the huge crowd was Mr. Freddy Shabangu, of Standerton, who won R200 in a side bet', nearly twice the average monthly wage of an African worker (*World*, 19 July 1964). According to Shogwe, gambling caused several riots at Pirates SASL matches. Shogwe resorted to hooliganism to avoid a costly gambling loss in May 1964, threatening a visiting goalkeeper with a .38 revolver.

> I showed him the gun, said Shogwe, and he ran away ... Then I heard, 'Goal!' and I asked the linesmen if it was official. It was a draw! I ran out of the stadium, collected my money and was gone. On Monday my boss got his money. (Alegi 2000a: 13)

Ironically, the increase in violent incidents coincided with women, teenagers and families attending matches in greater numbers than ever before.[13] In a letter to the popular black weekly *Post*, a Soweto fan writing under the pseudonym 'Fullback' poignantly captured the effects of spiralling football violence in the mid-1960s on the common spectator:

> My wife and I are both keen sports fans, and have a lot of pleasure watching soccer matches at the many Reef grounds. But now a lot of that joy has gone out of our lives, because we are becoming afraid to watch now. So much so that my wife, who is now pregnant, says that she won't go to any more matches. It is all because of the way certain people behave when they get to the soccer grounds. Don't these people who throw stones, use sticks and swear at people realize that in the excitement of a soccer game it takes very little to start big trouble and spoil the game for thousands of people who have come along, not for trouble, but because they love the game and want a good afternoon's entertainment? (*World*, 14 November 1965)

Violence at SASL games presented the government and officials of white sport with a convenient excuse to crack down on integrated professional soccer. Aided by the propaganda of a powerful print media, the white alliance waged 'a war of attrition ... against the facilities, spectators and finances of the nonracial footballers' (Archer and Bouillon 1982: 196).

The strangulation of the SASL

The first shots in the war of attrition had been fired in 1962 by Interior Minister Jan De Klerk, Johannesburg Non-European Affairs Department (NEAD) manager W.J.P. Carr and NFL chairman Viv Granger who conspired to shut out 34 Transvaal Second Division clubs from municipal grounds (*Drum*, November 1962; SAIRR 1963: 292). By squeezing out the 'People's League' from municipal grounds, the state and its local agents sought to eradicate nonracial sport from the social geography of apartheid (Archer and Bouillon 1982: 194–8). In doing so, the NFL and FASA hoped to achieve three goals: to attract black fans to 'non-European' stands in segregated stadiums, to gain control of domestic soccer, and to get South Africa's suspension lifted at FIFA.[14] The political and sporting establishment's all-out assault on the SASL was sparked by a Durban magistrate's acquittal in May 1962 of members of the SASL's Lincoln City Football Club of Pietermaritzburg charged by the state of violating a provision of the Group Areas Act by playing mixed soccer (*South African Law Reports*, 1963 [1]: 261–4).

Judge J.L. Pretorius ruled that because Lincoln City's Indian, coloured and white players had not entered any building to socialize or share refreshments as intended by the Group Areas Act but rather had simply played football at the Curries Fountain ground, this kind of integrated sporting contact was not illegal. This decision – upheld by the Natal Supreme Court in October 1962 – confirmed what the SASL and the anti-apartheid sport movement had argued vociferously at home and abroad: there was no law prohibiting mixed sports teams in South Africa (ibid.: 261–4).[15] The legal triumph, however, was a pyrrhic victory. In the wake of the court decision, white authorities and administrators of white football moved decisively to suppress the SASL. FASA actively cooperated with the government by, among other things, 'send[ing] SASF letters addressed to them to the Government in the hope that action will be taken against SASF officials' and by 'writ[ing] to all Municipalities throughout the country, to prohibit the use of playing fields to SASF units [especially the SASL]' (SASF Memo to FIFA members, 1964).[16]

Therefore, when the municipal Non-European Affairs Department removed the goalposts at Natalspruit on 6 April 1963 the action was part of an overall strategy to strangle the oppositional SASL. Denied access to Natalspruit, the SASL could not survive for long since the facility was home to the league's Johannesburg area teams, including Soweto giants Orlando Pirates and Moroka Swallows. These two clubs had gained national popularity and accounted for nearly a third of SASL's total attendance and income. In a meeting with SASL representative Reggie Feldman, Viv Granger described white officialdom's vicious attack as 'a war to the death ... we're doing our best to obliterate you' (*Drum*, November 1963).

A prolonged, costly legal battle resulted in the Supreme Court in Bloemfontein taking Natalspruit away from the Johannesburg Indian Sports Ground Association, which leased it to the SASL, and turning it over to the Johannesburg City Council in 1964 (*South African Law Reports*, 1964 [4]: 779–85). The SASL survived one more year playing a truncated schedule. It staged its Johannesburg area matches at Kliptown, near Soweto, on the open ground that hosted the historic anti-apartheid Congress of the People in June 1955 (Clingman 1998: 233). Ironically, the gradual suffocation of the SASL in Johannesburg coincided with Moroka Swallows winning the 1965 league title – the first national championship ever claimed by a Sowetan side (*The Leader*, 26 November 1965). Swallows' victory inspired the first known South African music recordings about soccer. According to Gallo Music archivist Rob Allingham (personal communication, 13 June 2000), unknown artists (probably session musicians) recorded an instrumental song in 1966 entitled 'Up the Birds' and, that same year, the Jabulani Quads recorded the single 'Okongo Mame' which praised a famous Swallows player named Kongo Malemane (ibid.). The league's growing imbrication with black popular culture, however, could not prevent a government eviction from the bare and bumpy Kliptown ground (*World*, 22 October 1964).[17] The SASL shut down operations in 1966 due to the lack of suitable playing grounds.

The SASL was, unquestionably, the most important force in the history of South African football before the 1990s. In five years, the 'People's League' galvanized domestic soccer as it evolved from amateurism to professionalism, and from popular pastime to mass phenomenon. The new tactical strategies, training methods and playing styles of popular SASL clubs Avalon Athletic, Orlando Pirates, Moroka Swallows and Cape Ramblers produced scintillating soccer that attracted record crowds of nearly 50,000 for big matches (Bonner and Segal 1998: 64). Africans, coloureds and Indians tasted professionalism for the first time and intermingled on the field, in the stands and in supporters clubs (*Drum*, July 1962; SAIRR 1962). Some whites participated in the black-run league: a handful as players; others as coaches and referees. Ultimately, the game's public demonstration of the social and political potential of nonracial sport in apartheid South Africa led to its demise.

The strangulation of the SASL by the state and its agents and allies resulted in a long period of stagnation in domestic soccer lasting until the end of apartheid in the early 1990s. The inextricable links between sport and the political economy of apartheid were clearly exposed as fans were denied the right to enjoy watching the country's best football talents compete on the same playing field. South Africa's suspension from international soccer in 1961 (renewed in 1964 after an executive reprieve in 1963) exacerbated apartheid's stunting effect. Isolated from World Cup and African Nations Cup tournaments, and unable to play friendly matches with any member of FIFA, South African soccer – black and white – remained frozen in time while world football experienced a major technical, organizational and commercial transformation.

Looking back on his experiences as a young professional in the 1960s, former SASL player Vince Belgeums spoke for the lost generations of South African football stars when reflecting on his wrecked sporting dreams:

> In my heart I am also cross for the government for not giving us that scope to develop ... In those times, those were my youth, and my goals were to go play against Pelé and to show that South Africa has also got a Pelé, or even better. Because we never had sponsors, and we never really got the right act to be recognized or to be taken overseas to give you that break, today I'm still cross. I feel I could have been in a better position today through soccer because this was my career. I was born to play soccer. And I was really robbed. (interview with Belgeums)

Acknowledgements

This study is part of a book manuscript under completion entitled *Laduma! Soccer, Politics and Society in Modern South Africa*. Research funding was provided by a Fulbright Fellowship in 1997–98 and a Boston University African Studies Center/Ford Foundation grant in 1996. My thanks to Richard Maguire for sharing with me his taped interviews with former members of Soweto's Orlando Pirates. I wish to thank Diana Wylie, Glenn Adler and Laura Fair for their constructive comments on earlier versions of this chapter presented at the Northeast Workshop for Southern Africa (University of Vermont, 1 May 1999) and the 42nd Annual Meeting of the African Studies Association (Philadelphia, 12 November 1999).

Notes

1. The term 'black' in this chapter refers to South Africans previously classified as African, coloured and Indian under apartheid law (Population Registration Act 1950). Group terms are used only where appropriate. In doing so, the author recognizes that 'race' is a social construction, but acknowledges that

South Africans themselves still consider racial boundaries and identities important.

2. The Kajee Cup (1952–76), donated by a wealthy Indian businessman and conservative politician from Durban named A.I. Kajee, featured African, coloured and Indian 'national' teams competing under the auspices of the anti-apartheid South African Soccer Federation (SASF). The Kajee Cup and the interprovincial Moroka-Baloyi Cup (for Africans), were the leading domestic football tournaments of the 1950s. Two other black South Africans had unsuccessful trials in the UK. Johanneson's teammate Gerald Francis went to Leeds in 1958–59 and Joseph 'Carlton' Moloi of Moroka Swallows went to Cardiff in 1961. Moloi's failure led Mokone to take an anti-professional league stance: 'Professional football isn't easy as people back home think ... Yes, "Carlton", a real star in South Africa, just couldn't make it' (*World*, 18 March 1961).

3. University of the Western Cape, Bellville, Mayibuye Archive, *Papers of the Western Province Association Football Board*, box 3 (unsorted): 'South African Soccer Federation Public Relations, History of Unity and Division', 1988.

4. My thanks to Vince Belgeums and Basil 'Puzzy' Jansen for sharing the match programme they kept in their personal archives.

5. The Group Areas Boards were local administrative units responsible for residential segregation under the 1950 Group Areas Act. The SASL never believed in absolute non-cooperation with the state as a guiding principle, unlike the more radical South African Council of Sport (SACOS) in the 1970s (Booth 1998: 153–60).

6. After 1960 the liberation movements adopted armed struggle and opened a sabotage campaign against military and state targets. The leaders, Nelson Mandela among them, were arrested in 1963 and then sentenced to life imprisonment on Robben Island. By the end of 1964, the apartheid state had succeeded in breaking down the underground resistance (Thompson 1990: 211).

7. Green Point Track, today a dog-racing track, is adjacent to Green Point Stadium, a facility reserved for white sport during apartheid.

8. This absolute figure was derived by dividing the number of black South Africans included in the 1960 Census (4,847,000) by the total SASL attendance (676,575). 1960 Population Census cited in Van der Horst (1964: 19). Newspapers and interviews revealed that there were few white spectators at SASL games.

9. Goal averages for the World Cup tournaments in 1954, 1958 and 1962 were 5.38, 3.60 and 2.78 respectively (Gardner 1996: 202). Data provided by the Association of Football Statisticians indicate that the goals-per-game average in the English First Division declined from 3.78 in 1958 to 3.00 in 1967. A similar trend occurred in the (more defensive) Italian Serie A; according to the *2001 Almanacco Illustrato del Calcio* (Modena: Panini, 2000) the average dropped from 2.93 in 1958–59 to 2.00 in 1966–67.

10. Founding of supporters clubs reported, for example, in *The Leader*, 9 March 1962, and *World*, 12 July 1962, 30 October 1962, 23 May 1963, 21 October 1964.

11. See Shirts (1988) for a superb analysis of football's emancipatory power in Brazil under military rule.

12. 'Non-white' support was the key to Durban City's popularity, providing as much as 50 per cent of the league-best average attendance of 12,477 at New Kingsmead Stadium in 1964 (Litchfield 1965: 54–5).

13. A group of young Sowetan women led by Jessie Maseko tried, unsuccessfully it seems, to run an Orlando Pirates Women's Football Club (*World*, 12 September 1962).

14. The professional and amateur white soccer establishment pursued this goal by branding supporters of nonracial soccer 'political agitators' (*Post*, 25 August 1963) and (mis)representing the affiliation of moribund or novel pro-apartheid African, coloured and Indian associations as evidence of progressive change.

15. While no law prevented racially mixed team sports, the Boxing and Wrestling Control Act of 1954 prohibited interracial professional boxing matches and training. Even so, it was common practice for whites and blacks to train and spar together (Draper 1963: 90–1).

16. Memorandum found in the Sir Stanley Rous Papers, University of Brighton. I am indebted to Alan Tomlinson for access to the Rous Papers.

17. Despite the atrocious playing conditions at Kliptown, a crowd estimated at between 16,000 and 20,000 watched Pirates defeat Swallows 2–1 in November. This was the only loss suffered by Swallows in 1965 (*World*, 22 November 1965).

7
Football and Ethnicity in Mauritius: (Re)Producing Communal Allegiances

Tim Edensor and Ibrahim Koodoruth

As the most popular sport in the Indian Ocean island state of Mauritius, football holds a particularly tenacious hold over the ways in which Mauritians express their identities. As a multiethnic nation whose ethnic mix was forged during the years of Dutch, French and British colonialism, football has proved to be one of the most important cultural elements by which ethnic distinction has been maintained. For in Mauritius, identity remains pre-eminently mobilized and organized along ethnic lines, prevailing over local and national identities. This communal identification is expressed in quotidian rituals and unreflexive knowledge, is embedded in everyday life, kinship networks, commercial activities and official and political organizations. Football is one of a number of cultural spheres around which expressions of belonging are organized, including religious practice, language use, TV and film viewing, music-making, clothing and eating, as well as ritualized demarcations arranged around specific symbolic sites and key festive dates.

The Mauritian population is usually classified into disparate categories: 'Creole', 'Franco-Mauritian', *'gens de couleur'*, 'Chinese', 'Hindu', 'Tamil' and 'Muslim'. It will be at once apprehended that these categories depend on unlike categories, which refer to colour, cultural mixing, national and regional origin, and religion. Nevertheless, these official denotations provide a commonsense framework for the ethnic distinctions. In the 1991 Census, the 1.2 million population was delineated as consisting of 51 per cent Hindu (which also included Tamils), 18 per cent Muslim, 27 per cent 'general population' (a peculiar category that assembles together Creoles, Coloured and other individuals), 3 per cent Chinese, and 1 per cent Franco-Mauritian. The still economically powerful, white Franco-Mauritians are the descendants of the original sugar plantation owners, the Creoles are the descendants of the African slaves shipped over from Tanzania and Madagascar to work on the plantations, and the Coloured population are the progeny of liaisons between the Franco-Mauritians and the Creoles.

The prevalence of ethnic identification is occasionally transcended by points of intersection, arenas for compromise and negotiation, and occasionally by adherence to what Eriksen (1998) has called a search for 'common denominators'. Nevertheless, those who wish to build a strong sense of shared national identity continue to be thwarted by communal sentiments and the organization of social and cultural life according to ethnicity, as we will see in the case of football. Economic, social and cultural changes have been dramatic since the 1970s in Mauritius, and in order to achieve stability in the face of these transformations, communal leaders often attempt to reify the symbolic importance of cultural attributes to draw boundaries between ethnic groups.

Thus, rather than conceiving ethnicity as a collection of definitive cultural traits, the responses to these changes by Mauritians strongly supports the notion that ethnicity is a dynamic process which depends for its common sense on the continual (re)drawing of boundaries between groups (Barth 1969). Despite the fluidity of the character of these boundaries, ethnicity as the key marker of identity has certainly not become less central. Moreover, these ethnic expressions have not merely been mobilized to create group solidarity, do not merely reflect ethnicity as 'the inherent capacity of any human society to create symbolic, linguistic and social codes to bind its members together' (Arizpe 1992: 6–8). Instead, they have veered towards *ethnicism*; 'the deliberate use of ethnic symbols and codes of conduct to rally around, to defend or to attack others in pursuit of what are perceived as the group's aim' on particular occasions (ibid.). In this context, football has been used to broadcast and express communal identity through support for ethnically identified teams. Such boundary-drawing also constructs ideas about the teams of 'others', and football officials, referees, journalists, trainers and players have their ethnic allegiance identified and frequently called into question.

To emphasize: it is vital that we understand this boundary-drawing as ongoing, for ethnicity is certainly not the identification of particular enduring and self-evident cultural qualities, but a process of differentiation and identification. There is then, between ethnic groups, a constant process of reconfiguring. In this chapter, we will explore the changing contours of ethnic expression in football.

Ethnicity, football teams and spectator violence

Since colonial times, in Mauritius as elsewhere, football has been ethnically overdetermined, partly though the creation of separate white (British) teams and, due to the social divisions wrought through colonial policies of classifying indigenous populations, the subsequent formation of ethnically distinct local teams. This colonial hangover persisted in the form of social clubs – both colonial and indigenous – which provided a space for members of ethnic groups to mix and engage in leisure pursuits. The legacy of these private clubs has meant that until recently they had a large stake in the organization of Mauritian league football. In 1952, the inaugural First Division contained Muslim, Franco-Mauritian, Creole and Coloured teams and these were subsequently joined by Hindu and Tamil clubs. Until the 1980s, clubs routinely rejected players from other communities which coerced players into joining clubs of their own ethnic affiliation.

The exclusively white Franco-Mauritian Dodo Club, formed in 1928, had already left the league in 1978 after becoming a focus for discontent against Franco-Mauritians, but also, some argue, because they were aware of imminent legislation to decommunalize football. As it was stressed by a club member to Tim Edensor, 'the day we open our doors to blacks we are finished'. Their members continue to purvey the racist stereotypes about the attributes different ethnic groups bring to the game: 'football is not only about strength but also about organization and intelligence', a racist assumption which finds echoes in a contemporary context, as we will see. At the same time, the four best-supported clubs in Mauritius were also ethnically constituted. As teams that emerged from social clubs or occupational groupings, they became a forum for ethnic expression, and were supported, managed and owned almost exclusively by members of particular communities. Thus Fire Brigade represented the Creole community, and Tamil Cadets, Muslim Scouts and Hindu Cadets were clear in their allegiance to communal groupings. There were also Chinese (the Dragons) and 'Coloured' (Racing Club) clubs.

It was not until 1982, when renewed communal hostilities led to a wholesale rethink about the organization of Mauritian football, that the ethnic dimensions of the game were seriously challenged. The move towards regionalization in 1984 is part of the policy of the ruling party of that era, the Mouvement Militant Mauricien (MMM), to develop an anti-communal strategy which they called 'Mauritianism'. Indeed, this was the culmination of anxieties engendered by the suspension of football in 1956, 1964, 1969, and 1975 after violent communal disturbances, especially in games between the Hindu Cadets and the Muslim Scouts. Accordingly, it was decreed that football must be decommunalized. Communal names were disallowed and teams were obliged to recruit players from more than one community. Thus Tamil Cadets became Sunrise Flacq United. Muslim Scouts and Hindu Cadets were officially retitled the Scouts and the Cadets respectively. However, communal ownership of Fire Brigade, Scouts and Cadets persisted and irrespective of the ethnic composition of the team, the fan base remained much the same as before, the clubs remaining ethnic emblems for the supporters. Only Sunrise made more extensive efforts to decommunalize, establishing a more professional ethos and higher standard of play, and accordingly, they attracted a more diverse fan base, including those fans disillusioned with the divisive effects of communalism amongst Mauritians.

Despite government attempts to enforce decommunalization, the mobilisation of ethnicity around football did not diminish, and a catalogue of violent incidents have taken place since 1982 – battles between rival fans and with the police, damage to stadiums, assaults on referees, players and officials, pitch invasions. These without exception involved teams that retained a communal identity, namely the Scouts, Cadets, Fire Brigade and Sunrise, signifying a wider intensification of ethnic tensions across Mauritian society and culture. Such incidents were often generated by suspicions held about government biases towards and against particular communities, football serving as a theatrical setting in which to express such grievances. For instance, outrage at the perceived history of refereeing bias against Scouts, was believed to symbolize the systematic mistreatment of Muslims in Mauritius, and Scouts fans would argue that their treatment by the police during and before matches likewise mirrored wider political injustice. In addition, loss to bitter rivals could trigger anger directed against their own team or management who would be accused of humiliating not just the fans but the community they supposedly represented.

The expression of communal identity was further reinforced by the parading of particular clothing and banners, and the rituals of fans included ethnically based songs and chants against opposing teams and their supporters. In the football arena, ethnic insults were routine during the passions of the match, but these are largely considered unacceptable outside the stadium. Derogatory terms labelling Hindus '*malbars*', Muslims '*lascars*', and Creoles '*Mozambiken*' are considered beyond the pale in public life. Mauritian football then, has been a potent stage for ethnic expression, even hatred, where racist insults, religious zealotry and political protest have found an outlet. Such manifestations reveal the dangerous tensions that underlie social life and disabuse the myth of harmony that often masquerades under the pretence that Mauritius is a 'rainbow nation' or an excellent example of 'unity in diversity'.

Nevertheless, it is clear that such effusions of ethnic belonging were also contributing to ethnic distinctions, not merely reflecting them. Widely reported in the media, such events tapped into discourses which distinguish between groups, confirming commonsense ideas about the naturalness of ethnic boundaries, and countering more progressive notions about the values of negotiation and the search for Mauritian 'common denominators'. Football seemed to be turning into a realm in which the common stereotypes held by Mauritians about each other, about the virtues of their own community and the vices of other ethnic groups (Eriksen 1998: 55), were veering into something more recursive, less open to negotiation, and potentially destabilizing. By contributing to increasing communal mistrust, exacerbating ethnic tensions, providing an outlet for grievances and the articulation of crude stereotypes, football has helped to reconstitute a regressive expression of ethnicity which threatens any nation-building project.

The legacy of destruction, including damage to buses, stadiums and sugar cane fields, and injury to fans, reached its culmination on 23 May 1999, on the final day of the football season, when violence followed the decisive game in which Fire Brigade beat old rivals Scouts to claim the league title. The aftermath of the game included riot and destruction which culminated in the death of seven people in an arson attack on a casino in the Mauritian capital city, Port Louis. This proved to be the last straw for the football authorities and the government who promptly suspended organized sport throughout the country pending a radical overhaul of the constitution of Mauritian football (*Le Mauricien*, 24 May 1999; *5Plus Dimanche*, 30 May 1999).

Yet these incidents are part of a wider picture whereby renewed ethnic tensions erupted into serious communal riots in Mauritius in February 1999. These actions were principally directed by Creoles against police and governmental authorities in protest about their subordinate position in Mauritian society and the ethnic discrimination which has prevented them from achieving parity with other ethnic groups in areas such as education, employment and housing. Significantly, the revolts followed the death in police custody of a very popular seggae singer, Kaya, who was apparently the latest in a long sequence of Creole deaths at the hands of the police. The singer, who had been arrested for openly smoking hashish at a pro-legalization rally, was renowned for his synthesis of reggae and sega (seggae), a Creole form of percussive music and dance which has been adapted by the addition of contemporary Western pop instrumentation, guitars, drums and keyboards. This musical form is paradoxically a commodity enjoyed by Mauritians of all ethnicities, and a syncretic form of Creole ethnicity forged through the search for points of identification with other black African diasporic populations. We will return to this significant process of reconstituting ethnicity through globalization later.

The country was under curfew for several days, during which rioting produced large-scale damage to property and several deaths, and there were a number of perilous stand-offs between Creoles and Hindus. The air of unease following these disturbing events made any subsequent exacerbation of communal tensions highly undesirable. This tension, a stern rebuke to complacent illusions of communal harmony, has declined, but it makes the suspension of organized football understandable.

The regionalization of Mauritian football

Mauritius is administratively divided into 13 regions: Port Louis, Beau Bassin, Rose Hill, Quatre Bornes, Vacoas-Phoenix, Curepipe, Rivière Noire, Savanne, Flacq, Moka, Rivière du Rempart, Pamplemousses and Rodrigues. In the format laid down in the previous set-up, each region contained teams which participated in the three divisions of the Mauritian league according to the regulations of the Mauritian Football Association (MFA). However, these regional and local teams competed against the far more powerful ethnically based teams already identified. These elite clubs vastly outweighed the other clubs in financial terms and in levels of support, and they generally ensured that their interests were catered for by the policies adopted by the MFA. Yet this influence was overridden by a scheme which put forward the total regionalization of football; the new Sports Act of 1999 which has formed the basis for wholesale reorganization.

Until the cessation of football, only three stadiums were deemed suitable to stage Premier League games, none of which were the 'home' ground of any of the most popular teams. Consequently, for the best-supported clubs – those clubs with an ethnic basis – there was never any sense that they belonged to a particular place or region, and thus their ethnic affiliation could not be countered by a regionally based form of support. Now, however, committees will be established in all 13 regions to sponsor local teams, provide training facilities and build the necessary infrastructure, including new stadiums. Regional support will be difficult to attract if the previous lack of home grounds persists yet a degree of financial commitment is required to establish this new infrastructure. Moreover, the regions are uneven in terms of population and financial resources, which could lead to some teams being able to draw on a large pool of talented players, whereas others have far fewer players to call upon. This may create an unbalanced championship dominated by one or two teams.

First and foremost, clubs are no longer permitted to retain any ethnic name or symbol. The new sports act also stipulates that each sports club is obliged to 'admit its members and elect its managers in such a way that no person is disqualified or ineligible by reason of race, community, caste, creed, or colour'. Accordingly, many teams have merged with regional counterparts. Whilst the (Hindu) Cadets and (Muslim) Scouts remain social clubs, the Scouts are debarred from participating in football following the catalogue of violent incidents, and Cadets have been disinclined to join a league which disallows their communal identity.

To help minimize the chances of communalism re-emerging, the newly formed clubs must have teams which include no more than 25 per cent of players who reside outside the region. Certain clubs have challenged this and argue that they want to attract the best talent available in order to attain a higher and more professional standard of play. For instance, Olympique de Moka (formerly Sunrise) have attempted to attract players from elsewhere and house them in residential facilities in the Moka region – a costly policy, but one which depends on wealthy sponsors, and this may encourage other clubs to do likewise.

In addition to this club, the former bastion of Tamil support, becoming Olympique de Moka, Fire Brigade, symbolically the 'Creole club', have joined forces with Le Real, a small regional team, to form Pamplemousses SC. The new league also includes L'Association Sportive Port Louis 2000, L'Association Sportive de Rivière du Rempart', Grand Port FC, Rivière FC, Curepipe Starlight Sports Club, Faucon Flacq Sports Club, L'Association Sportive de Quatre Bornes, Maurice Espoir (which includes players from the Centre National de l'Ecole de Football), and L'Union Sportive of Beau Bassin. Thus far, the regions of Vacoas-Phoenix and Savanne are not represented by any team in the new league.

Although widely welcomed, not surprisingly, several team managers and fans of popular clubs strongly objected to the discontinuity in the historical constitution of football. For 'tradition' and history are fundamental constituents of club identity, reverently referred to and used by fans. The creation of entirely new teams and the erasure of those clubs with strong traditions will be difficult to achieve. As we have emphasized, most Mauritians continue to identify with the ethnic group to which they belong before expressing any regional affiliation or even national identity. It seems, therefore, that regionalization will not be adopted readily since communal allegiances will not be easily replaced by support for regional clubs. This is likely to cause the competitive edge formerly present in the league to diminish, and hence the standard of Mauritian football to decline. Already the new league seems beset by very poor attendance figures, and most matches are attended by fewer than 100 spectators, in contrast to the large gates present at games between the popular clubs (in fact, attendances had already decreased with restrictions placed upon numbers by police and football authorities, and by spectators staying away because of antagonistic communalism and the fear of violence). It may well take several years before Mauritian football retains its previous popularity. However, it is envisaged that the measures will eliminate the scourge of communalism from the game and remove the salience of ethnicity from football. The aims of the policy do indeed seem to have stimulated a circulation of players which is not determined by any ethnic allegiance, and so far there seems to be no sign of a re-emergence of clubs being associated with particular ethnic groups. Nevertheless, since high concentrations of particular ethnic groups characterize the population of certain regions, it remains a possibility that managers and players will be over-represented by these communities.

In the complex affective geographies of Mauritius, there are symbolic sites of ethnic allegiance – religious places, particular areas of habitation and historical landscapes. There are also places of national significance to which most Mauritians identify – such as the botanical gardens and racecourse. Yet there are few locations in this small island state that resonate with regional particularity. Whilst the pre-existing stadiums did occasionally serve as national sites when the national team played there or they hosted cup finals, they have never symbolized any regional allegiance. Possibly, any subsequent regional stadium-building programme has the potential to contribute to the development of a topology of regional belonging.

The increasing predominance of Creoles in Mauritian football

We have discussed above the profound association between football and ethnicity and the attempts that have been made to extinguish this link. However, although the insistence that Mauritian football must be regional and decommunalized might suggest that ethnicity in sport is disappearing, other issues are leading to a renewed awareness of the links between sport and ethnicity. As emphasized, ethnicity is a dynamic entity which is always in process, and likely to mutate. As old boundaries between ethnic groups become blurred, new ones are erected. In football, this reconfiguring of ethnicity is primarily constituted by the increasing predominance of Creole players amongst all league teams.

As we have described, teams were originally established in Mauritius around particular ethnic groups, and in the case of the Franco-Mauritian Dodos, Hindu Cadets, Tamil Cadets, Muslim Scouts and the Creole Fire Brigade, these clubs were emblematic of their community. Whilst Sunrise (formerly Tamil Cadets) made genuine attempts to decommunalize in their aim for higher professional standards, and the Dodos refused to consider any decommunalization and withdrew from competitive football, the other clubs made only cosmetic attempts to introduce a few players from other communities. And even latterly, the Scouts and Cadets clubs felt it was important to feature at least some players from the communities which made up the bulk of their support. Now, however, Hindu, Chinese, Tamil and Muslim players are rare in organized football, although there is widespread participation at village and less organized levels.

The tendency for Creoles to comprise the majority of players in all teams is not recent but has been an ongoing process since the 1970s, when players from other communities were far more prevalent in the league. Before the 1999 shutdown of organized football, Creoles made up at least eight of the eleven regular players in all teams, irrespective of the club's ostensible ethnic identity. Now, under the new regional structure, more than 90 per cent of all teams are made up of Creoles.

Although, as we have said, the 1984 changes did not alter the existing affiliation between certain football teams and ethnic groups, it nevertheless paved the way for any player to play in a team without necessarily sharing the ethnic affiliation of that team. Accordingly, whereas previously the intention was to feature teams comprising a majority of players from the ethnic group associated with the club, the competitive ethos of the league ensured that increasingly clubs sought the best players available in their quest for success. Consequently, the inclusion of players from outside the community clubs represented did not necessarily lead to disillusionment amongst fans if the team was successful. And this meant that there were increasing opportunities for players to find clubs irrespective of their ethnicity. Gradually, organized semi-professional football became a sphere in which Creoles started to predominate. Leading the way were the former Tamil Cadets club, Sunrise Flacq, who attempted to bring more professionalism in football. They attracted players by employing and accommodating them in one hotel, organizing regular training sessions and paying them to play football. For Creoles then, playing football became a way of earning one's living, but this was a strategy not shared by other ethnic groups. For instance, members of Indian ethnic groups have tended towards intellectual endeavour and the pursuit of a professional career.

Although a rather recent development, the fact that Creoles now form a large majority of players with the subsequent diminution of participants from other ethnic groups has reinforced racist ideas about the distribution of distinct ethnic qualities. It provides 'commonsense' evidence to support stereotypical notions about why Creole economic, political and educational underachievement persists: Creoles are good at sport but not academically inclined, and work less hard, putting greater emphasis on pleasure. The notion that Creoles live in an entrenched, present-time oriented culture, whereby there is no deferral of gratification, is of course easily grafted onto popular ideas about why they excel in the sphere of sport (and music and dance). In the same way, it is commonly believed that Hindus and Muslims succeed in business, 'Coloured' people do well in the media, Chinese excel in trade and Franco-Mauritians are the best farmers. There has been, therefore, a reinscription of ethnicity upon football which has served to confirm stereotypical views about ethnic attributes and characteristics. This must be understood as part of the ongoing reconstruction of ethnicity and its relation to wider economic, political, social and cultural changes. Such wider developments get mapped onto identities in a context in which ways of understanding self and others remains focused on ethnic distinction. Rather than confirming essentialist ideas about race and ethnicity, this highlights the ways in which ethnicity is a process of identification, both from within ethnic groups and from without.

Yet in the case of the Creole preponderance in football, rather than signifying sporting prowess, there is clear evidence that other employment avenues are blocked off, signifying a degree of social exclusion and economic marginalization. The educational progress (see Bunwaree 2001), unemployment rates and occupational profiles of Creoles are markedly inferior to comparative figures for Mauritians of Indian and Chinese descent. Indeed, an analysis of the socioeconomic background of Creole players reveals that most of them come from the underclass of this ethnic group.

This marginalization has emerged out of a particular historical context. Ever since their liberation from the harsh regime of the cane fields, most Creoles have avoided working in the sugar industry in which their ancestors were forced to work as slaves. The move towards working in marginal realms such as fishing has led to a tendency to work outside the formal economic system, which has meant that many Creoles occupy a position somewhat removed from the rest of Mauritian society. This has been partly exacerbated by the politics of ethnicity amongst Creoles, notably the fact that Creole 'leader' Sir Gaetan Duval, commonly referred to as 'King Creole', campaigned against the political independence of the country in the 1968 elections. After his lack of success in that election, he encouraged and helped many elite members of the Creole ethnic group to settle in Australia, Canada and other European countries, arguing that they would be severely disadvantaged in an independent Mauritius in which Indian ethnic groups would predominate. Moreover, there is a commonly held belief that the stereotypical cultural attributes of Creoles, specifically the idea that there is an 'easygoing' attitude to work, social responsibility and familial mores, was reconfirmed by Duval, who celebrated this relaxed disposition and spawned such attitudes amongst his supporters.

In addition, it has been charged that the dearth of educated Creoles following their emigration after independence has led to a lack of leaders amongst the community. This criticism also takes account of the fact that the key religious leaders of the Catholic Church, to which most Creoles belong, tend to be Franco-Mauritian clergy who have little interest in developing the social and economic ambitions of their flock. This assumed dependency, which reproduces the colonial relations between Franco-Mauritians and Creoles, has been argued to have held Creoles back from material and economic advancement, and is contrasted with the ways in which other ethnic groups have been able to mobilize their members through religious organizations to achieve political and economic goals.

However, the economic and social marginalization of the Creole community should not be exaggerated nor serve as a kind of functional explanation for the trend for football to be dominated by Creole players, for an underclass is identifiable across ethnic groups. In fact, there are a number of other reasons which contribute to the tendency of Creole youths to veer towards football, and likewise for other ethnic groups to retain an affection for the game whilst considering it unsuitable as a career.

The geographical distribution of ethnicity is partly responsible for determining the access players from different communities have to the necessary facilities for playing sport. Most Creoles live in residential areas known as '*cites*' in the urban regions of Mauritius, where sports facilities are available, in contrast to rural areas which lack such amenities, and also may not possess the transport whereby they can be reached. The playing of sport after work and school hours is thus curtailed. There have been attempts to overcome these obstacles amongst football fans from other ethnic groups. For instance, many Hindus, lamenting the dearth of Hindu players, notably in their 'own team' the Cadets, argued that the real reason for Creole predominance was the preferential treatment shown by the Ministry of Sport towards them, clearly evident in the distribution of sports scholarship schemes allegedly favouring Creole youths at the expense of Hindu talent. Immediately prior to the move towards regionalization, some Cadets fans were campaigning for the recommunalization of football, since they were concerned that the lack of Hindu players would cause a drastic decline in support. Accordingly, designs were wrought to develop coaching schemes solely devised for primarily rural players that could fit in with Hindu aspirations, lifestyles and patterns of family life.

Possibly most importantly, though, is the modes by which other ethnic groups have developed strategies for raising their status, and the ways in which these have become normative. Although of recent origin, such ethnically constituted strategies depend on support networks and are explained within discourses about ethnic differences. The economic growth of Mauritius since independence has been dramatic, and what writer V.S. Naipaul (1972) once referred to as an 'overcrowded barracoon', and decried for its squalid poverty, is now an esteemed example of economic success, classified as a 'middle-income' country. Whilst redistribution policies do not reflect this 'economic miracle' at all levels of society, certain individuals and groups have profited from the scale of this growth. Accordingly, the potential for economic advancement for many has led to a range of strategies which emphasize the acquisition of status. Primary amongst these has been the value placed on the education of one's children, and the significance of a range of career options which are believed to maximize economic opportunity. The importance of the cultural capital gained through a 'good' education is particularly important to the Indian Mauritians who have now established a network of contacts, tutors and teachers as well as an ideology which stresses educational achievement. The implications of the priority accorded to investing in education is that sport becomes relegated in importance. Like most Mauritian children, Hindu children finish school at 2.00 p.m. and yet thereafter the afternoon is taken up with supplementary private tuition, leaving little time to practise sport. The conventional belief has arisen that sport and education do not mix.

Creoles tend to be less economically able to buy into this extra-curricular education, and moreover are reluctant to condemn sport to such a subsidiary role. Often unable to compete in the educational field, they look for other occupational routes and alternative means to achieve status, football among them. We can see here the different ways in which ethnic groups are able to organize to represent their own interests and establish occupational and educational values, mobilizing ideas, institutions and networks in different ways. Ethnicity thus is dynamic in this instance: it emerges out of the divergent collective strategies to establish prominence in certain fields. So it is that occupational sectors in Mauritius continue to be dominated by specific ethnic groups. Where certain spheres of employment may now be more mixed than hitherto, others become subject to colonization by distinct groups. Football is one such sphere, formerly mixed, which has become dominated by one ethnic group as a result of interethnic competition within the Mauritian occupational structure as a whole.

The ethnic formation of identity must not be conceived of as fixed but as an ongoing process, whereby it is internally and externally contested and is subject to redrawing by using newly available cultural symbols and practices to assert new ways of belonging. There are signs in Mauritius that there are processes whereby areas of shared practice and meaning are being found between ethnic groups. Eriksen (1998: 103–36) cites the slight increase in mixed marriage, the common participation in political democracy, membership of trade unions, participation in the economic growth of the country and common celebration of economic growth. There are also cultural symbols which rather than being the property of particular communities are shared by most Mauritians, including the 'Father of the Nation', Sir Seewosagur Ramgoolam. Yet even apparently self-evident common denominators which are used by all sections of the Mauritian population are subject to contestation. Irrespective of its ubiquity, Kreol, the spoken lingua franca, cannot be accepted as the national tongue because of its association with the ethnic group implied by its name.

These battles over ethnicity then run alongside two versions of nationalism, a mosaic version constituted by ethnic diversity and a universalist version in which ethnic identities are transcended (Eriksen 1998: 144). Football exemplifies this well in that it has been both a forum for the parading of ethnic allegiances whilst constituting a shared focus for enthusiasm. Whilst the move to regionalization has foregrounded a non-ethnic Mauritian-ness, the predominance of Creole players in the game rekindles ethnic forms of identification.

To complicate the picture, global processes have fed into the dynamic (re)production of ethnicity, adding to the potential for the mobilization around common denominators but also offering the possibilities for renewed ethnic allegiances, constructed at greater scale. Global processes offer the delights of Western consumer capital, including renowned symbolic goods of the global marketplace such as soft drinks, cigarettes and fast food, as well as forms of information technology, media forms dominated by European and American newspaper and TV magnates, Hollywood cinema and Anglo-American pop music. As Hannerz (1990) has argued, globalization also produces forms of cosmopolitanism and renewed localisms, forms of resistance to the effects of global flows. In Mauritius, such cosmopolitans attempt to transcend the particularisms of ethnicity by proffering models of less recursive forms of identity and lifestyle, but cosmopolitanism is also evident in the lifestyles and tastes of the young who are drawn to fashionable Western popular culture. Yet these forms of cultural reaching out are countered by defensive reactions amongst those who perceive such developments as threatening Mauritian – or more usually, ethnic – identities. As Appadurai (1990) has pointed out, global flows of people, technologies, ideas, information, images and money are marked by disjunctures – they flow unevenly, impacting upon some places with powerful consequences whilst bypassing others. Thus, in Mauritius, many Indo-Mauritians have increasingly looked to India for their cultural practices, consuming Bollywood movies, pop music and clothing, as well as certain forms of religious fundamentalisms that have emerged from India. So for instance, sega, formerly understood as a shared *Mauritian* musical form, has faced competition from Bollywood soundtracks amongst Indo-Mauritians.

In the context of football, globalization is manifest by the huge, passionate support for English football teams, now far more fervent in expression than the diminishing support for local teams. Yet the Mauritian following for teams such as Arsenal, Liverpool and Manchester United is not shaped according to ethnic allegiance but transcends such adherence. Perhaps this is an example of what we might term 'everyday' or 'popular' cosmopolitanism, which depends on complex media systems to inculcate interest in products and cultural forms from far away. Yet in a notorious incident in 1996, a faction of Mauritian Muslims cheered on Egyptian club side Zamalek in an African Club Champions Cup game against Sunrise, the Mauritian champions, and likewise lent support to the Egyptian Under-23 side in an African Nations fixture against their Mauritian counterparts. Clearly providing evidence of identity construction at a global scale, such forms of allegiance undercut any national sense of identity. Growing familiarity with football as a global game also feeds into these ethnically aware practices. We might suggest that the lack of Indian players at an international level, particularly in the ubiquitous English Premier League, means that there is a dearth of role models for young Indo-Mauritians to emulate. On the other hand, for Creoles there are a host of famous black players from the top teams who can serve as exemplars.

Not only has league football been affected by the ethnic conflicts – and now the lack of allegiance felt for the new clubs – but the disappearance of support for Mauritian club teams is matched by the decline in spectator numbers for international matches. This is often explained as resulting from the Creole dominance, with occasionally only one other player from another ethnic group being selected to represent the country. It is argued by some that a 'representative' team should be selected in which all ethnic groups feature, irrespective of ability, so that it would appeal to all fans.

Throughout this chapter, we have attempted to highlight the ways in which football, traditionally an important signifier of ethnicity and a realm for ethnic expression, is part of the changing configuration of ethnicity and identity in Mauritius. Ethnicity becomes mapped onto processes of social, political, economic and cultural change, and recoded in the process. Certain processes are acting to decentre ethnic particularisms, but the power of ethnic allegiance in a Mauritian context means that new modes of expression form as others are curtailed, new boundaries are erected as others tumble.

8
Chasing the Ghosts: Narratives of Football and Nation in Morocco

Gareth Stanton

In his Arabic-language survey of the history of Moroccan football, the Moroccan journalist and writer, Hussein Hayani, notes that the first professional Moroccan player was called Buona. Mysteriously, however, Hayani was unable to find out which team he played in or what city he was from (Hayani 1992). Nobody in the country knew of the footballer's background. The life of Buona appears like something ephemeral. He has left only a trace, there exists nothing to give substance to his being. It is as if he was a ghost. This chapter searches for the ghost in a process intended to help us come to a better understanding of the role of football in Moroccan society and enable us to understand some of the political dimensions of the game from a historical perspective.

In some senses, football represents a certain democratic tendency in Moroccan civil society, albeit ghostly and repressed. In an account of his time spent as a political prisoner in the mid-1970s in one of Morocco's most harsh jails, the central prison in Kenitra, Jamal Benomar, a young student activist, describes one sign of a liberalization in general conditions at the time:

> From 3 o'clock and until 6 o'clock, there occurred the second historical event: for the first time, and after many battles with the prison administration, we – the political prisoners – won the right to have a television set, though only occasionally, for an important football match.[1]

After independence from the French in 1956 the Moroccan monarch, King Hassan II, who succeeded his father Mohammed V in 1961, had attempted to impose his own will upon the kingdom that nineteenth-century Europe had often known as 'Barbary'. Hassan's harsh autocratic rule and the blatant clientism and corruption it fostered met with popular resistance from many quarters but notably from members of left-wing secular parties and certain ethnic groups who felt they were being marginalized from power. By 1971 the strains in the system had become so extreme that certain sections of the military attempted a full-scale putsch. The King narrowly avoided death and acted swiftly to execute many of the officers involved. In the midst of this repression, football stood for a form of liberty.

There still today remains, however, a certain fear of football and the popular forces that it is capable of unleashing within society. Read the words of a Moroccan academic who published an account of giving up his car for financial reasons and then having to take the bus through the more, as the French might say, 'popular' (i.e. poor) districts of south-west Rabat. He documented this experience in his book *Carnets du Bus*:[2]

> [T]he city's big football stadium is next to the neighbourhood. Match days are days of huge flux. It's like a controlled explosion from the districts of the south-west. To the stadium and back the walk has the feel of a great diffuse insurrection, without reason or explanation. The smallest incident might set off an explosion. The young take the route to the stadium in small groups or bands. The caretakers are vigilant on match days and everybody who owns something is on the lookout. (Saaf 1999: 28, my translation)[3]

This fear of the popular crowd, its volubility and instability, is not particular to Morocco, but the way in which football had been manipulated in the country is of special interest.

Since mass tourism began to develop into its modern form in the late 1950s and early 1960s Moroccans have increasingly been exposed to the manias of other nations for sport (see Urry 1990). Anybody taking a holiday in the exotic location of Morocco in the 1960s and 1970s could not help but be impressed by the ardent dedication with which young men on beaches applied themselves to football. The game played an important part in the very definition of what it was to be Moroccan in the modern world and has been a focus of both nationalist agitation and a tool through which modern Moroccan identity has linked to the person of the king and of the monarchy more generally.[4] The Moroccan national team has a proud history performing on the world stage. It was the first African side that had *qualified* for the World Cup, in Mexico in 1970. In the 1986 World Cup, also in Mexico, they were the first side from the continent to progress to the second round. I shall not be discussing these successes here; rather, I want to explore the way in which soccer knits together contemporary Moroccan identity and the pitfalls of the close identification that Morocco has with its national sport. These are pressing enquiries for the simple reason that great political changes have been taking place in the country since the mid-1990s. The death of King Hassan II[5] in 1999 and the reforms he instituted saw an opening up of the Moroccan body politic. One needs in what follows to interrogate and understand the position of football in this new landscape.

From Tangier to Rabat: travelling south

During the 40 days of mourning demanded by Islam as a mark of respect for the dead, in this case of King Hassan II of Morocco, I asked at the well-known Librairie des Colonnes in Tangier if there were any books on Moroccan football. I received a kindly response. One, perhaps two, had been published, the assistant thought. But they were not available. Instead I purchased a copy of Moroccan novelist Driss Chraïbi's autobiography, *Vu, lu, entendu* (1998).[6] His 1981 novel, *Une enquête au pays*, features a police character, Inspector Ali, rescued from a life of poverty by 'the beautiful game', i.e. football. Ali, the child of rural migrants to the city, is saved from a life of petty crime on the streets by his footballing abilities. A career as a 'thunderous striker' for the Nehdad Settat club of the city of Settat brings him to the attention of the police force which he joins and where he slowly moves up through the ranks. In the later autobiographical book, Chraïbi recalls memories of football when in 1947 American forces were digging up the wastelands of Casablanca where 'the unemployed urchins had the habit of devoting themselves to their passion for football' (p. 147, my translation). Already in 1947 then, the dispossessed were expressing their hopes on any available space with a round ball.[7]

The Morocco edition of the young traveller's companion, the *Rough Guide*,[8] makes a similar point in respect of contemporary Morocco's young footballers. Playing on such waste-grounds develops a certain style which the guide tells us is likened to the Brazilian playing style epitomized by an absence of long balls – as nobody has any kit, identifying teammates over any distance is problematic – in such circumstances short balls or selfish dribbling make for more sensible and safer football. I pondered what all the guidebook detail really meant, reflecting on Roland Barthes' (1973) own dissection of the travel book genre.[9] Now the guides talk of meeting actual people, the Morocco *Lonely Planet*[10] guide proclaims that every visitor will almost certainly have at least one opportunity to eat in a real Moroccan household. Individuals in their individuality are what this new tourist discourse foregrounds, an offshoot of the 'authenticity' sought after by the modern traveller (see MacCannell 1976). The old Fodor[11] guide (1981) to Morocco used to announce that venturing into the Medina (old city) of Tangier could be a painful experience for those who do not expect harassment. The new-style guides do not ignore the problems of hustlers, but indicate that any genuine traveller should be able to find coping strategies quickly and use the guide to help them gauge what they can handle.

For the first time in this city I allowed myself to fall in with a guide.[12] Ali took me around and showed me the 'Berber market' and much else beside. He rushed through the various sites regarded as 'of interest' and recited snippets of history, but really he was only going through the motions. The city was dead now, he said, and even the Mediterranean cruise ships no longer stopped here. He had worked as a barman in the 1950s when the city was full of Europeans, but now he was older he was a regular visitor to the mosque. His children were migrants to be found in France and Belgium, but he remained here. He hired a cab to take me out of the city over the hills covered with the villas of the verminous drug dealers and criminals who, in his opinion, now ran everything in this overcrowded city. He overstated his case, but that is not to deny the opulent evidence of corruption. He told how, in recent memory, a local criminal had been asked by police to make a substantial contribution to the diminished coffers of a Tangier football team rather than a more straightforward bribe – corrupt policemen love football too.

On our return to the city we passed the prison. 'Seven star hotel,' said Ali with a smile, 'free board and lodging', but the city, he claimed, had turned against him, while the monarchy and the government was against the city.[13] The politicians in the capital lined their own pockets and nothing was left for Tangier. The world too was against the town and the tourists no longer came in any numbers. The glamour was now gone. It was all political, he said, even the fact that Tangier's leading local football club, Ittihad Tangier FC, was no longer amongst the best of the Moroccan clubs.[14] As he overcharged me by a blinding sum for the taxi I could only agree with him.

In Rabat, I asked for books on Moroccan football at one of its best-known French-language bookshops. I got one of those looks that suggests that books on such trivial matters were not sold there. The stock on some of the shelves looked old; the climate had played its part, but some books do sit for a long time. No case of sale or return here. None the less, after rummaging below the general displays, a volume was located. Thirty dirhams (around £3) in 1989 when it was published, it remained so.

Inaccessible to the shop's computerized stocktaking system, it had no barcode and required manual entry on the till. The book itself was falling apart – the spine long cracked and individual pages breaking loose at the slightest handling. The grey marks on the once pristine paper indicated not the years on the shelf so much as the number of pairs of hands that had picked it up. The book, the helpful assistant stated, talked a little of football. Its title was *Krimau: je suis comme ça!*[15] and told the story of a footballer called Abdelkrim Merry. The fans came to know him as Krimau. I bought the book, but the assistant seemed somewhat bemused by my enquiries into football.

Nearby on Avenue Allal Ben Abdellah stands Aalam al Fikr, an Arabic bookshop. 'Are there any books on Moroccan football in the shop?', I asked. 'No.' 'Are there any books on Moroccan football at all?' 'There are', he stated, 'but only in Arabic.' He showed no inclination to elaborate or to share any knowledge. Not out of some disgust of the common, but rather as a defence of something still sacred. Finally, he relented, producing a hugely expensive volume. At 200 dirhams, (approximately £20) Hussein Hayani's *Al-Rayatha al-Maghrebia* (*Moroccan Sport*) (1992) represented a considerable investment, out of the reach of most local football fans. In countries where we are constantly bombarded by commercial football ephemera it is perhaps refreshing to be confronted by such an absence. Is this simply a reflection of the absence of ready cash on the part of the fans? Or are we looking at processes of 'identification' which differ from our expectations and are not typically mediated by such trappings of commercial culture? What can we say of popular memory in a country with such a demographic profile, heavily weighted in favour of youth?

People on the move: travelling north

On the same day as my book-shopping trip, Morocco's most read newspaper, *Le Matin du Sahara*, carried various match reports from the English Premiership, the German Bundesliga, the Belgian Jupiler League, and the Italian Serie A. Authorless and ghostly, the urgent presence of the match report denied an author. I thought of Krimau's biography – so new, yet already so old. On how many shelves can it be found? In how many libraries?

Krimau became the first Moroccan football export in the modern period,[16] but Morocco has long exported human beings to Europe. Just as European tourists flooded south in search of the exotic from the 1960s, trails of Moroccans have made the journey north seeking work. This less heralded form of movement takes even harsher forms now. On 26 August 1999 *L'Opinion*, a Casablanca-published paper, noted recent interceptions of clandestine migrants to Europe. Ten kilometres out to sea east of Melilla on Morocco's Mediterranean coast, nine *'candidats à l'émigration clandestine'* (an expression encountered so frequently it achieves a significant distance from the reality of what it actually expresses, 'candidates for clandestine emigration') were stopped by the Moroccan Royal Marines. That was on the Sunday. The next day, another group of Royal Marines stopped a boat to the south-east of Melilla and ten migrants were stopped, nine Senegalese and a Mauritanian national – all without papers. The July–August (no. 18) issue of the enterprising Tangier magazine *D3* carried a piece of imagined reportage written by François Trotet entitled 'Passage' – it featured a story of two journalists embarking on this perilous crossing which, as in the story, so often ends in death.[17]

The export of footballers, however, does not necessitate such dire measures and has itself become a growth industry of late. And not just to the European mainland. In England alone, Southampton, Coventry, Aston Villa and Fulham have signed Moroccan players in recent years, although there has been some swapping around. Indeed, in 1999, there were febrile mutterings in Morocco about the imminent signing of the Moroccan national captain Noureddine Naybet by Manchester United. In the 2001–02 season Tahar El-Khalej was playing for Southampton. Aston Villa were fielding Moustapha Hadji and Hassan Kachloul, while at Coventry fans could watch the two Youssefs, Safri and Chippo.[18] Further north, the stands at Aberdeen have been enlivened by fez-wearing supporters paying tribute to their club's Moroccan signings, Hicham Zerouali and Rachid Belabed.[19]

The main story in the day's papers, however, is the reaffirmation of allegiance given to the 'Sultan du Maroc' (a significant expression, given Hassan's adoption of the title 'King' back in the 1960s, to signify the modernity of his reign) by the Ahl Maâ El Aïnine, a tribal grouping from the deep south. This had also been announced the day before in *Le Matin du Sahara* which at first sight somewhat bizarrely carried a large announcement on page 7 conveying the most sad and profound condolences of Dr Lâarbi Habza and the staff of La Pharmacie Alaswak in Laayoune on the death of the king. Why should such an advert be significant and what might it have to do with football? The answer lies in the aspirations of Hassan II and the search for a cause that would further galvanize the people of Morocco behind his reign. That came in 1975 when the Spanish withdrew from the Western Sahara. Hassan orchestrated a huge civilian march into the territory, the 'Green March', which made Morocco's territorial claims clear and generated huge popular nationalistic support amongst Moroccans. They did not reckon, however, with the original inhabitants, the Sahrawis, who had fought the Spanish as the Polisario[20] and would wage war in turn against the Moroccans. For a long time there has been talk of a referendum. But slowly the area has been filled with Moroccans from the north of the country, encouraged to move south to tip the demographic balance against the Sahrawis and make the result of any referendum increasingly difficult to interpret. The allegience of the Ahl Maâ El Aïnine is of far greater import than that of the doctor and his staff in the chemistry of the new provincial capital, but the latter represents the Laayoune of migrants and the territorial ambitions of the late king and here, now, in the midst of the desert is a 30,000-seat stadium, as the *Rough Guide* notes, with real grass. Indeed, as journalist Hassan Benadad has noted, football has become the king of sports in the disputed region, with the top club Jeunesse Sportive Al Massira, based in Laayoune, challenging at the highest levels.

The formal structure of the message of allegiance brought by Cheikh Maâ Al Aïnine is the other side of two modalities at work here, both the need to meld the nation through building of stadiums financed by the state and the atavistic remembrance of the threat posed in the past by such groups (as Ibn Khaldoun, the great muslim sociologist of the Middle Ages, recognized long ago, it is ragged tribes from the desert that have displaced urban rulers in the north, softened by decadent urban living). Flying in the face of such historical evidence, the Ahl Maâ El Aïnine affirm the allegiance that has always existed between the Sahara and the Sultans of Morocco. The mutual alliance of monarchy and people is further evidenced by the lead sports story. Hicham El Guerrouj's brilliant victory in the 1500 metres in the World Athletics Championship in Seville is announced with the banner headline *'Félicitations royales pour El Guerrouj'*. The new king had been quick to send his congratulations to this superb athlete and his solemn face stares out from the page, linked forever to that of the celebrating athlete. Let us return, however, to an excavation of the past of Moroccan football in the shape of French journalist Thierry Niemen's biography of Krimau.

Krimau in Corsica

Exploring the biographical homage which is the lot of world sport, I want to tease out from Krimau's biography some of the peculiarities of this particular example of the hagiographer's art. There is a preface from the 'black pearl' himself, star Moroccan footballer Larbi Ben Mbarek. He played football in a pre-independence age – in France, Spain, Sweden, Germany and elsewhere. The notes to the biography tell us that he was born in Casablanca in 1914, but he, like Ibn Khaldoun's desert hordes, was originally from the south, Tata in his case. In the seasons 1934–35 and 1935–36 he played for Club Ideal, created by Marcel Cerdan, the pride of French middleweight boxing.[21] He was picked for the Moroccan national side in the latter season. In 1937, he signed for USM (United Sport Meknes). In that year he played again in the national side which beat France 4–2 in a famous match.[22] He played in France and Spain, finishing his professional career in the 1955–56 season with Olympic Marseilles. He went on to work as the manager of the Algerian side Sidi Bel Abbes[23] before managing a number of Moroccan sides, including the national side in the 1961–62 season. The 'pearl' chooses the preface to 'pay tribute to the old players: Abderrahmane, Kadmiri, Madani, Kacem-Kacimi, Benaissa, Karroum'. All these names, he suggests, are better known in foreign parts. It's the ghosts again: 'It's a problem of information that must be sorted out by putting the journalists in touch with the past', he writes (p. 10).[24]

As for Krimau, his life passes into hagiography along familiar lines, like Mbarek, another black 'child of the desert'.[25] But the fifth child of Lahcen Merry, Abdelkrim, was in fact born in Casablanca (January 1955), in the 'popular quarter' of the Medina. The biographer expounds on the multiple wives of the father, the large number of children, the father's strictness and adherence to Islam. No one dared cross the father, although rare moments of leisure were to be snatched in the streets (with *'le ballon rond'*). This is a rags-to-riches football life, with a Moroccan inflection. The first event of importance in his young life was the journey of the nine-year-old to the site of his parents' birth, tracing one of the tourist routes towards the Sahara – to Rissani[26] and Erfoud, after which the road slowly disappears, 'defeated by the desert'. There, beyond this spot, his parents were born. Here young Krimau received his first shock. The child discovered that 'immensity' rhymes with 'beauty': 'His roots were here, amongst the dunes, under the unpitying sun' (p. 13).

Here the father spoke to the son as a man for the first time: 'Aim high, but never forget your roots' (p. 14). Twenty years later, the man, now mature and familiar with glory and success, recalled that journey still. The holidays had to end, however, and the young footballer asked at a family gathering why they had to return to Casablanca. The grandfather replied, that in the village, Erfoud, the people were resigned and fatalist, but his father was ambitious and wanted to make it in the biggest town of the country.[27] The return was miserable; suddenly the cramped spaces of the Medina 'contrasted cruelly' with the spaces of the desert, but at least he knew where he came from now.

One point which is made in the biography is the importance of the arrival of television in Morocco and the Merry household in 1970. This was also the year that Krimau signed as a junior for the Casa side Asptt before moving on to Esperance of Casa and then to Rapc (both of Casa).[28] In those early days he was playing in defensive positions despite the fact that in later life he would be known for his attacking flair. This flexibility, what Krimau terms 'polyvalance', is something owed to the *'football de quartier'*. It was also 1970 that saw Africa admitted to the World Cup for the first time, via qualifying stages. Morocco was to represent the continent. The West Germans were to defeat England in the quarter-finals, but the first game of their qualifying group against Morocco came as a shock when the Moroccan side went 1–0 up. One member of this team, Petchou, ended his playing career at the Saudi Arabian club Wahada of Mecca. He died of cancer in 1980 and his body was transported back to Casablanca[29] where it was buried in front of a huge crowd in the Cemetery of the Martyrs. The years following this first showing on the World Cup stage were disappointing ones for Morocco, with a number of defeats. The national side needed to reform from the ground up. In the search for new players Krimau was discovered by one of the national junior coaches and found himself in the line-up for the 1974 international junior championship at Bastia in Corsica. The Moroccan side won the tournament with a crushing 4–0 defeat of England and victory against a West German side. Krimau, then wearing the number 10 shirt, was the hero of the tournament. Following his performance the management of Sporting Etoile Club Bastia flew out to Morocco in order to sign the young Krimau. His European journey began. He was the first Moroccan in modern times to play in Europe. In the eighteenth- and nineteenth-century accounts of North Africa the inhabitants are often referred to as Moors. Bastia play in blue and the club badge features (dubiously perhaps, for modern tastes) the stylized head of a Moor. In the words of the biography, Krimau became a *'bleu aux tête du maure'*, a 'blue with the head of a Moor'.

In an exclusive interview reported in one of the Moroccan papers on 28–29 August 1999 (in the final days of official mourning) there was an interview with a Moroccan national, Adbelhafid Rahmani, who was on trial for his life in Orlando, USA. He had killed his wife and her lover in a 'crime of passion'. Before his death the king had personally sent $60,000 in order for him to conduct his defence. It struck me that it was a strange monarch that made such a gesture, but then things are different in the

Moroccan context and this sort of real involvement as opposed to more symbolic gestures is part and parcel of one side of the way in which Morocco has been run since independence.

If a writer such as Driss Chraïbi represents one sort of life trajectory in modern Morocco, then Krimau can stand for another. If both ended up in Europe, their journeys were very different. Chraïbi is self-assured, a product of 'high culture', even if his version of 'culture' does extend to crime-writing and football. Chraïbi is in thrall to a certain 'ideal' of Morocco, epitomized in the sensuous cuisine of Imperial Fez, but he has little time for its rulers. Krimau displays an equally vital sense of being Moroccan, but for him this is linked to the person of the king and comes across clearly in the chapter of the biography entitled *'Notre Premier Supporter'*. Talking of King Hassan II, it begins thus:

> He is our chief supporter. We feel that he is so close to us it is like having a twelfth man on the pitch. In Mexico in 1986 we were in telephone contact with him both before and after the match. His support for us was infinitely precious. (p. 185)

As Krimau is keen to attest, every time something has been required to be done for the sport the king has been there. Despite residence overseas, questions of identity have never troubled Krimau:

> I left Morocco in 1974 and France has become my second home. But I've never forgotten my origins. Wear the shirt of your country, it's a privilege and a responsibility.[30]

He goes on to state how there is extra motivation to believe that 'the king is there, near to us ... He is the link that unites us all across the seas and continents' (p. 187). On page 164 of Krimau's biography we get a further insight into the relationship fostered by the Royal Family with football. Photographed to the left of Krimau in a national team photograph are the 'two princes', who, like their father before them, have always supported and been very attentive to the development of football in the country.

What then is this relationship between royalty, nationalism and football? Stéphane Bernard's monumental study *The Franco-Moroccan Conflict 1943–1956* (1968), has nothing to say about sport, let alone football, but the book I purchased in Aalam al Fikr, Hayani's *Al-Rayatha al-Maghrebia*, reveals some tantalizing snippits concerning the way in which the king had involved himself in sport from the earliest days.

Wydad had been founded as a Casablanca swimming club in 1937, but it had increased its activities to include other sports such as basketball and football. The heir actively sponsored the Wydad football team and it is clear that in many respects this was a substitute for out-and-out nationalist activity and many of those behind the club were of a nationalist persuasion. It has been said that the heir was as busy with the results of Wydad as with any other national issue. He requested that the French authorities keep the team provided with phone lines so that he could call them. And he would – calling the players, especially at half-time, to remind them of their responsibilities towards their homeland and the monarchy. He would hold receptions for the players at his palace in Rabat and present the players with gifts and bonuses. Wydad had great success in the early 1950s both in Morocco and across French North Africa. Wydad remains among the most powerful presences in Moroccan football and the club makes much of its association with the nationalist struggle.[31] The origins of the club actually stem from what might be called 'banal' forms of exclusion during the Protectorate period in the country. Along the Atlantic coast of Casablanca, up from the staggeringly huge Hassan II mosque (completed in 1993, by public subscription), one can still see the remains of seafront swimming pools that were part of the recreational focus of colonialists during the Protectorate period. Moroccans were allowed to join the clubs that ran these pools in the mid-1930s, but when their numbers reached a certain level European fears led to a backlash and Moroccans were expelled. It was in this context that the idea was hatched for the creation of a Moroccan club. Following initial setbacks Wydad was created after the intervention of Resident General Nogues who approved the club as long as it was secular, non-political and anti-racist (seats on the committee were to be reserved for French members!). The statutes of the club were of a general nature, allowing for the creation of a football section in 1939. For club historians, Wydad was the incarnation of Moroccan resistance to the Protectorate and in this early period operated as an unofficial national side, channelling resistance to the French despite prohibitions on 'political activities'.

Interestingly, it was not only Hassan who recognized the political implications of football's political possibilities. Moroccan journalist Hassan Benadad has written about the footballing interests of the new socialist Prime Minister, Abderrahmane Youssoufi, leader of the USFP (Union Socialiste des Forces Populaires) and long-term opponent of the monarchy. Youssoufi too, back in the 1940s and 1950s, was treating the great game as a cover for nationalist agitation. Youssoufi, in Benadad's account,[32] fled Tangier in 1944.[33] He fetched up in Casablanca and, like

Chraïbi at the same time, took note of the huge enthusiasm for football of the town's youth. Working as a teacher and attempting to organize resistance cells amongst the workers, he realized that through football he could win young converts to the nationalist cause. A great number of youngsters thereby came into contact with the message of nationalism through football, an area that the French authorities at the time never imagined could be used to such ends. With the coming of the Second World War, however, the colonial authorities suspended the leagues and the Moroccan clubs stopped their activities. After the war, however, Youssoufi was involved in another initiative. With the banishing of Mohammed V, the throne and the national struggle had become associated in the popular mind and the Fête du Trône[34] became a day of national resistance. It was Youssoufi who argued that a *Coupe du Trône* be inaugurated to commence annually on the same day. He continued the political struggle and involvement in football in the 1950s, the environment in which today's two big clubs Wydad and Raja evolved. Raja, too, was formed as a consequence of the national struggle. The Casablanca district of Derb Sultane was home to a number of clubs in the 1940s. In 1949, the teams Mansour Dahbi, Fath and Abdelmoumen joined together under the name Raja in order to unite both footballing energies and nationalist zeal.

Morocco gained its independence in 1956, but Hassan kept up his association with football. In 1959 the magazine *Maroc-Football* was launched. The opening issue contained a message from the prince:

> It is with sincere joy that I salute the appearance of this revue. For my part, I think that it will have a great and warranted success among the popular masses because it reflects all the problems, all the questions and, above all, all the perspectives of Moroccans interested in sport ... (cited in Hayani 1992: 45).

The contemporary period

In the postcolonial period, interest in sport, and football in particular, has been spirited, but despite their achievements in the two Mexico World Cups the record of the national side has not been as exalted as the Moroccan population's expectations. They won the African Nations Cup in Addis Ababa in 1976 but it was ten more years until their appearance in Mexico in 1986. There were great expectations when a 1–0 victory over Zambia at Casablanca gained them a place for USA '94, but the campaign dissolved in acrimony and they lost all their group matches, including a 2–1 defeat at the hands of Saudia Arabia. While some fingers were pointed at players for apparent lack of commitment, it was a general failure of organization that led to their speedy departure from the tournament.

Many commentators, such as *Maroc Hebdo International*'s football writer, Hassan Benadad, are very critical of the Moroccan footballing authorities in print and argue that Moroccan football is caught between false amateurism and psuedo-professionalism. Sponsorship has proved difficult to find. Indeed, only the most privileged clubs tend to benefit from such arrangements and there is an increasingly large gap between the footballing haves and the have-nots (mirroring the more general social reality). It was such difficulties, along with a fallow period for the national team culminating in the poor performance in the USA World Cup in 1994, that led to a shake-up in the structure of Moroccan football and the appointment by the king of a no-nonsense military man, General Housni Benslimane, to head a *Comité provisoire*. The fallow period between 1988, when Morocco hosted the African Nations Cup, and failed to impress,[35] and the World Cup of 1994, was attributed to the poor running of the Fédération Royale Marocaine de Football (FRMF).

It was the General who was responsible for the development and delivery of TV exposure for Moroccan football. This was represented by a deal struck with the French communications group Darmond. In tandem with then newly appointed French coach Henri Michel, Moroccan football hopes were lifted once more and by the time they qualified for France '98, commentators were once more placing the 'Lions of the Atlas' on the highest rungs of world football.

At the domestic level, however, the televising of matches resulted in a drain on actual gate receipts at matches and for the small clubs revenues declined to dangerous levels and were not being recuperated through the TV deal, the details of which were far from transparent and seemed to benefit Darmond rather more than might have been expected had the deal been negotiated with some financial acumen on behalf of the Moroccan footballing authorities.

After four years of reviewing the situation the FRMF came up with a series of proposals to improve the game (see *Le Matin du Sahara et du Maghreb*, 2 December 1999). None the less, after a disappointing showing in the African Nations Cup in 2000 when they were eliminated in the group stage, *Le Matin du Sahara* (4 Febuary 2000) was talking of starting again and getting rid of the old structures of the game in the country. Michel, who had been hired personally by King Hassan II, has since been shown the door subsequent to this performance. He was replaced by the

Pole, Henri Kasperczak, who lasted only six months and was himself replaced by the Portuguese coach Humberto Coelho. When Morocco failed to qualify for the 2002 World Cup, Coelho too looked set to be relieved of his responsibilities until the new king intervened. Morocco was in the running to host the 2002 World Cup, but the death of Hassan had drained the energy from the campaign. On the domestic front the Moroccan First Division is to be professionalized in 2003 and reduced from 16 to 12 clubs. It is hoped that this move will help to nurture talent and feed through into national performances.

Hayani begins his book with a tale that could have been penned by the Argentinian writer Jorge Luis Borges. He tells of the existence of a book from the Moroccan town of Taza dating from the seventeenth century, *Al Mkhtasar al-Fared (Short-cut to the Unique)*. The author, one Sheik Znoof al-Tazi, discusses the rules of football. But, as Hayani ruefully points out, none of the rules mentioned in the book were practised at the time in Europe and because of this it would seem likely that the book was 'invented for a purpose'. In the Moroccan case it is tempting to argue that football itself was invented for a purpose – that of building a modern state and providing a unifying force which identifies a people with its rulers. However, the stakes are high in such a strategy for failure breeds discontent, but there is no turning back. Morocco is bidding to host the 2006 African Nations Cup and will bid once more to host the World Cup in 2010. This time there is the distinct possibility of success. Then the ghosts of the Moroccan game might return and receive their proper recognition.

Acknowledgements

I would like to thank Gary Armstrong for inviting me to contribute to this volume. Versions of this chapter have been aired at a staff seminar in my own department at Goldsmiths College, at the Birmingham Crossroads in Cultural Studies 2000 conference and at the British Academy symposium 'Travel and Nation' held in London in July 2000. My thanks to the organizers of these events and to Joke Hermes and John Hutnyk in particular. I would also like to thank Khalid Hmeid for his translations. I'm grateful for financial support from Goldsmiths College. Finally, thanks to the staff at the British Council in Rabat for their assistance.

Notes

1. Jamal Benomar to Joyce Edling, in Edling (1996: 127).
2. The full title of his book translates as *Bus Notebooks: An Essay on Daily Life in the Neighbourhoods of South-West Rabat*.

3. Echoes are apparent here of Victorian fears of the masses in Britain. See, most notably, Matthew Arnold's *Culture and Anarchy* (1869).
4. Football and national identity have been usefully explored in great detail in the Latin American context by Mason (1995) and Archetti (1999). See also Armstrong and Giulianotti (1998).
5. As noted, King Hassan II ascended to the throne in 1961, on the death of his father Mohammed V. Parliamentary reforms in 1996 and local and national elections in 1997 were indications of moves in the direction of greater democracy and saw the leader of the opposition USFP (Union Socialiste des Forces Populaires), Abderrahamane Youssoufi, appointed as Prime Minister. Critical accounts of Hassan's rule can be found in Waterbury (1970) and Perrault (1990).
6. Chraïbi was among the first Moroccans to be given a French education. He went to France to pursue studies in chemistry. Here he composed his first novel *Le passé simple* (1954); many more were to follow. He remained resident in France.
7. The quotation reminded me of Archetti's description of the *pibes* in Argentina. He wrote of how aspects of Argentinian play could be traced back to the kids ('*pibes*') who learned their football in the empty and uneven urban spaces known in Argentina as '*potreros*'. Archetti writes 'In the *potreros*, with so many other players in such a confined space, the only way to keep control of the ball for some time was by becoming an inveterate dribbler' (Archetti 1999: 180).
8. *Rough Guides* were started in London in the early 1980s by Mark Ellingham who saw that there was a gap in the market for guides for younger travellers on a small budget. In two decades it has become something of a publishing phenomenon and an integral part of the luggage of many tourists. The Morocco guide was one of the earliest and, according to the publishers, is the one that excites the most correspondence, due, they suspect, to the challenge posed by the country.
9. He was discussing the *Hachette World Guides*, known in French as *Guide Bleu*. Barthes noted that this genre of guide has little to do with people, 'the human life of the country disappears to the exclusive benefit of its monuments' (1973: 74–5).
10. *Lonely Planet* is another series of guide books for the budget traveller. Started by Tony and Maureen Wheeler in 1973, it is now a global industry producing over 400 guides.
11. Fodor is an American company, producing guides for a more affluent market than that targeted by the likes of *Lonely Planet* and *Rough Guides*.
12. For an indication of the role of the guide in Orientalist travel literature, see Stanton (1988).
13. There is a long and complex history of tribal insurrection in Morocco, even into the Independence period (see Gellner 1962). The tribesmen of the Rif mountains, the range to the south-east of Tangier, have a reputation as fierce fighters. As a result of famine and economic dislocation many Riffis migrated to coastal towns such as Tangier. Some indications of the state of the regional economy in the contemporary period can be found in Boraki (2001).
14. His pessimism on this point was overblown. The team does now play in Morocco's first division.

15. Krimau's biography, *Krimau: 'I am Like That'*, was ghosted by a French journailst, Thierry Niemen (Niemen 1989), but the salient details covering Moroccan footballing history had been provided by Belaid Bouimid, sports writer for the left-wing daily *Al Bayane*. The book itself was published in 1989, which meant it had been standing on the shelf for ten years. More importantly, in a footballing context, it was published by a Casablanca publishing house, Eddif. In 1988 the managing director of this concern, Abdelkader Retani, became the director of one of the most successful Moroccan club sides of the 1990s, Raja of Casablanca.

16. For a point of comparison, see Archetti's account of the export of 'sporting bodies' (Archetti 1999).

17. For a more detailed analysis see Vermeren (2002).

18. Of these five, El-Khalej, Hadji and Chippo were part of Morocco's 1998 World Cup squad.

19. Belabed is slightly exceptional in that he was actually born in Belgium, to Moroccan parents.

20. A shortened form of Frente Popular para la Liberacíon de Saguia El-Hamra y Rio de Oro.

21. Cerdan was the son of a Casablanca butcher, but of French descent. Described by Jake LaMotta 'as the greatest boxer ever to come out of Europe', he was equally well known for his liaison with the French singer Edith Piaf. Cf. *Observer Sport Monthly* (20 December 2001): 6–7.

22. Which in its significance we might compare with the first home defeat of the English cricket team by a touring West Indian side.

23. In his influential book *The Black Atlantic*, sociologist Paul Gilroy (1993) describes the movement and circulation of black bodies between Europe, the West Indies and the Americas. Ben Mbarek's criss-crossing of the Mediterranean might hint at a 'black Mediterranean' equivalent.

24. The world wide web is changing these things, but even the web master for the site The Atlas Lions Forum (<www.theatlaslions.com>) suggests that Ben Mbarek deserves to be kept alive in the memories of Moroccan football fans. Visitors to the site are referred to the Athletico Madrid website at <www.at-madrid.es/espanol/historia/leyendas/index.html>. The name of the national side derives from the range of mountains known as the Atlas mountains, where lions once roamed.

25. The journey has something in common with Ibn Khaldoun's political formulations and their more recent codification in the work of Gellner (1981) in his 'pendulum theory of Islam' which restates the line that urban political power in Islamic history is constantly being displaced by stricter adherents of Islam emerging from the desert, but themselves being softened by urban life and, in their turn, being displaced by further pretenders from the desert. Were he still alive, Gellner might argue that the pendulum action has been frozen by Western interference. The theme of the child of the desert has also had literary resonances of late, notably in the work of French novelist Michel Tournier and his book *La goutte d'or* (1985) and Moroccan writer Tahar Ben Jelloun's novel *L'enfant du sable* (1985).

26. *'Avec ses ksour'* ('with its castles'), notes the biographer, echoing the language of the guidebooks.

27. In the most brilliant piece of ethnographic writing on Morocco in the last decade, Pandolfo (1997) reflects on another aspect of the movement north from the desert regions when she talks of the arrogance of the young men who dig the traditional irrigation wells in the south (often 'blacks') and handle dynamite without fear, sometimes blowing themselves up – or those who put on city shoes and jeans and head north to work on the building sites of Casa, high on the scaffolding.

28. As one of the continent's largest cities Casablanca has many football clubs. The three top-flight clubs are Racing Casablanca, Raja Casablanca and Wydad Casablanca.

29. Susan Ossman's otherwise fascinating account of modern Casablanca, *Picturing Casablanca* (1994), contains no reference to the big Casa clubs. In fact, her sole reference to football manages to place a World Cup in 1988 (cf. p. 77).

30. Krimau's remarks need some updating in relation to the current situation in France. Silverstein (2000) provides a good starting point.

31. See the club website, <www.wydad.com>.

32. This article can be consulted at <www.maroc-hebdo.press.ma/SiteArchives309/Une%20passion.html>.

33. This is somewhat curious in that Tangier then had the status of an international city and was the site of a great deal of nationalist plotting against the French Protectorate. Cf. Landau (1952).

34. A widely celebrated secular holiday in Morocco.

35. They topped their group, but went out to Cameroon 1–0 in the semi-finals. They lost the third-place play-off to Algeria on penalties.

Part Three
Off the Ball Movements

9
France in the Cameroonian Football Imagination

Bea Vidacs

The Indomitable Lions of Cameroon are one of the best known and most successful national football teams of Africa. In 1990 they surprised and delighted the world by reaching the quarter-finals of the World Cup in Italy – the first African country ever to do so – and in 2000 in Sydney, Australia, they enthralled millions of television viewers when they won the football Olympic gold. As a result of these exploits players such as Roger Milla, Thomas Nkono, Joseph-Antoine Bell, François Omam Biyick, and more recently Patrick Mboma and Carlos Kameni, became household names amongst millions of football lovers. The Lions have also won the African Nations championship three times in 1984, 1988 and 2000.

Cameroon, a small Central African country, has an unusually varied colonial history. It was first colonized by the Germans in 1884, but following the First World War, when Germany lost its colonies, the country became a League of Nations Mandate jointly administered by France and England. The division was not equal; the larger Eastern part was under French rule and the smaller Western part was administered by the British. The legacy of the duality of British and French rule remains to this day. In addition to having a large number of ethnic groups and languages the country is divided along the lines of the colonial legacy of English and French language use. The preponderance of Francophones over Anglophones, as well as the fact that France maintains a much closer relationship (in political, economic and cultural terms) with its former colonies than does Britain ensures that the relationship to France is the determinant one (cf. Mazrui and Tidy 1984).

France granted independence to Cameroon in 1960, but in fact Cameroonians, led by the Union des Populations Camerounaises (UPC), waged a bloody struggle against the French beginning in the late 1950s which was ultimately unsuccessful.[1] The fact that independence came about more at the will of the French and with many compromises made

169

in their favour created a sense that it is less than complete and undermined the legitimacy of subsequent governments in the eyes of many Cameroonians (cf. Bayart 1985; Mbembe 1986). Opposition to France is thus never far from people's minds, all the more so as Cameroon's largely unpopular governments are seen to be propped up by the French. On the surface, however, France is projected by the official propaganda of the Cameroonian government and by the French themselves, as the 'mother country', suggestive as it is of somehow being a benefactor of Cameroon (and of its other former colonies).

Much has been written about this closeness between France and its former colonies. In part it is due to differences in the colonizing styles of the French and the British. The former were more committed to imparting their cultural values to the peoples colonized than the latter. In the present, this is also a question of France's wish to maintain the primacy of the French language, '*la francophonie*' (a hegemonic quest if there ever was one, to counterbalance the spread of the influence of the English language, and American culture). Jean-François Bayart also argues that this closeness, or as he calls it 'inter-continental cultural sociability' (1993: 197), plays an important role in the creation of 'postcolonial historic blocs', which successfully dominate African politics. This may well be true on the level of elites, and apart from the very real sense of cultural connections it may also bear the stamp of realism and pragmatism.[2] However, on the level of the 'little people', as Bayart refers to them, opposition to the French is never far from the surface, and football appears to be one of the areas where this otherwise submerged dislike surfaces.

Football's symbolic nature makes multiple interpretations possible. Among others it can be seen to crystallize national as well as ethnic identity and sentiments, and can be and has been analysed as an instrument of political control as well as of political resistance (cf. Armstrong and Giulianotti 1998). This analysis attempts to illustrate how football allows Cameroonians to express their latent and not so latent anti-(neo)colonialist, anti-French feelings. Most of what has been written by social scientists about the relationship of the colonized and colonizers in relation to sport concentrates on the colonial period (Baker 1987; Fair 1997b; Martin 1995; Ranger 1987; Stuart 1996). These authors by and large see sports as an area where Africans could challenge the status quo of the colonial order by appropriating the imported organizational forms and by aspiring to beat the colonizers at their own game while at the same time forging new identities for themselves. But in fact due to the pervasive effects of colonization and the continuing neocolonial ties that still bind former colonized peoples to their erstwhile masters in the 'postcolonial' period, the relationship continues while acquiring new twists.

While this chapter focuses on how the events of the 1998 World Cup brought to the surface anti-French sentiments among Cameroonians and reinforced their negative views of France, I have shown elsewhere (Vidacs 1998) that during the 1994 World Cup when the Cameroonian squad did not do well, one of the targets of Cameroonian ire was the French coach of the national side. It was not merely that people criticized the choice of a foreign coach to lead the Indomitable Lions, but the fact that it was a Frenchman irked many because many people interpreted it as a clear indicator of the survival of ties to France, in effect a continuation of colonialism. Others went further and constructed a conspiracy theory arguing that Henri Michel, the French coach of the national team, was a 'special agent' of France, sent to prevent the Indomitable Lions from passing to the second round. This was seen as quite plausible given that France could not even qualify for the 1994 World Cup; proponents of this view thought it was illusory for Cameroonians to think that the French coach 'in his heart of hearts' could really wish for the Cameroonian team to succeed. Though this conspiracy theory may have been, in part, an attempt to look for scapegoats, it was also a profound expression of how Cameroonians see the French and their relationship to them. It expressed not only their condemnation of the close relationship their government maintains with France, which props up the unpopular political regime, but more deeply it was also about seeing the French as essentially unwilling to let go of their colonial habit of domination, going so far as to actively prevent (though obviously by what exact means this was done is not clear) the Cameroonians from advancing. It also reflected the Cameroonian perception of the French as wishing to demonstrate that Cameroonians, and by extension Africans, could not aspire to those heights where the French, and by extension Europeans and whites, rightfully belonged.

The significance of France as the venue of the 1998 World Cup

It should not be surprising that the fact that the 1998 World Cup took place in France was especially significant to Cameroonians even before the event. A Francophone university professor told me in 1995 that for him it was essential that Cameroon should qualify for the 1998 World Cup because it was going to be a unique historical moment for the country to play against France, the erstwhile colonizer. As it happened Cameroon was eliminated after the first round under circumstances which were highly irregular (cf. Vidacs forthcoming). None the less, similar attitudes were echoed by people from all walks of life during the entire competition and manifested themselves in special attention paid to the matches France played. The wish that France be defeated by any opponent was oft-repeated throughout the event. In what follows I will examine the ways in which Cameroonian anti-colonial attitudes to France were played out and how Cameroonians, at least on a symbolic and rhetorical level, managed to wrest the victory from France.

These anti-colonial sentiments should not be seen as rooted exclusively in the past, nor even in the neocolonial constellation of things in Cameroon, but as responses to the events of the present; in this case, to what took place at the World Cup. Analysis needs to examine a number of contexts, like concentric circles, which, taken together, elicit the responses I describe below. If we think of the matches played by France as the centre then the matches in which France played no part are the first of the concentric circles. The performances and the treatment of Cameroon and other African countries can be seen as the second circle as perceptions of these also influenced how the French performance and the entire World Cup was evaluated. These impressions were also influenced by the commentary of Canal+, the French cable television company which broadcast the matches to Africa. Beyond the immediacy of the World Cup as an event – but as we shall see, closely related to it – is what Cameroonians perceive of France today, in particular the way immigrants are treated and the influence and electoral appeal of France's extreme right-wing politician Jean-Marie Le Pen, leader of the Front Nationale (FN) party. Outside these spheres of reference lies the history of Cameroonian–French relationships, which leads Cameroonians to see France as an ungrateful recipient towards the people whose exploitation led to its greatness. It is within these expanding circles that the attitudes and explanations described in what follows must be understood.

The general characteristics of the 1998 World Cup for Cameroonians

The general impression of most people in Cameroon was that there was biased refereeing against Third World teams in general and African teams in particular throughout the World Cup. This view was reinforced by what seemed to be an overwhelming number of red cards given to Third World teams for less than obvious infractions. Among these, naturally, the highly controversial refereeing decisions made in the Cameroon v. Chile match had a special significance for Cameroonians. In addition to expelling two Cameroonian players the referee refused – for no obvious reason – a crucial goal which would have allowed Cameroon to advance to the second round. This provoked anti-white riots in Yaoundé and Douala after the match (cf. Vidacs forthcoming). The elimination of Morocco due to the awarding of a controversial penalty to Norway against Brazil on the same day also reinforced the perception of anti-African bias (cf. Dauncey and Hare 1999).

Only Nigeria of the five participating African countries made it to the second round. In general, this perceived bias was explained as being due to a fear of 'outsiders' among the powers-that-be of world football, which forced the latter to resort to 'dirty tricks' to protect *their* interest in maintaining the footballing status quo, i.e. the domination of European and a few Latin American teams, especially Brazil. In seeking to find explanations for this bias Cameroonians drew upon two further issues. One was the change in the leadership of FIFA, the governing body of world football, just prior to the beginning of the competition; and the other, closely related to it, was the issue of the number of places allotted to Africa in the competition.[3] In early June 1998 Joseph (Sepp) Blatter was elected as the new President of FIFA, replacing João Havelange who had dominated the world football body for 24 years. This surprised many commentators, as Lennart Johansson, the head of UEFA (Union of European Football Associations), seemed to be the favourite candidate immediately prior to the elections. In fact, John Sugden and Alan Tomlinson (1998), British academics who had studied FIFA, as good as predicted Johansson's election in their work. As they clearly demonstrate, African countries and the African Football Confederation (Confédération Africaine de Football – CAF) represent an important voting bloc in FIFA, therefore whoever they support has a good chance of winning such an election. One of the cornerstones of their argument for their prediction was that Johansson had been supportive of Issa Hayatou (the Cameroonian president of CAF) who waged a long battle within FIFA to secure more places in the final phase of the competition for African countries. In the event, however, the African countries were split and Blatter was elected.

Thus – to some extent extrapolating from their experience of politics in their own country – as they were watching the unfolding of the World Cup, Cameroonians wondered aloud whether the distribution of red cards and the favouritism shown towards European teams was not a reflection of Blatter's 'revenge' towards those countries whose delegates voted against him in the elections, or alternately whether the early elimination of African countries did not have to do with a wish on the part of FIFA/Blatter to revert to having fewer African teams in the final phase of the competition, thus maintaining a European monopoly on the game.

The World Cup through French lenses: hegemony and subversion

I watched most of the matches of the 1998 World Cup in one of two bars. One was a large popular place attracting an audience consisting predominantly of poor people (mostly men). The other was more upmarket and expensive, in the administrative centre of town. Here the audience was largely made up of civil servants (again mostly men), often formally dressed. In both places commentary flew freely on all aspects of the game, including the broadcasting.

We may add to the list of injustices the nature of the commentary on Canal+, the French chain broadcasting the matches to Africa. Cameroonian TV had its own broadcast of the World Cup with bilingual French and English commentary, but for a variety of reasons most people preferred to watch the French broadcast.[4]

Watching the World Cup on Canal+ was an unsettling experience. The French commentators wholeheartedly and unashamedly praised their own team, even when at the beginning of the competition the 'Blues' (as the French team is familiarly called) faced teams that were rather weak or at least less likely to win. It should be said that this kind of unbridled nationalism is nothing new in sports broadcasting, and certainly not limited to the French, but what was discomforting about this was the fact that they were broadcasting to an international audience which was likely to have loyalties elsewhere (cf. Blain et al. 1993), and there did not seem to be any acknowledgement of this in the coverage. It was as if the commentators expected everyone to share in their admiration of the French team.

There were instances when the associated programming was in bad taste, if not downright racist, as, for example, in two sketches where two Cameroonian players in a pre-match light entertainment were seen demonstrating the 'wake up call *à la française*', and the 'wake up call *à la camerounaise*'. In the first sketch, upon hearing the alarm the two players jump up immediately and run to wash and get ready, whereas in the second one they turn over and continue to sleep!

The not so latent racism of the commentators was also evident during matches. For example, when Nigeria defeated Bulgaria the French commentators explained Nigerian superiority by arguing that it was very hot in Paris and the heat favoured the Africans. Most of the players on the Nigerian team play in Europe and thus are as used to or unused to the heat as the Bulgarians. An older man, sitting a few places away from me, also noted the partiality of the statement and, using me as a reference point, exclaimed with feeling: 'The heat! They are only looking for excuses, always excuses, they can't accept it that Africans can beat them. During the summer it's hot there too, isn't it? Madame, in Greece it is 40 degrees – hotter than in Africa!'

The overwhelming majority of Cameroonians wanted France to be beaten. After the wish that Cameroon should meet France, the second choice expressed by many was that Nigeria, standing as proxy for the whole of Africa, should encounter and beat France. Beyond that the majority of the population supported whomever was France's adversary.

The matches of France through Cameroonian lenses

Naturally the opposition to France was most evident in the response during the matches the French team played. Apart from rooting against France the tenor of these comments also tell us about the larger concerns of Cameroonians, such as their perception of inconsistency in refereeing decisions and how they fitted into a broader discourse about the relationship of Cameroon and France.

Saudi Arabia v. France

The Saudi Arabia–France match took place the day after Cameroon lost to Italy, and one of its defenders (Raymond Kalla) received a red card, which many Cameroonians considered terribly harsh. This perceived injustice influenced Cameroonians' reactions to what happened in the Saudi Arabia–France match. After about ten minutes of play the referee expelled a Saudi player for an infraction that was less than clear – supposedly for tackling from behind. My companion, a coach who is something of a free thinker and also an upholder of the rules, said to me in great disgust that 'This World Cup is no good. It's not worth it.' Obviously others were of the same opinion because following the expulsion of the Saudi player, every time there was an action where they took the ball away from the French, people started to mockingly shout 'Red! Red!', sarcastically urging to the referee to dismiss more Saudi players. Furthermore, the spectators in the bar expressed their general sentiment by clapping ferociously when the French failed to score. The impression of biased refereeing was not lessened by the expulsion towards the end of the match of the French team's star player and playmaker, Zinedine Zidane. Despite the French broadcasters' boasts to the contrary, many people I spoke to also insisted that France was in a rather weak group for the first round, some going so far as to suggest that the draw for determining these groups had been rigged to favour France.

France v. Italy

The first really serious opponent the French team faced was Italy in the quarter-finals. The match was one of the most tense of the World Cup. The bar where I watched the game (the more popular of the two) was full to capacity with 80 people, which was double the regular crowd. Everyone seemed to be supporting Italy. After 90 minutes the game ended in a goalless draw. The match went to extra time and eventually was decided by penalty kicks, which France won. People left quietly and very disappointed. On the street I crossed paths with a young stranger, who asked me whom I had supported. When I answered 'Italy' he replied with great feeling: 'We were together!' This sense of *communitas* (cf. Turner 1969) that emerged through opposition to the French speaks volumes to how football unites people, and how easily anti-French sentiment, despite or perhaps because of the close ties with France, can come to the surface at the slightest provocation.

France v. Croatia

The semi-final saw France face Croatia. The latter were the surprise team of the World Cup, having beaten Germany in a dramatic game. I saw this match in the smaller of the two bars, but even here, where some of the lower echelons of the state bureaucracy congregated, the mood was decidedly anti-French. When the French conceded fouls there were comments calling attention to the arbitrariness of the distribution of cards by the referee. Seconds into the second half Croatia scored and everyone cheered. Half a minute later when the French equalized, only three people cheered. One of those cheering was a man, who exclaimed that 'Now there is match!' His remark indicated that to him it was the spectacle rather than the anti-colonial political agenda that counted. When Laurent Blanc, one of the French players, received a red card, there was jubilation. Suddenly the French were in disarray. A viewer exclaimed: 'Come on, you are not the first ones [to play at a numerical disadvantage]! We have played eight against fifteen!' Amid general laughter he explained, 'Against eleven Chileans and the centre judge, and the [two] linesmen and even against the fourth referee who is now there!' This was of course a reference to Cameroon's above-mentioned match against Chile, where two Lions were expelled and the refereeing was seen as completely biased.

The speaker actually made a mistake, because Cameroon played with nine and not eight players, but the hyperbole only heightened the effect.

When France won 2–1, people were subdued. One person said with equanimity: 'Brazil is going to cure that.' Another exclaimed: 'Brazil is going to correct the French!' This was in anticipation of France's next and last match in the finals of the World Cup, against Brazil, the acknowledged best team in the world.

Scrutinizing the ethnic composition of the French team

During the match against Croatia, a portly gentleman in suit and tie remarked that 'France's best goalkeeper is on the bench because he is black.' He was talking about Bernard Lama. Scrutinizing the ethnic composition of the French team seemed to be a favourite pastime for Cameroonians. I have heard remarks on other occasions as well, asking what kind of French team this was when all the players were foreigners. Indeed many of France's players bear the stamp of France's colonial past: Lilian Thuram is of Guadeloupean origin; Christian Karembeu is a Kanak from New Caledonia; and Zinedine Zidane, the star of the French team, is the son of Algerian Kabyle immigrants.[5] During this particular match someone remarked that there were no French players on the team, to which somebody else replied that no, there were some, and started enumerating them. The portly gentleman interrupted and said 'Oh, they are Germans, as they are bordering on Germany, the people of Strasbourg!' By hyperbolically denying the presence of any 'French' players in the national team he was playing with the notion of divisions within France that have nothing to do with race. When France won the match with two goals by Lilian Thuram, this fact did not go unnoticed and was cause for jubilation. Even though people wanted France to lose, if that was not to be at least France should win through a representative of the very people whom the French wish to eliminate from the competition, and, according to the French far-right propaganda, from France itself.

Cameroonians take vicarious pleasure in the fact that 'foreigners' (naturally they have to be nationals of France in order to qualify for the team) play such a prominent role in French football. Some of this is the triumph felt by the underdogs, who are aware that France, through stringent immigration laws, is forever trying to prevent them from migrating there, and that there is racism and discrimination against foreigners and especially Africans. Nobody in Cameroon is ignorant of the progress of the extreme right in France, and Jean-Marie Le Pen's political career is watched with care.

This scrutiny is not limited to ordinary people. It is reflected in the Cameroonian newspapers as well. The front page of *La Nouvelle Expression* (no. 387, 10 July 1998), one of the two most important opposition newspapers in the country, carried Thuram's photo with the caption 'Lilian Thuram, the Guadeloupean who qualified France'. Inside the paper two articles discussed the paradoxes of the composition of the French team and French racism. One was entitled 'The Black Heroes of a Racist France', the other 'Blues, Whites and Blacks' (Kala-Lobe 1998a, 1998b). In addition there was an article about immigrants in Paris, the title quoting one of the interviewees: 'God has chosen Thuram to speak to the French' while the subtitle was 'Ingratitude' (Mvie 1998). Another typical response was that after the final, when France had won the World Cup, the headline of *Le Messager*, Cameroon's other widely read French-language opposition paper, was 'Africa Saves France', and the caption under the headline again played with the nickname of the French team and the French tricolour, referring to them as the 'Blues-Whites-Blacks' (no. 787, 13 July 1998). The article draws a parallel between African participation in the liberation of France during the Second World War and the role of Africans in this victory (Tocke 1998). Underlying this emphasis on the presence of black players on the French team is the sentiment that France would be nowhere without the very people who are otherwise looked upon with disdain by large parts of the French electorate. In many ways these are concretized instances of a much broader argument that the wealth of France is due to France's colonial past.

The ethnic composition of their team also raised eyebrows in France. Previously in 1996 Jean-Marie Le Pen objected to the number of 'foreigners' on the national team (cf. Marks 1999). When Thuram's ability helped France to victory against Croatia, his ethnic and racial background did not escape French notice either, and it was reported to me that according to the press review of Radio France International one French journal carried the headline: 'France–Croatia 2–1, France–Le Pen 2–0'.[6] From what I saw of the eventual celebration of victory in the World Cup, notwithstanding the less than sensitive coverage that Canal+ provided, the French media did present the event as a cause for celebrating multi-culturalism.[7]

It is evident from reports in the French media of the World Cup that the French themselves were not at all certain of their victory and that it came as not only a great surprise but also as a source of great relief. This was due partly to French self-doubt about France's chances of doing well in the tournament. The uncertainty may explain in part the boasting evident in the commentary of Canal+; rather than a sign of strength it could be seen as an attempt to bolster a fragile French self-confidence. It is an interesting question as to how and why this aspect of the French discourse about the World Cup did not make it to Cameroon. While on the one hand the Cameroonians were turning Le Pen's arguments upside down by calling attention to the multiracial and multiethnic nature of the team, they also insisted that the French should both be grateful for and acknowledge the contributions of 'foreigners'. Yet when Le Pen's French enemies celebrated the victory as a coup for the racial inclusiveness in France, such a sentiment was ignored in the most part, especially in popular commentaries. In an insightful paper about South African township football Grant Farred argues that the working-class coloured community of Cape Town could overlook the racism evident in English football when identifying with English clubs, because these details were 'lost in the process of cultural translation' (1999: 77). In the same way some of what was significant in the World Cup victory for France was also lost in translation to Cameroonians. As Cameroonians attempted to make sense of what they saw happening in the tournament they disregarded those aspects of the question that were irrelevant to them. The details that fill in the gaps left by the loss reflect their own concerns.

Give us the honour and we'll give you the money

The final of the World Cup produced an interesting discourse which again highlighted the anti-French sentiments of Cameroonians, but at the same time exhibited a certain kind of accommodation to the realities of life. Within a day of the French semi-final victory against Croatia, people in taxis, bars and alongside football pitches were convinced that a French victory was a foregone conclusion.

I heard one of the fullest expositions of this view in a taxi. The argument was that France had bought the match from Brazil. The French had gone to the Brazilians and said: 'You have had the honour four times. Give us the honour and we'll give you the money.' When I hazarded that the Brazilians might not wish to forgo the honour the answer was immediate: they are a Third World country, they are poor, they cannot but accept the money. I tested this view on as many people as I could. Most were convinced that this was the case, and this included one of Cameroon's foremost intellectuals. He went so far as to call me the day after the final to explain that he was right; that you only had to look at the 'purposeful' misses of the Brazilian team, the bad positioning of the players, etc. He even suggested that the fact that France's victory celebrations, including signs, banners and fireworks, were already in place clearly indicated that they knew in advance that they were going to win.[8]

There were some exceptions to this view. One of them was my friend the coach, who, being a devoted football buff, and a coach, found it impossible to credit that any team in the world, and especially the Brazilians, would 'throw' a match. He also added that there were enormous financial interests behind the Brazilian team and they did not need France's money to benefit financially from the World Cup. Another person said that he could not believe it because the Brazilians could not do such a thing to all the poor people in Brazil who had been putting aside their money for four years (since the last World Cup) in order to go and see their team win the World Cup in France. One of Cameroon's eminent opposition figures and intellectuals found fault with the argument, not on the merits of whether Brazil would or would not sell the match – he is one of the few people I know in Cameroon who professes to have no interest whatsoever in the game – but rather with the framing of the whole issue. Upon hearing the rumour he wondered aloud whether this meant that Cameroonians thought their own team would do so in a similar position, and then queried the notion that Brazil should even be considered a Third World country in the same way as Cameroon.

There is a certain kind of logic to these assumptions. In part they follow from the observation made throughout the competition that the World Cup seemed to be going against Third World peoples. Therefore the idea that whites in general, and the French in particular, would do anything to win the competition was already well rooted. As people's wish that France be beaten and drop out of the competition failed to materialize, the only possible explanation that remained was that France would win by cheating, and thus not really win. Also, as was suggested above by the noted opposition figure, this particular explanation would be readily comprehensible in a country from which Jean-François Bayart could borrow the expression 'politics of the belly', to characterize the entire continent.[9] Money will get most Cameroonians out of trouble, and their identification of Brazil as a Third World country made the assumption perfectly plausible while at the same time denying France the glory that it had strived for.

France v. Brazil, the final

The World Cup final between France and Brazil did nothing to allay these feelings. Not only did France win 3–0, but it looked as if the Brazilian team was not even there, thus confirming in Cameroon what everybody already knew. When it was disclosed that Ronaldo, Brazil's star player, who had not played too well throughout the competition and was unrecognizable in this game, had suffered a mysterious seizure only hours before kick-off, this 'rational' explanation came too late to change the conviction shared by so many Cameroonians that France had 'taken' but not 'won' this World Cup.

As metaphor, football serves in part to explain social reality but, like a folk tale, it also improves on that reality, symbolically setting the world to right. Faced with the seeming inevitability of a French victory, Cameroonians were quick to work out an explanatory system which, although it acknowledged the French victory, at the same time denied its legitimacy and strengthened the general view that France deserves the disdain of Cameroonians.

Notes

1. Founded in 1948, the UPC was in the forefront of the Cameroonian nationalist, anti-colonial struggle. Its most important objectives were independence from France and reunification with British Cameroons. In 1955 it was banned by the French colonial administration. After its banning the UPC went underground and waged a guerrilla war against the French. Reuben Um Nyobe, the leader of the movement, was killed in unclear circumstances in 1958. Following his death the guerrilla struggle continued and was bloodily suppressed by the French and later by Ahmadou Ahidjo's independent Cameroonian government (cf. Joseph 1977; Mbembe 1986).
2. An example of this proximity between France's and Cameroon's ruling elite could be heard from Gervais Mendo Zé, the director of CRTV (Cameroon Radio and Television). In the opening ceremony of the World Cup broadcast on Cameroonian TV in a quasi-religious ceremony where French- and English-speaking priests prayed for the success of the Lions, he also asked that France, as the organizing country, be especially blessed. He also declared on national radio that he supported France and Cameroon in equal measure, a comment which upset quite a few people.
3. Until 1982 Africa only had one place in the World Cup final and even that was shared with Asia. From 1982 there were two and this remained in effect until 1994 when, in no small part due to Cameroon's stellar performance in 1990, Africa was allotted three places which was enlarged to five in 1998.
4. One reason given was that there were technical hitches on Cameroonian TV, at least at the beginning of the World Cup. For example, there was considerable delay between sound and picture. Some people explained to me that they preferred the French broadcasts because of the quality of the commentary. There were often famous non-participating football players commenting on the game, and during breaks and after matches the French broadcasters had greater access to coaches and FIFA officials and other experts for quick commentary.
5. In fact 13 out of the 22 players originated from countries other than France, including Armenia, Ghana, Guyana, Italy, Tunisia and Spain amongst others (cf. Marks 1999: 52–3).
6. I am indebted to André Ntonfo for calling my attention to this in a personal communication.

7. It is also clear from Western coverage of the 1998 World Cup that some of the French public as well as commentators considered the victory to be of tremendous importance in combating the National Front. As Mignon comments: 'The celebrations of 12 July were indeed a symbol of a call for unity precisely because that unity is far from real. The multi-racial nature of the French national team exemplified a diversity which is not accepted by everyone, in particular not by those for whom the experience of life is not one of successful integration, but the experience of the difficulties young people have, whether "white", "black" or *beurs*, in integrating themselves in society' (Mignon 1999: 96). A similar appreciation of the unusual nature and importance of the effects of a victory by a multiracial team on French consciousness is expressed by Lucy McKeever in the same volume: 'It is hard to conceive the following eulogy to multi-racial France appearing in *Le Figaro* [which she characterizes as a right-wing paper] before or since: "What would we be without our ethnic communities? Thank you to our overseas territories, thank you Africa, and thank you Kabylia"' (McKeever 1999: 163).

8. The host country often wins the competition. Whether this is due to some kind of favouritism or to the well known advantage that home teams have on all levels of competition is open to debate. However, suspicions of partiality among referees in World Cup competitions is not limited to Cameroonians. François Thébaud (1998), a veteran French sports journalist, analysing the decisions of referees throughout the history of the World Cup, suggests that many times the results of past World Cups were dictated by politics with the collusion of referees. Thus he cites as a clear case of favouritism the quarter-final match of the 1934 World Cup where Italy, the eventual winner, was pitted against Spain, and the Swiss referee allowed seven Spaniards to be injured without penalizing the Italians. He was afterwards recalled to Switzerland and banned from refereeing. Thébaud also sees the same pattern in the 1954 World Cup where Hungary, then the best national team of the world, was beaten in the final by West Germany. In the author's analysis this was the result of a Cold War political necessity to make sure that a communist country did not win, and at the same time led to the first public recognition of West Germany since the ending of the Second World War, significantly followed by Germany's admission into NATO in the same year, as a final act of that country's postwar political rehabilitation. Interestingly, this explanation did not gain currency in Hungary. Most likely this is because it would have benefited the communist regime, to which by and large all Hungarians were opposed at the time, and thus it would have sounded like official propaganda to them. In fact, the loss gave rise to the first open expression of popular dissatisfaction with the regime (cf. Handler 1994).

9. The expression 'politics of the belly' refers to the intertwining of wealth and political power in Cameroon and elsewhere in Africa. A person who receives political office is seen to have access to wealth and is expected to deliver some of this wealth to his constituency. Bayart warns, however, that this is not merely a question of corruption. 'The expression … must be understood in the totality of its meaning. It refers not just to the "belly" but also to "politics." This "African way of politics" furthermore suggests an ethic which is more complicated than that of lucre. A man of power who is able to amass and redistribute wealth becomes a "man of honour"' (Bayart 1993: 242).

10

Life, Death, and the Biscuit: Football and the Embodiment of Society in Liberia, West Africa

Gary Armstrong

The man referred to in his native country as the Godfather of Liberian football by virtue of his prolific career at both international and club level is Josiah Johnson, better known as 'J-J'. Following his retirement from playing in the 1970s J-J was the first Liberian to be funded by the then President of the country to travel to Germany to take a coaching course. His return saw him coach the two top club sides in the capital city of Monrovia and later the national side with whom he held the position of Technical Director until 1999. Shortly after he was appointed as Deputy Minister of Youth and Sport. He was thus well qualified to pontificate on both the state of domestic football and the wider issues affecting Liberian society. A quote he gave to a journalist in the 1980s was oft repeated to me when informing football enthusiasts of my meeting with the man. With a smile on their faces fans would repeat his mantra that 'Football is like a biscuit ... you never know how it's going to break.' Whilst not exactly Oscar Wilde in its wit nor Solomon in its wisdom, the metaphor was demonstrated to me as I sat having lunch with the man in a Monrovian diner in 1999. Snapping a wafer bread he argued that with the best will in the world and the most precise application of force, no two outcomes, be it breaking biscuits or playing games of football, will ever be identical. It is an image and tale that has remained with me, not least every time I am faced with a biscuit. Aside from preaching parables around football-related physics J-J attempted to explain to me the problems that his country faced as it attempted to rebuild after a nine-year civil conflict:

> The end of the conflict saw our society turned upside down ... We saw thousands of young people return to Monrovia or come into the city from their homes up-country and they proved to be young men

who had lost discipline. Their respect for authority is very poor. Money is their new god; they have no respect for traditional behaviour because now parents seek in their children support for themselves. In the past they would have had three meals a day and presents at their birthday. Today kids have to do things for themselves and they have no respect or fear for their elders. They earn more than their parents and this lowers their authority.

His words were significant in that he was a father of two teenaged sons. His somewhat pessimistic outlook on contemporary Liberia came with a message to the young combatants:

Put down your guns and go to the stadium and enjoy the game, you don't become a millionaire shooting someone, you might if you can play good football.

In J-J's thinking football offered some way out of the multifarious problems his country faced. For him the game could be considered functional in being able to provide both a stable career and material wealth for those whose lives hitherto had lacked direction.

Many people believe that sport has an inherent property to integrate people at odds with each other. Certainly it can contribute to the quest for a shared identity. But beyond these two issues lies the deeper problem of seeking to answer what it is exactly that sport is expected to promote. Which begs the further question as to what state of existence or, to use a more fashionable term, what 'civil society' is it that a people wish to attain, share and sustain? In a postwar milieu we would do well to ask what it is that provides for a sense of national consciousness and where this can be most obviously witnessed. With these questions in mind we can address the contemporary situation in Liberia, West Africa, and ask what it is that can provide for diverse and recently antagonistic people recognition of or a shared sense of values, territory and citizenship. Can sport – in this instance specifically football – produce the collective conscience that will integrate people to believe that their shared identities are more significant than that which divides them? One could argue that such a project might be simplified if some form of national consciousness could be established, sustained and shared, but the very term 'nationalism' is perhaps too complex an issue for the current enquiry when one considers that the root of much of the current situation might be found in the contrast between a civic and an ethnic nationalism, the former freely chosen and therefore disposable and the latter allowing little way out. But to talk of this dichotomy simplifies matters and ceases to give credence to the reality of lived-out experiences and the ability of people to construct abstract social relationships. What therefore should analysts seek in a sporting context that should somehow represent and indeed reconcile the fractious forces that constitute contemporary Liberia?

Playing away: Liberian footballers

Football is Liberia's national sport par excellence. Every available piece of flat (and usually sand-covered) ground sees boys and men (and more recently women) play informal games at all hours of the day. The game has in the past 15 years provided the country with its most internationally renowned export – the human personnel that are international footballers. No fewer than 33 Liberian-born players currently ply their skills in twelve countries in Europe, the Far East and the Middle East, and the Liberian football enthusiast will proudly tell an outsider that their country is third only to Nigeria and Ghana of sub-Saharan African countries in exporting footballers. Such comparisons are somewhat impressive when one realizes that Nigeria has a population of 120 million and Ghana is home to 33 million, whilst Liberia is home to a mere 2 million. Football in Liberia, like no other public gathering, can attract crowds of up to 50,000 for internationals and 25,000 for high-profile domestic fixtures. The expatriate footballer has taken on a role in Liberia that did not exist ten years ago – that of the returning hero. Paid at times astronomical wages by anyone's standards, even the more mediocre talents will earn an income abroad that makes them a virtual millionaire in their homeland. For this reason the foreign-based player is fêted on his return by hangers-on and well-wishers. This could be seen as a classic form of supplication or even client-patronage in a land of acute economic scarcity, but at times it is genuinely performed out of heartfelt admiration for the man's footballing ability and courage in seeking pastures new. The footballer plays his part by sporting the seemingly de rigueur uniform of tight-fitting designer T-shirt and jeans with the heavy gold neck-chain accoutrements. The more preposterous the imported sports car that can be used to drive along the devastated streets of Monrovia acting the 'big man', the more the legend grows.

People like to be associated with the game. Local football clubs attract the patronage of local 'Big Men' and entrepreneurs. All the top clubs have people who contribute towards boots and kit and the general costs of running a team. Whilst reflected glory will always provide some motive, the actions of such people are not always to be considered in a cynical light. Liberian society encourages a willingness to be generous. Thus many a footballer, established or aspiring, will speak of his 'patron' or 'sponsor', terms which describes the man who recognizes a footballing talent and pays towards the player's footballing footwear and sustenance. The same man will be expected to finance the cost of the air fare should a trial be offered in Europe or elsewhere. The sponsor stands to have his money returned ten times over should his prodigy hit the big time.

Whilst these observations are the reality of contemporary football a central problem remains: namely, that if there is no homogeneous political identity that is capable of constituting 'Liberia' then what use is a game of football which would seem to be no more that an artificial creation allowing a 90-minute delusion, albeit one that permits a Turnerian (1969) *communitas* before a return to the reality of a de facto fission and fusion wrapped up at times in hatred and mistrust? In seeking to answer if football might embody the values of a nation we should step back and question what these 'national values' are. The answer in this instance might prove hard to find.

Matters of life and death

Issues of life and death have become terribly relevant in Liberia over the past 20 years. Political upheaval beginning in the late 1970s resulted in a civil conflict lasting eight years between 1990 and 1997. The conflict, as British academic Ellis (1999) has argued, was at times nihilistic in its practices and confused in both its origins and factions. The conflict resulted in the death of 10 per cent of the population, i.e. 150,000 people, and the displacement of around a million people from a pre-conflict population of around 2.5 million both domestically and throughout West Africa. The conflict touched upon the life of every Liberian. All knew someone or were close to someone murdered. Some – those we might call the fortunate – survived the likelihood of death to live a life of permanent disability. To a military strategist the hostility was a guerrilla conflict fought by irregular armies using a range of weapons ranging from primitive machetes to state-of-the-art machine-guns. The combatants' demeanour and deportment was frequently characterized by a dependence on a cocktail of drugs and alcohol, the bravado further enhanced by a pervasive belief in the mystic-induced powers of indigenous cults. The enduring international image provided by TV footage was of boy soldiers carrying guns at times almost the same size as them whilst dressed in a bizarre variety of looted clothing which at times included women's dresses and wigs. The logic that informed the combatants will never be known, suffice to say that the conflict was, as Ellis (ibid.) notes to a Western audience, atrocious in its brutality yet highly theatrical.

Around 10 per cent (15,000) of the combatants were aged 15 or under, the victors – the National Patriotic Front of Liberia (NFPL), led by Charles Taylor – even had a Small Boys Unit containing armed combatants as young as eight. When hostilities ended the former combatants and civilians had to come to terms with a plethora of personal traumas provided by, variously, bereavement, rape, torture, mutilation and witness to massacre. Then came the added problems of starvation and malnutrition, not forgetting mass-displacement and homelessness. Many adults blamed the young for prolonging the conflict, and those that survived their families found little by way of compassion in a people who were too preoccupied with their own personal survival to worry about others. Those children without families, the orphaned, the dispossessed and the abandoned, were left to fend for themselves on the streets of the capital city, Monrovia. Living in bomb sites and cargo containers and preyed on by older children, they had to fight for survival and food any way they could and at the same time had to avoid the attentions of unscrupulous adults who would take advantage of their youth for services both sexual and akin to indentured labour in both the domestic and industrial economies.

The multiple tasks of post-conflict reconstruction are today played out in a society where current life expectancy is just over 40 years, and which has one of the world's highest rates of teenage pregnancy alongside one of the highest levels of illiteracy. A school teacher can expect a monthly salary of US$3 a month and must attempt to instruct in a country with a devastated infrastructure, containing few buildings with running water, no public electricity system (bar that powered by personally owned generators) and a near total absence of freely available medical care. The post-conflict rebuilding which attracted UN food programmes costing over $5 billion and the involvement of around two dozen NGOs was thus characterized by scarcity, with that which could be called prewar Tradition either dead – or, at best, mutilated beyond recognition.

Land of the Free: the American Dream?

In the turbulent history of postcolonial Africa, Liberia – the oldest republic on the continent – was regarded by the more naive of political analysts, ignorant of the dominant political role of the Firestone Corporation of the US with its huge rubber interests, as a beacon of light untainted as it was by white colonial rule. This political history, unique to the continent, explains both Liberia's decades of political stability and the ferocity of the conflict once the existing civil society broke down. The initial 100 years of relative political stability was due in no small degree to its never having been the colony of a European power. Instead Liberia was able to preserve its independent status and nomenclature as the 'Negro Republic of Liberia'. However, this status arose out of a form of colonialism which had its origins initially in enlightened political thought some 3000 miles away in the United States where the 1790 abolition of slavery saw immediate freedom offered to over 160,000 Africans, a figure that would rise to 250,000 by the 1820s. Freedom, however, did not come accompanied with economic assistance and the ensuing racial tensions and periodic revolts of those who remained in conditions of indenture in the state of Virginia inspired the local political elite to seek to repatriate the former slaves. Those that boarded ships to Africa and survived the journey were taken to the West Coast and the land that was to become Liberia.[1]

History and loyalty, so crucial to a football fan, are matters that have created huge problems for Liberia. Ethnicity was manipulated both prior to the war and during it. Four of the 16 ethnic groups were prominent in the troubles. The question which concerns us at this stage is whether the conflict could have been avoided and, in seeking an answer, one has to consider both the internal politics of Liberia and then analyse the response of the outside world. From the former viewpoint one could argue that Liberia was a one-party state for all its history and the dominant 'settler' group, resident in Monrovia, treated the rest of the population with disdain and contempt.

It took until 1944 when William Tubman assumed the role of President before the exclusivity of the ruling class was lessened. In a rule lasting until 1971 Tubman encouraged other ethnicities to become involved in politics. Despite this brave encouragement the reality remained that from 1870 to 1980 politics was controlled by the True Whig party who managed to pass the presidency on without any trouble to their political hegemony. This tranquillity ended in 1971 when Tubman was succeeded by his former Vice-President, William Tolbert, who presided in a dictatorial and authoritarian manner and met his demise in 1980 when he was assassinated during Liberia's first military coup. Taking control of government was Sergeant Samuel Doe who assumed the role of the Armed Forces Commander-in-Chief. From the renowned warring ethnic group called the Krahn, Doe became the country's first indigenous President in 1986 following rigged elections a few months earlier. Such democratic deficiencies did not seem to worry the US, which supported him via Chester Croker, the Under-Secretary of State (see Berkeley 2001). The ensuing years of Doe's rule saw widespread corruption, economic decline and violence merited on political opponents. The fall of Doe was inevitable but the overthrow unleashed a variety of hitherto latent ethnic tensions.

A civil war began in December 1986 originating in the district known as Nimba County adjacent to the border with the Ivory Coast. A militia numbering 209, trained in Libya and known as the National Patriotic Front of Liberia (NPFL), was led by Charles Taylor. Seeking to overthrow the dictatorship of Doe the conflict took on dimensions of ethnicity; the Mamo and Keo people were fighting the Krahn of Doe. This ethnic division continued even after the death of Doe, who was shot dead in September 1990 on a beach in Monrovia after prolonged torture at the hands of his captors. A video exists of this procedure (see Kapuscinski 2001). Following his death the conflict became confused as a variety of individuals claimed to be the new head of state. But seeking the precise cause of the conflict is impossible. Without a doubt the dislike of the government had taken on an ethnic angle but other factors were as significant. Analysis by Ellis (1999) cites the following factors: an over-centralized state following a failed coup attempt on Doe in 1985 resulted in pogroms against those he perceived as his ethnic opponents. This also resulted in an over-representation of Krahn people in positions of power. The over-concern with security was detrimental to the economy and the good years that characterized the country from the mid-1950s began to crumble 30 years later, particularly when the wage-labourer jobs in the plantations ended. In the ensuing unemployment and hardships, Ellis argues that 'war became thinkable'. A further factor was the core–periphery dichotomy. The dominant position of Monrovia, with a population of about 800,000 and the home to all foreign banks, business interests, and the centre of politics and cultural life, was in sharp contrast to a neglected and underdeveloped hinterland (see Tonkin 1981).

In these latter regions religious belief had a sometimes understated role to play in what was to follow. The population is nominally two-thirds Christian, 14 per cent Muslim and 18 per cent Traditional African. As Ellis (1999) argues, the traditional societies found in abundance outside of the capital meant that people looked to religious leaders to solve their problems and not politicians. Furthermore, the fighting took on the characteristics of a country that had little by way of industrial production and mercantile capitalism. Unable to move easily, and being distant geographically, politically and morally from the government, meant that people looked to strong leaders in times of distress or threat. As a consequence, when armed conflict began a variety of 'Big Men' were to assume the role of faction leaders or 'warlords'. At one time no fewer than eight rival factions existed who were to make various alliances only to break them. One might argue, as Ellis has, that these individuals could be termed 'military entrepreneurs' because whilst in part they were motivated by a form of tribal based ideology, they primarily sought a share in the profits of the diamond, iron ore and timber trades and found a market from the British and French who traded throughout the war (Berkeley 2001). This very rational economic motivation was combined with traditional forces of indigenous cults and the secret societies which were the major political and law-enforcement agencies that predated the creation of the Liberian state. These became the recruiting grounds for the young men who would take the advice of the elders and, often armed through mysticism with a belief in immortality, join the militias.

If confusion reigned as to when the hostilities began the question as to what the war was all about is lost in history or what Ellis (1999), drawing on Clausewitz, calls the 'fog of war'. Ideology seemed to play second string to the economic opportunities offered by controlling by force the mining and export of diamonds and to a lesser degree, timber. The conflict formally ceased in July 1997 following an election contested by 13 candidates that Charles Taylor won with a landslide 75 per cent majority. Taylor's victory was attributed to a number of factors – including some technological factors in that he was the only candidate who could canvass – assisted by a helicopter – the war-weary who believed that he was worth electing because, having started the war, he was assumed to be the only person capable of ending it. At times the election had a madness of its own when pro-Taylor supporters orchestrated groups of children to chant 'He killed my Ma/ He killed my Pa/ But I will vote for him'. Whilst not classic in its democratic aims it did give a clear mandate even if one disregards the issue of Taylor's control over large sections of the media, of voter illiteracy, threats to voters from Taylor's henchmen and bribery by way of bags of rice being given away to those who voted for Taylor. Thereupon the 49-year-old Taylor assumed the role of President. The reality however is that hostilities have not ended, they have merely been reduced and what does occur does not always make it into the agenda of the Western news media. Four years after the elections the country is not at ease, political opponents are in exile or have died in various circumstances and politicians of the ruling party state publicly that they fear for their lives. The President's movements from his personal residence in the suburbs of Monrovia to the various buildings of government in the centre includes a cortège which at times numbers over 20 armed vehicles containing both uniformed and plain-clothed personal bodyguards. This could be seen in a cultural context as an admirable and impressive show of power to a people who were willing to fall in with the demands of Big Man politics. Equally the armed paraphernalia – which includes rocket launchers, armoured cars and a decoy Mercedes saloon car, which seem de rigueur for the most elementary of movements – suggests a President aware that opponents are never too far away.[2] What happens here cannot be dismissed as a small war in Africa which has little significance to anyone outside the borders. The conflict has repercussions for the outside world both in terms of the threat the instability offered – still offers, in fact – to those countries that border Liberia and what it tells the wider world about the realpolitik of the post-Cold War New World Order.[3]

Reconciliation through sport: the rhetoric

The cessation of hostilities in 1997 left thousands of young men who had been involved in militias since their mid- and even pre-teens, and who hardly knew any mode of life other than violent conflict and looting. Many young men had up to five years alone in the bush devoid of education and at times deployed to attack their own community. Older prewar notions of understanding and existence were destroyed; consequently new idioms of social incorporation must be invented. This is where sport and specifically football might have a role to play. As Richards (1997) argued in his seminal work on a similar scenario in neighbouring Sierra Leone, what wider reference points the former boy-soldiers have are provided by the popular cultures of youth; namely music, sport and world religion. The vital source of all three is the electronic media, which in particular provides for images of music and football from around the globe. The shared enthusiasm for football is interesting because the game is considered a 'neutral' pursuit – a common cultural property unspoiled by war. But in the Liberian context the former war combatants are only part of the equation. Thousands of young men and women did not take up arms but when hostilities ended were left to face a frightening and inhospitable future. The boy-soldiers might have been photogenic and the cause célèbre of certain Western aid agencies but it is important to note that they were not the full picture.

Very few girls were child soldiers and those that were visible were often there in their role as concubines of the male combatants. That said, many girls were subject to rape and brutality and others were witnesses to various atrocities. Which trauma should take precedence for those who wish to apply Western intellectual and psychotherapeutic ideas of counselling to such victims is a question I cannot answer. What can be said without contention is that most young women enjoy sport, and are as poor as the men and face a life equally as hard – if not harder – as a consequence of having to raise children at a very early age. Hitherto women's sporting participation was confined to kickball, a game which seems from an African perspective to be unique to Liberia, having been introduced in 1959 by an American-born Episcopalian nun. The nine-a-side game is basically baseball played with a football, with the 'pitcher' bowling underarm and the 'batter' striking the 'pitch' with their feet in pursuit of a home run. The recent proliferation in women's football teams is a direct consequence of a 1999 FIFA-inspired promotion of the game amongst women and a realization that kickball was too parochial and would therefore never provide a conduit for the Liberian sporting authorities seeking, via sport, some form of world recognition (see later in this chapter).

The role that sport can play in divided societies raises many issues which are relevant to both theoretical debates within the social sciences generally and to sport's sociology in particular and, because of the huge implications they may carry, are of concern to those involved in policy-making in the area defined as 'development' (cf. Grillo and Stirrat 1997). This latter paradigm includes both governmental departments and non-governmental organizations (NGOs). The former have recently used football in the British and European spheres in a variety of attempts to challenge, variously, racism, sexism, truancy, illiteracy, and to promote world peace. The NGOs alongside the game's governing bodies have funded schemes in parts of the world that are recovering from war. Thus as Giulianotti (1999b) has chronicled, one can read of the International Red Cross using well known football personalities to preach their opposition to anti-personnel land mines. The administrators of European football – UEFA – have donated 1 million Swiss Francs to such a scheme. At an international level FIFA launched the expensively funded Goal! project, which aims to rectify social problems in developing countries via football-inspired projects. Organizations which are not founded on football have also financed altruistic schemes using the game as an entry point to facilitate a message. In 1990 Action Aid began the One World One Goal campaign which sought to bring antagonistic peoples together via sporting participation. A few years later Spirit of Soccer was launched by UNICEF in the former Yugoslavia, the aim being to arrange games for the young which would be followed by lessons on the perils of unexploded land mines. Suffice to say then that the topic of football and reconciliation is relevant and even fashionable, and the influences the game can have on people are thus recognized by a whole host of organizations.

However, the outcomes of the various projects are not made obvious. There are possibly two reasons for this. The first is that many projects are recent in their implementation and in the arena of postwar reconstruction are difficult to evaluate. The other is that some projects seem to be celebrity-led with little evidence of long-term planning, but the organizers seem happy to promulgate clichés via glossy brochures and photo opportunities. These processes raise controversial issues: some organizations possibly use the game and its celebrities as part of what Giulianotti (ibid.) has termed their 'marketing melodrama'; others naively see football as the answer to what might be considered by those more informed as either immutable problems or ones that centuries of government and politics were unable to solve. Bearing these reservations in mind we need to turn to the evidence that Liberian football presents in relation to these optimistic beliefs.

Liberia's Big Two: football clubs and social responsibility

The first football club in Liberia was founded in 1934 and was known by the acronym Bama, a title which could be elaborated on as meaning 'We die before you can beat us'. Founded by seafaring men from the Kru ethnicity (one of the three seafaring peoples alongside the Bassa and Grebo) who had travelled to Britain on ships and brought the game home, the game as played in Liberia was possibly unique in its development in having no colonial authorities to play and no games against visiting sailors from either military or merchant ships. The game developed largely indigenously with tactics coming from the Liberians who watched the coaching conducted in the Atlantic ports of Freetown and Lisbon and when sailing further north in Liverpool. From the 1960s new tactics appeared courtesy of videos of matches imported from both Europe (particularly Britain) and, from the 1970s, from South America, particularly Brazil. Out of this fascination with the game came two teams who were to dominate Liberian football.

Begun in 1943, Invincible Eleven (IE), nicknamed the Sunshine Yellow Boys (by virtue of their kit, which was in turn derivative of the yellow and maroon colours of the pepper bird), were associated with and named by the settlers from the elite College of West Africa. The somewhat boasting name was explained to me by club officials as a way of describing a club that variously 'creates miracles' and 'does things that inspire people'. The club had an ideology which officials explained to me was 'Self-help, modesty, and the striving to become better people.' The founders were Monrovian property owners and entrepreneurs who funded the club, which also drew finances from past pupil subscriptions. Claiming to have no religious or political affiliation, officials stressed the inclusive 'broad-based' nature of the club which extends to their non-denominational supporter base. That said, IE has a history of saying prayers and singing hymns from the Presbyterian Church and one former player was a Lutheran bishop. Dominating domestic football in the 1940s and early 1950s their hegemony was then challenged by two other clubs, Jet and Mighty Barrolle. However, between 1977 and 1986 IE won the league in consecutive years and saw many of its best players depart to clubs in both the US and Europe. In the 1980s the main sponsor of IE was a fishing magnate, and by the late 1990s finance came by a variety of sponsors but was sufficient to ensure that IE was the only club with the services of a doctor. This and their renowned international contacts meant that many a promising player would turn down the greater pay on offer at other clubs to be part of the IE set-up. Training on the multi-functional and public 'Airfield' pitches, IE attracted crowds numbering in their hundreds to the evening training sessions. IE also had a membership card, which did not have too much use in this war-torn society but, as one enthusiast explained, 'it gives you authority in any argument about football'. They were keen to impress on me their tolerance of outside and even rival spectators at their training sessions and explained, in the time-honoured fashion of those who never see themselves except as the virtuous people in a symbiotic relationship with a cultural Other, that should any of their officials similarly watch Mighty Barrolle train they ran the risk of violence from their hosts.

Founded in 1956, Mighty Barrolle (MB) were formerly known as Eleven Basa Boys and later Gbazon Star of Buchanan City, Basa County. In origin the name reflected ethnicity, i.e. the Basa people, and even today MB remain the only club with an ethnic identity, but one which is more bound up in their support than the team players who have been drawn from all ethnicities for over two decades now. The nomenclature is a reminder of past political patronage as Jimmy Barrolle was butler to President Tubman and was influential in directing funding to the club. The glory days of MB came in the years 1963–74 when they won the championship nine times in a row. Their all-red kit is seen by many as a legacy of their being a 'traditional club'. Such a description carries with it a belief that the pre-match practices are not Christian but animist and bound up in traditional beliefs about medicines. The red is considered indicative of animistic practices. Christian practices can sit well with animism in the Liberian footballing context. As generations of missionaries will testify, the Christian doctrines as practised locally are more flexible than as manifested now in Europe and the US and many a believer feels no guilt in drawing upon divine and otherworld intervention in pursuit of what they desire. Pragmatism is everything.

The big two of Liberian football are thus in origin representative of the dichotomy that has produced the current political situation. Somewhat strangely, disorder around football matches has not been considered a problem historically or contemporarily. Fan disorder always seemed to involve the supporters of the big two teams, if not with each other then with fans of the smaller teams. But nobody I spoke with was ever aware of a 'hooligan' problem and the fixtures were not the occasion for the manifesting of chants and fights bound up in ethnic and sociopolitical antagonisms. Disorders tended to arise as a consequence of disputed refereeing decisions or cheating by players. In such instances games have been abandoned after assaults on match officials. However, an observer would not have been able to predict the coming conflict from watching Liberian domestic football, nor would a spectator today find clues in football fixtures as to why the country self-destructed.

Politics, patrons and peacemakers: Big Men and football

Politicians in Liberia, like politicians since antiquity, have seen the benefits that patronage of sport, specifically football, can bring to their political profile. In 1964 President Tubman began a football tournament known as the County Meet. The aim was an attempt to generate a feeling of national unity via football. The tournament was organized and promoted by the Sports Commission – a body appointed by the President and funded by the government – who would liaise with the Superintendents of the then nine counties and five territories. The two-week Monrovia-based tournament sought to bring people together as well as encourage the idea of sport and sporting participation as a useful pastime. The 14 teams would be funded for their stay via the finances of their respective county councils, assisted in many instances by the largesse of wealthy patrons (usually resident in Monrovia). The league system saw two games a day played at the stadium that the President built in the centre of Monrovia and named after his wife. The Antoinette Tubman Stadium

(ATS) was thus the host for crowds of up to 30,000. Ethnic and geographical identities were inseparable in some teams, yet in others matters were more complicated. The tournament was prestigious and so competition was open to financial manipulation. As a consequence, whatever the initial spirit of the tournament, the teams in later years contained gifted players with no connection to the counties, bought in by benefactors. Residency and ethnicity ceased to matter in the pursuit of glory. Under the Doe regime Grand Geda County twice won the Meet. By coincidence Doe was from the county and paid a considerable sum to have the best players represent his home.

Tubman's successor, William Tolbert, was instrumental in the building of the national stadium, opened in 1986 and host ever since to all national team games. Begun in 1980, the stadium was finished six years later. In the interim, Tolbert had been murdered by the forces of Samuel Doe. The latter was a keen amateur footballer and at the opening ceremony named the stadium after himself, Samuel K. Doe. The stadium even today is referred to as the 'SKD', a monument to a man's vanity and a tribute to the ingenuity and engineering of Taiwanese money and construction workers respectively. The Taiwanese in return were given logging and iron-ore concessions.

There are instances in the 1990s wherein football could be said to have stopped armed conflict. The only occasions that produced a sense of national unity during the civil conflict were football fixtures, albeit few and far between. Playing on this, politicians (in particular Sokar Wilson from the Ministry of Youth and Sport), foreign embassies (in particular the Taiwan delegation), churches and the Liberian Football Association (LFA) patronized local football tournaments in 1992 and 1993 with the aim of getting regional teams to meet so as to prove to each other that over the hill did not live dragons but human beings with the same hopes and fears as those who ostensibly despised them.[4] After the first phase of the 1990 conflict the Monrovian teams tried to organize fixtures whilst in Banga (a stronghold of Taylor's forces) and the County Meet fixtures continued on a limited scale. In fact Taylor proved to be very supportive of football; during ceasefires and before the election he would invite Monrovia teams to play in Banga in return for gifts and money and would spectate. Both Mighty Barrolle (the team he supported) and St Joseph's played his teams, but IE were too afraid of him to travel. They did, however, fulfil a 1992 fixture against Bassam, a Banga team sponsored by a Lebanese trader which drew a crowd of 30,000 to the Airfield (mainly Monrovians curious as to what Taylor's men looked like). They received a very warm reception.

International fixtures also saw the combatants cease hostilities – for the duration of the game at least. In 1992 Liberia played Tanzania, Senegal and Togo in the African Nations tournament in front of a crowd of 40,000 at the SKD in a game funded by the then Interim Government of National Unity as part of the peace process. The game is remembered as the occasion when thousands of combatants attended unarmed and went their separate ways afterwards. The faction combatants were recognizable to each other but agreed to leave their weapons aside for the day. Normal hostilities were resumed in some cases just days later.

Goodwill and the king: George Weah

In 1998 only one statue existed in the city of Monrovia. It stands in the middle of Broad Street, the busiest street in the city. Cast in bronze, it is dedicated to George Obbong-Weah, and was paid for by well-wishers. His brilliant dribbling skills and goal-scoring ability as a 16-year-old with Young Survivors of Claretown saw him become, by the age of 17, a very dependable player with IE. By the age of 18 he was the league's highest goal-scorer and had won three awards for his abilities. Then came a tournament to celebrate the 50th anniversary of the founding of the LFA. Five teams took part. The Liberian big two competed against Flamingo of Nigeria, Fisheries of Sierra Leone and Tonnerre Yaounde of Cameroon. The performance of Weah against the latter saw the club refuse to leave the country without him as part of their entourage! A two-week trial saw them pay his club the grand total of $5000 in 1987. After six months with his new club, Arsene Wenger, the then coach of Monaco, visited Africa, noticed him and bought him for less than $20,000. Weah was to become the star of the French municipality team for the following three seasons. Other transfers followed, the biggest being a move to AC Milan from Paris St Germain. With the transfers came the awards, most notably European Footballer of the Year, not once but twice. In 1995 Weah was awarded the accolade of World Footballer of the Year. Other titles followed; the most unusual for a footballer being the one given by UNESCO that saw Weah carry the title of Goodwill Ambassador for Sport. Later he was to become FIFA Ambassador for Football. And on top of all this Weah became known in his homeland as 'The King' and in return bankrolled the national team's away games and paid all the costs so that they could compete in the African Nations tournament in South Africa in 1996. Owning a large residence on the beach in a swish part of the capital and a large house on the edge of the city, Weah seems to support a whole industry of Weah worshippers frequently found in his hotel and bar. Not only is he the de facto patron and Technical Director of the national team since 1998, he also acts as a conduit for Liberian players who attract the interests of European clubs. For many in Liberia he is a national hero and a figure of hope as to what hard work can produce.

But being a Liberian hero is not easy. His departure and subsequent success did not produce plaudits from all amongst his former employers. At an IE training session in 1998 a group of officials and fans told me that Weah was not welcome in their midst because following his departure in 1994 IE were trying to rebuild their team and had appointed Weah as President of Foreign Affairs with the dual aim of negotiating deals in Europe for Liberian players and bringing the club kits and boots from any source available. After a while Weah decided that IE should establish a feeder team, which was agreed with Archibald Bernard, the President of IE. The task was to be given to a coach of Brazilian-South African origins credited with discovering Weah and who coached IE before moving to Guinea for the duration of the war, returning at the end of hostilities. The team was to be called Junior Pro and the idea was for the coach to find promising youngsters and train them in the morning before training the IE first team in the evening. This arrangement worked for a year. Then Weah decided to take five of the players to France for mid-season trials. Over the next few months IE lost a number of games and ultimately the championship. The disgruntled fans asked rhetorically what was Weah's motive? The answer they gave me was that he and the President were attempting to line their own pockets with transfer fees. Faced with such accusations Weah broke with IE and invested in Junior Pro, appointing the former IE coach as manager with instant success.[5] Weah does not seem to harbour any ambitions to stand for election in Liberia, but it was significant that in January 2000 when three British TV documentary makers were arrested and imprisoned by the Liberian authorities on suspicion of subterfuge, that the British press and politicians seeking their release turned to Weah (at the time resident in England) for help. In response he announced he would have a word with his 'good friend' the President and plead on their behalf. The men were released, but the extent of his intervention in this remains unclear. What is significant is the presumption on the part of the British that a footballer could in this context alter the course of events. Football, it could be argued, had arbitrated in matters of life and death.

'The King', having signed for a club in the United Arab Emirates in September 2001 and residing in the millionaires' playground that is Dubai, is living proof of J-J's message that a young man becomes a millionaire by football, not killing.[6] But he carries the unenviable burden of being both icon and ambassador to a nation by virtue of being able to coordinate thought and movement in pursuit of a football quicker than most people on earth. Such a status is precarious. In July 2001 a World Cup qualifier saw Liberia lose 2–1 at home to Ghana. A victory would have almost certainly seen Liberia qualify for the first time for the World Cup tournament to be co-hosted the following year by Japan and South Korea. The defeat resulted in Weah being vociferously denigrated by a crowd of 30,000. After the game he vowed both never to play again for his country and never to return to Liberia. He was talked out of these threats within a week after a meeting with Charles Taylor, but the Liberian footballing public considered the behaviour of the Liberian squad in the day preceding this vital game reprehensible. Some of the players were seen out partying on consecutive nights prior to the game. The eve of the game coincided with one of the squad's wedding anniversary which saw celebrations late into the night in a city-centre bar. The first-choice goalkeeper, driving to a party the previous night, crashed his car and sustained an arm injury. Controversy arose when $10,000 given to him by the President as an incentive to recover caused consternation in the squad as to who were the rightful owners of the cash. The line-up the next day was both under-strength and contained players on the bench who it was well known had fallen foul of Weah. The most important game in the nation's history ended with an angry mob approaching the home of Weah, which saw him become a recluse for days as armed police kept permanent guard outside. Players fought out their animosities via the press and eventually the President called the warring factions together in an attempt at reconciliation. Football in this instance was not the harbinger of national unity and pride.

Beyond rhetoric: the reality of reconstruction

The politicians of contemporary Liberia are well aware of the value of football in the reconstruction of their nation, not least the 'Chief Patron of Sport' Charles Taylor. On assuming the Presidency in 1997, amongst his appointments was a Minister for Youth and Sport, a position held between 1997 and June 2001 by Françoise Massaquoi, a former warlord of the Lofa Defence Force from the remote North West Lofa County. Assuming control of a newly created ministry, Massaquoi took office as a consequence of the desire to reconcile the various factions under one government. His two deputies were former professional footballers. In 1998 he stated in an interview with me how he saw the importance of the game to national image:

Football brings recognition and status to a country. Success in football is vital to our rebuilding. Failure reflects badly on self image.

Aware that footballing standards needed to be raised so as to compete at international level, in 1998 he had approached one of the former coaches of Ajax Amsterdam. The latter's financial demands were for $200,000 per annum plus travelling expenses for overseas scouting purposes. South American or European footballing standards would not consider such remuneration unreasonable but the annual budget for the ministry in 1998 was $225,000, a sum meant to fund schemes amongst a population that is 70 per cent under the age of 18. A year later I spoke in London with Victoria Refell, Chair of the government-funded National Reconciliation and Unification Committee. She spoke of a forthcoming Football and Basketball Reconciliation tournament funded from 'UN sources' and plans to build playgrounds containing multipurpose sports courts with video and reading facilities and areas for families to meet. Further questioning revealed the extent of the tournament funding – two footballs to each of the 15 counties to be distributed by 'local politicians'. The tournament never took place and two years later no playground had been built.

Perhaps recognizing the dire financial reality of Liberia and keen to promote the idea of football as a medium for social good, the international footballing authorities have been well disposed to Liberia. A visit in 1997 by Michel Platini (in his capacity as FIFA Ambassador) produced a promise of $1 million under the Goal! project for the building of an artificial pitch. Politics played a part. As part of his campaign to be elected President of FIFA in 1998, Sepp Blatter, then Secretary-General of FIFA, also visited Liberia and became a good friend of both the President of the LFA, Edwin Snowe, and George Weah. The latter was to become part of Blatter's election campaign; the former received a promise that should he be victorious and Liberia had voted for him then the country would be rewarded. Once elected Blatter was true to his word and Liberia was the first African country to receive a donation of $1.2 million as part of the Goal! project. The money was to go towards the laying of an artificial surface on the ATS stadium and a general upgrade of the facilities on offer there. By late 2001 the money had been used up but the project had not been finished. The pitch had been laid but the floodlights and enclosures were not fully functional. Despite this Blatter had conducted the opening ceremony for the refurbished facility in mid-2001 and watched two local select XI's play a game in front of a packed house allowed in free. Further FIFA funding of $5 million over four years began in 1998 following an application from the LFA under the National Assistance Programme. This funding, the LFA President told me, was meant to go towards technical assistance, youth development, the development of a footballing infrastructure and assisting the national team. However, fundamental problems of national unity remained unresolved.

The politics of football funding

The core–periphery division of Liberian society was a critical component of the civil conflict. The contemporary administrators of football in Liberia realize that the game has to address this issue if it is to promote national consciousness amongst people beyond Monrovia. Consequently a Decentralization Programme was begun in February 2001. Such a scheme was actually begun in 1996 by the then LFA President Willy Russell but was abandoned. In the meantime only one team in the Liberian Premier league came from outside of Monrovia, and they were unable to provide a team from 1999 onwards. This situation had not changed by summer 2001. Hence the funding for the out-of-towners provided by the LFA (via gate money from the national team fixtures) and FIFA. The scheme aimed to work by identifying a variety of clubs in the 15 counties and giving them 50 footballs and up to $2000 to buy kit and offer scholarships to promising players. Those interested in the game's development told me to be aware of the realpolitik of the seeming largesse of the LFA. The election for the position of LFA President was to be contested in the autumn. To many the distribution of equipment and money to those with a vote was too much of a coincidence.

At the same time as the regional initiative was being promoted, so was women's participation in football as a consequence of FIFA funding which specified the promotion of the women's game. A Women's Football Programme was begun under the Doe regime after he had seen the game played by women in Europe. The demise of Doe and the ensuing conflict killed the initiative. The FIFA-funded promotion in 2001 launched by George Weah before an exhibition game at the Monrovian Zion school began, inevitably, in Monrovia and later spread to Basa, Bomi, Kakata and Firestone. A ten-team women's league was begun in late 2001, drawn exclusively from Monrovian neighbourhoods with players ranging in age from 13 to 28 and in occupation from school pupil to entrepreneur. The female game had a subtext – namely the desire to reduce teenage pregnancy. The LFA President explained:

We've no playgrounds. They've nothing to do. They come out of school and hang around with boys and end up going behind the shacks. With football we're hoping to build after-school constructive activity.

Well intentioned proposals for football are not in short supply. But closer enquiry can illustrate the magnitude of the task set for football and present the realities that such ideas are up against. Speaking to the Minister of Youth and Sport in 1999, decentralization projects were placed in the local geopolitical context when he explained:

We can build the pitch but these facilities need coaches and administrators to move up-country, but who will go there when the good life is really only available in Monrovia? Besides, all talk of decentralization is based upon knowledge that Lofa County, 180 miles by road, takes four days to travel there. The government has no money because the outside world won't help it so it cannot finance much in the way of sports development.

A similar sentiment was heard in the same year from Gus Doe-Williams, the Secretary-General of the FA:

Reconciliation needs the inclusion of the people from all the counties. We hope we can do this via football. But the last County Meet was three years ago. At the moment all the teams in the league are from Monrovia or its suburbs, the others cannot afford to play or travel.

Not all football-related problems were logistical. In 1998 an Under-13 national selection was planning to tour Sweden at a cost of $77,000. The Minister of Youth and Sport told me he had managed to extract $55,000 from the Minister of Finance after a huge argument, which he claimed nearly came to blows and required the personal intervention of Charles Taylor as mediator. The squad flew out one day before the tournament began with a budget of $10 a day in Scandinavia, which meant they were dependent on the generosity of the host country to survive. The following year a 25-strong Under-15 national side was set to go on a one-month tour of the US and Europe. The government gave the party $75,000, which would equate to around $100 for each squad member for a month: or put another way, around $3 a day. Between the money being released and being handed over to the tour organizers a sum of $15,000 went missing. Enquiries from the media pointed the finger at a deal between the Minister of Youth and Sport and a travel agent. Such a scandal did not force the former's resignation but J-J resigned from his position in the Ministry, angry at the turn of events – an anger exacerbated by the fact that his two sons were part of the tour.

The Minister of Youth and Sport was to leave his post involuntarily in June 2001 when ambushed whilst travelling to his home region of Lofa County. He died instantly in circumstances no one was able to explain, assassins unknown.

Shelter, hope and football: the 'Papeye Sport' project

Beyond words and good intentions, where, one might ask, is it possible to find a football-related project that is proving to be of use? The answer to this author would seem to lie on the outskirts of Monrovia in the person of the 40-year-old Reverend Joe Glackin and a football club scheme that began by accident and grew and grew so that by July 2001 it accommodated 116 neighbourhood teams. Space does not permit an elaborate history of the project; suffice to say that the Scottish-born missionary of the Salesians of Don Bosco, who has lived in Liberia for a decade and remained throughout the war, has a knowledge of the country which is peerless amongst non-natives.[7] His ignorance of the world game has been little hindrance to him being nicknamed 'Papeye [Father/Patron] Sport' by his legion of native admirers. His footballing knowledge and interest was minimal until a few years ago when the young homeless boys (and in many cases former child combatants) the Bosco projects sheltered upon the cessation of hostilities, asked for him to provide a ball and football shirts so they could kill the long hours of the day and Joe could get them away from his Mission for a time. From such a small acorn grew a football club that took the name Bosco United Sports Association (BUSA) and entered the Premier League within two years of its founding. Nursery teams followed, then came the neighbourhood network and with it recognition and praise from George Weah, UNICEF and Save the Children personnel in the region.

In origins the first team stressed self-help and demanded discipline from all its players. Miscreants, be it for drug use or violence or rape, were thrown out. The rewards for inclusion were more social than financial as only travelling expenses were ever paid. But in a society of displaced people the squad was a surrogate family and a resource network for many. The religious input was and remains negligible. Few of the original BUSA team were Catholic (some were Muslim) and none attended Mass. Individuals in the Salesian hierarchy had asked about the quantifiable evangelistic side of his work as evidenced in Catholic births, marriages and burial ceremonies. In response to the same question from me, Joe replied:

> I guess I could say that the schemes are in many cases saving lives, in which case I'm saving souls so that they can make more of their lives. There is no official preaching in the project but there is shelter, hope and football.

Saving the lives of children is what the Salesian project aimed to do and has done. Instrumental in this has been football and football clubs. As stated earlier, the children of Liberia are open to abuse of various kinds. All of it must be addressed and the best way of doing this was considered to be via the promotion of community football teams which, once established, would give the project some degree of structure and permanency. The Bosco-sponsored tournaments that the creation of such clubs would no doubt seek to compete in would also be the occasion for the promotion of talks on child rights.[8] Ideally, having learned of the rights of the child, the players and their adult officials would return to their neighbourhoods aware of what they must not tolerate or suffer.

Football and child protection go hand in hand. What Father Joe has established over the past three years is the de facto child protection agency of Monrovia (and more recently the towns within a 50-mile radius of the capital) in a project that employs some 120 people and has 4500 children under its aegis. The immediate problem facing any child found destitute is finding a home, and this is where the project workers act and seek out a home that the child can be taken in by. The aim is to reunify and reconcile children with parents. The family is the desired cohabiting unit because it is meant to provoke a two-way responsibility. The adult heads of the household are expected to care for the child and provide for their basic necessities and listen to their needs as they grow, and support them if found to be in conflict with the law. In turn the children are given instruction as to their responsibilities to the family, the community and the state. Open days and lectures combine with street theatre and posters to remind them of the need to live within the law and to respect elders and property. The need for education is also stressed, which means attending school regularly. The adult guardians must stress the undesirability of taking up arms. Whilst the project has trained and employs outreach workers who actively seek children at risk, their task has now been supplemented by football teams and the neighbourhood activists who assist in their running.[9]

What the children of Liberia have now is some form of protection thanks to football clubs made up primarily of young men who know it is their duty to report the abuse of children to the project who in turn will send personnel to visit the alleged perpetrator and discuss the situation, often attracting a crowd of locals in the proceedings. Shame can be a powerful tool. Should gentle reason not work, the perpetrators are told that police might well be informed; the very mention of police strikes fear into many. A middle way for the more sadistic and recalcitrant of perpetrators is a visit from some of the biggest and less reasonable members of the football team.

Life, death and biscuits: football as sustenance?

All nations have some ideology as to how to use the body, often linked to the defence of territory. There is an irony evident here in that whilst sport historically was a way of preparing for war, the late twentieth and early twenty-first century have seen Western governments and NGOs recognize in the floundering wish to 'do something' in war-zones that sport and particularly football is possibly a way to prevent armed conflict. Liberia's perennial problem remains that of building a sustainable civil society, central to which is the need to make people think of themselves as homogeneous or at least not too different. Central to this are the following issues: access to land, gainful employment, a more egalitarian distribution of income, elementary health provision, the construction of decent and affordable housing, elementary educational opportunities, the availability of clean water and a campaign that might somehow address the growing incidence of AIDS. In the meantime the fear of abduction of young boys to be forced to fight for the militias should war break out again remains, as does the over-centralization of the state in relation to the hinterland. Teenage pregnancies are still happening. Football alone cannot solve these issues.

For West Africa the game offers, as Richards (1997) states, a neutral place in which ex-combatants and the wider society might begin to seek mutual accommodation before assisting in the hard task of re-forming Liberian social identities and social understandings. Across the country, rich and poor, women and men, Muslims, Christians and animists enjoy the game and football pitches are found in the remotest villages as well as the densest urban areas. The game is providing an avenue for linking local populations and groups of displaced 'outsiders'. The burgeoning community football clubs have provided a justified source of pride for thousands of young people, be it in playing, spectating or organizing. In the absence of any other opportunities to hone their organizational talent, for some young men whose principal skill had hitherto been reserved for war or various forms of violent or acquisitive crimes, running and managing football competitions may be one way of building quickly and constructively on such tenuous social capacities. What can best be hoped is that football might provide a network of neighbourhoods which, having learned to coexist via football fixtures, should the call to arms come again, might refuse to go running to join the militias.

The game can undoubtedly provide for national heroes and recognition from the wider world, but footballing heroes are fragile objects, not least because no one criterion ever defines a nation. It would be difficult to argue that any sport could be emblematic of a nation as devastated as Liberia. What we can say with confidence is that football clubs the world over are significant in creating neighbourhoods and wider identifications. They can also offer educational narratives, but whether the game can inculcate nationally agreed values pertaining to justice and egalitarianism remains to be seen (cf. Barry 2000). The best that football can claim to be able to offer is a reflection of life. Occasionally it can act as a workable metaphor, but mostly it is flippancy.

So what can watching the development of football in Liberia tell us about the health and hopes of the society as a whole? The most obvious answer is the striking manner in which young Liberian bodies are sought for inclusion in one or another football scheme. So many different reflections of the fragmented, disintegrative and even dysfunctional nature of Liberian society is reflected in football. Nothing seems to work in a straightforward manner. What Liberian football seems to represent is the embodiment of both national and civic disintegration counter-balanced by a pulsing and highly human determination for survival. This can variously take the form of calculated attempts to mine Liberia for commodifiable football talent or the beneficent project of the Salesians to help vulnerable children survive. There is at the same time a desperation about the manner in which football is meant variously to keep young girls from getting pregnant or to encourage young boys to become millionaires rather than murderers. On top of it all, football's governing bodies in their initiatives seem to be just about as fully out of touch with reality (or as cynical) as the European and Asian powers that permit the disintegration of Liberia to proceed as long as the flow of assets out of the country is not seriously threatened.

Football by itself cannot possibly solve the multifarious problems that Liberia currently faces, but in some cases the game might offer in a variety of ways a useful form of mediation. Certainly, from the work being done via the BUSA football club and Father Joe's community teams, children in danger are being rescued from their appalling predicaments and in such instances the game can be said to have saved lives. To borrow from J-J, war is like a biscuit. No one for certain can ever know when it will break out or what form it will take when subject to various pressures. In war as in football, no one knows the outcome in advance, but having endured this state of affairs for too long the biscuit metaphor must stay strictly in the realm of football. People need to see that footballers are more significant to their future than military Big Men. George Weah never held a gun, nor did he kill anyone; he ran around and kicked a ball and did more for his country than the tens of thousands of combatants dead or alive ever did. Sport, and specifically football, can act as a metaphor for life. In places like Liberia it might even be considered a replacement.

Acknowledgements

My sincere thanks are due to the Reverend Joe Glackin and the hospitality of the Salesians of Don Bosco. I am also grateful for the insight into Liberian football offered by coach Sam Cooper.

Postscript

The simmering hostilities in post-election Liberia came to the surface in 2003 when the civil conflict resumed on a nationwide scale. In some six months of heavy fighting an estimated 10,000 people lost their lives and around 1 million became refugees. The forces backing Charles Taylor made use of child combatants in their efforts to resist the forces of the Liberians United for the Restoration of Democracy (LURD) who also recruited children. Combat in the streets of Monrovia destroyed much of what had been restored over the previous four years. In one week in July some 600 civilians were killed by combatants from both factions.

Marines from the US military landed to wild acclaim from Liberian civilians as they helped evacuate the US diplomatic personnel. Peace-keeping forces from West African states entered Monrovia in August. Pressure from neighbouring countries and the US, the UN and the EU brought the warring factions together in Accra, Ghana. Facing military retreat Charles Taylor resigned in August ending his 17-minute speech with the words 'God willing, I will be back.' He now resides with his entourage in Calabar, Nigeria. The factions agreed to replace him with a Liberian businessman who was to head a transitional government which was expected to yield to an elected government in 2005.

Father Joe was forced to leave Liberia in 2002 when cumulative illnesses took their toll. He is currently convalescing in the UK. George Weah retired from football in 2002 and currently lives in the US. The BUSA football clubs remain albeit some key personnel have fled the country. Some of the children who played in the neighbourhood teams were killed in the hostilities.

Notes

1. Adopting a model of the US Constitution in 1847 was in hindsight an inappropriate political doctrine to this new nation. A Senate and House of Representatives headed by a President and cabinet became the preserve of the newly arrived (or returned) people who were to become known then and even 150 years later as Americo-Liberians. The governmental seat of power is adjacent to the police HQ which is a stone's throw from the University of Liberia, all found in an area known as Capitol Hill. The neocolonialism of the Americo-Liberians subjected the indigenous 90 per cent of the population, consisting of 16 ethnic groups, to their political whims which were to see them emulate that which they were subject to in the US, namely slavery. This time, however, the settlers enslaved the indigenous people on their plantations. The latter in varying degrees of contempt referred to the new arrivals as 'the settlers' and 'congo-people' – a derivative of the statement 'People who come and go'. Such terms are still heard today. The minority was to dominate the political, economic, judicial and social life of Liberia for the next 130 years in their metropolitan society modelled on the Southern states of the US. The transatlantic influences are evident to any outsider. The national flag, known as the 'Lone Star' was invented in the nineteenth century and consists of a single star in the top left-hand corner and eleven horizontal stripes to signify the eleven signatories of the Declaration of Independence – from the American Colonization Society, not the US. Socially one can witness a plethora of female beauty pageants, school – even kindergarten – graduation ceremonies, the game of basketball, and instructors of various sports being referred to as 'coach'. A multitude of Pentecostal and Baptist churches originating from the Southern states and the Midwest are evident throughout Monrovia, competing with the recent arrival of the Evangelicals. Adverts for such denominations are regularly broadcast on state TV.
2. The life of Charles Taylor makes for a fine study in the abilities of adventurism. A former politician in Liberia under the Doe regime, he fled the country when wanted for embezzlement of state funds. Washing up in New York, he was arrested, only to escape from prison and flee the US. Before training with his militia in Libya and eventually entering Liberia via the Ivory Coast there are 'missing years' when all that is known is that he was travelling in, variously, Central America, Southern Europe and West Africa.
3. When the conflict was underway in July 1990 the US sent 2000 marines and six warships into Liberian waters. This force could have been very influential in imposing a cessation of hostilities. However, having evacuated all those of US and European nationality that wanted to leave, the fleet left the scene – to

fight the Gulf War, a war fought, in the words of President Bush, to 'preserve the American way of life'.

4. Local tournaments were promoted by other bodies, both NGO and military. Various NGOs distributed football kits to neighbourhood teams and arranged mini-tournaments. The ECOMOG peacekeeping forces (the military wing of the Economic Community of West African States, ECOWAS) arranged games for their soldiers against local teams. Two Nigerian soldiers so impressed some onlookers that after the withdrawal of the peacekeepers in 1999 they returned to sign for the Junior Pro club.

5. In 1994 Junior Pro won promotion from Division Two and were promoted again the following year. The next season saw them lose the Premier title following a protest about an ineligible player.

6. As recently as July 2001, Weah, when still a player with Marseilles, proclaimed his joy upon learning of the resumption of the Concorde supersonic flights between the US and Europe, thereby enabling him to continue to live in New York until Sunday and yet be at work in France by Monday.

7. The Salesian society was founded in Turin, Italy, in 1859 by Don Bosco. The man based his principles and subsequent society on the ethos developed by St Francis of Sales and sought to serve the needs of poor and abandoned young people. The Mission that first entered Liberia in 1979 with the aim of converting and preaching bears no relation to the work that is being done today.

8. The Salesian project follows the definition of a child as that defined by UNICEF, which states that the term defines anyone under the age of 18. The promotion of children's rights draws on the 1959 United Nations Convention on the Rights of the Child (UNCRC) which arose out of the 1948 Declaration of Human Rights and was made an addendum to the 1948 Declaration and adopted some 40 years later in November 1989 by the UN. The Liberian government of 1992 ratified the convention. Central to the doctrine of rights is the 'foundation of freedom, justice, and peace in the world'. For an overview of the various issues involved in Human Rights see Forsythe (2000).

9. The project is not a bottomless pit of free footballing equipment. A ball is given to clubs on condition they turn up at the open days and participate in the discussions on the Rights of the Child. Further largesse from the project to any club is dependent on their being seen to actively pursue the aims of the project.

11
Playing Against Deprivation: Football and Development in Nairobi, Kenya[1]

Hans Hognestad and Arvid Tollisen

Take the number 46 bus from downtown Nairobi and some 15 minutes later, depending on traffic, you enter Juja Road and the Mathare shanty town. The pot-holed streets are alive with people selling vegetables, fried corn and second hand clothes. Handymen, known as *fundis*, try to make a living by repairing anything that can be repaired which in many African nations means most things. Homes are shelters made of mud, corrugated iron, cardboard and whatever else may offer protection. The population is not officially drawn, but estimates vary from 500,000 to 1 million people drawn from a variety of tribal and ethnic backgrounds. Some 70 per cent of Mathare households are one parent families, invariably mothers bringing up kids. The heavily polluted Mathare river runs through the district and in the absence of any state-provided sanitation the rubbish is everywhere and rotting. One of many criminal activities evident is the illegal brewing of *chang'aa* (beer) with water drawn from the contaminated river. As a consequence stomach-related diseases are common. The few open spaces, if not filled with garbage, host kids playing football. Most play in bare feet, their football made from plastic bags tied into a ball with rope. Despite this the youngsters play with joy as they aspire to emulate their TV idols of Manchester United, Liverpool and Arsenal.

Along the Juja Road there are signs indicating the way to the office of MYSA (Mathare Youth Sports Association). A visitor may well ask why one should bother building a sports organization in a great slum area where people's main concern is survival. After all, as any scholar in this field knows, the principal tasks for development and aid programmes have traditionally been health, education and food. But even with apparently well thought-out programmes and the best of intentions, African postcolonial history has seen many failures with the result of increased

210

dependency. MYSA is different. Its point of entry is based in a local interest for sport, particularly football, which has involved young people to an extent rarely seen in developmental projects. The success and high profile added by the successes of Mathare United in the Kenyan Premier League has amplified the process. MYSA sees its task as strengthening self-esteem and belief in 'home-made' ways by locating individual skills and applying them in collective action. As such it hopes to change both the established public images of the slum and the distorted images of Africa (MYSA document).[2] This is no small ambition. The achievements of MYSA, hailed by the Canadian researcher Owen Willis[3] (1999: 158–9) as 'a brave and innovative initiative', have attracted considerable interest among aid workers, researchers and politicians dealing with development. MYSA's expressed ambition is to unite people across gendered, tribal and religious divides and it claims to be an organization for and run by the youth themselves.

In this chapter we will take a look at MYSA's history and reality in relation to its ideological body and the influence of patrons and sponsors. We will also view its stated ambitions in relation to Kenya's colonial and postcolonial history. We also ask how, if at all, football can provide a basis for social development in deprived areas.

The dawn of MYSA and the role of patrons and donors

From humble origins in 1987, MYSA has grown to become the largest youth organization in Africa.[4] Today MYSA is a non-governmental organization (NGO) involving around 14,000 members (Lindøe 2001: 7). Its main focus is still football, but MYSA has become, even to those not interested in the game, a very visible and appreciated factor in tough and often hopeless surroundings.

Canadian-born Bob Munro was a key agent in the founding of MYSA and has since remained a patron and a 'father figure' for the organization. He has lived in Kenya since 1985 as Managing Director of a consulting group working for African governments and the United Nations on economic planning and environmental policies. For more than three decades he has worked with issues relating to international environment policies. In 1987 he visited Mathare and observed children playing with their home-made football. The enthusiasm with which the kids played, caught Munro's interest and he offered to referee a game. This proved to be the start of a social programme using football as a central activity for children in Mathare. In Munro's own words: 'What started out as a charitable instinct, and it was charitable when MYSA started in 1987, was in a couple of months transformed into respect and admiration as I saw the tremendous energy and focus and talent of these kids' (interview with Bob Munro, August 1999).

Initially there was seemingly no clear ideology involved other than a hunch about the potential a popular sport such as football might have as a means of social development. When the boys he got to know as a referee told him they would remove garbage if he gave them a new football, this laid the foundation for the MYSA principle: 'You do something, MYSA does something. You do nothing, MYSA does nothing.' This principle is still well known by the members and permeates all levels of the organization, which currently includes a range of sports activities and an educational programme described in further detail below. Francis Kimanzi, one of the boys who met Bob Munro in 1987, is currently the chief manager of the organization. Known to everyone as Kim, he recalls the early programme: 'To get a new ball was a great motivator for the effort. It was hard work through community service to achieve something' (interview with Francis Kimanzi, April 2000). In view of this, footballs were not given because the children were poor and needy, but as a way of developing opportunities to explore and develop skills and talents both in football and community activities.

Today MYSA organizes a league system throughout the Mathare area. Some 100 MYSA leagues exist for around 1000 teams for players ranging from 9 to 18 years of age. Since 1992, 200 girls' teams have also been established.[5] The football activity and leagues are organized in different zones according to location. There are 16 such zones grouped in two regions. In each zone they elect a Sport Council and a Community Service Council to run the activity in the zone. From these councils members are elected to the supreme council or board in the MYSA organization, called the Executive Council (Lindøe 2001: 22). The organization relies heavily on volunteers, but as the organization grew rapidly, the need for paid administrative staff became obvious. Sixty people, all locals from the Mathare area, are currently employed to administer MYSA activities. Activities are funded through partnerships and donors from both Kenya and abroad. The Norwegian aid agencies NORAD[6] and the Strømme Foundation[7] represent the bulk of the foreign financial support. Bob Munro established contacts with NORAD through a number of Norwegian visitors in Mathare, among them a TV reporter who made a TV documentary about MYSA which was shown on Norwegian TV in 1992. From 1990 NORAD paid the costs for bringing an MYSA football team to Oslo to compete in the annual Norway Cup,[8] regularly hailed by the Norwegian organizers as 'the world's largest football tournament'. Private and personal initiatives by various Norwegian agents were important in the process of getting NORAD involved, and among them was former Norwegian Kenya Ambassador Arman Aardal. Subsequently the Strømme Foundation succeeded NORAD as MYSA's main international partner in 1994. This foundation, in cooperation with NORAD, is currently the largest donor with an annual contribution of around $300,000[9] (ibid: 25, and information from the Strømme Foundation). Dutch agencies[10] and the American-based Ford Foundation[11] have also contributed to the development of MYSA (Lindøe 2001: 24). Another important Kenyan-based contributor is an Indian-born company director who in the early years helped to cover travel expences for MYSA teams (interview with John Muraya, April 2000).[12] The financial support of MYSA's activities has been established because of its intertwining of football with environmental responsibility. Every weekend 50 football teams armed with shovels, rakes and wheelbarrows clear garbage and drainage ditches around their homes. For this they earn six points for their league standing.[13] The voluntary clean-up service is now backed by a full-time MYSA-sponsored garbage cleaning team counting eleven full-time MYSA-staff-members. (Lindøe 2001: 71).

In 1992 MYSA received an invitation to attend the United Nations Earth Summit on Environment and Development in Rio de Janeiro.[14] It seems reasonable to assume that the influential Bob Munro and his network within the environmental sections of the UN contributed to this invitation. At the summit MYSA were awarded the UNEP Global 500 Award.[15] The UNEP Executive Director called MYSA's effort 'a unique and innovative environmental activity'. The Eco '92 Youth Football Games were held as a part of the summit. This tournament was promoted by the famous Brazilian footballer Pelé. An MYSA team was invited to participate in this tournament and Pelé personally paid MYSA's expenses during their stay in Brazil (Willis 1999: 96–7).

Mathare United between professional football and community service

Mathare United, the MYSA senior football team, was formed in 1994 by MYSA 'graduates',[16] when they also became a member of the Kenyan Football Association and the Kenyan football league. Between 1994 and 2000 the Norwegian company Norsk Hydro was their main sponsor.[17] Today KD Wire, a local Kenyan steel and barbed wire company, is the main sponsor. Having worked their way up the divisions Mathare United are currently an established team in the Kenyan Premier League. In 1998 they won the Moi Golden Cup,[18] prompting a media headline of 'Slumboys Realize Dream' in a national newspaper (*East African Standard*, 30 October 1998). This achievement rewarded them with a place in the African Cup Winners Cup for the first time ever the following season (Odanga 1999: 31). They repeated this success in 2000, while they narrowly lost the final in 2001.[19] All of the team players are products of the MYSA organization and still have to take their share of the work in the organization. Players in the senior team are also involved as coaches for junior teams, football referees or AIDS counsellors and also take part in community service such as collecting garbage. Every month the team as a whole put in 80 hours of work for the organization.

MYSA's community responsibility is extended to cover information about AIDS, a serious and well known threat to most African countries. The organization has trained 300 of its youths to be peer counsellors on AIDS. By its own admission, 'MYSA has no resources to give care treatment to those who already are infected, but we can inform and prevent by providing knowledge and information' (interview with Isac Kere).[20] In pursuit of prevention, peer counsellors deliver an AIDS information session to the players for a few minutes prior to every football match, focusing on precautions. In recent years drama and dance performances have also been used to entertain people and spread information. Part of the funding received from the Strømme Foundation is directed to MYSA's own outreach programme. Many of the numerous 'street children' living without their parents in Nairobi are taken into custody by the police. MYSA's 'Jail Kid' programme tries to offer a helping hand to these kids by providing them with meals and establishing contact with their families in order to get them released. Since the start in 1997, more than 18,000 street children have received meals through this programme (Lindøe 2001: 51).

As a way of controlling their own publicity, 16 boys and 16 girls were equipped with simple point-and-shoot cameras in 1997. With basic camera training they began work on a photographic documentary of Mathare.[21] The result was an impressive book published in 1999. Initiated by American-based photographer Lana Wong together with MYSA leader Francis Kimanzi who received his camera training on a scholarship to a Norwegian college, the objective of the project was 'to change the public perception of the Nairobi slums and help generate positive stories and images about Mathare and its inhabitants' (MYSA document). Except for contributions from editor Lana Wong, the project used only photographers/authors recruited from MYSA. Another recent project within MYSA intended to teach basic computer and web-design skills for selected youths has resulted in their own home page on the internet (<www.nairobits.org>).

Part of the funding received by MYSA provides scholarships. School is expensive and therefore impossible for people with a low or no income. The scholarship programme was established in 1997 and each grant is equivalent to approximately $170. So far 250 boys and girls have benefited from the programme between 1997 and 1999 (Lindøe 2001: 47). MYSA has established a point collection system where the youths make themselves eligible for a possible scholarship. The system is based on the five major categories: player, coach, referee and linesman, community service, elected posts and meetings.[22] Scholarship candidates are picked from reports on their talents, disciplinary behaviour and level of involvement in the various activities in accordance with the founding MYSA principle mentioned above. Similar criteria are applied in the selection of members picked to attend a year's study in Norway[23] and also with regards to the selection for teams who participate in the annual Norway Cup in Oslo.

A focus on discipline and abiding by the social rules within the MYSA system is evident in MYSA's Fairplay Code.[24] This gives directions for 'proper behaviour', stressing respect and self-discipline towards teammates, coaches, opponents and officials both on and off the field. Sanctions are applied by the MYSA governing bodies if rules are violated and a number of youths have been expelled for various reasons. If a player verbally abuses the referee, for instance, this results in automatic suspension until the offending player has refereed ten games (Willis 1999: 99).

The focus on discipline must be understood in view of the otherwise anarchic Mathare reality, ridden as it is with poverty and misery. There have been no reported incidents of robbery carried out against either an MYSA youth or a visitor (Lindøe 2001: 36), which is noteworthy in an area otherwise troubled with crime and violence. This may be interpreted as a testimony to the respect the organization holds in the community and how MYSA membership is regarded by many as protective in relation to the harsh realities of the slum. On the football field, Mathare United players have not received any red cards since the team was formed, and the average number of yellow cards received is around one-third that of opposing teams (ibid.: 62). Hence their loyalty to the Fairplay Code has seemingly not affected their success. In many ways the Fairplay Code reads like disciplinary rules generated by the British public school system (cf. Holt 1989b). Thus it might appear as a bit of a puzzle that social rules clearly reflecting the values of the former colonial power have been applied in the stated ambitions of generating social development through football in a postcolonial society such as that of Kenya which begs the question: how does the development and relatively brief history of MYSA, focused on reconciliation and the bridging of ethnic, religious and social gaps, relate to historical and current realities of tribal conflict and colonial domination?

Colonialism and beyond: the Kenyan backdrop

Commentators from Western countries have a tendency to consider Kenya as a young country, with its *uhuru* (the Kiswahili word for freedom) achieved from Britain as late as 1963. If the independent nation-state of Kenya is young, the history of its different peoples is ancient. Recent discoveries in the Great Rift Valley suggest that the first people on earth came from this area.[25] A dramatic shift in African history occurred with colonization and the resulting partition of the continent using often arbitrary border-drawing by the European imperial powers in the aftermath of the so-called Berlin Conference of 1884–85[26] (Tenga 2000: 37). Kenya became a British Protectorate in 1895 and remained formally under British control until 1963. Left with arbitrary borders, Kenya, together with many other countries, therefore had to overcome the fact that in building the new nation its population is comprised of ethnic and tribal groups often with little in common historically and culturally.

Independence from the British saw the arrival of the first President, Jomo Kenyatta, who faced what one author has termed the challenge of making a nation out of the past (Atieno-Odhiambo 1996: 1). Despite almost 70 years of colonial rule Kenyatta encouraged the British colonialists to stay. Norwegian TV correspondent and frequent visitor to numerous African countries, Tomm Kristiansen (1994: 142–56), describes this generosity as typically traditionally African in its belief that democracy should be based on consensus. In traditional African societies the tribe, the group and the family had to stick together in order to survive with scarce resources. The modern political parallel is manifest in compromise and coalition. The stress on consensus was also evident during the years of negotiations between former Presidents of South Africa F.W. de Klerk and Nelson Mandela prior to the abolition of the apartheid system in 1993. Both of them agreed that the transitional constitution should be based on consensus and not voting. Colonial powers rarely disturbed the traditional local democracy, but when they left it was generally not the chiefs of consensus who won political power and influence. In most postcolonial African nations a local elite gained power, but with no integrative forces socially and culturally, resulting more often than not in social destabilization and conflict (Kristiansen 1994).

Kenya currently consists of more than 40 ethnic groups, the largest of which are the Kikuyu (22 per cent), the Luhya (14 per cent), the Luo (13 per cent), the Kalenjin (12 per cent) and the Masai (1.5 per cent) (see <www.bsos.umd.edu>, article by Danso, 1999). The transition to an independent Kenya was never fuelled with the sort of anti-British antagonism manifest most overtly by the Mau Mau uprising. However, while the bureaucratic structures from the colonial partition were inherited, the new political alliances of independent Kenya were based on traditional linguistic and tribal loyalties. Antagonism towards the politically dominant Kikuyu was evident in the 1960s and 1970s, even though violent confrontations did not generate a state of civil war (Monnington 1986: 149). Kenyatta was a Kikuyu, and his concerns were primarily aimed at maintaining friendly ties with the British. Kenyan professor of history William R. Ochieng argues that Kenyatta's call to forgive and forget became the keynote of his government and the authorized line of policy. Many of the British who remained took Kenyan citizenship and felt safe under Kenyatta who rebuked those who spoke of revenge. Just weeks after liberation Kenyatta even asked British troops for assistance when an army unit threatened with mutiny (Ochieng 1996: 93). Kenyatta managed to keep the young Kenyan nation in a state of political stability until his death in August 1978, even though this did not entail a Western-style multiparty democracy. The issue of his successor did not initially result in any major political conflict. Kenya became gradually, and formally in 1982, a one-party state under the new president Daniel Arap Moi, belonging to the Kalenjin ethnic group. During the next decade the Kenyan government was increasingly accused of corruption, political oppression and the violation of human rights. It was not until December 1991 that Moi agreed to organize democratic elections after sustained diplomatic pressure from abroad[27] (Corneliussen 1995: 51).

The events leading up to the election the year after also catalysed a number of tribal animosities in the Kenyan Rift Valley where the Kikuyus and other immigrant tribes had coexisted peacefully with the Kalenjins until trouble first erupted in mid-1991. Corneliussen analyses these conflicts in relation to the increasing pressure from Western countries towards the Kenyan government to introduce multiparty elections: 'Democracy was equated with the multiparty system, parliamentarism and elections based on the British model ... instead of focusing on how basic democratic ideals and values could be developed in a Kenyan context'

(Corneliussen 1995: 53). Since the founding of political parties in Africa in general is often based on tribal identities, it is understandable that tribal clashes occurred simultaneously with the international pressure put on Kenya around 1990.

These were the apparent paradoxical consequences of the international pressure on the Kenyan government. *'Harambee'* is the Kiswahili word for 'pulling together' and, despite tribal conflicts and problems with bureaucratic corruption like in any other African state, Kenya may be described as a relatively successful *harambee* African country. The national football team call themselves the Harambee Stars, indicative of how football is regarded as a potential for social reconciliation. The construction of a postcolonial Kenyan identity built upon the principles of *harambee* has been a prime political task in postcolonial Kenyan society (Maloba 1996: 11). Both Kenya's first President, Kenyatta, and former head of state, Daniel Arap Moi, have valued the political significance of using sports and sporting success in the creation of a national identity and unity. 'Sport is one factor that unifies all people regardless of their race, tribe ethnicity or denomination' (Moi 1987, quoted in Godia 1989: 270). Many current football clubs in Kenya were founded in the 1960s and the first decade of Kenyan independence.

Attempts at using sports for national unification cannot hide the fact that tribal rivalries linked to sport do occur. The 2001 Moi Golden Cup winners, AFC Leopards, is regarded as the team of the Luhya tribe (see <www.Kenyapage.com/football>). Influential politicians such as Oginga Odinga and Tom Mboya[28] were linked to the formation of football clubs with ties to the Luo tribe. A substantial amount of people from the Luo tribe support Gor Mahia FC. Tribal animosities between players of Gor Mahia and AFC Leopards have been evident also within the national team, the Harambee Stars. In 1988 the national team went on tour to Brazil to prepare for the African Nations Cup. The latent rivalry and animosity between the Leopards and Gor Mahia resulted in intra-squad fights and the hospitalization for two weeks of one of the players (ibid.). The increasing influence of larger modern enterprises in Kenyan football has diminished the ethnic impact in the Kenyan Premier League in recent years and a 'modern' club such as Mathare United hosts players from a variety of ethnic backgrounds, reflecting the ethnic mix of people in the Mathare area as a whole.

The construction of modern Kenyan identities is influenced by various social and cultural impulses and it is within this context that the paradoxical image of Britain as both a former colonial oppressor and a possibility for growth and welfare must be understood.

Building self-esteem through football

The Norwegian TV correspondent Tomm Kristiansen lived in Africa for several years and was once asked by a local in Harare, Zimbabwe, where he came from. He replied: 'Norway!' 'But you can't come from nowhere?', said the puzzled local. 'Norway, the upper part of Europe', Kristiansen replied, by way of further explanation, to which the Zimbabwean responded: 'I would never live in Europe, there is a terrible tribal war going on up there in Bosnia, and I have heard that they burn black people's homes in Germany. And a lot of unemployment. No, Africa is much better.' The bemused Norwegian tried to explain further: 'But Norway is not Bosnia and Germany. It is further north.' But this only served to provoke further images of distress: 'North? Northern Ireland. There is war everywhere up there. And so cold!' (Kristiansen 1994: 63–4). If this is the image an African has of Europe we might ask, what are the dominant images Europeans have of Africa? Images of starvation and hopelessness would most certainly be on that list. The young people in MYSA and the Mathare district leave an onlooker with a slightly different impression even in an environment where poverty and a daily struggle for existence is dramatically real: you meet people with dignity, guts and optimism, a sense of humour and a level of reflection arguably beyond most of the youth found in contemporary Northern Europe.

Former Norwegian ambassador in Tanzania, Gunnar Garbo, is critical of much of the way that Norwegian governmental aid channelled through NORAD was transferred to Tanzania. In the 'receiving country' (in itself a humiliating word) a local Norwegian elite made all the decisions with salaries 200–300 times above what locals were paid. As Garbo (1993: 94) argues: 'No one will learn much by having others doing the work for them.' In a recent Norwegian TV commentary MYSA was introduced as the 'Norwegian football project in the slum' (Norwegian TV2, 10 April 2001). There are indeed Norwegians involved in MYSA, but this TV presentation leaves us with the familiar image of Westerners representing the know-how in development projects, hence extending manifestations of African dependency on Western capital and resources. Giulianotti (1999b) presents some of the endeavours that have sought to use sport in a development and rehabilitation context: However, his seven points are all Western-dominated organizations such as the International Committee of the Red Cross, FIFA and the International Olympic Committee. As important as these global organizations and their influences may be, it is also indicative of a lack of knowledge about more locally based African initiatives and how they work and what they manage to achieve.

As a United Nations employee Bob Munro was important in the founding of MYSA. Yet his approach never consisted of bringing a staff of 'experts' in to show locals how to build the organization in the slum. He was an important agent in the establishment of the organization and he has no doubt enjoyed considerable personal rewards for his involvement, of which the Global 500 Award mentioned above is a visible example. Munro has no formal power in the organization, but is undoubtedly a much respected authority and is highly regarded among the many MYSA members and the community. In 1999, Arvid Tollisen, co-author of this chapter, asked Munro why they had chosen an originally British sport such as football and not a more traditional African game as a means to social development. Munro responded: 'What African game? You just ask the kids. They want to play football.' Munro's point was that the issue of building identity and self-esteem does not depend on culture-specific activities, but more on how activities are applied in accordance with the popular significance of those activities. And during the twentieth century, football grew to become the most popular sport in most parts of the African continent (cf. Richards 1997).

Football was brought to Africa with the colonial powers. Guttmann (1994) describes how sport spread throughout the globe. The colonial masters saw sport as an important part of their attempts at 'character building' in accordance with the norms and values of the ruling forces. Kenya was no different: 'The colonial administrators and settlers who came to Kenya brought their sporting tradition with them. They built up a sports culture in Kenya which was a copy of the one in Britain' (Godia 1989: 269). Sports were organized in community clubhouses and were exclusively for the Europeans. Godia mentions golf, swimming, tennis, rugby and cricket, but leaves football out of that list (ibid.). This is perhaps no coincidence. Football was never among the premier colonial sports in Kenya or indeed other British colonies, but was introduced to children attending missionary schools (Guttmann 1994: 65–6). Consequently the game of football was a game with significance and resonance at a grassroot level.[29] Mazrui (1987) states that football is generally experienced in African nations as a more culture-neutral sport than, for example, lawn tennis. There is also one very practical and very obvious reason, especially in a slum area, for taking up football. You can play it on any available field and it is cheap. Combined with the fact that football has no specific hegemonic social or cultural reference (cf. Richards 1997), the choice of football becomes understandable. Football in Kenya has a long history.

The Football Association of Kenya, founded in 1922, may have been the first African sports federation for black players (Guttman 1994: 67). As Wagner (1990: 402) notes: 'Bringing sports into new cultural contexts probably serves more as examples available for people to pick up or trade if they wish, rather than any imposed or forced cultural change ....' MYSA picked up football and found the game to be a suitable device for building the organization.

Football between reconciliation and violent anarchy

Mathare and other slum areas have grown parallel to the growth of the city of Nairobi itself. From a population of around 10,000 in 1906, Nairobi was home to 1.6 million in 1994 (Obudho 1997). Despite regulations, land allocation is fraught with corruption and disregard for regulations (ibid.). Mathare has a history of anarchy (Lindøe 2001: 20). Members of MYSA confirm this picture. [30] Mathare United's home games are not played in the Mathare valley, but in the 60,000-capacity stadium at the Moi International Sports Complex. This stadium is located within easy walking distance along Thika Road, a few kilometres from the Mathare valley. In MYSA's recently built headqarters in the Mathare valley they would, according to MYSA volunteer Bonface Mbugua, never allow football matches involving the senior team due to fears of violent clashes. Fans of the two teams mentioned above, Gor Mahia and AFC Leopards, have an especially notorious reputation and according to a variety of sources hooliganism is generally increasing in contemporary Kenyan football (see, for example, *Daily Nation*, 2 November 2000). For fans of these two teams, 'post-match violence is deeply rooted in tradition ... a match is not over until the fans have caused mayhem' (*East African*, 16–22 April 1999). More often than not, these incidents are related to the respective clubs' links to conflicting tribal identities and backgrounds.

There have been no reports linking supporters or players of Mathare United with violent conduct. Perhaps this should be viewed against the fact that the football team was established out of a principle of social reconciliation rather than local or ethnic rivalry. MYSA appears to have brought some stability and safety in an area where there previously was none. James Waithaka, Mathare United's bus driver, told us that before MYSA became a reality, the area around the current MYSA office on Juja Road would have been dangerous to walk for a white person.

The coupling of violence and football is well known in Europe and Latin America. British anthropologist Paul Richards (1997) argues for the possibility of reconciliation through football rather than conflict from a different reality than that of an abundant post-industrial society. For the young irregular militias of Sierra Leone, which he bases his study on, there are few options of rule-based social interaction. From his observations Richards argues that football evokes a sense of mutual understanding among children and youngsters tormented and traumatized by warfare experiences about the necessity of abiding by basic shared rules (ibid.). Such a scenario could easily be adapted to the anarchic slum realities of Mathare. The general interest for the game is an obvious reason for its suitability. The tool is there if it works, as Richards argues: 'Perhaps soccer is one of the basic ways in which conditions of radical desocialization can be reversed' (ibid.: 154).

With half the African population under the age of 18 (ibid.: 146), the importance of having innovative, democratic organizations among that particular age group is obvious. Adelman (1995: 102) argues that any democratic organization or society needs to be built from the realities on a grassroots level. This is a stated ambition of MYSA's governing body, the Executive Council, which consists of elected members from each of the 16 MYSA zones mentioned above. Willis questions the real influence children and youths in MYSA have when he states that, 'While opportunities for the youth themselves to sit on councils do exist, whether they have the capacity of being influential is more open to question' (Willis 1999: 137). Nevertheless, field observations indicate that the feeling of ownership is strong among members of MYSA, as stressed by one of the young leaders in MYSA, Salim Mohammed: 'Youth are talking now, before youth were forgotten' (ibid.).

What makes MYSA different?

Many development and aid projects initiated by Western agencies have failed over the last 50 years. The Norwegian anthropologist Tord Larsen relates this to a lack of knowledge about local cultural practices and beliefs: 'All forms of social pathology and client-making of populations have been a consequence of invalidating people's cultural codes and depriving them of their means to create valuable social communities' (Larsen 1989: 19, authors' translation). MYSA seems to have succeeded with a different approach. As an organization it has been built and maintained with financial support from different Western agencies. Foreign agencies fund various projects and programmes run by MYSA, and Western social and cultural influences are evident in anything from the stress on discipline and fair play to the fact that their main donor was founded on Christian Lutheran ideology.[31] The significant difference between the MYSA development project and more traditional aid programmes is that MYSA's activities are conditioned by local participation and administration, despite its continuing dependency on Western agencies. Its subsequent successes may be explained via its ability to engage young people in activities that are meaningful to them and to offer them a new direction and opportunities in their lives.

Football is the number one sport, not only in Mathare, but in Kenya, and indeed Africa in general. In Kenya this is evident in the massive coverage of national and international football in daily national papers such as the *Daily Nation* or the *East African Standard*. 'Soccer as a spectator sport is found in every town and village of the country' (Godia 1989: 276). MYSA and Mathare United have during their short existence become popular members of the Kenyan football family. Mathare United has not been latched onto by Kenyan politicians attempting to create popular goodwill for themselves, as has been the case with a number of other clubs, and hence it has maintained a politically and ethnically neutral position.

After 15 years of existence MYSA is still growing and engaging in new projects. As a consequence the need for partners and donors will probably increase. Today it is heavily dependent on the financial support from a small number of foreign partners, such as NORAD and the Strømme Foundation. The management are aware of this. The potential for revenue through Mathare United is evident, where both the sale of players and sponsorship deals are potential sources of funding. Over the years MYSA has produced numerous good coaches and instructors. Revenue can be gained by providing commercial sport instruction for people able and willing to pay.[32] To become sustainable it is important to avoid economic dependency on other parties. MYSA is in the process of becoming famous and is attracting attention from various aid agencies.[33] Such attention may provide a possibility for further development, yet also a possible threat as agencies may wish to be associated with the name. MYSA has grown to become something of a model for other clubs in Kenya as well, yet operates independently of the Kenyan Football Federation (KFF). MYSA has been successful on a grassroots level and economic support has never been channelled via the national football administration. The KFF has a reputation charged with fraud and corruption and officials in the KFF have repeatedly demonstrated a negative attitude towards MYSA.

A grassroots organization building on apparent democratic principles in a country struggling to overcome corruption, nepotism and non-democratic use of power should be welcomed and appreciated. Maloba (1996) stresses the significance of regaining African dignity. The poverty remains, but people there have a new focal point, and with this, dignity and self-respect for creating a basis for identity-building. In Giulianotti's words: 'The social identity of people is rooted in a twin process, of identifying themselves within a community, and also, as a consequence, by identifying themselves against other people and other communities' (Giulianotti 1999b: 3) MYSA has given its members a group identity and a feeling of ownership of the organization in an environment where it can be hard to find reasons for pride against the outside communities. If we combine Giulianotti's key point that 'sportification of Africa can indeed be a positive rather than a negative component establishing peaceful and viable social relationships' (ibid.), with the urge of Blacking (1987) to diminish the Euro-American pressure as mentioned above, we seem to get close to the recipe for MYSA success. In an area with a multitude of ethnic groups and severe social deprivation, MYSA has managed to build a foundation for improving material conditions and generating a new Mathare identity charged with an improved sense of self-esteem.

Notes

1. This chapter is based on fieldwork conducted by Arvid Tollisen in the Mathare district of Nairobi, Kenya, between 1999 and 2001.
2. MYSA produce information in the shape of printed handouts covering their policy, history, rules and regulations. These 'publications' are low-cost photocopies used within the organization and for promotional purposes.
3. Owen Willis wrote his PhD thesis on Sport and Development. The thesis is based on fieldwork conducted in Mathare, April/May 1999, and personal contact and correspondence with persons connected to MYSA.
4. Information obtained during interview with Banu Kahn who is an associate with the Population Council, Nairobi office. The Population Council is a non-governmental research organization with headquarters in New York.
5. The way MYSA has included girls in a traditionally male-dominated arena such as football is interesting in itself, but a closer scrutiny of MYSA's gender dimension goes beyond the scope of this chapter.
6. The Norwegian Agency for Development Cooperation (NORAD) is a directorate under the Norwegian Ministry of Foreign Affairs.
7. The Strømme Foundation is a development organization based on Christian values. The main office is in Kristiansand, Norway. Regional offices are located in Lima in Peru, Bamako in Mali, Kampala in Uganda and Dhaka in Bangladesh. Their budget derives from church collection and fundraising supported by NORAD and the Norwegian Ministry of Foreign Affairs (UD). The organization operates typically in a partnership entirely relying on local partners (see <www.strommestiftelsen.no>).
8. The Norway Cup dates back to 1972. This youth tournament is administrated and run by Bækkelaget Sportsklubb. They were awarded a UNICEF award in 1995 for their international involvement and involvement in aid programmes.

In 2001 around 25,000 young footballers participated (<www.norway-cup.no>).

9. NORAD has a policy of adding four times the amount of what is initially raised by voluntary organizations like the Strømme Foundation based on approval of the projects. Hence NORAD is no longer directly involved as a partner in Mathare, but channels its financial support through the Strømme Foundation.

10. The Dutch agencies include a variety of development cooperations and the Netherlands Olympic Committee (Lindøe 2001: 24).

11. The Ford Foundation is an independent, non-profit, non-governmental organization and a resource for innovative people and institutions worldwide with the stated aim of 'Strengthening democratic values, reducing poverty and injustice, promote international cooperation and advancing human achievement' (<www.fordfound.org>).

12. Muraya is the Project Manager for the garbage clean-up programme in MYSA.

13. MYSA has its own independent league system linked to the different 16 zones. MYSA sets up and administrates these leagues through its staff and volunteers.

14. The United Nations World Commission on Development and Environment, which presented its report at this summit, was headed by the former Norwegian Prime Minister, Gro Harlem Brundtland.

15. In 1987, the United Nations Environment Programme (UNEP) established the so-called Global 500 Roll of Honour for Environmental Achievement. All recipients of this award become ex officio members of the Global 500 Environmental Forum, which was set up at the Rio conference in 1992 to promote awareness of the work of grassroots organizations engaged in environmental issues.

16. The oldest league within the MYSA system is the Under-18 league. After the age of 18, young players can try to get a contract with Mathare United or another team in the Kenyan league. The term 'graduate' refers to those who have been through the MYSA league system. It is still a criterion that to play for Mathare United you must have been 'brought up' within the MYSA league system.

17. Norsk Hydro is one of the largest public companies in Norway and has been involved in numerous development projects supported or run by the Norwegian government. This sponsorship deal was worth $44,500 each season between 1994 and 1998 (information from the Strømme Foundation).

18. Moi Golden Cup is the nationwide Kenyan cup competition, named after President Daniel Arap Moi.

19. Evans 'Valdo' Nyabaro was the first Mathare United player who made a footballing career abroad. Since 1998 he has played for the Norwegian club Start FC, reflecting the numerous links between Norwegian partners and MYSA.

20. Kere is the Project Manager for the AIDS Information Programme in MYSA and a player at Mathare United.

21. The MYSA sponsoring by the Ford Foundation was linked to this project.

22. Elected posts and meetings include, for example, serving as an elected official in a league committee or representing MYSA in external meetings.

23. The first MYSA youth who went to Norway on a college scholarship was Francis Kimanzi in 1996/97. Since 1997 this opportunity has been funded as

a consequence of a cooperation between Norwegian colleges and the Strømme Foundation. Between 1997 and 2001 14 MYSA students have been involved in this programme.

24. MYSA's Fairplay Code is a written document which states that 'Fairplay is only for those who want to be winners on and off the field.' It consists of the following eleven paragraphs: 1. No indiscipline, 2. No unfair play, 3. No retaliation, 4. No fouls, 5. No appeals, 6. Respect the coach, 7. Respect the captain, 8. Respect teammates, 9. Respect opponents, 10. Respect the officials, 11. Respect myself and the environment.

25. Findings by Meave Leakey and colleagues at the National Museum of Kenya throw the origins of humankind into question (see *Los Angeles Times*, 22 March 2001: p. A1).

26. The Berlin Conference 1884–85 was the peak of the 'Scramble for Africa'. Invited by the German Chancellor Otto von Bismarck, the colony powers agreed on African territory possession. The borders drawn and signed in the 26 February 1885 agreement are largely the borders seen after the independence of the African states (*Aschehoug/Gyldendahl Encyclopedia* 1995: 278).

27. This included the Norwegian government who had broken diplomatic relations with Kenya following the imprisonment of the oppositional politician Koigi Wa Wamwere.

28. Oginga Odinga and Tom Mboya were both key figures in the 1950s nationalist struggles for Kenyan independence (Ochieng and Atieno-Odhiambo 1996: xii).

29. Blacking (1987: 5) suggests that modern sports had their analogues in traditional African societies and as one consequence thereof African countries will be better off by choosing sports corresponding with their own cultural configuration rather *than succumb to the pressures and fashions of Euro-American sport world*.

30. See Wainaina (<www.g21.net>) who claims that 'The name Mathare is so notorious it strikes terror in any owner of fixed property.'

31. MYSA itself does not have a stated Christian ideological basis, yet the practising of Christianity is evident among many of its members. However MYSA documents contain no religious statements. Information obtained from the Strømme Foundation confirms this religious neutral profile of the MYSA organization and according to the Strømme Foundation's own statements, religious belonging is not a criterion for becoming a partner to the foundation. The overall denominational composition of Kenya is: Protestants 38 per cent, Catholics 28 per cent, indigenous religions 26 per cent, Muslims 7 per cent, others 1 per cent (see <www.keyalogy.com>).

32. Nairobi is a city of great economic contrasts. For the affluent population the market for leisure activities could be a way for MYSA to gain revenue by providing instruction (interview Bob Munro, April 2000).

33. One example here is the way former track and field star Edwin Moses and former football world champion Bobby Charlton handed over approximately $60,000 on behalf of a charity organization to MYSA in April 2001 (Norwegian TV2, 10 April 2001).

Part Four
Moving with the Ball

12
Three Geographies of African Footballer Migration: Patterns, Problems and Postcoloniality

John Bale

Introduction

The changing geography of labour is one of the characteristics of globalization. Among both skilled and not-so-skilled elements of international labour migration are the African male footballers who ply their trade in football's global markets. How might such migration be examined? Where in Africa do migrant footballers come from and where in Europe are their sojourns? How are these Africans received by their hosts? How are they read by the world of sport? This chapter seeks to present three geographical ways of looking at the migration of African migrant football-workers. The first adopts a traditional sports-geographic approach that, literally, maps the geographical variations in the migratory flows of African soccer professionals. This seeks to show the extent of such migration and also the heterogeneity of Africa – that it is a continent of contrasts with respect to the 'production' and 'export' of football talent. My second geography of African football migration adopts a quite different approach and seeks to excavate the surficial 'facts' of migration. Broadly speaking, the second section of this chapter takes a neocolonial view of African football by drawing attention to continuing colonial practices in the 'processing' of African sports-labour and the recruitment of young African players. Thirdly, postcolonial analysis is employed in exploring the textual construction and the 'imaginative geographies' (Said 1978) of African footballers. I show how Europe writes 'the African' (potential or actual) migrant footballer. There is no monolithic European discourse, postcolonial rhetoric being polyvocal and fractured. The second and third parts of the chapter therefore rewrite the contemporary migration of African footballers in a less benign way than is commonly the case.

Of the 311 players making up the 16 national squads in the 2002 African Nations Cup, 193, or 62 per cent, were employed full-time in Europe. In the cases of Cameroon, Nigeria and Senegal, every squad member was domiciled in Europe (Moore 2002). In 1999, over 890 African professional footballers were listed on the rosters of European professional clubs (Ricci 2000). The emergence of substantial numbers of African footballers playing/working on foreign teams is relatively recent but as the names of such stars as Bakayoko, Kanu, Weah, Radebe and Kachloul testify, the African migrant footballer has become an established figure. Beyond Europe, African footballers have been recruited in the Americas and Asia. The growth of an African presence in the global football arena is not simply the result of the 'development' of the game in Africa itself, the outcome of a century of sporting proselytizing both by missionaries (in the early days), military, schools, plantation owners and, latterly, by the global football federation (FIFA). African sports talent has become more accessible as a result of the growing commercialism of the football industry and the compression of time-space that brings potential professional sports labour closer than ever to the global markets for its employment (Darby 2000b, 2002).

Before attempting to chart some of the lineaments of African soccer player migration I need to define, for this section, the term 'African footballer'. By this I refer to sports-workers who are either immigrants or recruits to nations outside Africa. However, given both the nature of much of the data that I use and the cultural construction of what is 'nationality', I also include those longer-term residents of non-African nations who have chosen to represent African countries at the international level. African migrant footballers may be, in Maguire's (1999: 105–6) terms, 'mercenaries' (motivated by short-term gains), 'settlers' (those who remain in the society in which they perform their labour) or 'nomadic cosmopolitans' (embarking on quests of discovering other lands and peoples, becoming strangers in foreign metropolitan cultures). A different form of geographical movement is made up of 'returnees'; that is, footballers making short-term visits abroad specifically to compete in international matches or competitions, thence returning to their African homes. To these could be added those whose stay overseas is limited to a few months or less, the return being the result of disenchantment or dissatisfaction. This classification, if it can be so-called, reveals the diversity of possible migrant types and experiences (see also Lanfranchi and Taylor 2001: 186–9). Additionally, diversity exists at an 'ethnic' level. The 'African footballer', as represented in this chapter, is not synonymous with the 'black footballer'. European and

American players of African extraction are not included (had they been, the numbers would have been substantially greater). The word 'extraction' to denote parentage is used advisedly because these players have been extracted from somewhere else before becoming Brazilian, American, English, French, Dutch, Swedish or Belgian (Quayson 2000: 177). In some nations, recent migrants from Africa are a minority of the black players who are said to bring African-ness or hybridity to the modern game of football. A further group is made up of African soccer migrants who are of European extraction, notably several from South Africa. There is also the arguable distinction between players from the 'oriental' north of Africa and those from 'Black Africa', south of the Sahara, a distinction drawn by both Africanists and Afrocentrists (Howe 1998: 232). Superimposed on these categorizations is the difference in national and regional origins and destinations, the patterns of which form the prime foci of the following section.

Geography 1: mapping migrations

The employment of African players by football clubs in Europe is not new (Darby 2000b; Lanfranchi and Taylor 2001) but space does not permit a detailed examination of the antecedents of such 'body trading' (Shilling 1993: 20). Nor is a review of the history of African teams visiting Europe to take part in various kinds of international competitions (e.g. Vasili 1995) possible here. However, the presence of African football-workers in Europe has clearly increased dramatically in recent years, as part of the growth in the number of foreign players per se (Table 12.1). For example, in the early 1990s, there were less than 20 foreign players in the English Premiership. By 2000 there were over 250, serving to remind us that the migration of African sports talent is but part of the broader globalization of skilled migrants per se. Africans have also formed a substantial part of the growing number of black players working at the highest level of European football (e.g. Szymanski and Kuypers 2000: 185). In this section I will review the extent of African footballer migration at the professional level at the start of the twenty-first century. This is, therefore, a snapshot at one point in time and variations will be found in different years for the precise extent of immigration and emigration by host and donor nations respectively. Two geographical dimensions of this migration can be reviewed; first, the international destinations, and secondly the African origins.

Table 12.1   Some dimensions of elite African footballer migration: selected countries, top division clubs only, 2000

Country	Total elite players[1]	Percent foreign (n)	Percent African (n)	African as percent of foreign
France	938	20.5 (192)	10.0 (94)·	48.9
Denmark	312	12.2 (38)	4.2 (13)	34.2
Belgium	504	41.3 (208)	11.9 (60)·	28.8
Netherlands	516	33.9 (175)	7.2 (37)·	21.2
Portugal	713	23.6 (168)	4.8 (34)·	20.2
Greece	269	29.0 (78)	5.6 (15)··	19.2
Switzerland	194	39.7 (77)	7.2 (14)·	18.2
Austria	209	33.4 (70)	5.7 (12)·	17.1
Italy	672	22.8 (153)	3.3 (22)·	14.4
Norway	336	12.5 (42)	1.8 (6)	14.3
Germany	601	38.9 (234)	5.5 (33)·	14.1
England[2]	764	33.5 (256)	2.5 (19)·	7.4
Spain	813	33.5 (272)	2.3 (19)	7.0
Scotland[2]	311	28.9 (90)	0.6 (2)	2.2
Sweden	322	7.8 (25)	0	0
Total	**7,474**	**27.8 (2,078)**	**5.1 (380)**	**18.3**

Notes: [1] Refers to top division squads of national leagues.
         [2] Excludes migrants from other nations of the UK.

Source: Soccerweb (2000).

Of the 894 African professionals in Europe in 1999, nearly 59 per cent were playing in four countries – France (16 per cent), Portugal (15 per cent), Belgium (15 per cent) and Germany (12 per cent). The overall distribution is shown in Figure 12.1, derived from data assembled by Ricci (2000). This reveals a widespread continental distribution of African players with almost all countries in Western Europe having recruited African players. There is also a scattering of such players in countries of Eastern Europe, notably Poland and Russia, each of which attracted more Africans than any of the nations of Scandinavia. In addition to migrants to Europe, African players work in the US, Australia, India, China and Saudi Arabia. In 2000, the rosters of the twelve clubs making up the US Major Soccer League revealed that only five Africans were included, comprising 7 per cent of the foreign total (MSL 2000). A small number of African football players are also recruited on 'sports scholarships' to American universities (Bale 1991).

    The extent of African participation in Europe can be refined by utilizing a second data set, that from Soccerweb (2000). While covering a smaller

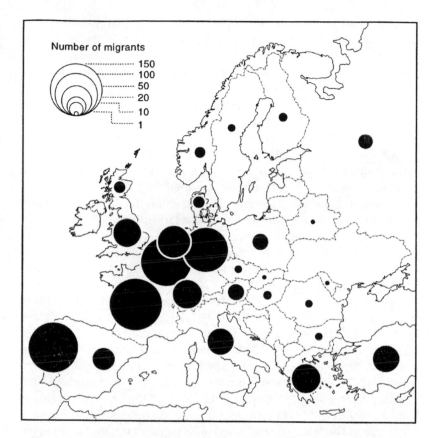

Figure 12.1 African professional footbailers in Europe, 1999

Source: Ricci (2000).

number of players than that listed by Ricci, the Soccerweb data provide details of the national composition of squad members of each top division club in a number of countries (Table 12.1). These data therefore provide indicators of the percentage of the total number of elite professionals in each country who are African and the number of African players as a percentage of all foreign players. An examination of 15 Western European countries, including the major footballing nations of France, Italy, Spain, Portugal, Germany, the Netherlands, Belgium and England, for which data were available for the year 2000, shows that foreign players made up about 28 per cent of top division players. African migrant players, on average, made up around 5 per cent of those employed in the premier division clubs. Around this average, however, there are considerable variations ranging from nearly 12 per cent in the Belgian top division to none in the Swedish equivalent (at the time represented by the data). Table 12.1 reveals a marked difference in the 'penetration' of African players. Although Belgium, of the nations included, has the largest proportion of its elite playing force made up of foreign recruits, the proportion of foreigners who are African is much higher in the case of France where nearly half of all foreign recruits are from Africa. At the other end of the scale, while the proportion of foreign players in England is not markedly different from the average for those countries considered (i.e. about one-third of all elite players), very few of them are from Africa. Additionally, very small numbers of Africans are recruited to Scotland, Norway and Sweden. Some of these migratory flows probably relate to the different traditions of respective former colonial relationships. The substantial African presence in French and Belgian football is mirrored in Spain and Portugal by high numbers of imported players from Latin America and in Britain by the long traditions of migrant footballers from its former colony, Ireland (McGovern 2000).

To some extent, the European destinations of the 894 elite African footballers identified by Ricci (2000) as working in Europe follow predictable patterns of former colonial relations. For example, most Algerian players are found in France. Three-quarters, one-half, and one-third of African elite players in Europe from, respectively, Senegal, Ivory Coast and Cameroon, likewise migrated to French clubs. Almost 60 per cent of players from the Democratic Republic of the Congo migrated to Belgium while over 93 per cent of those from Angola moved to Portugal. Such apparently strong residual colonial linkages are not found, however, in the case of African players from the former British colonies. Nigerians, Ghanaians and South Africans found destinations throughout Western Europe with only a slight sign of any concentration in Britain. While suggestive of differing colonial attitudes and government – Britain was simply 'uninterested in its colonial resource', according to Lanfranchi and Taylor (2001: 182) – the differences between the adoption of sojourn in a particular former colonial power by some African footballers and not others requires much more detailed historical, social and cultural enquiry.

It is widely presumed that the majority of foreign migrants in many sports gravitate to the major leagues. The assumption that foreign migrant footballers are established stars leads to the conclusion that it is only the richer clubs that can afford them. In some countries this may indeed be the case. In Switzerland 59 per cent of imported African players are with top division clubs; in Italy, 62 per cent play in Serie A; in Spain the equivalent figure is 65 per cent and in Holland 80 per cent. However, the situation in other nations suggests that substantial numbers of African migrants are either not elite, not yet elite or are no longer elite. In both France and England, 54 per cent of the African professionals play in the lower divisions and in Portugal the figure is 56 per cent. In Belgium and Germany the percentage of the total number of African migrants playing in lower divisions substantially outnumbers those in the top division, the figures being 62 per cent and 66 per cent respectively. These variations suggest that many African football migrants can be viewed as relatively 'cheap labour', in Western terms. This has traditionally been the case in Belgium which has lagged behind the minimum wage for first division footballers found in other Western European nations (Castle et al., 2000; Lanfranchi and Taylor 2001: 182–3).

My second analysis focuses on the geography of migrant origins. The production of migrant African professionals is highly concentrated in a small number of nations. Five countries (Nigeria, Cameroon, Ghana, Morocco and Angola) supply over half the African 'output'. Add four other nations (Democratic Republic of the Congo, Ivory Coast, Senegal and Algeria) and over 70 per cent of those moving to Europe are accounted for (Table 12.2). Two major zones of production of African professional footballers are evident. First a band of coastal nations of West Africa including Nigeria, Cameroon, Ghana, Ivory Coast and Senegal. Each of these nations produces a substantial number of talented soccer players, Nigeria being the major single national provider, supplying about 15 per cent of all African players to the European soccer market. A less productive region lies in North Africa and is composed of the two major producers, Morocco and Algeria. The more sparsely populated

Table 12.2   Major African sources of migrant footballers to Europe, 1999

Nation	Number	Percentage
Nigeria	140	15.7
Cameroon	97	10.9
Ghana	88	9.8
Morocco	72	8.1
Angola	66	7.4
Dem. Rep. Congo	63	7.0
Ivory Coast	43	4.8
Senegal	40	4.5
Algeria	30	3.4

Source: Ricci (2000).

nations of Libya and Tunisia are modest suppliers, but so too is North Africa's most populous nation, Egypt. Figure 12.2 reveals the relatively empty heart of Africa with some large nation-states supplying relatively small numbers of footballers to Europe's major leagues. This is notably the case of nations in East Africa such as Kenya, Zimbabwe and Tanzania, though the latter has had a tradition of sending players to Saudi Arabia (Tenga 2000). At the same time, it is clear from Figure 12.2 that most African countries supply few players to Europe, an important reminder that Africa is not an undifferentiated continent of 'natural' footballers, a subject I return to later.

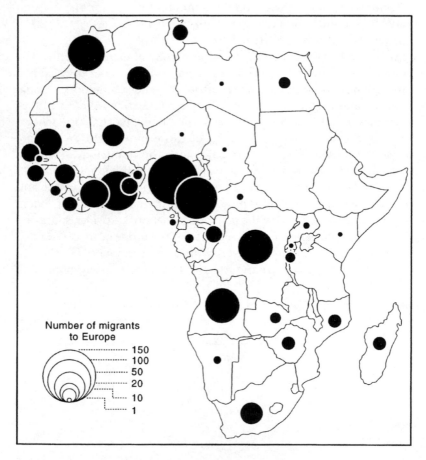

Figure 12.2   National origins of African players in Europe

Source: Ricci (2000).

Geography 2: neocolonial 'exploitation'?

It is impossible to examine in detail the social and cultural problems that may accompany the migration of the kinds of African soccer stars who startle the world's audiences with their skills. Given the constraints of space, all I can do in this (and the following) section is to excavate the kind of status quo geography outlined above and to humanize the generalized patterns shown in Tables 12.1 and 12.2 and Figures 12.1 and 12.2. As David Ley pointed out in critiquing such sports geographic approaches, they may be of considerable interest but

> exemplify a research style where description takes precedence over interpretation. Maps of the spatial origins of professional sports players … invite interpretive accounts of the places and practices which produced such social facts. (Ley 1985: 417; note also Cresswell 2001)

In response to this critique, there is a need, I think, to examine some of the practices involved in football-worker migration, reflecting the fact that the maps and tables shown earlier are not, beneath their elegantly crafted surfaces, as neat and tidy as first impressions suggest.

The German soccer coach, Dettmar Cramer, is quoted in the (former West) German parliamentary gazette as stating that

> we can systematically comb thoroughly one continent after another and help our friends in every country to leap in order to smooth their path towards the top of world football. This is their aim. That they may reach it, this is our task. (quoted in Eichberg 1994)

The systematization of recruitment, migration and work of African footballers can be read as a form of neocolonialism and exploitation in the well worn European traditions of scrambling for Africa, as reflected in Cramer's statement above. I want to illustrate the neocolonialism of African player migrations through three examples. The first is the establishment of 'farm clubs' by European mega-clubs in Africa; the second is the exploitation of young African recruits in Europe; and the third alludes to the role of 'agents' in the exploitation of African sports talent domiciled in Europe.

Cultivating and processing footballers can be read as a reduced mirror image of the plantation system of colonial Africa. In his study of baseball in the Dominican Republic, Allan Klein (1991: 42) observes that the euphemistically termed 'baseball academies' set up by North American baseball clubs are latter-day counterparts of the 'colonial outpost'. Similarly, like any other major international company, the emergent 'farm clubs' for footballers in Africa, owned and operated by major European outfits, seek to (a) find raw materials, i.e. talented players; (b) refine them, i.e. train the players, and (c) ship abroad the finished products, i.e. football players (ibid.). In 1999 the Dutch club, Ajax, became the first European club to purchase a South African club 'with the aim of nurturing young talent' by establishing an extensive scouting network (Milner 1999). A new club, Ajax Cape Town, was formed by a merger of two Cape Town clubs, each of which had previous links with Ajax. In a not dissimilar situation, FC Copenhagen have set up a 'Soccer School of Excellence' in South Africa for the search and processing of local soccer talent. US$10 million has been spent by FC Copenhagen on the development of this project. The 'production' of one star could lead to this investment more than being matched by the sale price of such a player. Football academies are said to be 'opening up all over the continent' involving European clubs such as Feyenoord, Paris St Germain and Monaco (Oliver 2000). Though not quite the same as the 'farm club' concept it may be worth noting that Manchester United collaborates with the Belgian club, Royal Antwerp, in finding players from Africa and elsewhere to work in the English Premiership. The primary aim of such initiatives is to enhance the playing power and economic wealth of European clubs. Associated with this is what Eichberg (1994) has termed a well meaning 'Pygmalion syndrome' – the pride and love of the producer in a neocolonial context. The trade in footballers between Europe and Africa inhibits development – or, at best, creates dependent development – within Africa. This usually occurs in three ways:

1. The transnational organizations at the 'centre' that drive a commodified global football industry have the power to generate wealth at the expense of clubs in nations at the periphery
2. The domination and appeal of the European clubs are enhanced by their ability to attract soccer talent from Africa, leading to a deskilling of players in African leagues
3. African countries tend to be excluded from the foci of decision-making in global football and are consequently unable to change these processes of domination (McGovern 2000: 402–3).

The players that leave Africa and reach Europe are placed with clubs in several ways. Some migrants arrive as a result of their own initiatives. In some cases they may be illegal immigrants possessing no official papers but with sufficient desire for a life in European soccer. A second group is made up of migrants who are recommended by an agent and may be drawn to Europe on the basis of a videotape or an invitation to demonstrate their abilities. In both of these groups, the European sojourn may be very brief, the result of the inability of the migrants to make the required grade. How many of those not making the required grade stay in Europe is unknown. The third group is made up of players who are known to European coaches or African scouts who have witnessed these promising players at first hand (Broere and van der Drift 1997: 85). A fourth group is made up of African players who are well established and are subject to transfer from one (often European) club to another. However, the growing number of African stars who hold European Union passports as well as those of their home nations in order to allow them to play in Europe without work permits, has led to concern within FIFA and UEFA. Many foreign players are thought to have illegally obtained passports, often in collusion with their European clubs (Chaudhary 2001).

My particular focus here is on the role of agents in the migration process. According to Broere and van der Drift (1997), an Italian agent whose interest is focused on Ghanaian players takes 12 per cent of their monthly salaries. He brings players of 15 and 16 years of age to Europe where often they live in squalid accommodation, and many return to Ghana impoverished and disenchanted. It has been noted that trade in footballers has a somewhat sour taste throughout the world. It is a world which has its own norms and laws, its own subculture. In Africa it seems that the player agents can go further than in Europe because in some countries there is no regulatory system. In addition, the motivation of players to find a European club is huge. Many African footballers are content to put up with a bad contract because they expect that in Europe they will eventually do better (ibid.: 84).

Once playing in Europe, African players commonly experience culture shock and abuse. African players suffer racial abuse, mocking, jeering and insults from spectators in a number of European countries, though this is not without ambivalence (Back et al., 2001). Outside the stadium, insults from team colleagues may assume the form of racist jokes. Although substantial amounts of money are made by some migrant players, culture shock and problems of adjustment are far from uncommon. And in Britain, at least, it has been found that 'black' players are paid less than 'white' players, despite the view that the average black footballer is better than the average white player, having longer careers and making more league and international appearances (Szymanski and Kuypers 2000: 183). The Zimbabwean, Peter Ndlovu, found that the initial financial package that he signed with Coventry City made him one of the club's worst-paid players (quoted in Darby 2000b: 227).

It is unlikely that the likes of George Weah and Nwankwo Kanu would admit to being exploited by the world of professional football. Their earnings should allow them to live in comfort for the rest of their lives. But they are at the pinnacle of the world football hierarchy. What about those at its bottom end? The worst-case scenario is arguably one in which African teenagers – the 'raw material' – are tested, trained and quickly discarded, ending up in menial jobs or, at worst, as street children (Hoberman 2000: 60). This is not to say, however, that being a street person in Brussels is worse than being one in Monrovia. However, the European concern about child footballers is graphically illustrated by evidence provided to the UK House of Commons Select Committee on Education and Employment. It referred to a report of the UN Commission on Human Rights that highlighted 'the problems of young African players being effectively bought by agents and then taken to Northern European countries to be offered to football clubs' and that there was 'a danger of effectively creating a modern day "slave trade" in young African footballers' (House of Commons 1999). What has been termed 'exploitation of the most cruel and blatant kind' by the President of the Sport and Freedom Association, a human rights group investigating the cases of young African footballers lured to Europe, results from non-materialized contracts and broken promises (see Box 12.1). From such perspectives, African footballer migration – like that of child sex workers – can be seen as raising serious issues concerning children's rights (Kidd and Donnelly 2000).

Box 12.1   Njiki's story

In 1996, Njiki, just 16, was a gifted and prolific striker enrolled in the youth training scheme at Olympique de M'Volye, the biggest club in Yaoundé, capital city of his native Cameroon. He dreamed of European football, where 'the stadiums are beautiful, the team strips are always brand new, the players get looked after and cosseted and cared for. It was what we all wanted.'

Foreign scouts were frequent visitors to the club, and every boy there hoped his turn would come. Njiki's came quickly: an offer from the French club Montpellier. He had never heard of them, but took the proffered plane ticket anyway. He was put up in a comfortable hotel, started training immediately and carried on with his schoolwork as French law required. He was not being paid, but he had all he needed. Within a month, his nightmare had started. Spotted by the Belgian First Division club Ghent, he was offered a professional contract

– impossible in France, where no player under the age of 17 can turn pro. Njiki headed for Ghent with a three-month visa, trained for a month, and was not paid at the end of it.

'They told me I should wait, be patient, there were small problems to sort out,' he says. 'I waited.' Two months later, Montpellier had had enough of his waiting and informed him they no longer needed his services. A week later, Ghent did the same. Njiki, still not 17, was alone in a foreign country, without even the money to pay his fare home. His visa would expire within weeks; he would soon be an illegal immigrant.

Fortunately, his talents did not go unrecognized. A Third Division club was only too happy to take him on. He signed a piece of paper, in Dutch, which he did not understand but which he understood to be a contract. In fact, it tied him to the club for no fixed wage. 'They slipped me R100 or R150 when they felt like it, here and there,' he says. 'I played for them like that all that season.'

Enter another nebulous figure in Njiki's two-and-a-half years of misery. A smooth-talking football agent appeared on the scene in May 1997 and promised to save his skin. The approach was tempting: another First Division club, Malines, was prepared to offer a two-year professional contract, full pay, all above board. There was just one condition: Njiki had to sign with the agent first. And the contract stipulated that he would be due a commission comprising 50 per cent net of all sums received by the player in respect of activities performed by him that were organized or arranged by the manager or any third party.

Njiki swears that 5 per cent inexplicably became 50 per cent after the contract was signed. 'But in any case, what was I to do?' he asks. 'I was depressed, illegal, without a penny. All I wanted was to play football, be housed and fed. The agent profited from my situation. I was at his mercy. I was being exploited, the victim of trafficking. But it took me a long time to realize it.'

Reduced to sharing a squalid one-room flat in Brussels with four other young African players, he found a Second Division club that wanted him – but not at the price demanded by his agent. So he approached them on his own, signed his dreamed-of contract, and could only watch helplessly as the scorned agent threatened both him and the club, Denderleeuw, with legal action and even physical violence unless he received his commission. The club, of course, dropped Njiki like a shot. Only now is he beginning to emerge from his trauma.

(Source: Henly 1998)

Geography 3: postcolonial ponderings

I want to take a final tack by outlining what can be termed the 'imaginative geographies' of African footballers. This approach is inspired by the writings of postcolonial analysts such as Edward Said (1978) and, especially here, David Spurr (1994). Such a postcolonial approach is hardly de rigueur in football studies. Yet I believe that a 'postcolonial geography' of football, involving the interrogation of (neo)colonial texts about African football and place, has much to offer. Here I want to explore how African footballers are both 'received' and 'constructed' in Western media. I seek to demonstrate how well-worn colonial rhetorics continue to be employed in the post/neocolonial representation of migrant African soccer workers. The importance of postcolonial studies can be argued to lie in their application to the present. Here, I mainly rework a variety of texts that allude to African football-workers and suggest the value of an awareness of the question (or 'crisis') of representation in football studies. I want to outline the continuing validity of Spurr's (1994) schema of colonial writing that encourages a move away from monolithic studies of, say, stereotyping. Instead, I focus on a number of conceptual categories of writing or, as Spurr puts it, rhetorical modes. Spurr recognizes twelve such modes, but for my purposes I will collapse them into four – surveillance, appropriation, idealization and negation. These reveal the discourse on the African footballer as being fractured and often contradictory.

In colonial texts African athletes who were often represented as fantastic athletes were 'othered' and 'ordered' by the European gaze. The Africans' corporeal practices could seemingly be recorded only in the terms of the European, but the rhetoric employed could range from that representing the 'idle native' to that of the 'noble savage'. The same applies today. However, there seems to be one important difference between the rhetoric used to represent athletic Africans in colonial texts and those used to represent many African football workers of the twenty-first century. When Europeans ventured into central Africa in the late nineteenth and early twentieth centuries, no modern sports existed there. Yet it has been shown how native peoples were often rhetorically appropriated and constructed as potential world-class sportsmen (the gendered noun is deliberate) in an idealized, yet equivocal, way (Bale 2002). Conversely, at the start of the twenty-first century, popular representations of black athletes who have, in actuality, achieved world-class status in the world of achievement sports, are often rhetorically 'reduced' to their (pre-) colonial state by the application of modes of debasement and negation, again equivocally. Certainly, the tropes of surveillance, naturalization and idealization continue, but negating of the African seems to me to be the most pernicious mode of representation in an ambivalent and ambiguous discourse. The continued excavation and interrogation of (neo)colonial texts is surely relevant to the study of contemporary 'imaginative geographies' of the modern, globalized, postcolonial, sportized body. Let me briefly illustrate four rhetorical modes employed in writing 'the African footballer'.

Surveillance in modern sport is a pervasive global phenomenon and is much more prevalent today than in the first half of the twentieth century. The quantitative recording of sport has become more spatially extensive and more sophisticated. Ranking and ordering of individuals and teams are central features of the global sportized gaze. The universal currencies of achievement sports – the record and the statistic – enable the employers of sports labour to stand back and take an 'objective' view of the sports potential among young people the world over. The videotape is an essential form of representation that has enabled the European recruiter to gaze at the African prospect from afar. Additionally, a website advertising the activities of Cennetsportlink International claims to be able to provide the 'easy availability of African soccer professional players to the rest of the world'. Through the collection of quantitative data (e.g. Ricci 2000) the West is able to record the extent of potential recruitment and monitor the success of the neocolonial project of sport 'development'. The quantitative data which facilitate the classification of individuals and of nations permit a mapping of the new global sports empires, in a similar way to the recording of the anthropologists' categorizations of 'native games and customs' in past decades. Underlying such forms of surveillance is the domination and power of those in authority and privilege.

The rhetorical mode of *appropriation* was displayed in Cramer's quote in the previous section. Global sports organizations today see the people of neocolonial states as belonging to the achievement sport movement, rather than to traditional folk-games. The emphasis here is to eliminate difference and to gather African and other athletes from the world's economic 'periphery' into the fold of modern sport – a new 'family of man' – on the West's terms. Football seems to have been projected as a necessary and fundamental human experience – a global human community – placed on the same plane as the two universal facts, those of life and death, as Roland Barthes (1973) might have put it. He might have also placed the universalistic claims and ambitions of world football against the irony of Western colonialism and racism.

The appropriative language used to describe African soccer players often reveals them as versions of a European ideal. Though projected in less blatant terms than those of Cramer, it can be illustrated by examples taken from work by British media analysts who examined European newspaper coverage of the 1990 World Cup in Spain (Blain et al. 1993). In this, and in the paragraphs that follow, I will concentrate on their findings concerning the representation of the Cameroon national team. For example, the Cameroon player Oman Biyik was referred to as 'a black van Basten', an 'African Gerd Müller' or a 'black Horst Hrubesch'. Africans are here defined in relation to Europeans (ibid.: 71–3). The Cameroon team was also viewed as a hybrid – 'well-versed in modern tactics [but] it plays its game without abandoning its indigenous style' (ibid.: 73). A 'native style' is not seen as enough and, at least, it needs to possess modern techniques.

Idealization is an equally familiar mode of neocolonial representation with idealized statements being juxtaposed to those of appropriation noted above. The survey of images of the 1990 World Cup revealed that the players from Cameroon were written as having 'football in their blood'; they 'obtained their skills as whippersnappers on the streets'; their play brought 'magic to the game'; they were 'instinctive footballers', 'refreshingly attacking' and 'not at all inhibited'. European soccer, on the other hand, was represented by 'modern' images – those of 'the artificial' and 'the machine' (ibid.). Among the implications of these idealized kinds of reporting of black athletes is the desire for a more 'pure' kind of sport, one not blemished by artifice or tactics, reflecting atavistic tendencies on the part of the writers. There is a longing for what Europe might have been, a romantic nostalgia, a view that sees in the African an untutored and ideal sportsman – what the European might have been, but for his loss of innocence and his gain in refinement. In a lengthy article in the German soccer magazine *Kicker*, Karl-Heinz Heimann noted that

> in Cameroon, everywhere (sic) in Africa and Asia the ball is the favourite toy of millions of children, they know no other. Neither surf board nor mountain bike, neither tennis courts or even computers are at hand to distract them from playing with the ball.
>
> There is no longer any 'street football' here in our country (Germany). Should children join a club, usually when they are considerably older, the first thing the trainer has to do is to apply his efforts to teaching them ball control. In most cases it's already too late. And tactics are already given too much importance in the youth work of our clubs. (quoted in Blain et al. 1993: 74)

Heimann yearns for kids playing soccer in bare feet, kicking a ball around for fun and pleasure, for a 'purification' of modern soccer through play rather than tactics. A mythical, idealized, romantic world of yesteryear – or of Africa – would ideally replace the corrupted and debased world of modern sports.

In the course of naturalizing the African sports-worker, the mode of *negation* evidently parallels it. The African athlete (not just footballers) has often been projected as a negative stereotype – 'great speed but little stamina' has traditionally been a widespread appellation (Wiggins 1989). During the 1990 World Cup competition, the Cameroon team could be labelled, in Western journalism, as 'harmless wild men', 'irrational' and 'less intellectual'; the soccer set-up in Cameroon was described as 'chaotic' with a 'deficient system'. The team 'knows nothing about tactics' and 'they need to hear the applause of the crowd more than the instructions of the trainer' (Blain et al. 1993: 73–6). African sports-workers are often negated by allusions to their 'natural' talent. It is said that their performances are unfairly enhanced as a result of their supposed innate ability, something that Adolf Hitler recognized as a reason for banning 'the Negro' from the Olympic Games. It is still possible in the modern world to see colonial modes of rhetoric such as negation and idealization, quantification and naturalization, lying alongside each other.

This chapter has focused on three characteristics of the intercontinental migration of African footballers. Some basic 'facts' of such migration were revealed in maps and figures. It was shown that in the top divisions of some European countries African soccer labour made up around 10 per cent of the workforce. Almost 20 per cent of all elite foreign professional footballers in Europe are African migrants. However, I emphasized that elegant though such maps and figures may be, they are, in essence, obfuscatory. They fail to indicate the lived worlds of African migrant players, the role of their agents and the neocolonial ideologies underlying the process of recruitment and relocation. I concluded with a view of the African footballer as found in football's imaginative geographies. In such cases, the players that are brought to Europe can be read as texts and re-presented in various rhetorical modes. My exploration of these modes revealed a degree of equivocation and ambivalence. Moreover, the modes that represented 'the African' are basically the same as nineteenth- and early twentieth-century discourses on African corporeality and athleticism.

Associated with new media has been the emergence of what might be called 'techno-Africanism', particularly in the coverage of sports. It has been suggested that the televisual mediation of 'events' and peoples make us all in the global North like anthropologists, surveying the world of 'others' via our television screens. Will the globalization of 'the African footballer' change our traditional prejudices? Not necessarily. It should not be assumed that technically improved communications media necessarily improve intercultural relations. Indeed, as part of an electronic world, stereotypes may have been reinforced (Said 1978: 26; Morley and Robins 1995: 133). The arrogation of African football-workers by 'Western' nations and the largely one-way flow of international communications are therefore intimately linked to the question of how 'the African' footballer is re-presented to those in his nation of sojourn.

Acknowledgements

An earlier version of this chapter was presented at the annual conference of the British International Studies Association, Bradford, January 2001, and at a seminar at Keele University, February 2002. I am grateful for comments made by participants at these presentations, and to Elsbeth Robson (Keele University) and Gary Armstrong (Brunel University) for helpful observations. I thank Andy Lawrence (Keele University) for crafting the maps. I take full responsibility for the final version.

13

The Migration of the Black Panther: An Interview with Eusebio of Mozambique and Portugal

Gary Armstrong

Eusebio was the first internationally renowned African footballer, and only Nelson Mandela is a more recognizable African-born individual. Labelled the 'Black Pearl', the 'Black Panther' and the 'European Pelé' by the footballing media, he had, at the age of 50, a life-sized bronze statue erected outside the main entrance to the Estadio da Luz (Stadium of Light) by his admirers at Benfica, Lisbon. Resident for over 40 years in his adopted Lisbon and aged 60 when interviewed in 2002, Eusebio is as imperious off the pitch as he was in his prime on it. The debilitating limp does not detract from what is still an impressive physique. His mystique remains and has obviously been passed down generations, which explains an interview process constantly interrupted by well-wishers both in their teens and in their late fifties. A walk around the Stadium of Light illustrates the aura that this football genius exudes amongst the Benfica fanatics; when coming across a group of 30 men, all over 40 years of age, silence prevails upon them until he speaks. His life was and remains a remarkable story, a classic 'rags to riches' wherein his ability with a football took him from the poverty of Mozambique to the fame and fortune offered by Portuguese society and the footballing world. It was a journey that took considerable courage and one which requires an understanding of both the history and politics of Portuguese colonialism and one of Africa's bitterest civil wars.

The presence of the Portuguese in Africa is a legacy of the expedition of Vasco da Gama who landed there in 1436 on his way to India. Having little funds to invest in this colony the Portuguese leased some two-thirds of the land to British and Belgian companies, which explains why Mozambique is a member of the British Commonwealth. At the 1885

Berlin Conference, Portugal was given Mozambique along with Angola and Guinea-Bissau. The modern boundary was a product of an 1891 agreement between Portugal and Britain. Between the fifteenth and late eighteenth centuries Portugal did not seek to impose a state or civil society on the indigenous people, being content to exploit the country's resources of gold, ivory and slaves – some 1 million of whom were forcibly transported to the Americas. In the early twentieth century colonial administration was left to private companies of Portuguese, French and British origin who imposed taxes and forced labour under an iniquitous system known as *chibalo*. In 1926 Portugal fell under the rule of fascist dictator Antonio Salazar, who was to end the rule of the charter companies. He encouraged Portuguese companies to develop trade and hundreds of thousands of Portuguese 'peasants' were encouraged to migrate. Furthermore, Salazar effectively divided the people of Mozambique via the 'Indigenous People's Rule' which awarded honorary status of 'assimilated' Portuguese to the 1 per cent of the black and mixed population who were literate in Portuguese and considered European in their thinking. The remainder were expected to work on colonial farms both in Mozambique and Rhodesia. As late as the 1960s the indigenous people worked by coercion for the Portuguese authorities on colonial plantations and road and rail building. Neglected in terms of education and health care and with little infrastructure supplied by the colonists who dominated every aspect of society, the life of the Mozambican-born majority was, at times, desperate.

Organized resistance to this state of being began in the early 1960s when a peaceful demonstration provoked the colonial authorities to shoot dead 600 protesters. At the invitation of Tanzanian president, Julius Nyerere, resistance-in-exile groups were founded in Dar es Salaam and joined together in 1962 to become the Liberation Front of Mozambique (Frelimo) led by Eduardo Mondlane, a former professor of Anthropology at Syracuse University, New York. Two years later the guerrilla war of resistance to Portuguese rule began and lasted over a decade. Armed and funded by the USSR, China and Cuba, Frelimo established health centres and literacy classes, and whilst this won them recruits and sympathizers it was events in Lisbon in 1974 that significantly affected the outcome of the struggle. The military coup by the Armed Forces Movement provoked in part by the heavy losses incurred in the colonial war ousted Salazar's successor. In 1975 the new rulers handed power to Frelimo under Somora Michel without calling for elections. Frelimo declared itself a Marxist/Leninist party and Mozambique a one-party state. It took almost 20 years before multiparty elections were allowed. Meanwhile thousands of European-born settlers left, political activity was suppressed and opposition figures were exiled or, on occasion, executed. Many of the educated *assimilatos* left for Lisbon in 1975 (a second wave followed them in the 1980s to join relatives established in Lisbon). Others migrated to work in the gold mines of Johannesburg and to take up menial tasks in neighbouring Zimbabwe, Malawi and Tanzania. At times some 50 per cent of adult males were migrant workers.

Throughout colonial times football was the main sporting pastime for men and boys. Whilst the precise origins of the game in Mozambique are not known, the Catholic Church, via its schools, was instrumental in the game's development. No other sport to this day can touch football for popularity, albeit basketball is played by many and, indeed, Mozambique were African champions in the late 1990s. Since the 1950s, radio commentaries of matches being played in Portugal have been listened to by huge sections of the Mozambique population every Sunday. TV only appeared in the late 1980s, some five years after independence and initially limited to the capital city, only reaching the rest of the nation in the mid to late 1990s.

Football in colonial times mirrored the political jurisdiction to a degree. The colonial powers divided the country into ten administrative areas. Each had a regional capital and each had football teams in the national football league. Some clubs were named after the most famous clubs of their mother country, i.e. Benfica and Sporting. All supporters of local teams also had an implicit loyalty to their Portuguese namesakes. The choice of club, whilst mostly subjective, did in some instances contain some objective factors. Sporting (Lourenco Marques – LM) was considered the team of the professional middle class and less receptive to black players than Benfica. The largest supported club, Ferroviario – founded by settlers – had no equivalent in Portugal and was the works team of the national railway. As the biggest employer in the country, Ferroviario had wealth by virtue of every worker having a contribution deducted from their monthly wage which went towards funding the football team. The national stadium, named Stadio Salazar, belonged to them; however, the official inauguration of this structure by the dictator was never completed – he never set foot in Mozambique. Years later the official ceremony of independence was held here.

Independence in 1975 led to a very short-lived peace. Soon a struggle began in 1977 against Renamo (Mozambican National Resistance Party) and continued for the next 13 years. Sponsored by Rhodesia and later South Africa (who conducted their own direct air and land attacks), Renamo was short on politics but effective in destroying the social and political structure of Mozambique whilst gaining a reputation as the 'Khmer Rouge of Africa'. In a conflict that took an estimated 200,000 lives (exacerbated by a famine in 1983–84 that killed tens of thousands) widespread atrocities from both sides displaced millions and economically ruined Mozambique. Peace talks begun in 1984 led by the Catholic Church and the late British tycoon Tiny Rowland did not prove effective. It was in 1990 when the Catholic charity movement of St Egidio managed to initiate a settlement assisted by the UN, Italy, Britain, Portugal and the US that peace came about and was facilitated inadvertently by the post-1989 fall of communism in Europe and the USSR, which saw the Frelimo government abandon the Marxist/Leninist ideology and open itself to world capitalism. The civil war officially ended in 1992 and the head of state implemented election by secret ballot in 1994, and with it religious tolerance and the promotion of free enterprise. But tragedy remains in Mozambique. Severe floods in the year 2000 killed over 800 people; Mozambique is currently one of the poorest nations on earth and struggles along on an economy exporting copra, cotton, sisel, cashew nuts, prawns and shrimps, and servicing trade to the hinterland neighbours of Zambia, Zimbabwe and Malawi. Reserves of columbotautalile (useful in nuclear reactors and missile technology) will always attract economic interests from Western arms producers. Ten major ethnic groups (with their own languages) vie for political power. The Ronga dominate Maputo, the Maqua dominate the north and the Shangana are over-represented in the ruling party. The country is further divided on religion with the centre and north mainly accounting for the 35 per cent who follow Catholicism whilst northern coastal regions house a 25 per cent Muslim population. The remainder are animists or have no formalized faith.

The victory of the Marxist/Leninist Frelimo in 1975 affected the domestic football scene in a number of ways. The new government banned the use of Portuguese names, instructing football clubs to use only African ones. At the same time the capital city of Lourenco Marques, 'LM', a one-time holiday resort for the wealthy of southern Africa with its Mediterranean villas and main thoroughfare named Whiskey Road, was renamed Maputo. Portuguese clubs did not tour for some 15 years. Between 1975 and 1987 footballers were forbidden by the government from migrating to play elsewhere. This dictat was not very effective; from around 1984, national team players moved to South Africa in ever increasing numbers. The legacy of foreign influence remains in the form of streets named Ho Chi Minh and Mao Tse Tung which stand not far from hotels opened by postwar South African entrepreneurs.

Since the post-1992 resumption of links with Portugal, indigenous football clubs have in some instances returned to their former nomenclature, often in the hope of attracting sponsors and fans. The post-conflict milieu has seen football promoted as a manifestation of normality. Former combatants played a tournament in 1992 sponsored by local businesses. Mozambique played in the 1994 finals in South Africa but did not make it past the first round and have yet to win a game at the African Nations Cup finals. Football clubs from Brazil and Portugal have toured and played exhibition matches. The national team have appointed coaches from Brazil, Portugal and the Ukraine in pursuit of success. A Ministry of Culture and Sport was established in 1999 as part of a recognition that sport (particularly football) had a part to play in integration and nation-building. However, poverty remains and crime is considered a massive problem. Mozambique remains one of the biggest debtor nations on earth. Few hold secure jobs; a minority have the benefits of schooling, and life expectancy is 45 years.

Two years before Frelimo began its armed resistance, a hairdressing salon provided the inspiration for Benfica's signing of Eusebio. Enthusing about this particular player was the coach of the Brazilian side São Paulo, who was with his team touring Portugal following a tour of Mozambique. His opinion impressed the listening Benfica coach, Bela Guttman, who within a week had flown to Lourenco Marques. He was to find a youth drawn from the Mafalala suburb playing for Sporting club (LM) with a reputation for speed and deadly finishing. Soon Guttman had this precocious talent (who could cover 100 m in eleven seconds) training with the Benfica squad as part of a four-team tournament. Days later Guttman bought Eusebio for £7500. To this day stories circulate about the contest between Sporting and Benfica for his signature. The latter are accused of having kidnapped Eusebio on his arrival in Lisbon and having held him in a safe house on the Algarve until the dispute had died down. Two weeks after signing, Eusebio was playing inside left for the Portuguese national side.

Eusebio had joined a club with a fabulous footballing pedigree. Established in 1904 by Cosme Damião, the originator had insisted the club choose players born in Portugal or from Portuguese colonies and 'possessions'. Consequently African-born players were no strangers to Benfica's colours – Mario Coluña had arrived in 1954. When the former African colonies gained independence a debate ensued between what might be termed the traditionalists and progressives at Benfica as to where the originator's request stood. The progressives won and the statute was changed. Since that day Benfica has signed players from all over the world.

In 13 seasons with Benfica between 1961 and 1975, Eusebio achieved almost everything the game could offer. At the domestic level he was in a team that won seven championships and two cups; he was also the league's top scorer between 1964 and 1968. In total he scored 317 goals for Benfica. At the European level he won the European Cup in 1962, and was three times in a team that finished as runners-up. He was awarded European Footballer of the Year in 1965 and retired having scored 46 goals in European competitions. At the International level Benfica were World Club Cup runners-up twice and the Portuguese national team finished third in the 1966 World Cup. This latter tournament saw Eusebio win the Golden Boot for being top scorer with nine goals, four of which came in the famous 5–3 victory over North Korea in the quarter-finals. He also had the supreme accolade of a wax replica exhibited in Madame Tussaud's in central London, much to the public's delight. With 64 caps he retired from international football in 1973 as the third most capped player in Portuguese football history. His 41 international goals is a Portuguese record that remains.

Such a career inevitably had its ups and downs. A first-team debut aged 18 in 1961 saw him score one goal and miss a penalty in a losing side. Less than two weeks later he turned out for the Portuguese national team. In 1962 he scored two goals against Real Madrid in a 5–3 European Cup victory only to find himself a year later earning a pittance whilst doing his military service in honour of his adopted nation. Initially playing under Bela Guttman, famed for his advocacy of the 'WM' formation, he later fitted into the plans of the Yugoslav Milorad Pavic and the Englishman Jimmy Hagan. At national level he was coached by the Brazilian Otto Gloria. In the summer of 1969 at the age of 28 Eusebio was involved in a contract dispute with Benfica. After ten years with them and with 30 national appearances behind him, he was earning around £4000 a year. A 17-day dispute ensued centred on his financial demands and requests for a three-year contract. The club considered such a request too excessive. Further disagreement arose over the extent of the signing-on fee, bonuses should trophies be won, bonuses for being leading scorer and the percentage of gate money for international friendlies played abroad. Lawyers for Benfica argued that whilst FA regulations permitted any player with ten years' service and 30 national appearances to enjoy a free transfer, the Benfica lawyers had found that under Portuguese law no player from the Portuguese empire could be transferred abroad without government sanction. In response Eusebio spoke emotionally of how he had given body and soul to Benfica and played games despite terrible knee pain. The resolution saw both sides shift their ground to accommodate the other.

He attracted the admiration of coaches the world over. In 1966 Helenio Herrera at Roma agreed a £500,000 transfer deal with Benfica. However, the Italian FA, so shamed by their team's showing in the World Cup (particularly their losing to North Korea), banned the importation of foreign players in pursuit of raising the standards of the native-born. Furthermore, the dictator Salazar was not keen to lose such a national asset. Later interest from Real Madrid was tempered by concern over his recurring knee injuries and a declining goal-scoring rate. In the end Eusebio only played for other clubs when his career was effectively over.

Stating his own unwillingness to enter politics, Eusebio was always reluctant to be drawn on issues of political debate. In 1975 Eusebio was quoted as stating he would return to Mozambique when his football days ended. He was to return repeatedly but was never to live there for long. His immediate post-Benfica career saw him play in Mexico with Monterey, then in Canada with the Toronto Metro Stars, and later in the US with the Boston Minutemen and Las Vegas Quicksilver. When his playing days were over he was to take on a public relations/ambassadorial function with both Benfica and the Portuguese national side. In recent years he has opened sports shops in Maputo and founded a fundraising project for the poor of his native country.

GA: In journalistic circles you are still referred to as the 'black pearl' and the 'black panther'. Do you like that?

E: It was the English press who first called me the 'Black Panther'. At the time, I had misgivings because in the USA there was a sect called the Black Panthers whose symbol was a cobra, and they kidnapped Patricia Hearst. I was worried about the connection but then I thought: they are in the USA, I live in Europe, I have nothing to do with politics, I am football. I got to like it when they called me that. Even today, I can be walking along a street and children will grab their mother's skirt or father's trousers and say: 'Look, it's the Black Panther.' It's nice, isn't it? The 'Black Pearl' came from the 'Pearl of Mozambique', coined by the French, but I like 'Black Panther' better.

GA: How did you obtain the childhood nickname of 'Nene' ['baby']?

E: 'Nene' was the nickname given to a Brazilian footballer. In 1957 we were a group of kids playing football in our neighbourhood team and the

Chairman told each of us to choose the name of a Brazilian footballer as a nickname – my cousin was 'Pelé' and I was *'Nene'*. My real name is Eusebio da Silva Ferreira.

GA: *Did you have a footballing hero?*

E: My idol was Alfredo di Stefano. I used to read the newspapers when I was ten, eleven, twelve years of age about Real Madrid being one of the best teams in Europe, if not the world. My eldest brother Jaime used to talk about this great footballer.

GA: *What influence did live radio commentary of Portuguese matches have on your aspirations to becoming a footballer?*

E: As we had no television, we would listen to the Benfica matches on the radio, as supporters of other teams would listen to their teams. Our parents would gather round the radio, and we would ask what the score was, but at that time I never thought I would one day be playing for them. Then, when I was about 17 years old, newspapers began to write about me, people were talking about me, and I started to believe in the dream that one day I could be a professional and go to Portugal. But when I was a child the idea never crossed my mind. Only when I was 17 did I start to think and believe in the dream and, as it turned out, it was Benfica, the team my family supported, who signed me.

GA: *What were the career options available to a boy of your age if football had not taken you?*

E: My late father was a mechanic on the railways. In my family we studied hard – my mother made us … study, study, study all the time – otherwise we would get nowhere! I was the only child in the family who did not finish school. I was born for football. My mother used to tell me off because I would stop on the way to school to play football with my friends. But there were opportunities to work in offices; typing, etc. My brothers and sister all ended up with good jobs – one became an engineer. We were six boys and two girls in our family. Three of my siblings have died: one had a heart attack, one died in an accident, and one of my sisters died in childbirth – the child was saved but there was no medical help in Mozambique in those days and my sister died.

GA: Was there money to make a living as a professional footballer had you remained in Mozambique?

E: There were no professional footballers in Mozambique – only amateurs. To become professionals we had to go to Portugal. The small clubs from each district would go 'fishing' for players in their own district. They were amateurs, therefore we were not obliged to play if we didn't want to. I sometimes would not play because I had to study. One day my club was playing, but my mother said I had to go to a party instead! The big official clubs (also amateurs) would send scouts out to watch the children playing football in the streets. These scouts would stop their cars, watch the game, see if there were any good players, call them over to ask their names, where they lived, and then go with them to talk to their parents. In the small villages, there was always someone who was a supporter of, say, Benfica or Sporting [Mozambique] who would spot the local talent, say to them 'You are a good player, why don't you go to Lourenco Marques and have a trial for Benfica/Sporting?' These clubs, Sporting, Benfica, Desportivo, were all based in Lourenco Marques. All the clubs were federated, each large town had its own football association. The people who controlled the federation were voted in for fixed terms by the associations.

GA: Did the Catholic missionaries and the Catholic Church play any role in the development of Mozambican football?

E: I never really noticed. We played football in school and the Dutch priests liked football, but they did not influence me much. When I played football, I always made the sign of the cross and said a prayer before going on the pitch, because I am a committed Catholic.

GA: Portuguese teams would visit Angola and Mozambique to play exhibition matches. How important was it for the pride of the Mozambican people when their teams played Benfica or Sporting?

E: This was a question of professionals against amateurs, and if we won it was extremely satisfying. I once played in the Mozambique national team when Belenenses (who had recently beaten Benfica to win the Portuguese Cup) came to play. I was 17 at the time and scored two goals – even though I was still really a junior – and we were all amateurs. I was extremely proud and the crowd watching were ecstatic. It was an incredible feeling, scoring two goals against professional footballers. The only payment we got was a Coca-Cola or orange juice and a sandwich at the end of the game.

GA: Were you influenced by African-born players who had previously travelled to Portugal to find fame in the game, e.g. Miguel Arcanjo, Luca Figueiredo, Mario Esteves Coluña, Rosario da Conceicao (Hilario)?

E: No, not really. My family was a football family – my father had played football, as had my elder brother, but not professionally. I never thought that one day I would be signed by a Portuguese club – it happened, but I was not influenced by the players who had gone to Portugal before me.

GA: Was there any reason why people in Mozambique chose to support or play for Sporting over Benfica or others?

E: Not really. I think it just depended on the fans and where the club's ground was located – people would support the team closest to their home. We would support and play for who we wanted. The clubs were created by the clubs in Portugal – for example, the amateur Sporting Clube de Lourenco Marques (the son) was created by the professional Sporting Clube de Portugal (the father), and the same goes for Benfica. The clubs in Portugal would send all the equipment (strip, etc.) for the Mozambique clubs to use, but with different lettering on the badges, although the strip was exactly the same. Officially, I played for Sporting and would play on Saturday or Sunday morning. Then I would come home for lunch and unofficially go and play barefoot for my local team.

GA: Who controlled the Mozambique versions of Benfica, Porto and Sporting?

E: There were representatives of Benfica, Sporting, Porto and Belenenses in Mozambique who represented the professional clubs of the same name in Portugal. However, they had nothing to do with the control of our teams in Mozambique. For example, the Benfica representative lived and worked there, watched the team and scouted for talented players to send to Portugal, receiving in return commission from Benfica. But he had no control in the club, and it was the same with the other clubs, who were affiliated to their Portuguese counterparts.

GA: What were the conditions like for those wanting to play football?

E: It is normal in Africa, even today, for the kids to play barefoot in their neighbourhood teams. When we played for our local team, we never had boots or shoes. Today some neighbourhoods have a 'pitch' to play on, but they play barefoot, and they don't even have proper footballs; they stuff women's stockings with rags to make a ball.

GA: Were the coaches native-born or Portuguese?

E: We were all coaches when we played in our neighbourhood! The coaches at the clubs were all locals, and a mixture of whites and blacks. However, some came over from Portugal, as part of their national service, and if they were footballers they stayed and played or coached football in the official clubs.

GA: What role did the Ferroviario club play in local football as it was the best supported club yet the only big team not connected to a Portuguese club?

E: Ferroviario was the team of the railway company and was not linked to clubs in Portugal, although the Portuguese scouts watched them. The company signed players – like my late father – and then arranged jobs on the railways for them, and paid them for their jobs while they played (the other teams were amateurs and didn't get paid) so that they could have a better life.

GA: Did you break a tradition by playing for Sporting Mozambique, only to sign for Benfica Lisbon?

E: A player will go to the club that pays more and offers a better contract; it has nothing to do with tradition. For example, 'Matateu' (Sebastião Lucas da Fonseca) came to Portugal to play for Belenenses; Coluña played for Desportivo Mozambique and came to Benfica; Hilario played for Sporting Mozambique and went to Sporting Lisbon. It all depended on the terms and conditions offered by the clubs in Portugal. It was my family, our lawyer and myself who decided I would come to Benfica.

GA: Who should take the credit for discovering Eusebio?

E: Bela Guttman was the manager, Benfica was the club. Benfica, like the other clubs, had directors and agents in Lourenco Marques who would write to their clubs in Portugal saying this or that player was good.

GA: In November 1960 you suddenly went from being a boy in a large family in Mozambique to, months later, the 18-year-old playing for the world-famous Benfica team in Portugal. What were your expectations and what were your fears?

E: We were a very, very close family – always together and always gathering at my mother's house. Even my brothers who had left home always came back and we would be together for Christmas, birthdays, etc. This went on for 18 years, then I left for Portugal. It was extremely difficult for me but the contract with Benfica gave me money which I could use to improve the family's lives. I could buy land and houses to give them a better lifestyle. It was not a sacrifice for me: I was going to do what I enjoyed most – playing football and helping my family at the same time. I wasn't afraid at all. My problem was my family – we were very close. I was 18 years old, had lived all my life surrounded by family. It was a long way in those days – there were no jet planes – and it used to take over 30 hours to get to Lisbon. My only fear when I arrived in Portugal was not realizing the extent of the rivalry between Benfica and Sporting – in Mozambique there was a lot of rivalry between the clubs, but here it was even worse, and I felt apprehensive. The situation was aggravated by the fact that Sporting also wanted to sign me.

GA: You've probably been asked a thousand times about the circumstances of the transfer to Benfica. What exactly happened?

E: Even today, and I am 60 years old, Sporting still says I was 'kidnapped' – it's a total lie [repeats 'lies', 'lies']. Let me explain: how could I like someone who kidnapped me, as I love Benfica? Another thing: the contract with Benfica was signed by my mother (I was a minor). I have a photocopy of that contract, Benfica has a photocopy of that contract, the flight to Portugal was paid for by Benfica. There has *never* been *any* document drawn up by Sporting and signed either by my mother or me – nothing. I think it was Sporting that wanted to kidnap me! To get me away from the confusion and controversy, Benfica sent me to a house on the Algarve. I played for Sporting in Mozambique, and Sporting Lisbon wanted to bring me over to Portugal for a trial. But why should I have gone for a trial with Sporting, when Benfica had the contract and the money ready to give me?

GA: How did a young boy from Africa find the confidence and the courage to negotiate the wages and captain a famous European team?

E: The first contract was signed in Africa by my mother and was for three years. By the time it was ready for renegotiation, I was older and more confident. I knew people I could trust and a lawyer helped me.

GA: Were your wages the same as your Portuguese-born equivalents?

E: My transfer fee was the highest ever at the time for an African-born player ... [other players like Hilario, Matateu and Coluña had cost one-fifth to two-fifths the amount of Eusbio's fee]. My contract stated what I earned, I didn't care what the others were earning, but I know I earned more than them ... [twice what they were earning]. When the first contract finished, I signed a new one for more money, but it had nothing to do with what the other players earned.

GA: You had one contractual dispute which lasted for two weeks over wages offered by Benfica ...

E: It was my final contract, when Jimmy Hagan arrived as manager (1970). By that time I had done everything: highest goal-scorer in the world, best player in the world, best player in Europe, five times the highest goal-scorer in Portugal – I had done it all. I was about to sign probably the last three-year contract of my playing career, and I had to get it right. I had put Benfica into the limelight, yet they wouldn't agree to my terms. So I put my family on a plane back to Mozambique and signed a power of attorney for my lawyer to act on my behalf. The Benfica team went to Africa, and when they caught the plane to return to Portugal, I caught one to Mozambique to join my family. The Benfica directors thought I would be there when they returned, but discovered I had gone. Training began for the new season, and I trained in Mozambique. Then Benfica telephoned me – I answered the phone, and told them not to speak to me, only to my lawyer. Finally, Benfica had to accept my terms; my lawyer phoned me and I came back.

GA: Did you ever find racial prejudice in your footballing career in Portugal?

E: No. I never encountered anything – here we are in the twenty-first century and you cannot go to a football match without hearing these so-called hooligans shouting racist taunts about black footballers – when I played for Benfica, almost all the clubs had black players and there was never any problem. I could go out, go to the cinema, and no one said anything bad; I never felt that I was different. The tradition of Benfica was always only Portuguese or Portuguese-speaking players from the colonies, no 'foreigners'. The manager, however, could be 'foreign'! Benfica's greatest successes were always with Portuguese-speaking players from Angola and Mozambique.

GA: Was there any resentment from anyone when a Mozambique-born footballer was made captain of Benfica?

E: They had already had African-born captains, José Aguas (from Angola) and Mario Coluña (from Mozambique). Besides, the team was like a family.

GA: Did you expect to stay for 40 years in various capacities with Benfica?

E: When I came to Portugal I changed from being an amateur to a professional. With my personality and my age at the time, I knew I had to show my class as a player, not to be afraid and to work hard. The other players could have resented me, thinking: 'I am getting old, this new player is going to take my place in the team.' But no, all the older players, José Aguas, Costa Perreira, Mario Coluña, were like a family there to support me and I didn't feel isolated at all. Therefore, I made greater efforts to show how well I could play and secured my place in the team. When I arrived, I went to watch the team training while Benfica sorted out my paperwork. I thought to myself: 'I will play in this team because I know I am as good as, if not better, than most of those players.' However, I didn't say this to anyone, I just knew in my head I could play better than them and be in the team.

GA: Which clubs tried to buy you in the course of your career?

E: I could have gone to Italy – Juventus wanted me and offered me a contract – but Salazar, the Portuguese dictator at the time, wouldn't let me go. That's why I stayed in Portugal. Then I had to go and do my national service in Queluz (some 30 miles outside Lisbon). After the 1966 World Cup, when Portugal came third, Roma managed by Herrera wanted to sign me, so I went there with my wife for a fortnight to look at everything – the house, etc. However, Italy had done so badly during that World Cup that the Italian Football Federation closed its doors to all foreign players. I had a three-year contract ready to sign for a vast amount of money – 90 million escudos when the rate to the dollar was 30 escudos.

GA: How did Benfica negotiate the 1975 independence of the Portuguese colonies, because then people would say players born in these countries were no longer Portuguese players?

E: Benfica had to change its statutes to allow foreign players in and allow the former colony players to continue to play.

GA: Were there dilemmas when having to choose which citizenship to take?

E: I have dual nationality – my passport and identity card are Portuguese, yet show that I was born in Mozambique. My family and I have Mozambican diplomatic passports.

GA: How did it feel to be Mozambique-born but be a conscript in the Portuguese army?

E: I did three years of national service, finishing just before the 1966 World Cup. The problem was that Angola, Mozambique, Cape Verde, São Tomé and Guinea-Bissau were Portuguese-speaking colonies. At that time, however, they were not yet independent. When I arrived in Portugal, the war for independence had already started in Mozambique. However, here in Portugal, my family and I had nothing to do with the war. I had my Portuguese identity card, indicating I was born in Mozambique, and my passport; both were exactly the same as issued here to Portuguese nationals. Coluña, Vicente, José Aguas, Hilario, all did their national service. I started national service like them, but at that time I was leaving to go back to Mozambique in transit to Italy – to sign for Juventus. However, the Portuguese government (a dictatorship) of that time under the regime of Dr Antonio Oliveira Salazar told me I could not leave the country – I was state property. What could I do? Although I was not paid by the government, in those days we could not argue, and if I tried to leave the country I could be arrested and imprisoned. They were very clever – if they put me in the army I would have to stay in the country. If I had fled, I would not have been able to play football. So I did my national service like everyone else, sleeping at home and turning up at the barracks every day. But it was a way of ensuring that I stayed in Portugal.

GA: I read of how in 1964 you returned to Mozambique and declined to take part in an invitation match which resulted in disorder. Can you explain the full circumstances?

E: I wasn't invited to play in the game – I was invited to watch it. I was on holiday in Mozambique, and near my house there is a pitch where they played barefoot. I went to watch – I have never seen so many people for such a game – and around me they were asking if I was going to play. I was dressed casually, in black trousers, a black shirt and a pullover – I shall never forget! At that time I also had my beard. This was the team I played for as a child, so they invited me to come along. The problems arose because lots of people had turned up expecting me play. The newspapers wanted a good story – they said I had been invited to play, but it was a lie and they blew the incident out of proportion. A few people were convinced that I was going to play and started creating problems when I said I was on holiday and had just come to watch. Things were said and there were a few scuffles, but nothing like the reports in the newspapers.

GA: Did you ever see yourself as a role model for other African players?

E: There are always young players who have their idols and who want to be like Eusebio. It is good for them that a captain of Benfica was born in Africa. When I came to Benfica, my captains were Coluña and José Aguas, both born in Africa. We were proud of the fact that we were captains of our team, and up to 1973–74 (from 1966) I was captain of the Portuguese national team. I am proud of the fact that I tried to teach new, younger players how to behave both on and off the pitch – for example, don't argue with the referee, it's not worth it, just get on with the game. There are thousands of people watching the matches, seeing how we behave and judging us. I tried to be a role model for them.

I was the youngest-ever national team captain when I took over from Coluña after the 1966 World Cup. In 1965 I was the first player from Africa and from Portugal to be awarded World Player of the Year. For me it was an enormous responsibility, but I was very proud to be the first African-born footballer to also win a Golden Boot. I realized the enormity of winning because by that time I was aged 25 – old enough to understand what an honour it was, and a responsibility. I represented Africa and Portugal, and there had never been a footballer from either to receive such an honour.

GA: Did football play a role in the Mozambique anti-colonial movement?

E: No, when I was playing for Benfica, we were football professionals. When we travelled as the national team, or as Benfica, we always had the government secret police (PIDE) with us, although we did not know who they were as they were always undercover. I'm not sure why, but I think it was to keep an eye on those of us from Africa to see if there was any connections made when we travelled, for example, to Bulgaria, Russia and other Eastern Bloc countries, as they were involved in the wars in Africa. There were African-born footballers and students who left Portugal to help the cause. José Julio was a white player for Academica de Coimbra Portugal – a team of university students, some of whom left Portugal – and he was linked to the Popular Liberation Movement in Angola which was like Frelimo in Mozambique. In my own case, I don't get involved in politics, I don't like politics – my only politics is football.

GA: In difficult times, particularly civil war, does the national football team take on a significance beyond that of merely playing a game of football?

E: I personally don't think about that. I had a contract with Benfica and I played for the Portuguese national team. If invited, I would also play for the Mozambique national team. If I was still playing in Mozambique and didn't want to play for the national team, I would be disciplined. You cannot compare football in the colonial days with post-independence football – it was a very sudden change. After independence, not only in Mozambique but also in Angola, the importance of football among the poorer people waned. Today they are beginning to rebuild.

GA: Did the ban on players moving outside Mozambique affect Mozambique football and the standard of Portuguese football?

E: There were Mozambique players who wanted to come to Portugal, but they had to pay the government under the Frelimo regime – an idea conceived by the Director of Sport. Why should the clubs in Portugal pay the Mozambique government? – they were already paying the parents or the player himself. José Julio sent a communiqué to all the football clubs in Mozambique that if a player wanted to turn professional, he had to be told. The problem then lay with the player's parents – they had to pay the government. As there was no money in Mozambique football, some players escaped to South Africa and changed their names in order to play. Some players returned to Mozambique eventually, but a lot stayed in South Africa to earn money and bring in food for their families. They were not paid in Mozambique and the conditions were bad – no food, etc.

GA: Were you ever offered the chance to manage the national team of Mozambique?

E: No – I support them totally but wouldn't want to be manager. Here in Portugal I have everything I want. There was a time when I wanted to be manager of Benfica (the only managerial position I would consider), but I have matured since then and know myself. I could never be a football manager, but I was one of Sven Goran Eriksson's first team coaches in 1994. For example, here at the Estadio da Luz there is a statue of me. If I became manager and things went wrong, it would be a difficult situation with the statue there. Here in Portugal, it's three months – no success and you're out. Can you imagine if I was manager here at Benfica? I would put the team together, but if the results were bad I would be sacked. Borges Coutinho, then President of Benfica, himself said to me: 'You can never be a manager – things could go wrong, the team could play badly and you will be blamed.' I know my position in life. I am always ready to help the Mozambique team when they need something from me. As an ambassador for the Portuguese national team and for Benfica, if Mozambique needs help as a member of FIFA, I will always go there, it's my homeland. I go to Mozambique every year, and I am always ready to help and support them, but not as a member of their management team.

GA: One of the recurring problems of player migration, certainly in English football, and I think increasingly in Italy and Spain, is the competing demands of club football versus country, especially when it comes to African players who have to travel sometimes arduous distances mid-season back to their homelands.

E: The problem is that the clubs are right – they are the ones who pay the player. However, the player has to play for his national team under his own country's flag. If the manager of the national team wants a player, the club has to let him go to play for his country – it's the law. All players want to play for their country – perhaps to qualify for the World Cup. It takes up a lot of a player's time, away from his club, but I don't see any way to resolve the problem.

GA: When teams like Manchester United, Ajax, FC Copenhagen, establish nurseries or buy teams in Africa to supply them with African-born players, is this going to assist or hinder the development of African football?

E: It helps. It provides better facilities – when there are no facilities there to play. When Ajax or Manchester United have teams there it is good because they have good living conditions, nutritional food, swimming pools – everything. I think it makes things better. Football can evolve.

GA: Why are there so few African-born coaches at international level?

E: There are coaches in Africa. The problem is that they have to come to Portugal or another European country to take a course. It is very difficult. Here in Portugal we have an excellent coaching school – in England and Germany too. Also, to be a coach you have to be lucky. That's why I chose not to become a football manager.

GA: Mozambique has many problems of poverty and dependency on the West. Has football got any role to play in the development and progress of Mozambique?

E: Sport can help. Not only football, but other sports such as basketball, athletics, etc. We have a world champion athlete in Maria Matola (world 800 metres champion). I think football also has progressed, but due to the lack of facilities and conditions in the country in comparison with other African countries such as South Africa, they can only try their best to make do with what they do have and progress in sport as far as they can. Mozambique today is one of the poorest countries in the world, and success in any sport can only help to raise its profile. SOS Mozambique was my own initiative: together with other former footballers. We all got together when Mozambique needed help because of the terrible floods a few years ago, which the whole world knew about. As a son of Mozambique I couldn't just stand there with my arms crossed and do nothing, so I organized everyone by knocking on friends' doors, saying: 'You are from Africa, come and help', collecting clothes, supplies, money, etc., and we flew to Mozambique to hand it all over to organizations like the Red Cross and Caritas [a Catholic NGO] to help the people directly, not the government. We are not politicians, we are footballers, and it had nothing to do with the government. In this way they received money, clothes and old footballs, which would probably have been 'kept' by officials if we had done things the usual way. This happens all over Africa – that's how things work there, but our aid got to the right place. The problem in Africa is that you can't just arrive there and hand aid over to officials, saying 'It's for the schools or children.'

GA: What is the Eusebio Foundation?

E: It's not quite ready yet – but nearly. I had the idea a few years ago. I am now starting to work on it and my daughters are also going to help me. I have the facilities to make a link between Lisbon and Mozambique.

GA: What is its aim?

E: To improve the lives of the children and use football to achieve this, as well as helping them in other ways. There is peace now in Mozambique, but there are children who have no facilities and I want to help them in any way I can. Principally, it is for the children – we must help them always.

GA: Is this organization a product of the generosity of Eusebio or is there a business involvement?

E: I have lots of support. Many people are interested, but we have to think hard about it. We don't want people putting money in just to get profit. I have plenty of time to work things out – I shall go to Mozambique and have more talks with the government there, and do the same here in Portugal. I'm trying to get it moving; however, these things take time.

GA: When do you see Africa being given the chance to stage the World Cup?

E: I believe that I will see a World Cup in Africa in my lifetime. South Africa or Morocco has the facilities to stage it. It would give me great pride to see an African country organize the World Cup. As far as I am concerned, South Africa is just as much an African country as Mozambique.

GA: Why has an East African nation never managed to get into the World Cup Finals?

E: They don't have suitable conditions or players for that level of competition. They are working towards this – look at the example of Nigeria. There are good players and good managers out there. The main problem is money.

GA: Do you think an African team will ever win the World Cup?

E: You never know – in football you can never tell.

GA: What do you see as the future for African footballers?

E: Players from African countries have already demonstrated their individual strengths, playing in England, Italy, Germany, Spain, here in Portugal, and other countries. They need to have faith in themselves and a good manager. Difficulties sometimes arise with the African mentality – they are distrustful and suspicious. They need to get rid of this mental trait, work hard and move forward.

GA: What advice would you give to a little boy running around the streets of Maputo wanting to be a footballer?

E: I go to Mozambique every year. When I go, I always take footballs, so that in my home district they have balls to play with. The problem is that they don't have as much space to play as I had when I was their age. It is a big problem, the lack of space. When I watch the young people play and speak to them, I tell them to study, finish school and then think about football. If I could go back in time, I would study a lot more and then go on to play football. I have a school for footballers called the Eusebio School here in Portugal. In Mozambique, the Eusebio Foundation will set up a school where children can go to study, play football and be well fed. If we find a promising footballer, we can bring him over to Portugal. The school here in Portugal runs for a week during the school holidays, sometimes in the national stadium where there is a hotel for them to stay, eat and sleep, and do football training with me. I travel from the north to the south of Portugal where I have weekend schools. The summer school runs for five weeks with different children each week. I am the head coach but I also have a goalkeeper coach, a striker coach, etc., all former Portuguese professional footballers (mostly internationals) who help me out. I want to do exactly the same in Mozambique when the Eusebio Foundation is set up.

GA: What would you consider is your greatest achievement in football?

E: There were so many: 1965, when I was voted European Player of the Year and received the Golden Ball; 1962, when we won the European Cup; 1966, the World Cup when we finished third; 1967, when I won the Golden Boot. They were all great moments.

GA: What is the greatest honour that football has bestowed on you?

E: I have received so many. In football terms probably when I was chosen as a FIFA Ambassador. I was decorated with a medal and became one of their ten best footballers of the century. We as a group are their ambassadors and we get together sometimes. Here in Portugal, apart from Benfica's 'Golden Eagle' medal, the government gave me the 'Cross of Christ' (for services to the country) which had never been given to a footballer. For me they made an exception. Also I am now an ambassador for both Benfica and the national team.

GA: In hindsight do you feel that you ever suffered exploitation at the hands of those who run the game?

E: I wish I could have kept on playing until I was 42, instead of 39. If I hadn't had the knee problem I would have wanted to carry on. I am perhaps the only footballer in the world to have six operations on the same knee and still carry on playing professionally. I was born on 25 January 1942, and there was a great footballer who I had the honour to play against, and who died recently, Sir Stanley Matthews. He played until he was 48, and I would have liked to do that too, but my knee problems prevented me.

GA: If you could live your life again, would you change anything?

E: I would change a lot. I would start in my own country, where I would want to see all the children have good facilities, hospitals, schools. Even though my family was poor, in my house we never went without food or drink or clothes. That's what I would want for Africa. Regarding my own life, I would change a lot of things. My life didn't turn out as I thought it would when I was young. As time passes, a person grows in stature, learns a lot more about life, what is happening in the world. I have been to many countries, but what I most would have liked to do is give more help to poorer countries. If I played football today, with the enormous amounts of money earned by players now, most of it would go towards helping the children in Mozambique. My family and I would have had a fantastic life (thanks be to God, we already have had), but we'd have had more than enough for all our needs and the money we didn't need I would have given firstly to help the children in Mozambique and then those here in Portugal.

Acknowledgements

The author is indebted to Eusebio for his time and opinions. Gratitude is due to Jackie Stewart (neé Hagan) for the personal introduction and translation. Manuel de Araujo, President of the UK Mozambican Association, helped immensely in providing historical background. Thanks are also due to John Garrett of Sheffield United FC for instigating a number of fortuitous meetings.

14
Extra Time

Peter Woodward

When approached by Gary Armstrong to contribute to this collection, I was not sure what was wanted. My instruction was to be a 'rapporteur', which struck me as rather grand for the game I have followed for over half a century: a bit like hearing Stuart Hall on *Sports Report* on a Saturday afternoon in French. At the same time the other contributors had had to do some work for their chapters, whereas I was just sitting down and reading: it felt like going on the pitch to be introduced to the players after the final whistle. Thoughts of the final whistle made me think that perhaps my part would be rather like extra time, after the real effort has been made and no conclusion reached. At the end of the 90 minutes it's often less than clear what can come next. Will all the players collapse with cramp; will a second yellow card be shown and leave ten already-tired men to run up the white flag; or will it produce a fresh, reinvigorated, all-too-short contest?

There was also the question: why me? In spite of years of following the game, I don't recall writing a word about soccer anywhere in the world, unlike my learned friends in the previous pages. But then I cast my mind back many years and remembered that I had one qualification that none of the others had claimed: I played football in Africa; regularly in Sudan from 1966 to 1971 and occasionally there and elsewhere on subsequent visits. It is those early years in Sudan that stand out most clearly. Arriving to live in a small town on the White Nile in central Sudan I swiftly became town commentator on the World Cup final from distant Wembley. Following crackly World Service radio commentary with far more than the usual quota of excitement was beyond the best local translator, so I sat in the store next to the market and kept what seemed like the whole town up to date on the score. At the final whistle (after extra time) I was warmly congratulated on the result, almost as enthusiastically as if I'd been Bobby Moore: it nearly compensated for not being able to see the game itself, which I only caught up with one year later when it was repeated on BBC television.

Shortly afterwards I discovered that on the dusty wasteland behind my house there were goalposts, and most days there would be a crowd of players in the late afternoon as the heat finally began to subside. So I joined in and was immediately adopted by the club on whose training ground I had stumbled. Furthermore I soon learned that it was one of the top two teams in town, Mereikh FC. On the other side of town were the great rivals, Hillal; and all over Sudan, from the mighty Mereikh and Hillal of Omdurman, the country's two leading teams, there were local counterparts: as if every town had an Arsenal and a Spurs, or a Rangers and a Celtic (I should add that I did later play for Hamilton Academicals of Reading). Off the pitch the Mereikh clubhouse was a local social centre, where I first tried backgammon and stumbling Arabic. The big game every week was on Friday afternoon, and played in the town's 'stadium': a walled ground, to keep out the goats, with the largest (almost the only) patch of grass in town. Occasionally we all piled into a converted Bedford truck and headed out on dusty tracks for other nearby towns (a mere 100 or so miles off) for the excitement of an away game. And when not playing with Mereikh, afternoons were often spent coaching or refereeing the school team where I was trying to teach.

But enough of my warm up, it's time to return to the extra time proper, though still with my personal 'memory lane' inevitably interwoven. This is of course a book by social scientists and we can't get away from Africa and all its reality in contemplating its football. Virtually all chapters are replete with various analytic and interpretative elements, several times drawing from that guru amongst Africanists in the 1990s, Jean-François Bayart, and centring around strains of politics and development.

Since the study of politics and international relations in Africa is a large part of my trade (having failed, like most other hopefuls, to make it through trials with a professional club), it was to that theme that I was particularly drawn and found the chapters both rich and varied: a true reflection of Africa. At the top stood the pretentiousness of politicians. Of course politicians everywhere try to identify with the game in some way or other, and given the centrality of 'Big Men' and patron–client relations in Africa, patronage of football clubs is to be expected and we are not disappointed here. The late King Hassan of Morocco stands out in this collection for the importance of his patronage of the game, but it goes on everywhere. Probably most active at the moment is Colonel Gaddafi of Libya, a born-again African, who is now indulging his younger son al-Saadi's dreams (he was named Libyan Striker of the Year in 2001) of football greatness; including hiring European teams for 'friendlies'. Al-Saadi is also buying into Italian football, where he sits on the board of Juventus, recently signed a cooperation deal with Lazio, and in late June 2003 signed as a striker for Perugia. It all sounds rather like Mussolini's Mare Nostrum in reverse. Little did I know it at the time, but in joining my local Mereikh I was attaching myself to one of the two largest Muslim 'sects' in Sudan (with Hillal attached to the other). This went beyond patronage of football since their respective spiritual leaders were also patrons of the major political parties: I was thus a bit-part player in a small-town manifestation of national politics.

However, political involvement can go beyond just the patronage of the mighty, for in the chapter on Nigeria, President Obasanjo and his fellow politicians actually play a match. Is it just a piece of populism (I recall Tony Blair playing head tennis with Kevin Keegan while electioneering) or middle-aged men playing out their fantasies? What they get up to in private is their business, but there is something rather absurd about middle-aged men, often overweight, squeezing themselves into gaudy modern football strips in public. Does it really appeal to the young, or do such caricatures of their real football idols bring only derision on these would-be sporting rulers? I don't know what reception Obasanjo received, though surely some derision was due when the game was stopped due to rain? I do though recall President Nimeiri of Sudan and his colleagues being jeered for their laboured efforts in similar circumstances. Perhaps we should be grateful that riding in her carriage and inspecting the runners is the closest the Queen comes to a horse at Royal Ascot.

The politics of football is not confined to rulers. In Britain it was for years the people's game ('a gentlemanly game played by ruffians'), and thus it can be in Africa as well. There may be no scenes there that quite equate with the factory closing at Saturday lunchtime decanting workers onto the terraces, so evocatively portrayed in Lowry's picture of Bolton Wanderers' Burnden Park (now replaced by the Reebok Stadium), but several of the chapters here include an 'us and them' dimension: whether based on race, ethnicity or class. Moreover, it is not confined to domestic politics, for the chapter on Cameroon brings out the international division of labour and its consequent resentments beautifully. The portrayal of the viewing public in a couple of bars watching the World Cup in France in 1998 is very evocative and revealing. I particularly enjoyed the elements of conspiracy, with France foisting a dud coach on the Cameroon team, ensuring their departure from the competition. And as if that was not enough, fixing referees and even the Brazilian team for the final (the latter explanation seems as convincing as any other for Brazil's extraordinarily vapid performance). While on this international tack, it is also worth noting the African solidarity in world football. Whereas supporters of European national teams care only for their own country, generally decrying the efforts of others, there is a feeling of pride in Africa as a whole for the performances in successive World Cups of the Indomitable Lions, the Super Eagles and all the rest.

From politics it is an easy step to 'development' and the uses of football. The Nigerian politicians mentioned above were not just trying to impress the people, there was also a reconciliatory purpose to Obasanjo and company quitting their flowing robes for tighter-fitting football kit. There had been tensions between the executive and legislative branches of government and it was intended to be a peacemaking gesture. Its success in this regard is not recorded, though hypothetically a draw might have been a more successful result than the 1–0 victory for the executive with the only goal being scored by the President himself. Going beyond seeking to improve intra-elite relations, there are in these pages at least two examples of ways in which football can contribute to community building. Anyone who has seen the Mathare shantytown in Nairobi can only be hopeful after reading of the Mathare Youth Sports Association, the local leagues and Mathare United Football Club. However, it is not just success on the field but the sense of purpose and social discipline that is revealed. I particularly liked the punishment for verbally abusing the referee: the offended player is suspended until he has refereed ten games ('those who can, play; those who can't, referee'). Likewise in Liberia, on the outskirts of Monrovia where 'Papeye Sport' has been at work in a project set up by the Salesians of Don Bosco. This fulfils a range of social functions, including teaching young men to abstain from activities such as drugs, rape and violence. The football clubs established under the programme also act as substitute families, providing protection for many of the orphans of the horrors of recent years in Liberia. It is heartening that something constructive can come out of that country's dreadful experiences.

However, sport can be a double-edged sword and divide as well as unite. The racial dimensions in South Africa, Zimbabwe and Algeria all surface here, although in post-apartheid South Africa there has been a general growing pride in the national team. At least football has not led to international conflict in Africa, as happened once in Central America. I do, though, recall seeing President Nimeiri deporting the Ghanaian football team for their, understandable if not condonable, response (refusing to collect losers' medals) to a defeat by Sudan that was entirely attributable to the referee, the most blatant 'homer' I ever witnessed.

Women and football I have never come across personally in Africa, but it several times appears here. It all sounds very joyful, but always one wonders how sustainable women's football will be. While we may think of it as a modern and growing phenomenon in Britain, it has in fact come and gone for years. Large crowds turned out in the early twentieth century only for the women's game to fade, and one wonders if it will be more lasting in Africa. Much may depend on situations, as the chapter on Liberia reminds us, for President Doe's attempt to promote women's football died with him.

In contrast to the novelty of women's football, I was much taken with the picture of cultural absorption in the case of Zanzibar. Football was presented less as a new activity brought in from outside that takes the place of indigenous activities, than as a further opportunity for the poor to show their skills competitively, alongside the existing competitions such as drumming, dancing and poetry. And after the final whistle, the bands take over to continue the ritualized atmosphere of the whole event.

Probably the most poignant chapter was the one on young players from Africa trying to make it in Europe. While we delight in the success of the few who make it, we may overlook all too easily the far greater number that manage one way or another to make the journey and then fail. It is one thing to be a European failing to make the grade in Europe, where after a brief disappointment one can take up something else; it is another matter entirely to be a young rejected African hopeful, who may end up penniless and drift towards the gutter. They may then lack the means to return to Africa, or feel unwilling to face the ignominy of failure once they do make it back. Failure may not reflect limited talent so much as an inability to adapt to the cultural differences of both football and life in Europe. I recall a young Liberian protégé of George Weah who signed for my local team Reading. In the few games he played in the Second Division he was streets ahead of any of the mainly journeymen players on the pitch, but, alas, he had trouble adapting himself to the disciplines of a work-oriented team and was in and out of the game; while off the field, rumours of all kinds circulated and were linked to his schizophrenic play on it. The chapter also illustrates the sleaziness of the game. Somehow sleaziness can be something of a joke among the rich of football – the George Grahams and others reputed to take their share of transfer 'bungs' – but small-time agents seeking to exploit and then cast off young Africans seems a much darker side to the game.

Failure in Europe for African hopefuls is a tragedy for individuals; the larger tragedy of Africa, not much mentioned in this collection, is that of HIV/AIDS. We are all aware of the scale of the tragedy but its social implications are only now being realized. Thus far studies have pointed to the impact of the disease amongst groups such as young professionals and the military, but it will be much wider and must, alas, include at least some of Africa's football talent.

Finally to the game itself. It's a commonplace to speak of the introduction of African children to the game. Not for them the latest kit from an early age, and ever more intense coaching by eager parents and coaches on grassy parks or even artificial surfaces. Instead, children's football in Africa is played in whatever is being worn, often little more than rags; mostly as an entirely informal activity; often on local wasteland or in the streets. Frequently it continues for hours on end, in groups large and small, and kicking anything that can be utilized, but rarely a shiny new ball of FIFA-approved size and pressure. The children themselves develop as young men to play in matches where they show high personal skills, especially in ball control and dribbling, rather than team play and tactical awareness. It may all sound like a truism, but for many, probably most, young Africans it is the reality: indeed, apart from the surfaces (rarely muddy grass) the picture is not so different from that experienced by many young people in Britain of my generation who grew up aspiring to the incredible close control and balance of Stanley Matthews, who had honed his skills on the streets of the Potteries. At the same time the displays of individual skills within the game in Africa are often what the crowd admires, rather like solo turns in a jazz number. The chapter on Zanzibar reminds us that there it is a game of aesthetics that regards 'bold, fast individual moves to be much more appealing than slow collective moves downfield'. Ray Wilkins, that king of the square pass, would find few admirers on the clove islands.

So the aim is the 'beautiful game' as Pelé dubbed it. And African players have certainly contributed to the beauty at the highest level, with the 'fast individual moves' providing some of the most memorable moments. Who can forget George Weah dribbling from his own penalty area to score for AC Milan in the mid-1990s, when both he and AC were at their peak: or more recently the contributions to the English Premiership of players as gifted as Kanu of Arsenal and J-J Okotcha of Bolton Wanderers (a team now unrecognizable in personnel to the generations of Lowry and Nat Lofthouse)? As Keats wrote, 'Beauty is truth, truth beauty, That is all you know on earth and all you need to know.'

Football, though is not only about beauty, it is also about winning. Bill Shankley, a great competitor as player and manager, once famously remarked that football is more important than life and death. But not winning at any price. The chapter on Algeria recalls Albert Camus, probably the most famous if not necessarily the best goalkeeper that Africa has produced: his contribution to the Philosophy Football series ('sporting outfitters of intellectual distinction') stated simply: 'All that I know most surely about morality and obligations I owe to football.'

Penalty shoot-out anyone?

Bibliography

Abdullahi, M.M. (2000) 'History and Development of Football: The Nigerian Experience'. Unpublished undergraduate final year thesis, University of Jos, Nigeria.

Abisuga, C.A. and H. Awurumibe (1991) *Genesis of Female Soccer in Nigeria,* Lagos: Kola Okanlawon Publishers Limited.

Abubaker, A. (1999) *Welcome to Nigeria. The Official Handbook of the Flying Eagles of Nigeria,* Abuja: NFA Publications.

Adelman, S. (1995) 'Alternative former for demokrati i Afrika', in *Fellesrådets Afrikaårbok,* Oslo: Gazette.

ADR (African Development Report) 2001, Oxford: Oxford University Press.

African Political Economy 27(85): 385–406.

Akindutire, O. (1991) 'The Historical Development of Soccer in Nigeria: An Appraisal of Emerging Prospects', *Canadian Journal of the History of Sport* (May).

Akpabot, S. (1985) *Football In Nigeria,* London: Macmillan.

Alegi, P. (2000a) '*Amathe Nolimi* (It is Saliva and the Tongue): Contracts of Joy in South African Football, c. 1940–1976,' *International Journal of the History of Sport* 17(4): 1–20.

Alegi, P. (2000b) 'Katanga vs Johannesburg: A History of the First Sub-Saharan African Football Championship, 1949–1950', *Kleio* 31.

Alexander, P. (2000) 'Zimbabwean Workers, the MDC and the 2000 Election', *Review of African Political Economy* 27(85): 385–406.

Aley, J. (1992) Interview with Juma Aley by Laura Fair (in Kiswahili), 30 May and 15 June.

Ali, R.M. (1991) Interview with Rajab Mzee Ali by Laura Fair (in Kiswahili), 5 March.

Allison, L. (1986) (ed.) *The Politics of Sport,* Manchester: Manchester University Press.

Ambler, C. (1996) 'A History of Leisure in Colonial Urban Africa'. A paper presented at a conference on 'Africa's Urban Past', School of Oriental and African Studies, University of London, June.

Ambler, C. (2002) 'Leisure in Urban Africa'. Paper presented at the African Studies Association Annual Meeting, 2001, revised and published as the introduction to a special issue on 'Leisure in Urban Africa', *International Journal of African Historical Studies* 35(1): 1–8.

Anderson, B. (1983) *Imagined Communities,* London: Verso.

Anthony, D. (1983) 'Culture and Society in a Town in Transition: A People's History of Dar es Salaam, 1865–1939'. PhD dissertation, University of Wisconsin, Madison.

Appadurai, A. (1990) 'Disjuncture and Difference in the Global Cultural Economy', in M. Featherstone (ed.) *Global Culture,* London: Sage.

Appadurai, A. (2000) 'Grassroots Globalization and the Research Imagination', *Public Culture* 12(1): 1–19.

Apraku, E. and M. Hesselman (1998) *Schwarze, Sterne und Pharaonen: Der Aufstieg des Afrikanischen fußballs*, Gottingen: Verlag Die Werkstaff.

Apter, A. (1996) 'The Pan-African Nation: Oil-Money and the Spectacle of Culture in Nigeria,' *Public Culture*, August.

Archer, R. and Bouillon, A. (1982) *The South African Game: Sport and Racism*, London: Zed Books.

Archetti, E. (1999) *Masculinities: Football, Polo and the Tango in Argentina*, Oxford: Berg.

Arizpe, L. (1992) 'Ethnicity, Nations and Culture', *Development* 1: 6–8.

Armstrong, G. and R. Giulianotti (1998) *Football Cultures and Identities*, Basingstoke: Macmillan (now Palgrave Macmillan).

Arnold, M. (1869) *Culture and Anarchy*, London: Smith, Elder & Co.

Askew, K. (1999) 'Female Circles and Male Lines: Gender Dynamics along the Swahili Coast', *Africa Today* 46(3/4): 67–102.

Atieno-Odhiambo, E.S. (1996): 'The Invention of Kenya', in B.A. Ogot and W.R. Ochieng, *Decolonization and Indepenence in Kenya 1943–93*, Nairobi: East African Educational Publishers Ltd/London: J. Curry Ltd/Athens: Ohio University Press.

Awolowo, O. (1960) *Awo*, Cambridge: Cambridge University Press.

Awoyinfa, W.O. (1957) 'Origin of Football in Nigeria', *West African Pilot* (November).

Aye, E. (1967) *Old Calabar Through the Centuries*, Calabar: Hope Waddell Press.

Aye, E. (1986) *Hope Waddell Training Institution*, Calabar: Paico Limited.

Azikiwe, N. (1970) *My Odyssey*, London: C. Hurst & Company.

Back, L., T. Crabbe and J. Solomos (2001) *The Changing Face of Football: Racism, Identity and Multiculture in the English Game*, Oxford: Berg.

Badenhorst, C. and C. Mather (1997) 'Tribal Recreation and Recreating Tribalism: Culture, Leisure and Social Control in South Africa's Gold Mines, 1940–1950', *Journal of Southern African Studies* 23(3): 473–89.

Bakari, A.S. (1995) Interview with Adija Salum Bakari by Laura Fair (in Kiswahili), 27 July.

Baker, W.J. (1987) 'Political Games: The Meaning of International Sport for Independent Africa', in W.J. Baker and J.A. Mangan (eds) *Sport in Africa: Essays in Social History*, New York: African Publishing Company.

Baker, W.J. and J.A. Mangan (eds) (1987) *Sport in Africa: Essays in Social History*, New York: African Publishing Company.

Bale, J. (1991) *The Brawn Drain: Foreign Student-Athletes in American Universities*, Urbana: University of Illinois Press.

Bale, J. (2002) *Imagined Olympians: Body Culture and Representation in Colonial Rwanda*, Minneapolis: University of Minnesota Press.

Bale, J. and J. Sang (1995) *Kenyan Running*, London: Frank Cass.

Barry, B. (2000) *Culture and Equality*, London: Blackwell.

Barth, F. (ed.) (1969) *Ethnic Groups and Boundaries: The Social Organisation of Culture Difference*, Boston: Little Brown.

Barthes, R. (1973) *Mythologies*, London: Paladin.

Bayart, J-F. (1985) *L'état au Cameroun*, Paris: Presses de la Fondation Nationale des Sciences Politiques.

Bayart, J-F. (1993) *The State in Africa: The Politics of the Belly*, London: Longman.

Beach, D. (1994) *The Shona and their Neighbours*, Oxford: Blackwell.

Bello, Sir Ahmadu (1962) *My Life*, Cambridge: Cambridge University Press.

Berkeley, B. (2001) *The Graves Are Not Yet Full: Race, Tribe and Power in the Heart of Africa*, New York: Basic Books.

Berman, B.J. (1998) 'Ethnicity, Patronage and the African State: The Politics of Uncivil Nationalism', *African Affairs* 97: 305–41.

Bernard, S. (1968) *The Franco-Moroccan Conflict 1943–1956*, New Haven: Yale University Press.

Berque, J. (1962) *Le Maghreb entre deux guerres*, Paris: Editions du Seuil.

BiMkubwa Stadi Fundi (1995) Interview with Laura Fair (in Kiswahili), 8 August.

Blacking, J. (1987) 'Games and Sport in Pre-Colonial African Societies', in W. Baker and J. Mangion (eds) *Sport in Africa: Essays in Social History*, New York: African Publishing Company.

Blades, J. (1998) *The Rainbow Game: A Random History of South African Soccer*, Lanseria: Bailey's African History Archives.

Blain, N., R. Boyle and H. O'Donnell (1993) *Sport and National Identity in the European Media*, Leicester: Leicester University Press.

Bonner, P. and L. Segal (1998) *Soweto: A History*, Cape Town: Maskew Miller Longman.

Booth, D. (1998) *The Race Game: Sport and Politics in South Africa*. London: Frank Cass.

Boraki, C. (2001) 'Les Contrebandières: Woman as Smuggler', *Women: A Cultural Review* 12(2): 176–91.

Bourdillon, M.F.C. (1987) *The Shona Peoples* (revised edition), Gweru: Mambo Press.

Bourdillon, M.F.C. (1994) 'Street Children in Harare', *Africa* 64(4): 516–32.

Broere, M. and R. van der Drift (1997) *Football Africa!* Oxford: World View Publishing.

Bromberger, C. (1995) *Le Match de Football. Ethnologie d'une passion partisane à Marseille, Naples et Turin*, Paris: Seuil.

Bunwaree, S. (2001) 'The Marginal in the Miracle: Human Capital in Mauritius', *International Journal for Educational Development* 21(3): 257–71.

Burke, T. (1996) *Lifebuoy Men, Lux Women: Commodification, Consumption, and Cleanliness in Modern Zimbabwe*, Durham, NC: Duke University Press.

Castle, S., A. Duval Smith and L. Rundle (2000) 'Inquiry into "Slave Trade" in African Footballers', *Independent*, 7 November, p. 16.

CCJP (Catholic Commission for Justice and Peace in Zimbabwe) (1997) *Report on the 1980s Disturbances in Matabeleland and the Midlands*, <www.mg.co.za/mg/zim/zimtitle.html>

CEMFZ (Commission of Enquiry into the Management of Football in Zimbabwe) (1997) *Report of the Commission of Enquiry into the Management of Football in Zimbabwe*, Harare: Zimbabwe Sports Commission.

Chattopadhyay, R. (2000) 'Zimbabwe: Structural Adjustment, Destitution and Food Insecurity', *Review of African Political Economy* 27(84): 307–16.

Chaudhary, V. (2000) 'Poverty Gap Threatens to Destroy League', *Guardian*, 26 August, p. 30.

Chaudhary, V. (2001) 'Police Mount Passport Enquiry', *Guardian*, 9 February, p. 34.

Chraïbi, D. (1981) *Une enquête au pays*, Paris: Seuil.

Chraïbi, D. (1998) *Vu, lu, entendu*, Paris: Denoël.

Clayton, A. (1987) 'Sport and African Soldiers: the Military Diffusion of Western Sport Throughout Sub-Saharan Africa', in W.J. Baker and J.A. Mangan (eds) *Sport in Africa: Essays in Social History*, New York: African Publishing Company.

Clayton, A. and D. Killingray (1989) *Khaki and Blue: Military and Police in British Colonial Africa*, Athens, Ohio: Ohio University Center for International Studies.

Clignet, R and M. Stark (1974) 'Modernisation and Football in Cameroon', *Journal of Modern African Studies* 12(3): 409–21.

Clingman, S. (1998) *Bram Fischer: Afrikaner Revolutionary*, Amherst, MA: University of Massachusetts Press.

Compagnon, D. (2000) 'Zimbabwe: Life After Zanu-PF', *African Affairs* 99: 449–53.

Cobley, A.G. (1997) *The Rules of the Game: Struggles in Black Recreation and Social Policy Welfare in South Africa*: Westport, CT: Greenwood Press.

Connell, D. (1993) *Against All Odds: A Chronicle of the Eritrean Revolution*, Lawrenceville, NJ: Red Sea Press.

Coplan, D. (1985) *In Township Tonight! South Africa's Black City Music and Theater*, New York: Longman.

Coquery-Vidrovitch, C. (1988) *Africa*, Berkeley: University of California Press.

Corneliussen, H.I. (1995) 'Har vestlig kondisjonalitet gjort Kenya mer demokratisk?' in *Fellesrådets Afrikaårbok 1995*, Oslo: Gazette.

Coronil, F. (1997) *The Magical State: Nature, Money, and Modernity in Venezuela*, Chicago: University of Chicago Press.

Couzens, T. (1983) 'An Introduction to the History of Football in South Africa', in B. Bezzoli (ed.) *Town and Countryside in the Transvaal*, Johannesburg: Raven.

Cresswell, T. (2001) 'The Production of Mobilities', *New Formations* 43: 11–25.

Cross, G. (1990) *A Social History of Leisure since 1600*, State College, PA: Venture.

Darby, P. (2000a) 'Football, Colonial Doctrine and Indigenous Resistance: Mapping the Political Persona of FIFA's African Constituency', *Culture, Sport, Society* 3(1): 61–87.

Darby, P. (2000b) 'The New Scramble for Africa: African Football Labour Migration to Europe', *European Sports History Review* 3: 217–44.

Darby, P. (2002) *Africa, Football and FIFA: Politics, Colonialism and Resistance*, London: Frank Cass.

Dauncey, H. and G. Hare (1999) '"33 jours de fête": A Diary of France 98', in H. Dauncey and G. Hare (eds) *France and the 1998 World Cup: The National Impact of a World Sporting Event*, London: Frank Cass.

Delves, A. (1981) 'Popular Recreation and Social Conflict in Derby, 1800–1850', in E. Yeo and S. Yeo (eds) *Popular Culture and Class Conflict, 1590–1914*, Atlantic Highlands, NJ: Humanities Press.

De Waal, V. (1990) *The Politics of Reconciliation: Zimbabwe's First Decade*, London: Hurst & Company.

Draper, M. (1963) *Sport and Race in South Africa*, Johannesburg: South African Institute of Race Relations.

Dzimba, J. (1998) *South Africa's Destabilization of Zimbabwe, 1989–89*, New York: St. Martin's Press.

Edling, J. (1996) *My Dear Jamal... Morocco Bound*, London: New Millenium.

Eichberg, H. (1994) 'Travelling, Comparing, Emigrating: Configurations of Sport Mobility', in J. Bale and J. Maguire (eds) *The Global Sports Arena: Athletic Talent Migration in an Independent World*, London: Frank Cass.

Elaigwu, J.I. (1986) *Gowon: The Biography of a Soldier-Statesman*, Ibadan: West Books Publishers Limited.

Ellis, S. (1999) *The Mask of Anarchy: The Destruction of Liberia*, Oxford: C. Hunt & Co.

Eriksen, T. (1998) *Common Denominators: Ethnicity, Nation-Building and Compromise in Mauritius*, Oxford: Berg.

Erlmann, V. (1991) *African Stars: Studies in Black South African Performance*, Chicago and London: University of Chicago Press.

Etienne, B. (1977) *L'Algérie, Cultures et Révolution*, Paris: Editions du Seuil.

Evans, I. (1997) *Bureaucracy and Race: Native Administration in South Africa*, Berkeley: University of California Press.

Fair, L (1997a) 'Identity, Difference and Dance: Female Initiation in Zanzibar, 1890–1930', *Frontiers* 17(3).

Fair, L. (1997b) 'Kickin' It: Leisure, Politics and Football in Colonial Zanzibar, 1900s–1950s', *Africa* 67(2): 224–51.

Fair, L. (2001) *Pastimes and Politics: Culture, Community and Identity in Post-Abolition Urban Zanzibar, 1890–1945*, Athens: Ohio University Press.

Farred, G. (1999) '"Theatre of Dreams": Mimicry and Difference in Cape Flats Township Football', *Polygraph* 11: 65–88.

Fereji, K. (1991) Interview with Khamis Fereji by Laura Fair (in Kiswahili), Zanzibar.

Feruz, H. (1991) Interview with Hamidi Feruz by Laura Fair (in Kiswahili), 16 September.

Fitzgibbon, Father (1960) 'Soccer in West Africa Began in Freetown and Nigeria', *West African Pilot*, 14 October.

Forsythe, D. (2000) *Human Rights in International Relations*, Cambridge: Cambridge University Press.

Foucault, M. (1982) 'The Subject and Power', in H.L. Dreyfus and P. Rabinow (eds) *Michel Foucault: Beyond Structuralism and Hermeneutics*, Chicago: Chicago University Press.

Franken, M. (1986) 'Anyone Can Dance: A Survey and Analysis of Swahili Ngoma Past and Present'. PhD dissertation, University of California, Riverside.

Frynas, J.G. (2001) 'Corporate and State Responses to Anti-Oil Protests in the Niger Delta', *African Affairs* 100: 27–54.

Gaitskell, D. (1982) '"Wailing for Purity": Prayer Unions, African Mothers and Adolescent Daughters, 1912–1940', in S. Marks and R. Rathbone (eds), *Industrialisation and Social Change in South Africa*, London: Longman.

Gallup, J.L. and J.D. Sachs (2000) 'The Economic Impact of Malaria', Center for International Development, Harvard University, Working Paper No. 52, July.

Garbo, G. (1993) *Makt og bistand*, Oslo: Spartacus.

Gardner, P. (1996) *The Simplest Game*, New York: Macmillan.

Gellner, E. (1962) 'Patterns of Rural Rebellion in Morocco', *Archives européennes de sociologie* III: 297–311.

Gellner, E. (1981) 'A Pendulum Swing Theory of Islam', in R. Robertson (ed.) *Sociology of Religion*, Harmondsworth: Penguin.

Gilroy, P. (1993) *The Black Atlantic*, London: Verso.

Giulianotti, R. (1999a) *Football: A Sociology of the Global Game*, London: Polity Press.

Giulianotti, R. (1999b) *'Sport and Development in Africa: Some Major Human Rights Issues'*, Paper given at 'How to Play The Game: Sport and Human Rights' Conference, Sydney, Australia.

Glaser, C. (2000) *Bo-Tsotsi: The Youth Gangs of Soweto, 1935–1976*, Portsmouth, NH: Heinemann.

Glassman, J. (1995) *Feats and Riot: Revelry, Rebellion and Popular Consciousness on the Swahili Coast*, Portsmouth, NH: Heinemann.

Godia, G. (1989): 'Sport in Kenya', in E.A. Wagner (ed.) *Sport in Asia and Africa: A Comparative Handbook*, Westport, CT: Greenwood Press.

Granger, V. (1961) *The World's Game Comes to South Africa*, Cape Town: Howard Immins.

Grillo, R. and Stirrat, R. (1997) *Discourses of Development. Anthropological Perspectives*, Oxford: Berg.

Guttman, A. (1994) *Games and Empires. Modern Sport and Cultural Imperialism*, New York: Columbia University Press.

Handler, A. (1994) 'From Goals to Guns: The Golden Age of Soccer in Hungary, 1950–1956', in *East European Monographs*, Boulder and New York: Columbia University Press.

Hannerz, U. (1990) 'Cosmopolitans and Locals', in M. Featherstone (ed.) *Global Culture*, London: Sage.

Hannerz, U. (1992) *Cultural Complexity: Studies in the Cultural Organization of Meaning*, New York: Columbia University Press.

Haruna, M. and S.A. Abdullahi (1991) 'The "Soccer Craze" and Club Formation among Hausa Youth in Kano, Nigeria', *Kano Studies* (special issue on football).

Hayani, H. (1992) (in Arabic) *Al-Rayatha al-Maghrebia*, Rabat.

Henly, J. (1998) 'Scandal of Belgium's Football Slave Trade', *Daily Mail and Guardian* (Johannesburg), 4 December.

Henry, I. (1993) *The Politics of Leisure Policy*, London: Macmillan.

Hilal, N.M. (1992) Interview with Nasra Mohamed Hilal by Laura Fair (in Kiswahili), 14 July and 25 October.

Hoberman, J. (2000) 'Behind the Mask', *Index on Censorship* 4: 57–61.

Holt, R. (1989a) 'Ideology and Sociability: A Review of New French Research into the History of Sport under the Early Third Republic (1870–1914)', *International Journal of the History of Sport* 6(3): 368–77.

Holt, R. (1989b) *Sport and the British – A Modern History*, Oxford: Clarendon Press.

Hope Waddell Training Institution (1894–1908) *Primary School Log Book 1894–1908*.

House of Commons (1999) <www.parliament.the-stationery-office.co.uk/pa/cm199900/cmselect/cmeduemp/218/0020903.htm>

Howe, S. (1998) *Afrocentricism. Mythical Pasts and Imagined Homes*, London: Verso.

Iyob, R. (1995) *The Eritrean Struggle for Independence: Domination, Resistance, Nationalism, 1941–1993*, Cambridge: Cambridge University Press.

James, C.L.R. (1963) *Beyond a Boundary*, London: Stanley Paul; reprinted Durham, NC: Duke University Press.

Jarvie, G. (1985) *Class, Race and Sport in South Africa's Political Economy*, London: Routledge.

Jeater, D. (1995) 'The Way You Tell Them: Language, Ideology and Development Policy in Southern Rhodesia', *African Studies* 54(2): 1–15.

Jeffrey, I. (1992) 'Street Rivalry and Patron-Managers: Football in Sharpeville, 1943–1985', *African Studies* 51(1): 68–94.

Jenkins, C. (1997) 'The Politics of Economic Policy-Making in Zimbabwe', *Journal of Modern African Studies* 35(4): 575–602.

Joseph, R.A. (1977) *Radical Nationalism in Cameroon: Social Origins of the UPC. Rebellion*, Oxford: Clarendon Press.

Juma, M. (1992) Interview with Mtumwa Juma by Laura Fair (in Kiswahili), 31 January.

Kaarsholm, P. (1990) '"Mental Colonisation or Catharsis?" Theatre, Democracy and Cultural Struggle from Rhodesia to Zimbabwe', *Journal of Southern African Studies* 16(2).

Kaarsholm, P. (1997) 'Inventions, Imaginings, Codifications: Authorising Versions of Ndebele Cultural Tradition', *Journal of Southern African Studies* 23(2): 243–58.

Kaarsholm, P. (1999) 'Si Ye Pambili – Which Way Forward? Urban Development, Culture and Politics in Bulawayo', in B. Raftopoulos and T. Yoshikuni (eds) *Sites of Struggle: Essays in Zimbabwe's Urban History*, Harare: Weaver Press.

Kala-Lobe, S. (1998a) 'Les héros noirs d'une France raciste', *La Nouvelle Expression*, 10 July.

Kala-Lobe, S. (1998b) 'Les Bleus, les Blancs et les Noirs', *La Nouvelle Expression*, 10 July.

Kalu, O. (1996) *The Embattled Gods*, Lagos: Minaj Publishers.

Kamati Maalum ya Kuchunguza Historia ya Michezo ya Riadha na Mipira Visiwani (1981) Unpublished confidential report conveyed to author by a committee member.

Kapuscinski, R. (2001) *Shadow of the Sun*, London: Penguin.

Kidd, B. and P. Donnelly (2000) 'Human Rights in Sports', *International Review for the Sociology of Sport* 35(2): 131–48.

Klein, A. (1991) *Sugarball. The American Game, the Dominican Dream*, New Haven: Yale University Press.

Kristiansen, T. (1994) *Mor Afrika*, Oslo: Cappelen.

Kuper, L. (1965) *An African Bourgeoisie: Race, Class, and Politics in South Africa*, New Haven and London: Yale University Press.

Landau, R. (1952) *Portrait of Tangier*, London: Robert Hale.

Lanfranchi, P. and M. Taylor (2001) *Moving with the Ball: The Migration of Professional Footballers*, Oxford: Berg.

Larsen, T. (1989) 'Kultur og utvikling', in T.H. Eriksen (ed.) *Kulturdemensjonen i bistandsarbeidet. Hvor mange hvite elefanter?*, Oslo: Ad Notam.

Leach, J. and G. Kildea (1975) *Trobriand Cricket: An Ingenious Response to Colonialism*. Video documentary.

Leseth, A. (1997) 'The Use of JuJu in Football: Sport and Witchcraft in Tanzania', in G. Armstrong and R. Giulianotti (eds) *Entering the Field: New Perspectives on World Football*, Oxford: Berg.

Lever, J. (1983) *Soccer Madness*, Chicago: University of Chicago Press.

Ley, D. (1985) 'Cultural/Humanistic Geography', *Progress in Human Geography* 9: 415–23.

Lindøe, P. (2001) *Making Dreams Come Through: Sport and Community Development in the Mathare Valley Slums*, Skarnes: Compendicus Forlag.

Litchfield, E. (1963) *Goals in the Sun*, Johannesburg: Simondium-Uitgewers.

Litchfield, E. (1965) *Eric Litchfield's Book of Soccer*, Johannesburg: Hugh Keartland.

Liwewe, P. (1999) 'The Zambian Air Crash', *African Soccer* 50.

Luke, Rev. J. (1929) *Pioneering in Mary Slessor's Country*, London: Epworth Press.

Lunn, I. (1999) 'The Meaning of the 1948 General Strike in Colonial Zimbabwe', in B. Raftopoulos and T. Yoshikuni (eds) *Sites of Struggle: Essays in Zimbabwe's Urban History*, Harare: Weaver Press.

Lyne, R. (1905) *Zanzibar in Contemporary Times*, London: Dart.

MacCannell, D. (1976) *The Tourist: A New Theory of the Leisure Class*, London: Macmillan.

McGovern, P. (2000) 'The Irish Brawn Drain: English League Clubs and Irish Footballers, 1946–1995', *British Journal of Sociology* 51(3): 401–18.

McKeever, L. (1999) 'Reporting the World Cup: Old and New Media', in H. Dauncey and G. Hare (eds) *France and the 1998 World Cup: The National Impact of a World Sporting Event*, London: Frank Cass.

Magubane, B. (1963) 'Sport and Politics in an Urban African Community: A Case Study of African Voluntary Organizations'. Unpublished MSS thesis, University of Natal.

Maguire, J. (1999) *Global Sport: Identities, Societies, Civilizations*, Cambridge: Polity Press.

Maguire, R. (1991) *The People's Club: A Social and Institutional History of Orlando Pirates Football Club, 1937–1973*. BA Honours thesis, University of the Witwatersrand.

Makame, A. (1991) Interview with Ali Makame by Laura Fair (in Kiswahili), 27 August.

Maloba, W.O. (1996) 'Decolonization: A Theoretical Perspective', in B.A. Ogot and W.R. Ochieng, *Decolonization and Independence in Kenya 1943–93*, Nairobi: East African Educational Publishers Ltd/London: J. Curry Ltd/Athens: Ohio University Press.

Mangan, J.A. (1985) *The Games Ethic and Imperialism*, London: Viking.

Mangan, J.A. (1987) 'Ethics and Ethnocentricity: Imperial Education in British Tropical Africa', in W.J. Baker and J.A. Mangan (eds) *Sport in Africa: Essays in Social History*, New York: African Publishing Company.

Marks, J. (1999) 'The French National Team and National Identity: "Cette France d'un 'bleu métis'"', in H. Dauncey and G. Hare (eds) *France and the 1998 World Cup: The National Impact of a World Sporting Event*, London: Frank Cass.

Martin, P. (1991) 'Colonialism, Youth and Football in French Equatorial Africa', *International Journal of the History of Sport* 8(1): 56–71.

Martin, P. (1995) *Leisure and Society in Colonial Brazzaville*, Cambridge: Cambridge University Press.

Martin, S. (1991) 'Brass Bands and the Beni Phenomenon in Urban East Africa', *African Music* 7(1): 72–81.

Mason, T. (1995) *Passion of the People? Football in South America*, London: Verso.

Mazrui, A. (1987) 'Africa's Triple Heritage of Play: Reflection on the Gender Gap', in W.J. Baker and J.A. Mangan (eds) *Sport in Africa: Essays in Social History*, New York: African Publishing Company.

Mazrui, A.A. and M. Tidy (1984) *Nationalism and New States in Africa*, Nairobi: Heinemann.

Mbembe, A. (1986) 'Pouvoir des morts et langage des vivants: les errances de la mémoire nationaliste au Cameroun', *Politique Africaine* 22: 37–72.

Mignon, P. (1999) 'Fans and Heroes', in H. Dauncey and G. Hare (eds) *France and the 1998 World Cup: The National Impact of a World Sporting Event*, London: Frank Cass.

Milner, M. (1999) 'Cape Town Soccer Club Goes Dutch', *Guardian*, 12 January, p. 1.

Mirza, A. (1991) Interview with Abaas Mirza by Laura Fair (in Kiswahili), 27 August.

Mohamed, S. (1992) Interview with Said (Nyanya) Mohamed by Laura Fair (in Kiswahili), 17 September.

Mokone, S. (1980) *The Life and Times of a Soccer Player*, Pretoria: De Jager-Haum.

Monnington, T. (1986) 'The Politics of Black African Sport', in L. Allison (ed.) *The Politics of Sport*, Manchester: Manchester University Press.

Moore, G. (2002) 'The World Tunes In to Mali's Showcase', *Independent*, 18 January, p. 22.

Morley, D. and K. Robins (1995) *Spaces of Identity: Global Media, Electronic Landscapes and Cultural Boundaries*, London: Routledge.

MSL (2000) Metropolitan Soccer league: <www.mslstl.com/home-page.htm>

Mtoro bin Mwinyi Bakari (1903) *The Customs of the Swahili People*, ed. and trans. J. Allen, Los Angeles: University of California Press. 1981. Originally published as Carl Velten, *Desturi za Wasuahili*, Gottingen: Vandenhoek and Ruprecht.

Murray, W. (1996) *The World's Game: A History of Soccer*, Urbana: University of Illinois Press.

Mvie, J.B. (1998) 'Dieu a choisi Thuram pour parler aux Français', *La Nouvelle Expression*, 10 July.

Myers, G. (1994) 'Ethnocentrism and African Urbanization: The Case of Zanzibar's Other Side,' *Antipode* 26(3): 195–215.

Mzee, M. (1992) Interview with Mbarak Mzee by Laura Fair (in Kiswahili), 31 January.

Naipaul, V.S. (1972) *The Overcrowded Barracoon*, London: Andre Deutsch.

Nauright, J. (1997) *Sport, Cultures and Identities in South Africa*, London: Leicester University Press.

Negash, T. (1997) *Eritrea and Ethiopia: The Federal Experience*, Uppsala, Sweden: Nordiska Afrika Institulet.

Niemen, T. (1989) *Krimau: Je suis Comme ça*, Casablanca: Eddif.

Nigerian Football Association (NFA) (1999) *Ghana–Nigeria 2000: Nigeria, the Super Eagles*, Abuja: Ghana–Nigeria 2000 Local Organizing Committee.

Obudho, R.A. (1997) 'Nairobi: National Capital and Regional Hub', in *The Urban Challenge of Africa 1997*, Tokyo/New York/Paris: United Nations University Press.

Ochieng, W.R. (1996) 'Structural and Political Changes', in B.A. Ogot and W.R. Ochieng (eds) *Decolonization and Independence in Kenya 1943–93*, Nairobi: East African Educational Publishers Ltd/London: J. Curry Ltd/Athens: Ohio University Press.

Ochieng, W.R. and E.S. Atieno-Odhiambo (1996) 'Prologue on Decolonization', in B.A. Ogot and W.R. Ochieng (eds) *Decolonization and Independence in Kenya 1943–93*, Nairobi: East African Educational Publishers Ltd/London: J. Curry Ltd/Athens: Ohio University Press.

Odanga, E. (1999) 'Cleaning Up', *African Soccer*, November, London: African Tele-Promotion.

Odegbami, S. (1993) *Goal Bound*, Lagos: Worldwide Sports Limited.

Oliver, B. (2000) '"Slaves" on a Fortune', *Guardian Unlimited*, 13 February.

Ossman, S. (1994) *Picturing Casablanca: Portraits of Power in a Modern City*, Berkeley and Los Angeles: University of California Press.

Othman, A. (1991) Interview with Abdulrahman Othman by Laura Fair (in Kiswahili), 14 June and 5 July.

Othman, A.S. (1995) Interview with Amina (Mapande) Seif Othman by Laura Fair (in Kiswahili), 19 July.

Pandolfo, S. (1997) *Impasse of the Angels*, Chicago: University of Chicago Press.

Parry, R. (1999) 'Culture, Organisation and Class: The African Experience in Salisbury, 1892–1935', in B. Raftopoulos and T. Yoshikuni (eds) *Sites of Struggle: Essays in Zimbabwe's Urban History*, Harare: Weaver Press.

Pateman, R. (1998) *Eritrea: Even the Stones are Burning*, Lawrenceville, NJ: Red Sea Press.

Perrault, G. (1990) *Notre ami le roi*, Paris: Gallimard.

Phimister, I. (1988) *An Economic and Social History of Zimbabwe 1890–1948*, London: Longman.

Poku, I. (2002) 'Poverty, Debt and Africa's HIV/AIDS Crisis', *International Affairs* 78(3): 531–46.

Powell, V.B.V. (1963?) *Preliminary Considerations Concerning the Provision of Sports and Recreational Facilities at the University of Ife, Western Nigeria*, Rhodes House Archives, Oxford University.

Quayson, A. (2000) *Postcolonialism*, Cambridge: Polity Press.

Ranger, T.O. (1968) 'African Politics in Twentieth-Century Southern Rhodesia', in T.O. Ranger (ed.) *Aspects of Central African History*, London: Heinemann.

Ranger, T. (1975) *Dance and Society in East Africa*, London: Heinemann.

Ranger, T.O. (1987) '"Pugilism and Pathology": African Boxing and the Black Urban Experience in Southern Rhodesia', in W.J. Baker and J.A. Mangan (eds) *Sport in Africa: Essays in Social History*, New York: African Publishing Company.

Ranger, T. and Vaughan, O. (1993) *Legitimacy and State in Twentieth-Century Africa*, Basingstoke: Macmillan.

Rashid, S. (1992) Interview with Said Rashid by Laura Fair (in Kiswahili), 27 July.

Rehani, M. (1995) Interview with Maulid Rehani by Laura Fair (in Kiswahili), 8 August.

Reid, D. (1976) 'The Decline of Saint Monday, 1776–1876', *Past and Present* 71: 76–101.

Ricci, F. (ed.) (2000) *African Football Yearbook* (third edition), Rome: Ricci.

Richards, P. (1997) 'Soccer and Violence in War Torn Africa. Soccer and Rehabilitation in Sierra Leone', in G. Armstrong and R. Giulianotti (eds) *Entering the Field. New Perspectives in World Football*, Oxford: Berg.

Robertson, R. (1992) *Globalization*, London: Sage.

Rostow, W.W. (1960) *The Stages of Economic Growth: A Non-Communist Manifesto*, Cambridge: Cambridge University Press.

Rotberg, R.I. (2000) 'Africa's Mess, Mugabe's Mayhem', *Foreign Affairs* 79(5): 47–61.

Saaf, A. (1999) *Carnets de Bus: essais sur le quotidien des quartiers Sud-Ouest de Rabat*, Casablanca: Eddif.

Said, E. (1978) *Orientalism*, Harmondsworth: Penguin.

Said, O. (1992) Interview with Omar Said (Kidevu) by Laura Fair (in Kiswahili), 23 July.

Salum, M. (1991) Interview with Mohamed Salum by Laura Fair (in Kiswahili), Zanzibar.

Seif, A. (1992) Interview with Abdalla Seif by Laura Fair (in Kiswahili), 31 January.

Sheriff, A. (1987) *Slaves, Spices and Ivory*, London: James Currey.

Shilling, C. (1993) *The Body and Social Theory*, London: Sage.

Shirts, M. (1988) 'Socrates, Corinthians, and Questions of Democracy and Citizenship', in J. Arbena (ed.) *Sport and Society in Latin America*, Westport, CT: Greenwood Press.

Silverstein, P. (2000) 'Sporting Faith: Islam, Soccer, and the French Nation-State', *Social Text* 55: 25–53.

Simonsen, A.H. (1995) 'Nigeria: Where Oil Kills – the Ogoni Tragedy', *Indigenous Affairs* 4: 52–5.

Skinner, N. (1996) *Burden at Sunset: Last Days of Empire*, Madison: University of Wisconsin, African Studies Program.

Smith, A.D. (1999) *Myths and Memories of the Nation*, Oxford: Oxford University Press.

Soccerweb (2000) <www.soccerweb.co.uk>

South African Institute of Race Relations (SAIRR) (1962–65) *A Survey of Race Relations in South Africa*, Johannesburg: SAIRR.

Spurr, D. (1994) *The Rhetoric of Europe*, Durham, NC: Duke University Press.

Stanton, G. (1988) 'The Oriental City: A North African Itinerary', *Third Text* 3/4: 3–38.

Strobel, M. (1979) *Muslim Women in Mombasa*, New Haven: Yale University Press.

Stuart, O. (1989) 'Good Boys, Footballers and Strikers: African Social Change in Bulawayo 1933–1953'. Unpublished PhD thesis, School of Oriental and African Studies, London.

Stuart, O. (1996) 'Players, Workers, Protestors: Social Change and Soccer in Colonial Zimbabwe', in J. MacClancy (ed.) *Sport, Identity and Ethnicity*, Oxford: Berg.

Sugden, J. and A. Tomlinson (1998) *FIFA and the Contest for World Football: Who Rules the People's Game?* Cambridge: Polity Press.

Suleiman, A.A. (1969) 'The Swahili Singing Star Siti binti Sadi', *Swahili* 39(1): 87–90.

Szeftel, M. (1998) 'Misunderstanding African Politics: Corruption and the Governance Agenda', *Review of African Political Economy* 76: 221–40.

Szymanski, S. and T. Kuypers (2000) *Winners and Losers: The Business Strategy of Football*, London: Penguin.

Tenga, S.T.M. (2000) 'Globalization and Olympic Sport in Tanzania: A Developmental Approach'. Doctoral dissertation, Oslo, Norwegian University of Sport and Physical Education.

Thompson, E.P. (1966) *The Making of the English Working Class*, New York: Vintage.

Thompson, E.P. (1967) 'Time, Work Discipline and Industrial Capitalism', *Past and Present* 38: 59–96.

Thompson, J. de L. (1935) *The Story of Rhodesian Sport. Volume One 1889–1935*, Bulawayo: Books of Rhodesia.

Thompson, L. (1990) *A History of South Africa*. New Haven: Yale University Press.

Tocke, A. (1998) 'Les Bleus conduits au sacre par des Africains', *Le Messager*, 13 July.

Tonkin, E. (1981) 'Model and Ideology: Dimensions of Being Civilised in Liberia', in L. Holy and M. Stuchlik (eds) *The Structure of Folk Models*, ASA Monograph 20, pp. 307–330, London: Academic Press.

Turner, V. (1969) *The Ritual Process*, New York: Cornell University Press.

Urry, J. (1990) *The Tourist Gaze*, London: Sage.

Van der Horst, S. (1964) *African Workers in Town: A Study of Labour in Cape Town*, Cape Town and London: Oxford University Press.

Vasili, P. (1995) 'Colonialism and Football: The First Nigerian Tour to Britain', *Race and Class* 36(4): 55–70.

Vermeren, P. (2002) 'Illegal Immigrants: "If I Die I'll Be An Economic Martyr", Morocco's Migrant Mexico', *Le Monde diplomatique* (June).

Vidacs, B. (1998) 'Football and Anti-colonial Sentiment in Cameroon', *Mots Pluriels* 6, <www.arts.uwa.edu.au/MotsPluriels/MP698bv.html>

Vidacs, B. (forthcoming) 'The Postcolonial and the Level Playing Field in the 1998 World Cup', in J. Bale and M. Cronin (eds) *Postcolonialism and Sport*, Oxford: Berg.

Wagner, E.A. (1990) 'Sport in Asia and Africa Americanization or Mundialization' in *Sociology of Sport Journal*, Champaign, IL: Human Kinetics Publishers Inc.

Waterbury, J. (1970) *The Commander of the Faithful*, London: Weidenfeld & Nicolson.

Watoto Club (1936) *Annual Report*, Zanzibar: Universities Mission to Central Africa.

Werbner, R. (1995) 'Human Rights and Moral Knowledge: Arguments of Accountability in Zimbabwe', in M. Strathern (ed.) *Shifting Contexts*, London: Routledge.

Werbner, R. (1999) 'Smoke from the Barrel of a Gun: Postwars of the Dead, Memory and Reinscription in Zimbabwe', in R. Werbner (ed.) *Memory and the Postcolony: African Anthropology and the Critique of Power*, London: Zed Books.

Wiggins, D. (1989) 'Great Speed but Little Stamina: The Historical Debate Over Black Athletic Superiority', *Journal of Sport History* 16(2): 158–85.

Willis, O. (1999) *Sport and Development: The Significance of Mathare Youth Sports Association*, Halifax: Dailhouse University Press.

Wilson, F.B. (1991) Personal communication.

Wilson, M. and A. Mafeje (1963) *Langa: A Study of Social Groups in an African Township*, London, New York and Cape Town: Oxford University Press.

Worby, E. (1994) 'Maps, Names, and Ethnic Games: The Epistemology and Iconography of Colonial Power in Northwestern Zimbabwe', *Journal of Southern African Studies* 20(3): 371–92.

Worby, E. (1998) 'Tyranny, Parody and Ethnic Polarity: Ritual Engagements with the State in Northwestern Zimbabwe', *Journal of Southern African Studies* 24(3): 561–78.

Younghusband, E. (1908) *Glimpses of East Africa and Zanzibar*, London: Long.

Zimbabwe Human Development Report (ZHDR) 1999, Harare: Statprint.

Web references

www.arts.uwa.edu.au/MotsPluriels/MP698bv.html

www.bsos.umd.edu, article on Kenya's ethnic composition by Danso (1999)

www.eastandard.net, 12 October 2001

www.footballunlimited.co.uk

www.g21.net, 'Jago of Mathare Valley'

www.kenyapage.com/football

www.mg.co.za/mg/news/98dec1/4dec-football.html

www.nairobits.org (a website produced by MYSA youth)

www.norway-cup.no

www.soccerassociation.com/home.htm

www.unisa.ac.za/dept/press/kleio/kleio31/soccer.html

Index

Compiled by Sue Carlton